25 Use parenthetical case explanations merely to show why you're citing the cases—not to present your argument.

D. EDITING FOR BRISK, UNCLUTTERED SENTENCES

26 Relax the tone: eliminate the jargon known as "legalese."

27 Avoid overparticularization.

28 Populate your sentences. Use real names (not procedural labels) for parties.

29 Work hard to replace *be*-verbs with action verbs.

30 Know what the passive voice is, and minimize it.

31 Uncover buried verbs—especially words ending in *-tion*.

32 When given the choice between a passive-voice verb and a buried verb, choose the passive voice.

33 Eliminate unnecessary prepositional phrases—especially those beginning with *of*.

34 Don't separate a short subject from its verb with a modifying phrase. Instead, start the sentence with the modifier.

35 Don't separate a verb from its object.

36 To write forcefully, end your sentences with punch.

37 Cut filler phrases such as *there is* and *there are*.

38 Eliminate throat-clearing phrases.

39 Ruthlessly cut unnecessary words.

40 Keep your sentences to one main thought, but combine related sentences if doing so will minimize choppiness.

41 Use parallel constructions whenever you can—but make sure the ideas are really parallel.

E. CHOOSING THE BEST WORDS

42 Replace humdrum phrases with snappy ones that spark interest.

43 State your ideas freshly; use clichés only when you can turn them to good advantage.

44 Strive for distinctive nouns and verbs—minimizing adjectives and adverbs.

45 Save syllables. Shoot for one-syllable words when possible; failing that, aim for two-syllable words.

46 Avoid heavy connectors.

47 Simplify wordy prepositions: *with respect to, as to, in order to, in connection with,* etc.

48 Don't use *However* to start a sentence: use *But* instead, move *however* inside the sentence, or collapse the preceding sentence into an *Although*-clause.

49 Strike *pursuant to* from your vocabulary.

50 Use *that* restrictively, *which* nonrestrictively.

THE WINNING BRIEF

OTHER BOOKS BY THE AUTHOR

Garner's Modern American Usage
(Oxford Univ. Press, 1998; 2d ed. 2003)

A Dictionary of Modern Legal Usage
(Oxford Univ. Press, 1987; 2d ed. 1995)

The Elements of Legal Style
(Oxford Univ. Press, 1991; 2d ed. 2002)

The Redbook: A Manual on Legal Style
(West, 2002)

Legal Writing in Plain English
(Univ. of Chicago Press, 2001)

Securities Disclosure in Plain English
(CCH, 1999)

Guidelines for Drafting and Editing Court Rules
(Admin. Office of the U.S. Courts, 1996)

The Rules of Golf in Plain English (coauthor)
(Univ. of Chicago Press, 2004)

BOOKS EDITED BY THE AUTHOR

Black's Law Dictionary
(West, 7th ed. 1999; 8th ed. 2004)

Black's Law Dictionary (pocket edition)
(West, 1996; 2d ed. 2001)

A Handbook of Basic Law Terms
(West, 1998)

A Handbook of Business Law Terms
(West, 1999)

A Handbook of Criminal Law Terms
(West, 2000)

A Handbook of Family Law Terms
(West, 2001)

Texas, Our Texas: Reminiscences of The University
(Eakin Press, 1984)

The Winning Brief

100 TIPS FOR PERSUASIVE BRIEFING
IN TRIAL AND APPELLATE COURTS

Second Edition

Bryan A. Garner

OXFORD
UNIVERSITY PRESS

OXFORD

UNIVERSITY PRESS

Oxford   New York
Auckland   Bangkok   Buenos Aires   Cape Town   Chennai
Dar es Salaam   Delhi   Hong Kong   Istanbul   Karachi   Kolkata
Kuala Lumpur   Madrid   Melbourne   Mexico City   Mumbai   Nairobi
São Paulo   Shanghai   Taipei   Tokyo   Toronto

Published by Oxford University Press, Inc.
198 Madison Avenue, New York, New York 10016

www.oup.com

Oxford is a registered trademark of Oxford University Press

Library of Congress Cataloguing-in-Publication Data
is available
ISBN-13 978-0-19-517075-7

13 15 17 19 20 18 16 14

Printed in the United States of America
on acid-free paper

In memory of Mariellen Griffin Garner
1931–1994

Contents

"The persuasive style requires two qualities: clearness and simplicity. If it is lacking in either of these it fails to persuade."

—Demetrius Phalereus
On Style 250 ¶ 221 (ca. 300 B.C.;
T.A. Moxon trans., 1943).

"If all the blunders of clever advocates were to be told, the student would come to the conclusion that practice makes us most imperfect; and that the art is more calculated to benumb the faculties than to quicken them. No one is more conscious of his faults than he who commits the fewest. One thing is certain: Advocacy never can be *mastered*; and the most we can do is to learn a little and unlearn a great deal."

—Richard Harris
Hints on Advocacy 312 (17th ed. 1937).

"[T]he written word is irrevocable. If it fails to convince or persuade the reader, there is no opportunity to switch to other ground. You make your play, and you cannot renege."

—Edward N. Teall
Putting Words to Work 146 (1940).

"[T]here are many good briefs that don't win cases, and assuredly there are poor ones (including some exceptionally poor ones) that do. But a brief that didn't win, however close to perfection it may have come, just wasn't an effective brief. . . . [I]t didn't persuade the court . . . ."

—Frederick B. Wiener
Briefing and Arguing Federal Appeals 125 (rev. ed. 1967).

Preface

In law, the quality of writing matters. Good writing can win cases, and bad writing can lose them. To some, this notion is self-evident. But to others it's dubious at best.

What explains these markedly divergent views? Ultimately, the disagreement hinges on the extent to which a given lawyer understands how language molds every human thought. Language is embedded in the very way we perceive the world. So it's impossible for a lawyer or a judge to focus exclusively on "the merits" of a case without being affected by the language used to express those merits.

When you write a brief, your implicit promise is that you'll give the judge good reasons for ruling as you request. This is all that matters: successfully persuading the judge to rule in your client's favor. Brief-writers tend to pity themselves and complain about judicial readers and their shortcomings—not reading closely enough, not allowing you enough pages, delegating study to law clerks, etc. But good brief-writers turn their complaints into challenges—challenges to mastering the writer–reader relationship. An objective observer would probably sympathize with some degree of self-pity because of the immense challenges you face. But an objective observer would probably pity your readers, too.

Until you understand why brief-readers should be pitied, you can't possibly write good briefs. Think of the judge's reading life. An endless stream of paper passes before the judge's eyes, with too little time to study each case in searching detail before the stream stagnates, becomes a massive stack of paper, and then becomes a fire hazard. And what does the stack consist of? Lots of rote phrases at the beginning and end of each document, loads of boring sameness, with everything spread out gradually through the middle—because the writers either can't or won't summarize. Sometimes law clerks read the briefs, not judges. It doesn't matter. Whoever the reader is, one thing is certain: run-of-the-mill brief-writing is pretty bad. It's slow and dull and abstract and digressive.

It's sobering to think that bad briefs can lose strong cases. But this surely happens all the time. Judge Thomas M. Reavley of the Fifth Circuit convincingly cites a case in point—a case that was very nearly decided wrongly because of bad briefing.

It was a wrongful-death case against the federal government, involving a patient who had been negligently misdiagnosed by Veterans Administration doctors. They told him he had a hernia that couldn't be operated on until he first lost weight. Actually, though, he had a tumor in his colon, which soon burst. He underwent emergency surgery and survived, but his blood transfusion infected him with HIV, and he eventually died of AIDS.

At trial, the decedent's family was awarded a judgment of $700,000. The VA appealed, filing what Judge Reavley called "a 28-page hide-the-ball brief." In it, the government lawyer danced around the real issues and made various irrelevant arguments. The plaintiffs' lawyer responded with a 32-page brief that "didn't uncover the ball"—it too was cluttered with fuzzy fact summaries and unconnected legal points.

Neither side's brief accomplished what it was supposed to do: focus the appellate court's attention on the issues. And this in what Judge Reavley called "a very simple case":

> The judgment found clear support in the evidence. But you would not know it from reading the briefs. And the appellate judge who got the case on the summary calendar wrote an opinion reversing the judgment. Fortunately, the next judge on the summary panel chose to let the case be argued. I was on the oral-argument panel. The argument shed no more light than the briefs did. But I read the record and, seeing ample support for the findings, affirmed. It was an excellent example of what ails us, and I assure you that this is not an unusual story.*

If not for the careful judge on the summary-calendar panel—and then for Judge Reavley himself—the plaintiffs would have lost $700,000.

Stories like that one are played out in appellate courts throughout the country. When the plaintiff ultimately prevails, the plaintiff's attorneys regale each other about how wonderful their briefing was. When the defendant ultimately prevails, the defense attorneys do the same. But the truth in many cases—certainly in far more than the lawyers would care to acknowledge—is that the briefing was poor on both sides. It's just that somebody had to win.

You can't say, of course, that superb briefs will always prevail. The merits of the case surely have something to do with winning. But statistically a good brief will improve your chances. It will help you highlight the merits for your side. It will entice judges by asking less of them—less elbow grease and less brain sweat.

All this can be pursued methodically. This book tries to chart the path.

———————————

This book—and the CLE course for which it was developed—resulted from three proximate causes. One was my nagging observation that, as writing is generally taught, even the most recurrent tips often surface merely by chance. They're part of the oral presentation but aren't to be found in the written materials. Or if they are there, they aren't in black-letter form. As one writing teacher has well said, "The means by which a person can gain help from the writing experience of others are not obscure; they are merely scattered."**

———————

* Remarks of Judge Thomas M. Reavley, Pepperdine Law School, April 1997.
** Charles W. Ferguson, *Say It with Words* 5 (1959).

A second impetus was my continuing dissatisfaction with both the literature and the practice of brief-writing. Rarely does the literature relate the brief-writer's special concern—persuading judges—to the larger field of rhetoric. And a large percentage of briefs are so poor that judges find them a grave disappointment: failed attempts at persuasion. Something must be done.

Third, my friend Jordan Cherrick of St. Louis urged me repeatedly to develop a CLE course designed exclusively for brief-writers. True, my "Advanced Legal Writing & Editing" course has long dealt with brief-writing. But it also deals with letters, memos, and reports. Jordan suggested in 1995 that I do a full day on nothing but briefs. And so, with his prompting, I decided to collect the 100 tips that I most commonly give to brief-writers.

The chief difficulty wasn't in reaching 100 tips. Hardly. As I had suspected, the chief difficulty was in narrowing the list down to 100: I could easily have made it 150.

Notice that I call them "tips." They're guidelines, not dogmas. Although I feel strongly about the advice here given, you are sure to encounter situations in which you'd be better off ignoring it.

Not all the tips are equal. Some are intellectually challenging (such as #8 and #88) and some are quite easy (such as #55 and #65). Brief-writers should work on the challenging points and assimilate the easy ones.

In June 1996, we made our first national tour with the program, holding it in eight cities: Chicago, Dallas, Houston, Los Angeles, New York, San Francisco, Seattle, and Washington, D.C. At each of those cities, the seminar proved quite popular. In 1997, we added Cleveland and Columbus. And in 1998, we added Minneapolis, New Orleans, and San Diego. Since then, we've occasionally added Boston, Detroit, Kansas City, and Sacramento to our June schedule, as well as a few other cities.

This book, like its earlier incarnations, owes much to the extraordinary skill and industriousness of my LawProse colleagues: Tiger Jackson, Jeff Newman, and David W. Schultz. Also, the book shows the strong influence of two other LawProse colleagues, both English professors at the University of Texas: Dr. Betty S. Flowers and Dr. John R. Trimble. Flowers, of course, laid the groundwork for the Flowers paradigm (tips #1–7). And Trimble's aura as an editor and teacher has greatly influenced me: not only is he quoted in various tips, but his seminal ideas pervade the book as a whole. I also thank Karen Magnuson for her excellent help in copyediting.

Finally, I continually learn from the participants in this and other seminars. I'm still collecting good examples of brief-writing, and I'm always grateful to participants who send me their work. So if you try to follow the principles in this book—or if you have an opponent who flouts them laughably—send me more stuff.

—Bryan A. Garner
Dallas, Texas
November 2003

Part A

Composing in an Orderly, Sensible Way

1

Plan every writing project by breaking it up— and carry it out in stages.

Quotable Quotes

"Lawyers are inclined to act too quickly and to think too little, if they ever think at all. A brief is not written even by a 'brilliant' lawyer in a single afternoon; if it is, the product is unworthy both of the client and of the court. Before writing a brief it is necessary to plot out the exact line of attack or defense fully. The brief should contain only one key point with possibly two or three material but subordinate points of attack or defense."

—Jean Appleman, *The Written Argument on Appeal*, 41 Notre Dame Law. 40, 41 (1965).

"How does one manage this feeling of being overwhelmed? It's like eating an elephant: You do it one bite at a time. Sit down and spend a few minutes breaking the project into logical bite-size units. Check your deadline. If it's a big project, figure out how far along you want to be with the job by when. Then mark these stages down on your calendar."

—Karin Mack & Eric Skjei, *Overcoming Writing Blocks* 57 (1979).

"Breaking down the various decisions involved in writing into separate stages reduces panic by making the job less awesome. It also makes writing a routine. No longer are moods of inspiration needed, no longer is writing only possible when you are exceptionally awake and fresh. The various stages can be worked through even when you are tired, or simply not feeling like concentrated creative thought. All professional writers learn this early in their careers. You probably use writing as an adjunct to professionalism in other spheres; but learning the divide-and-conquer techniques of the professional writer is still a valuable career asset."

—Christopher Turk & John Kirkman, *Effective Writing: Improving Scientific, Technical, and Business Communication* 43 (2d ed. 1989).

"Before actually beginning to write, do two things. *First*, ensure that you have a strong thesis. There's a good way to tell if you have one, but it takes courage. Write on some notepaper, 'I contend that——,' and complete the sentence. . . . *Second*, have on hand a list of concrete details and apt quotations, and be

ready to use them. Remember, if you lead off with a string of abstract generalizations, your reader may impatiently mutter, 'Sheesh,' and tune you out."
—John R. Trimble, *Writing with Style* 29–30 (2d ed. 2000).

Explanation

Most writing advice focuses on the end product. But we shouldn't neglect the process by which writers produce their words—because, in important ways, the process determines the product.

Now, I can't tell you what type of pen to use or what to sip while you're working. You can't teach the *physical* aspects of writing. But it's quite possible to teach the *mental* aspects of writing.

Before we get to that, though, think of the ways in which legal writers so frequently get mired:

- By starting to write in earnest before they fully understand what they're writing about—and then treating that draft as something sacrosanct.

- By sidestepping the creative stage altogether, so that the brief isn't nearly as imaginative as it could be.

- By writing and sharpening sentences before knowing what the overall structure will be—and thereby wasting valuable time. When structural changes later emerge, as they inevitably will, this early work will have to be changed.

- By allowing their critical side to interrupt throughout the process.

How can you avoid these pitfalls?

The Flowers Paradigm:
Madman–Architect–Carpenter–Judge

Several years ago Dr. Betty S. Flowers, a LawProse instructor who teaches in the University of Texas English Department, devised a method that dramatizes the writing process. Her method helps minimize the problems and maximize both efficiency and effectiveness.

It's called madman–architect–carpenter–judge.* It breaks down the writing process into four steps—each one based on a "character" or personality that we all have within us.

The madman "is full of ideas, writes crazily and perhaps rather sloppily, gets carried away by enthusiasm and desire, and if really let loose, could turn out ten pages an hour" (p. 7). Typically, the legal writer doesn't really "write" at all during this stage, but instead takes copious notes, jotting down ideas and possible approaches to a problem.

---

* Betty S. Flowers, *Madman, Architect, Carpenter, Judge: Roles and the Writing Process*, 44 Proceedings of the Conference of College Teachers of English 7–10 (1979). Page citations in this explanation are to this article.

The madman's nemesis is the judge—your critical character who really needs to be reined in until the final step. But many legal writers have an out-of-control judge, who is easily recognizable. As Flowers describes the judge:

> He's been educated and knows a sentence fragment when he sees one. He peers over your shoulder and says, 'That's trash!' with such authority that the madman loses his crazy confidence and shrivels up. You know the judge is right; after all, he speaks with the voice of an English teacher. But for all his sharpness of eye, he can't create anything. (*Id.*)

The secret to defusing this battle between madman and judge is to keep the judge at bay until the end of the writing process. Otherwise, the judge will stifle the madman altogether.

But what about the other steps?

Once the madman has generated lots of ideas, the architect takes them, makes connections between them, and starts planning their structure. In the first instance, the architect's work is nonlinear, but it will end up in the form of a linear outline. This means that the outline will finally have the form that seems obvious to most people today but was a great insight when Aristotle devised it: a beginning, a middle, and an end. And if the architect functions satisfactorily, ultimately producing a linear outline, you'll know each intermediate point—step by step—through the middle parts of the brief. In fact, the more detailed the architectural plans are, the better.

Then comes the carpenter, who starts building the draft. At this stage, the writing begins in earnest. And because you've planned the draft, the carpenter's work is greatly eased: it's more or less a matter of filling in the blanks. That may overstate how easy the carpenter's work is. But the process of building is greatly simplified when you have the architect's specifications laid out in front of you.

Charles Alan Wright makes this very point in the *Scribes Journal* essay in which he describes his writing process:

> For my kind of nonfiction it is necessary first to have a complete grasp of whatever subject it is I am going to be writing about. This we can take for granted, though the research is often long and tedious. The next stage, and to me the hardest of all, is organization. I never sit down to the keyboard—in the old days it was a typewriter, then an electronic typewriter, and in recent years it has been a computer—until I am clear in my mind how I am going to organize whatever it is that I am doing.**

That's why, earlier in his essay, Wright says that writing is easy—the preparation is the difficult part.

The most important thing about the carpenter stage is to write rapidly, without editing along the way, simply filling in the details according to the architectural specs. If you edit, then the judge starts getting active—and this is just the type of interference your carpenter doesn't need. If

---

** Charles Alan Wright, *How I Write*, 4 Scribes J. Legal Writing 87, 88 (1993).

you get stuck in a certain part, then move to the next section: you may have to leave a little hole here and there.

You'll notice, too, that the carpenter has some discretion—deciding how to finish off a corner, how to build the passage from one room to the next. Some architectural details, in other words, are left to the carpenter.

Once your carpenter has built a draft, the fun begins for your judge, who can start looking for ways to improve the draft. The judge will check many of the things that the rest of this book is devoted to: whether there are transitions between paragraphs, whether you've used passive voice where you really shouldn't have, and so on. And the judge will check many things that aren't mentioned in this book, from comma splices to misplaced modifiers to subject–verb agreement problems. The judge is a quality-control inspector.

Each of these characters needs time on stage—at the forefront of your brain. If you neglect any of them, your writing simply won't be as good as it might be.

Two Qualms Answered

But is it possible, in the hurly-burly of a busy law practice, to go through these four steps with every writing project? Of course. Even in the space of an hour-long writing project, you can spend 10 minutes on madman, 7 on architect, 20 on carpenter, and 10 on judge. What about the rest of the time? Well, you need breaks in between, both to get away from the project momentarily and to shift your focus to that of another character.

But isn't it true that we all approach problems differently? Isn't that the lesson of Myers-Briggs and other personality tests? Yes, and Flowers designed the paradigm with this in mind. Everyone is most comfortable working in a particular compartment of the brain. This approach ensures that you benefit from all that your brain has to offer, not just from the mental realm you're most comfortable with.

I, for example, spent years neglecting the architect. I wrote highly polished sentences and paragraphs, and people who read my stuff generally thought of me as a good writer. But when I now look at what I wrote in those days, some of it appears to be a highly polished mishmash. The organization was unpredictable. Now that has changed—and writing has become relatively painless for me, and much quicker. I do what Professor Wright mentioned: I plan my writing better than I used to.

Advantages of the Flowers Paradigm

In her original essay, Flowers pointed to eight advantages of her paradigm, rewritten here with my glosses:

1. It's easy to remember.

2. It stresses the sequential nature of the writing process—that you're likely to get better results if you work through the madman stage first rather than going back to the idea stage after you've spent three hours crafting sentences.

3. It dramatizes the need for rewriting and gives a sense of individual purpose to every draft.

4. It breaks the writing task down into manageable stages and allows you to enjoy each stage; that is, it shows you how to do one thing at a time.

5. It defuses the conflict that often arises when you try to write for an authority figure.

6. It offers a way to deal with self-image problems that sometimes interfere with the writing process. That is, if you see yourself as a creator, you might be impatient with the polishing and careful proofing that the judge can provide—and that every draft needs. And if you see yourself as a consummate critic, you may have a highly "repressed" style characterized by dry and unmemorable (but technically correct) prose.

7. It gives a new language for critiquing drafts, one that doesn't shove the editor exclusively into the role of judge. Now, an editor can look at a brief and say, "Try playing the madman more with this section," rather than just picking up a red pen and marking away.

8. It clarifies what you can and can't teach about writing. The madman stage is personal and subjective, a private area left almost exclusively to the writer. The judge can be taught from good writing texts. But in the architect and carpenter stages—where many writers are least experienced and usually least well trained—a teacher can be very helpful.

Many writers need more help with the writing process than with anything else. For those who do, the Flowers paradigm can be invaluable.

You'll likely find that you can most readily apply the rest of the tips on process—#2 through #7—if you capitalize on the paradigm.

2

When first working on a writing project, let the madman run loose for a while.

Quotable Quotes

"Ordinarily—not always, but more often than not—writing proceeds like this: Collecting material—trying to find a good approach—spending some time on something else—getting a sudden bright idea—planning and organizing—writing—revising. The most mysterious—and most fascinating—part of the whole process is the one you don't read about in the handbooks: the search for a good approach, the period when you abandon the search, and the moment when, out of nowhere, an idea pops into your mind.

"Maybe you won't believe me when I say that this is common experience. All right, I'll cite chapter and verse. This is the way the human mind works in creating *anything*—whether it's the mind of a poet or a mathematician, a philosopher or a historian, a scientist or an advertising man."

—Rudolf Flesch, *The Art of Readable Writing* 55 (1949; repr. 1967).

"[T]he attorney [must] allow his ideas to develop over a period of time. He should jot down ideas as they come to him, even developing ideas in their entirety but taking care not to write the full argument. As he does research upon the facts or the law, more and more ideas will come to him so that his notes should begin to grow and even overlap each other, but it will be simple to organize the material at the proper time. Until this meditating process is complete, a lawyer should not attempt to write his brief."

—Jean Appleman, *The Written Argument on Appeal*, 41 Notre Dame Law. 40, 41 (1965).

"The point is that a deeper level of thinking can go on when you relinquish your conscious grip on your material. A kind of letting go is necessary for this deep cooking. Having a beer, taking a walk or a bus ride, taking a nap or a shower—these all serve some people as ways of letting go."

—Peter Elbow, *Writing with Power* 40 (1981).

"Your subconscious mind does more writing than you think. Often you'll spend a whole day trying to fight your way out of some verbal thicket in which you seem to be tangled beyond salvation. Frequently a solution will occur to you the next morning when you plunge back in. While you slept, your writer's mind didn't. To some extent a writer is always working. Stay alert to the currents around you. Much of what you see and hear will come back, having percolated for days or months—or even years—through your subconscious mind, just when your conscious mind, laboring to write, needs it."

—William Zinsser, *On Writing Well* 126 (5th ed. 1994).

Explanation

Few legal writers seem to think of their work as being essentially creative. They often think that writing well is simply a matter of finding the law and getting it down.

In fact, though, every brief presents opportunities for creativity—for imaginative approaches that will convey the point most effectively. In Example A below, Mike Hatchell of Tyler, Texas, begins a motion for rehearing with a play, in which the lawyer tries to make sense of an intermediate court's holding. Not only did Hatchell succeed in persuading the court to accept the appeal it had earlier rejected, he also succeeded in having the lower court's decision altered.*

Example B, by Neal Goldfarb of Washington, D.C., also contains a "Prologue," but it's not in the form of a play. Instead, he uses a series of hypotheticals to open an amicus brief on behalf of three victims'-rights organizations. In doing so, he takes a difficult constitutional issue and frames it favorably for his clients.

All of this is not to suggest, of course, that you should start writing fictional prologues in your briefs. Instead, you should think hard about how best to get your point across. You may think of apt illustrations, analogies, diagrams, and other devices. Don't stop when you've thought of the most obvious approaches. Delve more deeply.

---

* *See Caller-Times Pub. Co. v. Triad Communications, Inc.*, 826 S.W.2d 576 (Tex. 1992).

Example A

[The "Prologue" follows a listing of points of error, which were required in Texas appellate practice until 1997.]

> "The court of appeals erred in failing to reach and sustain Caller-Times' Point of Error No. 13, because there is no evidence to support Triad's tortious interference claim, as submitted and determined in Questions Nos. 7–8 (Tr. 113, 125–127, 129–130, 153–154; IV S.F. 113–114; V S.F. 113–114, 120; MFR Assignment No. 50.)"

9.

The court has erred in failing to grant Caller-Times' application for writ of error and to reach and sustain Caller-Times' Conditional Assignment No. 2, which reads as follows:

> "If it is determined there is a scintilla of evidence to support Questions Nos. 7–8, the cause should be remanded to the court of appeals to rule on Caller-Times' Conditional Point of Error No. 14, which is in the exclusive jurisdiction of that court, reading as follows:

> '*** (T)he trial court erred in failing to grant defendant's motion for new trial, because the jury's answers to . . . [Questions Nos. 7–8] . . . are not supported by factually sufficient evidence or are against the great weight and overwhelming preponderance of the evidence.' " (MFR Assignment No. 51.)

PROLOGUE

"Well, apparently not in Texas . . ."

Scene: Corporate board room of Widgets & Surfboards/Plus, Inc., a manufacturer of widgets, surfboards, and gadgets with a major share of the Corpus Christi market and minor facilities in El Paso and Texarkana.

Players: The Chief Executive Officer, three directors, and the corporate counsel.

Staging: A conference table, a Black's Law Dictionary, a Webster's Dictionary, a telephone, a newspaper, and a large bottle of Tylenol.

CEO: Gentlemen, I got good news and bad news. The bad news is that sales have been soft this quarter and, with the payment of our retainage to settle that injury suit against one of our truck drivers, profits are "zilch" this quarter; in fact, we've sustained about a 10% loss. Now, we've got to do something to turn this around.

Director/1: What do you suggest?

CEO: Well, I think the price of our widgets is at the limit, and, if we lower it about 20%, we ought to be able to increase sales, reduce our per product overhead by using up some idle plant capacity, and, maybe, even permanently increase our market share. That oughta turn profits around real quick.

Director/2: Great, let's do it!

Counsel: Not so fast! That may be illegal!

Director/3: Come again?

Counsel: Yeah, there's this new case out of the Corpus court construing the Texas Anti-Trust Act—Caller-Times versus Triad. It says: if a business tries to increase its market share—in other words, if it takes business away from its competitors—by cutting its prices and the price is cut by a percent greater than the business's profit margin, that's evidence of what's called "predatory pricing," and we can be sued by a competitor for treble damages.

CEO: You've got to be kidding?

Counsel: I'm dead serious. And, you see, since we have a zero "profit margin," we can't lower prices. In fact, this case is so dangerous, I was prepared to suggest we raise our prices 10% on all products, because, under that case, if we maintain our present prices in the face of this loss, that might be considered a *de facto* cut and our present prices might be illegal—or might become illegal even as we speak.

The court didn't distinguish between product lines in that case, either—didn't seem to make any difference. So, even if the price of our widgets is way over what it costs to make them—especially with higher production—we still run the risk of predatory pricing—because, you see, the evidence in that case was just overall "profit margin."

Director/3: But, look, to raise our prices now when we need to lower them—and we can lower them and still make money—that's economic suicide. It's just insane!

Director/2: Now, wait a minute. Look at today's paper. Here are all these businesses advertising 25% off, 33% off, 50% off, here's one even 75% off. You know, Oriental rugs are 50% off all the time. Now, I know none of these businesses have that kind of profit margin—except maybe Oriental rugs. Are you telling me they're all violating this law?

Counsel: Well, let me put it this way. No one can say they're not—that's because you can't say what their profit margin is when these cuts are made. I bet they don't have a clue about what their profit margin is during these sales. They're all at risk under this case.

Director/1: Let me get this straight! I can understand why someone might say we can't lower our prices to a point that we consciously take a loss on that product just to increase our market at a competitor's expense, but what does profit margin have to do with that? It's just some balance sheet deal—a function of overall operations, bookkeeping transactions, maybe bad investments, off-the-wall accounting theories, like FASB-38, and all that—none of which has anything to do with whether we make money selling a product—like widgets.

My gosh, you just heard that our profit margin—or the lack of it—is due to stuff that doesn't have anything to do with making money from sales—especially widgets. This is crazy!

Counsel: I know—but it's the law.

Director/1: Well, at what point in time do we compute this "profit margin" test? Is it today's or last month's or last quarter's?

Gosh, we might actually have a favorable profit margin next quarter after we lower prices—especially if we can increase cash flow and we don't have these extraordinary expenses unrelated to production. Are we stymied because we didn't make money this quarter?

Counsel: That's a good question. This Caller-Times case doesn't really say. The testimony they used didn't identify if it was today's margin or last year's or just some historical average—as I say, it was just "profit margin." There were just a couple of lines of testimony about it.

Director/2: Well, can't we just refigure our "profit margin" under some other theory? Is it cast in stone how you compute that? I mean, how did the Corpus court figure it?

Counsel: They just took a definition from *Black's Law Dictionary*. Here it is:

"Sales minus all expenses as a single amount. Frequently used to mean the ratio of sales minus all operating expenses."

Director/1: They define an economic concept from a law dictionary?

Counsel: Yep!

CEO: But I still don't understand what "all operating expenses" has to do with the profitability of the price of one product. Is Black's definition related to antitrust law? What reference does Black's give for that?

Counsel: It doesn't—no texts, no cases, no nothing. You can't tell what they're talking about.

Director/3: Look, Webster defines it differently.

"The minimum return or reward, barely covering the costs of production."

Now, that seems to me to be more what we're talking about here. The cost to produce one product.

Which dictionary definition do we use?

Counsel: Don't ask me.

CEO: Well, if the lawyers don't know, I certainly don't.

Counsel: Don't get mad at me. I didn't write the silly thing.

Director/3: Call the accountant. Maybe he can help.

CEO (after dialing): Charlie, this is Mack over here at Widgets & Surfboards/Plus. We need some help. How do accountants figure "profit margin"?

Offstage Voice: Well, that's not an accounting term. We don't recognize it in any official way. It can mean just about anything. In the eye of the beholder, so to speak. I can give you a bunch of textbook definitions, but they're all different.

CEO: Oh, great.

Offstage Voice: This must be about that Caller-Times case. Everybody in town has been calling me about that. You seen today's paper? All the guys running sales are in a sweat. Nobody believed this case was for real. Pretty weird, huh?

CEO: Yeah, and scary, too. Makes you wonder if this is the USA or "The Twilight Zone." Well, thanks.

[Hangs up phone.]

Terrific! The lawyers can't tell us what we can do or what test to follow, the accountants can't tell us. What did the trial court tell the jury in that Caller-Times case?

Counsel: That's an interesting question. In fact, in that case the plaintiff said there wasn't any test other than intent to target your competitor's customers with low prices, even if they were profitable, and Caller-Times said you should use a test out of the federal Fifth Circuit that asks whether the price is below "average variable cost." That's a complicated economic term, but at least you can figure it out using standard economic data.

So, what happened—the court didn't tell the jury anything. This "profit margin" business was invented in the appeals court.

CEO: All right, what you're telling me is that this case was—what do you lawyers call it—"affirmed"?—on some theory that neither party said applied, that the judge didn't tell anybody about, and the jury didn't know anything about?

Counsel: Precisely.

Director/2: Is that legal?

Counsel: Well, it happened. Now "fair" or "logical" is another matter altogether.

CEO: Is it correct to say, then, that the only way we can know if our prices today are legal or illegal is to get ourselves sued? Then some months or years down the road, a jury tells us, but they don't have any rules to go by—other than maybe big guys versus little guys? And, that jury finding can be upheld by looking at some law dictionary and, then, figuring out what our profit margin was sometime—doesn't make any difference when?

Counsel: That's about the size of it.

Director/3: This Caller-Times case—is that the last word?

Counsel: Well, at least here in Corpus it is. Now, I don't know what the other courts of appeals will do.

Director/1: Well, what can they do?

Counsel: They can adopt some different test and different evidence rules.

Director/2: Get serious! You mean if our prices here in Corpus are illegal, still, the same kind of prices under the same circumstances can be okay in Texarkana or El Paso?

Counsel: That's exactly right. Corpus decisions just bind Corpus. There could be as many as 14 different tests.

In fact, it's pretty certain there will be other tests. The federal circuits—and our act is supposed to be construed in line with federal precedent—have adopted various definitions of "predatory pricing," but they all use an economic test based on "cost" of the goods versus price.

There isn't any case anywhere that's allowed "profit margin" to prove cost to make one product. And, for obvious reasons—you can see, our profit margin says very little about what it costs to produce and sell our widgets—in fact, it may be terribly misleading in that regard. We make good money on widgets.

Director/3: Tell me this is just a bad dream! I mean, won't the Supreme Court just straighten this thing out?

Counsel: Well, you would think so. The specialist antitrust lawyers are in an uproar about the case—really, it's so ludicrous, they just laugh at it. There was this speech in Dallas last week about it—pointed out that even the test Corpus purports to adopt makes "***mince meat***" out of its reasoning and result.

So, everybody has just assumed the case will be reversed or sent back because it was tried on the wrong theory, or something. But, bad news! The supreme court dodged the issue. It denied writ of error on September 6.

CEO: What did it say?

Counsel: Nothing.

Director/1: What's the basis for that?

Counsel: Well, about all you can tell is that the court thinks this just isn't important to the jurisprudence of Texas—that's their test for hearing cases.

CEO: You mean, stating a test for predatory pricing under this statewide act

. . . and saying how we can figure out whether or not we're violating the act today so we can stay out of court and stopping all these different tests from being created for different parts of the state

. . . and keeping businesses from being dragged through the courts maybe with different results in different parts of the state for the same conduct—all because nobody knows what the test is

. . . that's not important?

Director/2: Yeah, I thought the whole purpose of law was to have one place you could go look and tell what the rules are so you know how to stay out of court—so we can obey the law and avoid all this litigation expense. What's more important than that? Results? Why do we even have a Supreme Court, if they won't speak on those kinds of problems?

Counsel: Good question. These are hard cases. Murky economic concepts and all that—they're really tedious.

CEO: I'm not sure that really explains anything. I mean, it's the *supreme* court, isn't it?

[Silence. All stare into space. CEO takes Tylenol.]

Anybody got any bright ideas?

Counsel: Well, I do have a couple. This is the good news Mack was referring to. Let's try to make the best out of a bad situation.

We've just learned that our principal competitor that has the lion's share of the market out in El Paso—since it had to pay a big fine to EPA last and used some loss carryovers—didn't show a profit last year. Now they're offering a 25% discount on widgets this quarter.

On the other hand, since we just collected on these big open accounts claims we had to sue on, plus a lotta prejudgment interest, that gives us a profit margin of about 45%—at least this quarter.

So, I say we lower our prices on widgets out there about 40%—at least to our competitor's customers; now we may actually have some losses on that, but it's clearly legal to do it—that's what happened in the Caller-Times case. At the same time, we write them a letter claiming their prices are "predatory."

One of two things will happen: They have to jack their prices back up under this Corpus case, and, then, we oughta be able to run them out of their market pretty quick—then, we will raise our prices back to super-profitable levels. Or, if we fail—and that might actually be the better thing to happen, since El Paso is marginal anyway—we close down the plant and sue them for treble damages.

Director/2: Good thinking! All we've gotta do is prove their "profit margin" last year, some price cut greater than that and the fact they want us out of the way—right?

Counsel: Right! And, that's a cinch. Then, we get the right jury and it's "Katy, bar the door."

Director/2: Well, sounds pretty unsavory to me, but the way I look at it, what's sauce for the goose—and all that.

Director/1: Yeah, if these laws work that way, there's no reason we shouldn't play the game.

Director/3: Now, this just sounds like another tort theory to me. And another thing, it pretty much allows us to control our competitor's business—kinda creates a reverse monopoly, so to speak.

CEO: One thing is curious to me. The customer gets the short end of the stick in all this. They pay our competitor's higher prices if we force them up. Or, they pay our higher prices if we force our competitor out. And, they pay higher prices that now have to be maintained because of fear of these suits under this Corpus case.

But I was always told these antitrust laws were supposed to benefit the public with more competition and lower prices.

Counsel: Well, apparently not in Texas . . . .

BRIEF OF THE ARGUMENT

This portrayal is not a figment of the imagination. It is already being played out in the offices of the financial advisers and legal counselors to businesses all across the state. Sadly, apart from the derision and ridicule to which the Corpus court's opinion has been subjected (it has yet to find a scholarly champion, only critics, e.g., Appendix A), the most common response is frustration and disappointment with the system.

Frustration because legal advisers who genuinely wish to give their clients sage advice on how to properly price products under the Texas Antitrust Act have no tools with which to do so; they have no definitive test from the court of last resort; they have no certain evidentiary standards; they only have a result that has no analogue in antitrust law anywhere, that resorts to bizarre, worthless criteria, and that is so internally inconsistent, it actually repudiates itself.

Example B

PROLOGUE: THREE CASES

1.

Consider the hypothetical case of Peter Alladyn and John Powell.

Alladyn was an enforcer for the mob; Powell was a small-time hood who aspired to move up in the criminal pecking order. Powell heard that there was a contract out on Thomas Hope, and he wanted to be the one who did the job. Since he had never before killed anyone, he went to Alladyn for advice. Alladyn spent an hour with Powell, giving Powell the benefit of his experience. Alladyn told Powell what kind of gun to use, how to alter the gun to make it untraceable, where to aim (the head, preferably the eye sockets), how many shots to fire (at least three), and many other helpful hints.

Powell followed Alladyn's advice. He used the kind of gun Alladyn had recommended, he altered the gun as Alladyn had recommended, and he shot Hope three times in the head as Alladyn had recommended, killing him instantly.

After an investigation, the police arrested Powell and charged him with Hope's murder. At the police station, Powell broke down and confessed. He told the police about the advice he had gotten from Alladyn. The next day, Alladyn was arrested and charged with aiding and abetting murder.

When Alladyn was arraigned, his lawyer moved to dismiss the charges. "Your honor," he said, "the charges against my client are barred by the First Amendment. The First Amendment protects freedom of speech. And the only charge against my client is that he spoke to John Powell; Mr. Alladyn isn't charged with doing anything other than speaking. Since speech is protected by the First Amendment, the charges have to be dismissed."

In the back of the courtroom, several lawyers tried to stifle their laughter. The prosecutor approached the lectern, but the judge waved her away. "I don't need to hear from the State," he said. "The motion is denied."

2.

Now consider a variation of the first case. The facts are the same, but with one change. When Powell went to Alladyn for advice, Alladyn didn't have an hour to spare. So he gave Powell a book, *Hit Man: A Technical Manual for Independent Contractors*, written by "Rex Feral" and published by Paladin Press. "Read this," Alladyn said. "It will tell you how to do it."

Powell read the book and followed its instructions. He killed Hope, he was arrested, he confessed, and he told the police about the book he had gotten from Alladyn. Alladyn was arrested and charged with aiding and abetting. His lawyer made the same motion to dismiss. "The only charge against my client is that he gave someone a book," he said. "Books are protected by the First Amendment." This motion, too, was denied.

3.

Finally, consider the case now before this court. The facts are similar to those of the hypotheticals, except that the killer was not John Powell but James Perry; that he obtained the book *Hit Man* not from Peter Alladyn but directly from the publisher; and that the victims were not imaginary Thomas Hopes but three real human beings.

Those differences aside, the three cases are in all important respects identical. Paladin acted with the same knowledge and intent as Peter Alladyn: Paladin stipulated for the purposes of its summary-judgment motion that in publishing and selling *Hit Man*, it "intended and had knowledge that [the book] would be used, upon receipt, by criminals and would-be criminals to plan and execute the crime of murder for hire." Moreover, the result in all three cases was the same. Both Powell and Perry followed the instructions in committing murder. And Paladin's motion in the district court was the same as Alladyn's motions in the hypotheticals. But while Alladyn's motions were denied, Paladin's was granted.

Paladin apparently agrees that in the circumstances of the first two hypotheticals, Peter Alladyn could not hide behind the First Amendment.[1] The question raised by this appeal is whether the hypothetical case of John Powell and Peter Alladyn is any different from the real-life case of James Perry and Paladin Press.

---

[1] *See* Paladin Memorandum in Support of Motion for Summary Judgment at 33 n.24 (D.E. 18).

3

Begin the architectural planning by stating the issues. Before writing in earnest, figure out how many issues there are—and what they are.

Quotable Quotes

"It is impact not dead pull that drives a pile."
—Oliver Wendell Holmes, 1 *Holmes–Laski Letters* 684 (Mark D. Howe ed., 1953).

"The basic admonition to the lawyer who is sitting down to write the Argument is simply this: never start to write until you have thought the case through and have completed your basic research. That doesn't mean every citation or footnote, but it does include a reading, and, whenever required, a rereading, of all the important cases—because the basic authorities are always full of suggestive leads for further development.

. . .

"Concentrate on your problem, turn it over in your mind, think about it in tub or shower, try out your hypotheses on associates, live with the case in every spare waking moment—but don't start to write until the sequence and direction of your points have fallen clearly into place in your mind."
—Frederick B. Wiener, *Briefing and Arguing Federal Appeals* 136–37 (rev. ed. 1967).

"Ask yourself the two most important questions: 'Do I understand this?' 'Can I explain it to my readers?' Don't be satisfied until the answer to both is yes."
—George Kennedy et al., *The Writing Book* 36 (1984).

"Before any portion of the brief is drafted, the brief writer must be completely familiar with the record and generally familiar with the relevant law. This familiarity should enable the brief writer to ascertain those issues he wishes to raise and to prepare an initial draft of them. These draft issues can then give focus to the preparation of the other sections of the brief. As these other sections are written, it may develop that some modifications should be made in the statement of an issue to reflect a more accurate reading of the record or assessment of the state of the law. The writing of the brief should begin, however, with a draft of the statement of the issues."
—Robert J. Martineau, *Fundamentals of Modern Appellate Advocacy* § 7.30, at 142 (1985).

"Here is a useful rule for beginning: Know the story—as much of the story as you can possibly know, if not the whole story—before you commit yourself to the first paragraph. Know the story—the whole story, if possible—before you fall in love with your first *sentence*, not to mention your first chapter."

—John Irving, "Getting Started," in *Writers on Writing* 98, 98 (Robert Pack & Jay Parini eds., 1991).

"The most important analytical step in the appellate process—in fact in most aspects of litigation—is framing the issues."

—Bryan A. Garner, "The Language of Appellate Advocacy," in *Appellate Practice Manual* 188, 189 (Priscilla A. Schwab ed., 1992).

"[M]ost legal writers who write a lot are weakest in architecture because that's the most subtle—it's the organization. That's where the argument comes in, through the organization, and that's the hardest part of writing to teach because they don't get it in high school."

—Betty Sue Flowers, "The Salt Interview: Betty Sue Flowers," 2 *Salt J.*, Nov.–Dec. 1999, at 10, 17.

Explanation

This tip counteracts what is probably the most significant fault in the way lawyers write briefs.

Advocates often seem to think they're "knocking out some of the preliminaries" before they think much about the core of the brief. Then they go ahead and "knock out" the first section because they have in mind what it deals with. And then what's left to do but the final section or two? With this kind of start, they're feeling as if the draft is virtually done.

For these writers, the issues come as an afterthought.

The problem, of course, is that a brief written in this way will simply "talk around" the issue without ever piercing to its center. And the writer will think that everything has been covered when in fact some key links are likely to be missing.

If you're serious about writing good briefs, you shouldn't compose sentences and paragraphs until you have a good working statement of the issues. That's the proper starting point—not, as so often seems to happen, the ending point.

How does the issue sometimes turn up at the end of a writing project? You see it in the flash of insight that somebody has the night before a brief is due. Suddenly, everything has to be reworked because the issue has finally emerged in the writer's mind. This is a prime symptom of starting to write too early.

If you find that you have written too early—that is, the issues crystallize only after you've been writing for some time—you'll have to be ruthless with everything you've written before that crystallization occurs. Don't become wedded to sentences and paragraphs just because you've invested time in them. Be willing to discard them.

So precisely where in the writing process should the issue-framing come? In the madman phase? In the architect phase? Although there's no final answer to this question, the best practice is to write the issues before the outline. But when you're working with cocounsel, this isn't always possible. Your colleagues might have outlined the topics without stating the issues in the meaningful form of the deep issue (outlined in #8–12). If so, it's still not too late: draft the issues before writing anything else. If you don't, the writing will probably end up being highly diffuse.

How common is the problem? My guess is that more than half of all briefs suffer from this fault. And it's typified in the first of the two examples below, the second having been written by a lawyer who firmly grasps the issue. Example A is the opener from a party's brief, Example B from an amicus curiae's brief. But many judges who have looked at these openers say there's no reason why the party's brief couldn't read the way Example B does.

A Bad and a Good Example from the Same Case

Example A

This is an appeal by Plaintiff, Dobbins Medical Center, under section 19 of the Administrative Procedure and Register Act, from an order of the Maryland Health Facilities Commission granting a Certificate of Need to Charter Fenton, Inc., a wholly owned subsidiary of Acland Medical Corporation for Fenton Hospital, Baltimore, Maryland. On December 10, 1994, the Commission accepted and dated the application of Fenton for a Certificate of Need to construct, equip, and operate an 80-bed psychiatric and addictive-disease facility containing 43,410 square feet to be located in Baltimore. Fenton originally proposed 60 psychiatric and 20 addictive-disease beds but later amended its application to 64 psychiatric and 16 addictive-disease beds. Plaintiff filed a Notice of Intent to become a party to the application of Fenton, which request was accepted by the Commission on January 11, 1995. Defendant, Purley Hospital Group, also filed and was accepted as a party to the application of Fenton.

Example B

This case involves two contradictory decisions by the Maryland Health Facilities Commission concerning three applications to build new 80-bed psychiatric hospitals in Baltimore.

The hearing officer who heard all the evidence found a "proven need for two of the three" new hospitals. The Commission voted 3–0 to adopt her report but voted 2–1 to deny as "unnecessary" one of the two hospitals she recommended.

Neither the Commission majority's stated findings of fact nor substantial record evidence supports this illogical result. The majority's action arbitrarily violated the Commission's own rules of procedure. The result, if not rejected, would prevent elderly psychiatric patients in Maryland from receiving care that neither the newly approved hospital nor any existing hospital will provide.

4

Once you've drafted issue statements, read more law and take plenty of notes. Tweak or even rewrite the issues as you continue researching. Then organize the issues from most important to least important.

Quotable Quotes

"[Y]ou seek an arrangement that will keep the reader intensely reading and make a *clear and memorable impression* (hang on to the underscored phrase, for it has the virtue of making your mental muscles pull hard)."
—Gorham Munson, *The Written Word* 109 (rev. ed. 1949).

"[T]he arguments in many appellate briefs are wholly without any recognizable form or shape. They begin nowhere, proceed along meandering lines, and end nowhere. They quote a sentence or two from a court opinion, make a couple of collateral remarks, posit a general principle, refer to a fact or two, quote some more, and end with a conclusion that the trial court was in error. The judge reads such a brief, rereads it to make sure he did not drowse the first time, and then tosses it aside as useless . . . . When a lawyer prepares the argument in a brief, he ought to recognize in his own mind what the nature of the argument is, and then he ought to cast it in that form."
—E. Barrett Prettyman, "Some Observations Concerning Appellate Advocacy," in *Advocacy and the King's English* 259, 266–67 (George Rossman ed., 1960).

"Organizing thoughts before writing is pleasant and profitable, but organizing after writing is wasteful, irritating, and inefficient. Planning is not the second, third, or fourth step; it must be the first."
—H.J. Tichy, *Effective Writing for Engineers, Managers, and Scientists* 9 (1966).

"The question will naturally arise, how does one know when 'the case has been thought through' or when 'the basic research has been completed'? The only answer is, you come to sense it. There isn't any gauge or instrument, it is just a feeling. How do you know when you have had enough to eat? It's the same sort of thing, an instinctive reaction that develops after a time. You will recognize it, never fear, and when you do, then you can safely start writing—but not before!"

> —Frederick B. Wiener, *Briefing and Arguing Federal Appeals* 136–37 (rev. ed. 1967).

"Let us assume you have the information all ready to assemble. Some of it is in your mind, some of it in charts or other reports in front of you, some of it in rough notes on a piece of scratch paper. The ideas you want to put across are clear enough to you, but expressing them will take at least a couple of pages—and maybe much more. You have lived with these ideas; you are literally steeped in them. 'How in the world,' you wonder, 'am I to put the gist of them in a short opening paragraph or section? They're just not that simple!'

"You need to do the same thing that practically every good writer has done since the first cogent stone tablet was delivered by a caveman messenger: Step back mentally from the details and try to see just the essence of the message. Admittedly, this is easier said than done; but any writer of any message, no matter how complex, *can* do it if he or she wants."

> —David W. Ewing, *Writing for Results in Business, Government, and the Professions* 56 (1974).

"[A]lways take notes in your own words."

> —Jacques Barzun, *Simple & Direct* 170 (1975).

"[E]xperience shows that you must take notes in a uniform manner, on paper or cards of uniform size. Some researchers favor notebooks, bound or loose-leaf; others prefer ruled or blank index cards—3 × 5 inches, or 4 × 6, or 5 × 8—but one size only for the main materials. Those who use notebooks, large or small, copy out facts or quotations as they come, regardless of subject. They leave a wide margin straight down one side to permit a key word or phrase to be put opposite each note as a guide to the eye in finding and classifying that note."

> —Jacques Barzun & Henry F. Graff, *The Modern Researcher* 22 (5th ed. 1985).

"For most of us, uncertainty about which words to use stems mainly from uncertainty about what we want to say. Usually, if we have the underlying framework of our ideas straight, the writing of the first full prose draft can go ahead much more confidently and rapidly than if we are still trying to work out what sequence of statements we should make."

> —Christopher Turk & John Kirkman, *Effective Writing: Improving Scientific, Technical, and Business Communication* 39 (2d ed. 1989).

Explanation

During research, go through several madman–architect cycles before you begin to write in earnest. Sketch out the big points you need to cover, and supplement this list throughout the process.

The madman and the architect work closely together. And during your research, you'll likely find yourself shifting from one to the other. This collaboration often works in either of two ways. There's the research mode and the intuitive mode.

Most brief-writers probably use the research mode. That is, they do book research first and write later. If you're working in this way, then every time you read a case, for example, you ought to be thinking creatively about how it fits into what you're writing. And at nearly the same time, you should be tying it with the other cases that relate to your subject. As you fill in the configuration of these cases, you'll be using your imagination as well as your spatial sense.

Some excellent brief-writers, though, work in the intuitive mode. They've worked in law for many years, typically, and know its contours pretty well. They are capable of organizing and even drafting a brief without any prior research, confident that there are cases in the books to support what they're saying. If you work in this mode, you'll conceptualize the brief and then write it, and you'll find the cases later—often tweaking what you've said about the law depending on what you find in the cases.

Now a word about taking notes on caselaw. Make your note-taking systematic—not just for one brief, but in case after case. It's not enough to print off cases and highlight them. That's passive. You'll need to write case briefs that look something like this:

(Front)

> **In re Banks**, 299 F.3d 296 (4th Cir. 2002) (per Baldock, J.).
>
> **Facts:** Banks filed for Chapter 13 bankruptcy. His reorganization plan would prevent his nondischargeable, federally guaranteed student loans from accruing interest before Banks was discharged by the Bankruptcy Court. Sallie Mae, which held the student loans, was told of the plan and given the opportunity to attend hearings but never did so and didn't object to the plan before the court confirmed it. Five years later, Banks was discharged. He then learned that interest had continuously accrued on the loans. The Bankruptcy Court agreed that Banks's request to bar the accruals was improper under the Bankruptcy Code but held that Sallie Mae had had an opportunity to object before the court confirmed Banks's reorganization plan and did not do so. So the Bankruptcy Court held that the postdischarge complaint was barred by res judicata. The District Court reversed, holding that the reorganization plan had not given Sallie Mae adequate notice.

(Back)

> **Question:** The Bankruptcy Code and Rules require a debtor to bring a special adversary hearing to prove that exempting from discharge any student-loan debts or interest on the loans would impose an undue hardship. Banks did not do this. Can the Bankruptcy Court's approval of his plan serve as res judicata against Sallie Mae?
>
> **Holding:** No. A general reorganization plan cannot be used to discharge a nondischargeable debt when a special hearing is required on what is ordinarily a nondischargeable debt. Affirmed.
>
> **Reasoning:** A creditor must be given specific notice of an attempt to discharge a student loan or interest and the opportunity to object in a special hearing. Because Banks did not request such a hearing, Sallie Mae never knew about the provision barring the accrual of interest. So Sallie Mae is not bound by the court's confirmation of the reorganization plan, and res judicata does not apply.

Many lawyers haven't done this type of case brief since their first semester of law school. Yet the skill is worth carrying into your daily work: until you acquire such a habit, you'll never really master the caselaw to the extent you should. Be sure, in writing these case briefs, to record similar categories of information in the same part of the page or notecard, case after case.

One way or another, you'll end up with a constellation of cases. And they'll be configured around issues.

Let's say you have three issues. If so, you'll have three parts in the body of the brief, typically proceeding from the strongest to the least strong. (Forget the lame arguments.) Each part will be organized more or less as follows:

- Elaborate the legal premises embedded in the issue statement (see #11).

- Show how the factual points fit into the legal premises (see #12).

- Deal with counterarguments (see #88).

- Drive the point home with an additional reason or set of reasons (see #97).

That's the basic way of organizing the discussion of each issue.

5

Outline your brief, but start with nonlinear outlining.

Quotable Quotes

"Few write the way an architect builds, who first sketches out his plan and designs every detail. Rather, most people write only as though they were playing dominoes, where the pieces are arranged half by design, half by chance; and so it is with the sequence and connection of their sentences."
—Arthur Schopenhauer, "On Style" (1851), in *Theories of Style in Literature* 251, 269 (Lane Cooper ed., 1923) (translation modernized).

"If the prewriting stage has been thorough, it will usually happen that there is little rewriting to do . . . ."
—Gorham Munson, *The Written Word* 157 (rev. ed. 1949).

"[T]he form and organization of a brief ought to conform to two rules: First, it should be so complete within itself that reference to extrinsic sources will not be needed to learn anything that needs to be known about the case, but only to confirm the accuracy of the presentation. Second, the presentation should be such that it may be grasped and understood by the court without the expenditure of unnecessary effort or time."
—Herman F. Selvin, "The Form and Organization of Briefs," in *Advocacy and the King's English* 405, 406 (George Rossman ed., 1960).

"[A] working outline, made to serve as a guide for a future composition, can prevent the sort of obvious muddles of ideas and grammar that often occur when we do not think something out before we formally deliver it . . . as a piece of writing."
—James William Johnson, *Logic and Rhetoric* 20 (1962).

"[I]f the outline is faulty, the thinking is faulty. Consequently, if the draft outline won't wash, your case needs further and clearer analysis, and you will have to labor over it some more. Work over it, slave over it if need be, turn to other matters to clear your head if the deadline allows you that luxury. But keep at it until the outline is sound. Then—and only then—are you ready to write."
—Frederick B. Wiener, *Briefing and Arguing Federal Appeals* 201 (rev. ed. 1967).

"[O]ne of the only virtues of linear outlining is that it looks neat, and that very virtue is its downfall. By working hard to make sure the outline is neat, we effectively cut off any additions or insertions, any new idea. After all, we do not want to mess up our neat outline. When we move sequentially in the world of ideas, we proceed to the next concept under the assumption that we are finished with the idea before it. The fallacy of this method is believing that the concepts we leave behind have been thoroughly thought out and need no extension . . . . Branching, on the other hand, which starts from the center and radiates outward, is an expansive approach to organizing material. By its very nature, it allows you to retrace your steps for easy additions and after-thoughts. And often the afterthoughts are the most valuable aspects."
    —Henriette Anne Klauser, *Writing on Both Sides of the Brain* 48 (1987).

"A brief must be carefully and thoroughly organized before it is written. There is nothing worse than a rambling document that sounds as if it had been dictated off the cuff and filed virtually without change. That kind of brief is difficult to follow, frequently repetitive, often internally inconsistent, and always unpersuasive."
    —Daniel M. Friedman, "Winning on Appeal," in *Appellate Practice Manual* 129, 131 (Priscilla A. Schwab ed., 1992).

"Except for simple correspondence, I would rarely begin any writing without an outline, however cursory it may be. Think how much easier exam-paper grading would be, and how much higher the grades could be, if students would outline their answers before launching into whatever comes to mind on subjects suggested by the question."
    —Thomas M. Reavley, *How I Write*, 4 Scribes J. Legal Writing 51, 51 (1993).

"I like to read a brief that reflects a carefully constructed outline. I can feel the effects, even if the outline is camouflaged by the text; one point leads to the next with the minimum number of words. Just as I salute the discipline of outlining for a judge . . . , so I commend it to a writer of briefs. The attorney who outlines well is invoking the sense of order to which the judge gravitates in crafting an opinion."
    —Frank M. Coffin, *On Appeal: Courts, Lawyering, and Judging* 119 (1994).

Explanation

When it comes to outlining, most people think of Roman numerals, cap-ital letters, and the like—and of old schoolmarmish rules about not having only one or two items under a heading (at least three being required). Some people gravitate toward outlining, but many are repelled at the thought.

    And even if you're good at it, you're going to be less good if you lock yourself into a linear structure early in the process. That is, as an outline-writer, you might start out with something like this:

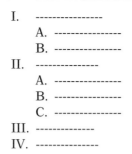

I.   ----------------
    A. ----------------
    B. ----------------
II.   --------------
    A. --------------
    B. --------------
    C. --------------
III. -------------
IV. --------------

If you did begin this way, you'd be unlikely ever to see it if there really should be a C, a D, and an E under heading I. They might end up being V, VI, and VII. In other words, as your architect works, your later thoughts might need to be integrated with your earlier ones, and you don't want to forestall this possibility.

An excellent way of improving this process is to use a nonlinear outline. I routinely create "whirlybirds" in this process. A whirlybird is a whorl of ideas resulting from the madman–architect collaboration. This gives the madman an opportunity to develop ideas, while the architect decides what's a major wing and what's just a feather on that wing of the whirlybird.

Essentially, you start a whirlybird by putting a smallish circle in the middle of the page—perhaps an inch in diameter. Then draw four gently arcing lines (or "wings") off that circle, like this:

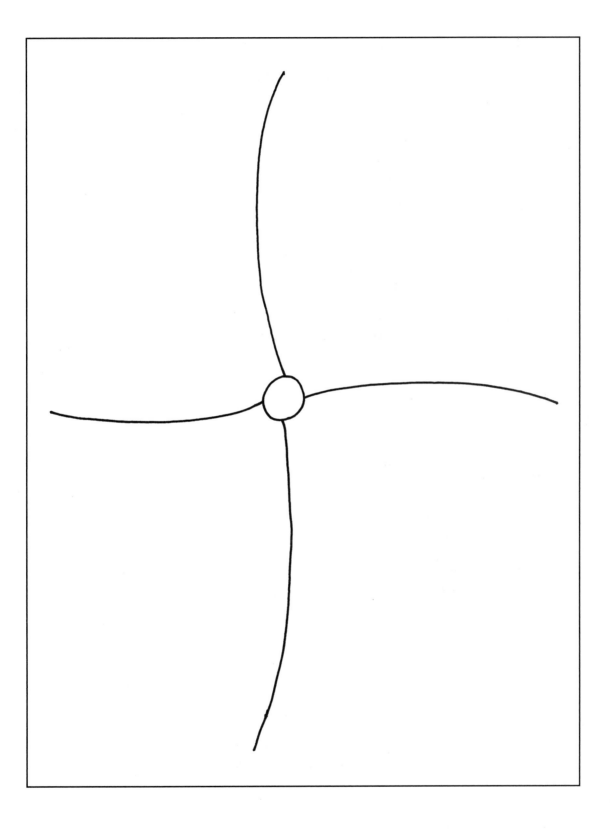

In the middle of the circle, write a shorthand name for your writing project (e.g., "Martin ADA Brief"). Think of one major point and write it on one of the wings. Then think of two or three others and put them on other wings. Then list, as "feathers" hanging off the wings, everything you can think of that relates to these points. Examine documents to gather more ideas. Read cases. Do whatever it takes to develop copious thoughts. If you need to add more wings straight off the circle, do so.

This process may take only ten minutes. It may take days. You're brainstorming. Whenever you think you're finished, force yourself to think of at least four more items—things you haven't yet recorded. When you've done that, force yourself to add two more. You need plenty of ideas. Challenge yourself to be creative.

Once you've truly exhausted your imagination, take a little rest. Turn to something else for a while—anywhere from a few minutes to a few days.

Now, having let the madman take the lead in getting abundant ideas down, you'll need to let the architect take over. Although the madman will still be present to fill in gaps, the architect will now be in charge. Study your whirlybird carefully to see which point will be your lead. Then start translating your whirlybird into a more traditional-looking, hierarchical outline. Think about what order best suits the subject matter, especially from the viewpoint of a stranger to your case. You'll probably find that a sensible order will emerge fairly quickly. Your architect will choose from among the items on your whirlybird, maybe rejecting several ideas, maybe collapsing two wings into one part of the outline, and maybe breaking one wing into two. The point is that the architect can work almost exclusively on *arranging* the material. There's no real pressure at this stage to develop material.

Although I was skeptical at first about this type of outlining—in fact, I refused to try it for more than two years—I now use it for almost every writing project. And I teach it to thousands of lawyers every year, many of whom are just as surprised as I was about how extremely useful it is. Here are the most common reactions:

- "I thought of things I would probably have missed."
- "I saw the interconnections between ideas."
- "I discovered what was really most important—an idea or theme that I might have otherwise buried."
- "I found out that I really know more about the subject than I thought."
- "The project seemed more manageable—it was a relief to see everything on one page without having to worry about order."
- "I'm amazed at how much progress I made in a very short time."

The progression of steps is illustrated in the example that follows—an 11th Circuit brief that I contributed to an ABA mock appellate argument in 1996. It's a plaintiff's brief in an ADA case. My fictitious client is Martin, an in-house lawyer who was dismissed after being diagnosed with a depressive psychological condition. The doctor prescribed a limit on his working hours and a limit on his travel. You'll see how the brief shaped up in the stages that follow.

The Whirlybird (Nonlinear) Outline of Issue 1

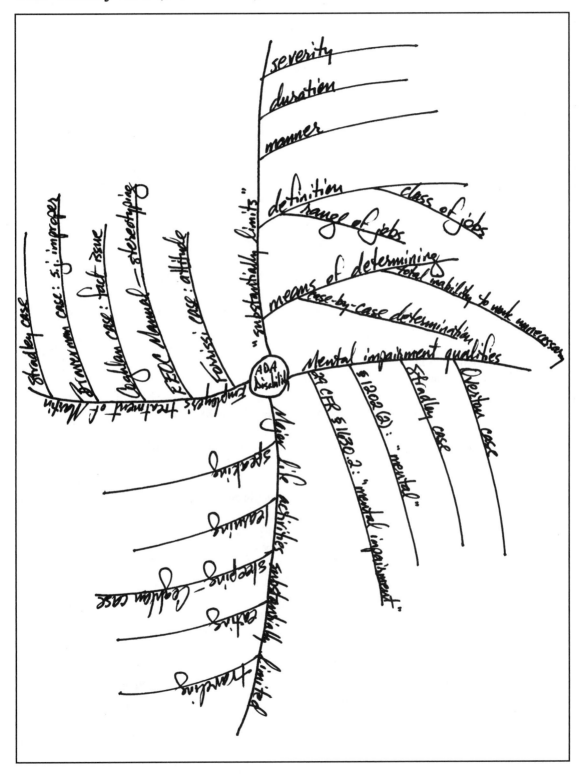

The Linear Outline of Issue 1

Outline of Appellant's Brief

Issue 1:

As the result of his supervisor's harsh criticism, Martin, an in-house attorney and lifelong overachiever, developed an adjustment disorder with anxiety and depression, and is suffering from sleeplessness, short attention span, intemperate behavior, and loss of appetite. His employer summarily fired him after learning his psychologist's opinion that for the indefinite future, he cannot travel, work a 40-hour week, or appear in court. Is there a genuine fact issue under the ADA about whether Martin: (1) has an impairment that substantially limits one or more major life activities; or (2) has been treated as if he has such a disability? [102 words]

A. Martin has a disability under the ADA—an impairment that substantially limits major life activities.

    1. A mental impairment qualifies as a disability. [§ 12101(2): "mental"; 29 CFR § 1630.2: "mental impairment"; *Overton* case; *Stradley* case.]

    2. Martin's condition substantially limits major life activities.

        (a) Martin's condition affects several major life activities [sleeping, speaking, learning, eating, traveling, interacting with others—§ 1630.2(i) list not exhaustive].

        (b) Martin's condition substantially limits one or more of those life activities.

            (1) The general meaning of "substantially limits." [Means of determining: case-by-case basis. Total inability to work not necessary.]

            (2) The factors indicating that Martin is substantially limited in major life activities [29 CFR § 1630.2(j)(1)].

            (3) The considerations for determining whether an individual has been substantially limited in his work.

B. Martin is regarded as having a disability under the ADA—an impairment that substantially limits major life activities.

The Brief on Issue 1

ARGUMENT AND AUTHORITIES

Introduction

The purpose of the ADA is "to provide a clear and comprehensive national mandate for the elimination of discrimination against individuals with disabilities"—a group of Americans that Congress has estimated at 43 million and growing.[94] The ADA prohibits an employer from "discriminat[ing] against a qualified individual with a disability because of the disability."[95] Martin stated a case under the ADA by alleging that (1) he suffers from a "disability"; (2) he is a "qualified individual"; and (3) he was fired from his job because of his disability.[96]

Congress intended that relevant caselaw developed under the Rehabilitation Act of 1973 would generally apply to analogous inquiries under the ADA.[97] The employment provisions of the ADA "merely generalize to the economy as a whole the duties, including that of reasonable accommodation, that the regulations under the Rehabilitation Act imposed on federal agencies and federal contractors."[98]

As this Court has recognized, Congress enacted the Rehabilitation Act because

---

[94] 42 U.S.C. § 12101(a), (b)(1) (1990); *see Vande Zande v. Wisconsin Dep't of Admin.*, 44 F.3d 538, 541 (7th Cir. 1995).

[95] 42 U.S.C. § 12112(a).

[96] R-4; *Stradley v. LaFourche Communications,* 869 F. Supp. 442, 443 (E.D. La. 1994).

[97] *Hogue v. MQS Inspection, Inc.*, 875 F. Supp. 714, 720 (D. Colo. 1995); *EEOC v. AIC Sec. Investigation, Ltd.*, 820 F. Supp. 1060, 1064 (N.D. Ill. 1993); *see White v. York Int'l Corp.,* 45 F.3d 357, 360 n.5 (10th Cir. 1995); *Bolton v. Scrivner, Inc.*, 36 F.3d 939, 942 (10th Cir. 1994) (noting that Rehabilitation Act caselaw defining disability is applicable to similar inquiry under the ADA), *cert. denied*, 115 S. Ct. 1104 (1995); *Sarsycki v. United Parcel Serv.*, 862 F. Supp. 336, 341 n.2 (W.D. Okla. 1994) (explaining that interpretations of the Rehabilitation Act are persuasive authority for ADA interpretations).

[98] *Vande Zande,* 44 F.3d at 542.

it decided that federal contractors and grantees should "bear the costs of providing employment for the handicapped as a *quid pro quo* for the receipt of federal funds."[99] Congress intended that federal contractors "shall take affirmative action to employ and advance in employment qualified handicapped individuals."[100] As a federal contractor receiving federal funds, then, Atlantic Coast had a long-standing legal obligation to advance qualified persons with disabilities—an obligation entirely ignored by Atilla when he abruptly fired Martin upon learning of his disability.[101]

Also useful in interpreting the ADA are federal regulations and guidelines, including those issued to implement Title 1 of the ADA.[102]

Issue 1: Fact Issue on Impairment

Martin, a lifelong overachiever and in-house attorney with Atlantic Coast, developed an adjustment disorder diagnosed by his psychologist as involving anxiety, depression, sleeplessness, and other physical symptoms. When Martin divulged his psychologist's opinion that he should not travel, work over 40 hours a week, or appear in court, Atlantic Coast summarily fired him. Under the ADA, is there a genuine fact issue about whether Martin has an impairment that substantially limits one or more major life activities?

Issue 2: Atlantic Coast's Action

In firing Martin because of his psychologist's diagnosis, has Atlantic Coast treated Martin as if he does in fact have such an impairment?

---

[99] *Moore v. Sun Bank,* 923 F.2d 1423, 1428 (11th Cir. 1991).

[100] *Howard v. Uniroyal, Inc.,* 719 F.2d 1552, 1553 (11th Cir. 1983); *see First Alabama Bank v. Donovan,* 692 F.2d 714, 716–22 (11th Cir. 1982) (discussing the requirement of an affirmative-action program under section 503 of the Rehabilitation Act).

[101] *See* 41 C.F.R. pt. 60-741.1 (1995).

[102] *Hogue,* 875 F. Supp. at 720; *see Bolton,* 36 F.3d at 942.

Under the ADA, the term "disability" means "(A) a physical or mental impairment that substantially limits one or more of the major life activities of [the plaintiff]; (B) a record of such impairment; or (C) being regarded as having such an impairment."[103] The record contains evidence on which a reasonable jury could conclude that Martin has a disability under either the first or the third prong of 42 U.S.C. § 12102(2). Martin produced evidence that would support such a finding, and thus raised a genuine fact issue on the element of disability.

A.   Martin has a disability under the ADA—an impairment that substantially limits major life activities.

1.   Martin's mental impairment qualifies as a disability.

Under the first prong of section 12102(2), a disability includes "a physical or mental impairment that substantially limits one or more of the major life activities."[104] Federal labor regulations specifically include emotional or mental illness in the definition of "mental impairment."[105] Depression and other mental conditions can thus qualify as disabilities under the Act.[106]

Martin has been diagnosed with adjustment disorder with anxiety and depressed mood, described in section 309.28 of the *Diagnostic and Statistical Manual of Men-*

---

[103] 42 U.S.C. § 12102(2).

[104] 42 U.S.C. § 12102(2).

[105] 29 C.F.R. § 1630.2 (1995).

[106] *See Doe v. Region 13 Mental Health–Mental Retardation Comm'n,* 704 F.2d 1402, 1408 (5th Cir. 1983); *Stradley,* 869 F. Supp. at 443.

tal Disorders (4th ed. 1994) (commonly known as *DSM-IV*).[107] A diagnosis is relevant in determining whether a party has a disability.[108]

Although an adjustment disorder, by definition, is said to "resolve" within six months of the termination of the "stressor," the symptoms may exist for longer than six months if the condition is diagnosed as chronic.[109] As Dr. Freud has testified, Martin would require accommodations for "the indefinite future"—an opinion that indicates a long-term or chronic disability.[110]

Moreover, Dr. Freud has also testified that Martin suffers from depression, a condition that is more severe and more permanent than an adjustment disorder.[111] As the Seventh Circuit has explained, " 'Depression' is a misleadingly mild term for an extraordinarily debilitating illness."[112]

"Major depressive disorder" is present when a patient has suffered from one or more major depressive episodes—which are characterized by at least two weeks of depressed mood nearly every day, accompanied by at least four additional symptoms of depression.[113] Dr. Freud's affidavit reveals that more than once, Martin has been

---

[107] *See* R-2 ¶ 13.

[108] *See* EEOC Compl. Man. (CCH) § 902.2(b) n.6, at 5307.

[109] R-2 ¶ 14 (citing *DSM-IV* at 623–24).

[110] R-2 ¶ 14.

[111] *See* R-2 ¶¶ 14, 17, 18–19.

[112] *Overton v. Reilly,* 977 F.2d 1190, 1191 n.1 (7th Cir. 1992) (citing William Styron, *Darkness Visible: A Memoir of Madness* (Random House 1900)).

[113] R-2 ¶ 19 (citing *DSM-IV* at 320).

depressed for at least two weeks, nearly every day for most of the day.[114] Further, Dr. Freud has testified that Martin's symptoms include: (1) sleeplessness; (2) loss of appetite; (3) difficulty concentrating; and (4) irritability.[115] These four symptoms are typical symptoms of depression.[116]

Finally, Dr. Freud has testified that he initially provides the least severe diagnosis possible for a patient because he believes that labeling a patient with a chronic illness may actually worsen the condition.[117] This phenomenon is especially true for depressed patients, whose depression often worsens upon being labeled as "chronically depressed."[118] In light of Dr. Freud's testimony that the condition will probably continue for the indefinite future and Martin's testimony about his symptoms, there is, at the very least, a fact issue about whether Martin has a disability under the ADA.[119]

2. *Martin's condition substantially limits major life activities.*

The determination whether a person is substantially limited in a major life activity is uniquely factual and must be made case by case.[120] Some impairments may be disabling for some people but not for others, depending on the stage of the im-

---

[114] *See* R-2 ¶ 18.

[115] R-2 ¶ 19.

[116] R-2 ¶ 19 (citing *DSM-IV* at 320).

[117] R-2 ¶ 13.

[118] R-2 ¶ 8.

[119] *See* R-2 ¶ 14; R-1 ¶¶ 20–23.

[120] 29 C.F.R. app. § 1630.2(j).

pairment, the presence of other impairments that combine to make the impairment disabling, or any number of other factors.[121] Because the inquiry is highly fact-specific and because Martin has at least raised a fact issue that his impairment and the associated symptoms are disabling to him, summary judgment was inappropriate.[122]

a.   Several of Martin's major life activities have been affected.

Major life activities specifically include learning and speaking, both of which have been affected by Martin's condition.[123] His short attention span may limit his ability to learn.[124] And Dr. Freud has recommended that he not make any more oral arguments, suggesting at least an indirect effect on his ability to speak.[125]

Mental and emotional processes such as thinking, concentrating, and interacting with others are also major life activities.[126] Martin's short attention span probably limits his ability to think and concentrate.[127] And because he suffers from irritability, short temper, and proneness to intemperate behavior, Martin may be limited in his ability to interact with others.[128]

---

[121] *Id.*

[122] *See Fehr v. McLean Packaging Corp.,* 860 F. Supp. 198, 200 (E.D. Pa. 1994).

[123] *See* 29 C.F.R. § 1630.2(i); *see* R-1 ¶¶ 20, 23, 24; R-2 ¶¶ 11, 16, 19.

[124] R-1 ¶ 23; R-2 ¶¶ 16, 19.

[125] *See* R-2 ¶ 11.

[126] EEOC Compl. Man. (CCH) § 902.3(b), at 5311.

[127] *See* R-1 ¶ 23; R-2 ¶ 16.

[128] *See* R-1 ¶ 20; R-2 ¶ 16.

Further, the list in section 1630.2(i) is not exhaustive.[129] Major life activities include any activity that an average person in the general population can perform with little or no difficulty.[130] Martin has been impaired in four such activities: sleep, eating, travel, and work. First, Dr. Freud has testified that Martin's mental disability has caused him to suffer from sleeplessness. And sleep, not surprisingly, has been held to be a major life activity.[131] Second, as Martin and Dr. Freud have testified, Martin's mental disability has also affected his eating—another major life activity.[132] Third, Dr. Freud has testified that Martin's disability precludes him from traveling, another activity that the average person can perform with little trouble.[133] Finally, Martin's condition may limit his ability to work, and working is specifically listed as a major life activity.[134]

b.   *There is a fact issue about whether Martin's life activities have been substantially limited.*

A person is "substantially limited" in major life activities if the person is significantly restricted in the manner and duration of performing these activities, as compared to the average person in the general population.[135] The evidence in this case

---

[129] EEOC Compl. Man. (CCH) § 902.3, at 5311; *see* 29 C.F.R. § 1630.2(i); *id.* app. § 1630.2(i) (noting that the list in section 1630.2(i) is not exhaustive).

[130] 29 C.F.R. app. § 1630.2(i).

[131] *See Coghlan v. H.J. Heinz Co.,* 851 F. Supp. 808, 814 (N.D. Tex. 1994); R-2 ¶ 16.

[132] *See* 29 C.F.R. app. § 1630.2(i); R-1 ¶ 22; R-2 ¶ 16.

[133] R-2 ¶ 11.

[134] 29 C.F.R. app. § 1630.2(i).

[135] 29 C.F.R. § 1630.2(j)(1).

certainly raises fact issues about whether Martin can learn, think, concentrate, or interact with others in the manner and for the duration that the average person can.
And as the evidence establishes, Martin is significantly restricted in the manner and
duration of his eating, sleeping, and traveling.[136]

In determining whether there is a substantial limitation, the fact-finder must
consider whether the impairment is severe and long-lasting.[137] Martin is afflicted with
a severe impairment, entailing both anxiety and depression. This impairment has affected not only his work but also his sleeping, eating, and other ordinary activities of
life.[138] An example in the EEOC Compliance Manual reveals that if an employee sus-
tains a concussion resulting in a short-term memory deficit, inability to concentrate,
and difficulty in learning and assimilating, then the employee's condition is substantially
limiting.[139] As Martin and Dr. Freud have testified, Martin suffers from similar thinking and learning problems.[140]

Moreover, a fact issue exists about whether Martin's impairment will be long-
lasting. As Dr. Freud has testified, accommodations will be necessary indefinitely,
suggesting that Martin's impairment is chronic.[141] Although Dr. Freud diagnosed the

---

[136] R-1 ¶¶ 20–22, 24; R-2 ¶¶ 11, 16.

[137] *See* 29 C.F.R. § 1630.2(j)(2).

[138] *See Weiler v. Household Fin. Corp.,* 3 AD Cases (BNA) 1337, 1339 (N.D. Ill. June 7, 1994)
(finding that anxiety and depression substantially limited plaintiff's ability to work, eat, and
sleep, and thereby met the ADA standard for a disability).

[139] *See* EEOC Compl. Man. (CCH) § 902.4(d), at 5320.

[140] R-1 ¶ 23; R-2 ¶ 16.

[141] *See* R-2 ¶ 14.

6

Write a draft straight through, without stopping to edit. Let it sit awhile before editing.

Quotable Quotes

"[P]olishing at an early stage usually is a waste of time . . . ."
—George J. Miller, *On Legal Style*, 43 Ky. L.J. 235, 239 (1955).

"When you have found your idea . . . write it down as nearly as possible as you would express it in speech; swiftly, unselfconsciously, without stopping to think about the form of it at all. Revise it afterwards—but only afterwards. To stop to think about form in midcareer, while the idea is in motion, is like throwing out your clutch halfway up a hill and having to start in low again. You never get back your old momentum."
—David Lambuth et al., *The Golden Book on Writing* 4 (1964).

"Poor writers are inclined to scorn revision and to assume incorrectly that good writers do not need to revise. Poor writers believe that articles, stories, and poems should pour forth in their complete and final forms. Until writers are disabused of this error, they are at best halfhearted about revising and at worst unwilling to change a word they have written."
—H.J. Tichy, *Effective Writing for Engineers, Managers, and Scientists* 10 (1966).

"What you must do, as a writer, is think about what you want to say and then let it flow in your usual way. Afterwards you will need to go over it and do some fixing—but, just as with the football play, that will not be hard if there are the right makings to begin with."
—David W. Ewing, *Writing for Results in Business, Government, the Sciences, and the Professions* 212 (2d ed. 1979).

"Convince yourself that you are working in clay not marble, on paper not eternal bronze: let that first sentence be as stupid as it wishes. No one will rush out and print it as it stands. Just put it down; then another. Your whole first paragraph or first page may have to be guillotined in any case after your piece is finished: it is a kind of forebirth."
—Jacques Barzun, "A Writer's Discipline," in *On Writing, Editing, and Publishing* 8 (2d ed. 1986).

Explanation

Mentally speaking, the writing function and the editing function are largely separate. That's why, in writing courses, the students who are the best editors are almost never the best writers, and vice versa.

And ultimately, the most accomplished writers keep the judge separate from the carpenter, who needs to work unimpeded. The judge is a kibitzer, a second-guesser. For the carpenter, the judge is a nuisance. For those with a well-developed judge, the great secret of writing is keeping the judge out of the way while the carpenter works.

Writers with an overbearing judge will find writing especially painful. They're the ones who squeeze out the draft word by word. They won't move on to a new sentence until the preceding one is perfect.

If you cheerfully acknowledge, though, that the judge will have time to work—that whatever you write at first will be subject to thorough revision and that the most important thing for now is to get a draft on paper—then you'll probably be able to let the carpenter work without distraction.

And as just about everyone knows, the more time you can put between the draft and the editing, the better your judge will work. In any event, the very switch in personality from carpenter to judge will function as a way of "sleeping on it," even if you allow only 15 minutes to pass between writing and editing. As judge, you'll look at your words through different eyes: those of a different personality.

As Alexander Pope (1688–1744) once said, "Compose with fury and correct with phlegm." Learn to write rapidly, without stopping to revise. For that matter, don't even take time to pick the right words. Just get your thoughts down by expanding on the outline that your architect has created. That's the way professional nonfiction writers typically work—at least the most productive ones.

When you learn to write this way, the prose itself takes on a different quality. The judicial reader will probably sense greater swiftness within your paragraphs. They won't be laborious reading.

7

Proof carefully;
have several others proof carefully;
learn and use standard editing marks.

Quotable Quotes

"No one can expect to write a finished essay in a single draft, and no one (except the green beginner or the newspaperman who is short of time) ever tries. Although students have been told the virtues of second and third drafts from the time they learned to write, they are still reluctant to take the trouble. The results are scandalous. Sentences don't parse; verbs are written in the wrong person and tense; the style is jerky; the order disconcerting; very frequently even the sense is gone. The only way to iron out the manuscript is to reread it (read it aloud if possible), correct it, revise it, and rewrite it."

—Sherman Kent, *Writing History* 69 (1941).

"I do not believe that the brief can be proofread too often or too carefully."

—Raymond S. Wilkins, "The Argument of an Appeal," in *Advocacy and the King's English* 277, 281 (George Rossman ed., 1960).

"Too often briefs [that] lawyers have dictated in part and handwritten in part and sent in that condition to the printer are filed without having been proofread and corrected. We attorneys have no right to criticize physicians who leave sponges in the bellies of patients if lawyers are equally cavalier of the rights of their clients."

—Jean Appleman, *The Written Argument on Appeal*, 41 Notre Dame Law. 40, 41 (1965).

"Check every citation, quotation, and record reference. *Check every citation, quotation, and record reference*! Check every citation, quotation, and record reference!"

—Frederick B. Wiener, *Briefing and Arguing Federal Appeals* 202 (rev. ed. 1967).

"Suppose that after making many small but painstaking corrections and improvements, you receive the manuscript back with a huge black comment scribbled in the margin: 'Nitpicking!' What to do? Respond neatly below in the margin and circle the whole thing so it won't be set in type but will remain for the author to see when reading proof: 'But who wants nits?' "

—Elsie Myers Stainton, *The Fine Art of Copyediting* 25 (1991).

Explanation

Like many other essential things, proofing can be deathly dull—especially if you've already proofed an earlier version of the brief. That's one reason why most writers can benefit from a fresh pair of eyes. If you've seen the page several times, you're likely to assume that things are as you expect them to be, not as they actually are. So enlist the help of support staffers, paralegals, or other lawyers in proofing.

Meanwhile, you'll be building an organizational culture in which everyone appreciates getting things right. That will improve not only your document-preparation, but also the many other tasks that you're involved in carrying out.

You'll save time in the process if people have a shared knowledge of editing marks. The legal secretary needs to know, for example, not only what an em-dash is but that the handwritten mark [⊥ₘ] means that an em dash should be inserted. (See #57.) And there ought to be some similarity in how readers mark text to be omitted, text to be inserted, and the like.

Because lawyers are professional writers, they and their staffs ought to feel at ease with editing marks. A well-edited page ought to have a familiar look.

Editing Marks

The Mark	The Mark in Text	Explanation
	question ~~as to~~ whether it applies	Delete
Write here	~~However,~~ *But* Illinois courts do not	Delete and replace
	They fully complied with	Delete and close up space
(*tr.*)	Rasch's record is unblemished (*tr.*)	Transpose
#	venue in thedistrict court	Insert a space
(*ital.*)	In Caponigro v. Navistar, the (*ital.*)	Make italic
(*rom.*)	In *Courtney v. Biosound*, the (*rom.*)	Roman—delete italics
(*bf*)	A. The Delivery (*bf*)	Make boldface
/ (*lc*)	To merit Summary Judgment, the (*lc*)	Lowercase
≡ (*cap.*)	The Village of niles claimed (*cap.*)	Uppercase
= (*sc*)	at 4:30 p.m. the next day (*sc*)	Small caps
(*write here*)	did not violate state tax laws (*federal or*)	Insert text
¶	factually supported. A detailed	Make a paragraph here
(*No ¶*) *Text* *Text*	linking his layoff to the tax issue. (*No ¶*) The evidence is uncontroverted,	No paragraph here

The Mark	The Mark in Text	Explanation
	C. 1995 Taxes	Move left
	D. 1996 Taxes	Move right
Word	can only be held liable when	Move word
	her administrative remedies The	Insert period
	In February 1994 at the time of the	Insert comma
	was not there; rather, she was	Insert semicolon
	no such claim Burton really said	Insert colon
	The company then in 1994 issued a	Parentheses
	He said, We quit.	Quotation marks
	entitled to attorneys fees	Apostrophe
	right-of-way law	Hyphen
	his claim namely, that	Em-dash
	1996-1997	En-dash
...... Stet	The court declined the proposal Stet	Let it stand (ignore the editor's mark)

A Well-Edited Page from a Brief

[Handwritten annotations are shown throughout this edited manuscript page.]

[Balloon note, top left:] "Bf. — upper & lower case large

ARGUMENT

Rinker's ~~Defendants'~~ requests for admission ~~do not seek "expert discovery," but~~ *ask the State to acknowledge*

~~rather acknowledgment by the State of~~ certain information that it either knows *[inserted: Because these requests are perfectly proper & and do not call for "expert discovery" it]* or, with reasonable inquiry, is capable of knowing. ~~Thus, the State should be~~ *[inserted: this Court should order the State to respond to Rinker's]* ~~ordered to provide responses to defendants'~~ requests.

[Balloon note, left: Flush left, w/ hanging indent. Lowercase bf.]

I. ~~DEFENDANTS'~~ *Rinker's* REQUESTS PROPERLY SEEK ADMISSIONS *by* BY THE STATE, NOT ITS TRIAL OR CONSULTING EXPERTS.

Although ~~The~~ State has ~~interposed only a single~~ *objected to Rinker's* objection ~~to defendants'~~ requests *[balloon note, right: the objection is grossly overbroad.]* for admissions, *claiming* ~~they seek~~ expert discovery. According to the State, ~~defendants~~ *Rinker's* requests would force the State "to make a judgment and to provide the defendants with expert opinions." * ~~Plaintiff is being asked to admit statements which are typically posed to experts on direct and cross-examination. Plaintiff's Response to Defendants' First Requests for Admission to Plaintiff at 2.~~ Thus, the State contends, "defendants are attempting to do by way of Rule 36 requests for admission what they are permitted to do only through Rule 33 interrogatories." Id. at 1. *But* ~~T~~*t*his objection ~~however, is completely without~~ *has no* merit *because ....*

~~Even the briefest examination of defendants' requests for admissions~~ shows that the State's blanket objection is hopelessly overbroad. It is difficult to understand, for example, how the State could plausibly assert that the following requests for admission require "expert testimony":

* *State's Response at 2.*

[Balloon note, bottom right: Capsulize the reason here: What is it?]

Part B

Conveying the Big Picture

8

Frame the deep issues at the outset so that you meet the 90-second test.

Quotable Quotes

"The best argument on a question of law is to state the question clearly."
—Rufus Choate, 1799–1859 (as quoted in Harley N. Crosby, "Mistakes Commonly Made in the Presentation of Appeals," in 3 Sydney C. Schweitzer, *Trial Guide* 1546 (1945)).

"Your business is to give the reader something of value he does not already possess. Do not bore him by putting in material he knows already, nor confuse him by including material that has no relation to your real point. Plunge in. An abrupt beginning is better than a dull one."
—James Weber Linn, *The Essentials of English Composition* § 11, at 17 (1916).

"[J]ust after being admitted to the bar, [I] was shocked when advised by S.S. Gregory, an ex-president of the American Bar Association—a man more than ordinarily aware of legal realities—that 'the way to win a case is to make the judge want to decide in your favor and then, and then only, to cite precedents which will justify such a determination. You will almost always find plenty of cases to cite in your favor.' All successful lawyers are more or less consciously aware of this technique. But they seldom avow it—even to themselves."
—Jerome Frank, *Law and the Modern Mind* 111 n.2 (1930; repr. 1963).

"In law the right answer usually depends on putting the right question."
—*Estate of Rogers v. Comm'r*, 320 U.S. 410, 413 (1943) (Frankfurter, J.).

"The wise man knows what the questions are. . . . The alternatives to asking answerable questions, and then making honest attempts to find answers to them, are clear—and disgraceful. We can ask no questions at all, either out of stupor or as a display of arrogance. We can ask questions that are misleading, or vague, or meaningless—to be answered, respectively, by mountebanks, the confused, and the very naive. Or, we may ask questions and then refuse to acknowledge them, as a gesture of fear, smugness, or irresponsibility."
—Wendell Johnson, *Verbal Man: The Enchantment of Words* 36, 41 (1956; repr. 1965).

"A lawyer who has never held a judicial office does not, I think, fully appreciate the importance of getting the principal facts and the main contention between the parties firmly fixed at the outset in the mind of the court. When he has done this, his labor is half over."
>—Alfred C. Coxe, "Is Brief-Making a Lost Art?," in *Advocacy and the King's English* 338, 341 (George Rossman ed., 1960).

" 'The difficulty with the average advocate is that he succeeds primarily in confusing the court rather than clarifying the issues.' "
>—Anonymous judge (as quoted in Frederick B. Wiener, *Briefing and Arguing Federal Appeals* 29 (rev. ed. 1967)).

"[T]he question presented in any case can be clearly and appealingly stated—or, contrariwise, unclearly and unappealingly."
>—Frederick B. Wiener, *Briefing and Arguing Federal Appeals* 77 (rev. ed. 1967).

"It may be argued that an essay involves so many complicated thoughts that no one sentence can be expected to summarize them all. But in most cases, and certainly in most brief essays, a failure to isolate the most important idea is usually an indication of sloppy thinking, not profundity."
>—Steward La Casce & Terry Belanger, *The Art of Persuasion: How to Write Effectively About Almost Anything* 13 (1972).

"[I]t is unwise to allow the court to read a factual statement without first having presented the issues involved. The court should not be forced to guess, even for a moment, what questions it is asked to decide."
>—Edward D. Re, *Brief Writing and Oral Argument* 117 (4th ed. 1974).

"Issues are the most important information attorneys give an appellate court. The courts decide issues, and determining what to decide is the sine qua non of any decision—an important truism. Rulings on the various issues in a case total up to a decision for the plaintiff or defendant . . . ."
>—Thomas B. Marvell, *Appellate Courts and Lawyers* 119 (1978).

"The issues should be stated so simply and so clearly that the judges will grasp them at once. Nowhere in the brief is clarity more important. Because the judges will normally examine both statements of the issues first, reading one after the other and comparing them, it is here that the brief writer makes an invaluable first impression."
>—Girvan Peck, *Writing Persuasive Briefs* 103–04 (1984).

" '[E]fficiency' does not mean the paper with the shortest length; rather, [it means] the paper that takes readers the shortest time to understand."
>—Michael Alley, *The Craft of Scientific Writing* 15 (1987).

"Unfortunately, the judge does not possess the luxury of time for leisurely, detached meditation. You'd better sell the sizzle as soon as possible; the steak can wait."
>—Ruggero J. Aldisert, *Winning on Appeal: Better Briefs and Oral Argument* 142 (1992).

"Start in the very first sentence with the problem in this case. Put it right up front. Start early. Don't bury it under a lot of verbiage and preliminaries."
—Nathan L. Hecht (as quoted in Bryan A. Garner, *Judges on Effective Writing: The Importance of Plain Language*, 73 Mich. B.J. 326, 326 (1994)).

"I like to see the most important issues framed up front. Of course, I expect to see what the writer considers her adversary's most vulnerable point; what I rejoice to see is a writer candidly recognizing what appears to the reading judge as her own most vulnerable issue and dealing with it."
—Frank M. Coffin, *On Appeal: Courts, Lawyering, and Judging* 120 (1994).

"Readers are impatient to get the goods. And they resent having to work any harder than necessary to get them."
—John R. Trimble, *Editing Your Own Prose* (forthcoming).

Explanation

Every brief should make its primary point within 90 seconds. But probably only 1% of American briefs actually succeed on this score. The ones that do are spectacular to read: within 90 seconds, the judge understands the basic question, the answer, and the reasons for that answer. These briefs are quick reads.

How does the brief-writer accomplish this? By cultivating a knack for framing issues well. To frame a good persuasive issue, you must:

- put it up front;

- break it into separate sentences, following a premise–premise–question form;

- weave in enough facts so that the reader can truly understand the problem; and

- write it in such a way that there is only one possible answer.

To do these things well, most lawyers must forget everything they ever learned in law school about framing legal issues. Forget the idea that you should begin with *Whether* . . . . Forget the notion that you should load all your points into one sentence (a format that ensures an unchronological presentation). Forget making the issue as abstract as possible.

What does a good persuasive issue look like? Take the following example:

As Hannicutt Corporation planned and constructed its headquarters, the general contractor, Laurence Construction Co., repeatedly recommended a roof membrane and noted that the manufacturer also recommended it. Even so, the roof manufacturer warranted the roof without the membrane. Now that the manufacturer has gone bankrupt and the roof is failing, is Laurence Construction jointly responsible with the insurer for the cost of reconstructing the roof?

Some briefs would take at least ten pages to deliver that information. And you wouldn't find this concise statement on page 10. Instead, you would find the tidbits within it strewn amid other facts throughout the first ten pages. To glean the issue, the judge would have to read slowly with intense concentration. That's quite a demand to impose on busy judges. And yet brief-writers seem to make this imposition routinely.

A big part of the problem seems to stem from fear—fear that if the judge doesn't see the issue in the same way as the advocate, the advocate is sunk. "How do I know what the judge will latch onto?" the diffident advocate asks. "I won't state the issue in a single way. I'll talk about the case and the parties in a way that gives the judge several handles on the case. But I'm not going to marry myself to a single issue or set of issues." The result of this understandable fear, unfortunately, is that the advocate has no clearly framed issues—no theory of the case.

And the judge becomes frustrated. Only one thing matters to the judge: what question he or she is supposed to answer. "If I can figure that out," thinks the judge, "I'll be ready to decide the case. But until I find out what that is, I'm just groping for it."

Framing the deep issue at the outset is a way of capturing the judicial imagination. Whoever does that in a given case is most likely to win.

I'm not much inclined to formulas, but if there's a good formula for beginning a court paper, I think it's this: "In deciding this [motion, etc.], the court need address only the following [two, three, or whatever number] issues: . . . ." What comes after the colon will be the most challenging thing you'll have to write: the deep issue.

What, precisely, is a *deep issue*? I've now used the term three times without defining it. Essentially, a deep issue is the ultimate, concrete question that a court needs to answer to decide a point your way. *Deep* refers to the deep structure of the case—not to deep thinking. The deep issue is the final question you pose when you can no longer usefully ask the follow-up question, "And what does *that* turn on?" The best form it can take is that of the syllogism (see #11).

The first example below typifies the leaden, slow, unduly complex style of so many modern briefs. Try reading it for just 90 seconds to see what you can glean. Certainly you'll get something from it—a subject matter—but (unless you're a rare genius) you probably won't understand the issue.

Then turn to page 68 to see how the brief might have begun. There, the issue is fully comprehensible in less than a minute—probably much less. This example shows just what it means to spill the beans on page 1.

The example beginning at page 69 shows the deep issue at work in a summary-judgment reply brief. This example had an interesting result. Both sides had moved for summary judgment, but only Firemen's reply brief had showcased a deep issue up front. When the lawyers appeared for oral argument, the federal district judge announced that he felt prepared to rule already, having read the briefs: he would rule for Firemen's unless the FDIC's lawyers could show him why he shouldn't. They tried but failed. The judge then ruled for Firemen's, without any argument from Firemen's lawyers. The judge essentially adopted the deep issue on page 69 as his own.

When you're framing your issues, remember the great Herbert Wechsler of Columbia University. As his former student Jim Damis recalls, Wechsler said this about his U.S. Supreme Court briefs: "Half my time in writing a brief is spent framing the issue."

A Typically Bad Example

In the Supreme Court of Indiana

APPEAL FROM THE COURT OF APPEALS
THIRD APPELLATE DISTRICT
MARION COUNTY, INDIANA

PLEBINOL CORPORATION,
Plaintiff-Appellee and Cross-Appellant,

vs.

THE TULL GROUP INC.

and

TULL AEROSPACE,
Defendants-Appellants.

**BRIEF OF DEFENDANTS-APPELLANTS
THE TULL GROUP INC. and
TULL AEROSPACE**

STATEMENT OF THE CASE

This lawsuit concerns an action for breach of warranty and/or fraud which was commenced in the Court of Common Pleas of Marion County, Indiana, in August of 1985. The plaintiff sought to recover certain specific damages from the defendants arising from an admitted breach of warranty. The plaintiff asked the jury to return a verdict in its favor in the amount of $1,076,347.64. Decision dated December 9, 1981 at p. 19.

This figure, $1,076,347.64, consisted of the following specifically enumerated items of damages:

1. $257,000—the amount paid by plaintiff to a third party in settlement of its claim related to the defective vinyl film; 2. $3,474.98—incidental expense incurred in the rental of a color meter; 3. $9,015.00—incidental expense incurred by hiring accounting firm of Ernst & Whinney; 4. $5,794.00—incidental additional salary expenses; 5. $2,596.43—incidental additional hourly costs; 6. $306,998.00—adhesion losses claimed to have been caused by breach of warranty; 7. $185,096.82—interest expense incurred by plaintiff; 8. $178,268.00—lost profits claimed by plaintiff; 9. $119,506.00—loss incurred by plaintiff on roll goods. Decision dated December 9, 1981 at pp. 20–28.

The jury ultimately returned a general verdict, untested by interrogatories, in the amount of $854,500.00. The defendants were permitted a credit of $15,500.00 and final judgment was entered in favor of the plaintiff in the amount of $839,000.00.

On appeal, the Court of Appeals for the Third Judicial District unanimously determined that items of damages totaling $262,532.84 were erroneously submitted to the jury by the trial court. Because there was no mathematical means to ascertain the extent to which the items totaling $262,532.84 were included in the jury's verdict, the Court of Appeals ordered a new trial. In its decision dated December 9, 1981, the Court of Appeals noted:

> "In light of the general verdict, *we cannot speculate* as to what elements of damages made up this differential. Therefore, we must reverse the judgment and remand the case for a new trial." (Emphasis added.) Decision dated December 9, 1981 at p. 34.

Then, in an abrupt turnabout, the same Court of Appeals, ruling on a Motion for Reconsideration filed by the plaintiff-appellee, over the dissent of Judge Bell, affirmed the judgment of the lower court in the amount of $813,814.80. After first determining (in its decision of December 9, 1981) that it was impossible to ascertain the extent to which the erroneously submitted items of damages were included in the jury's verdict, the Court subsequently "determined" in its Decision and Journal Entry of December 23, 1981 that only $40,685.20 of the erroneously submitted items of damages ($262,532.84) not from the verdict ($854,500.00) but from the total damages sought by the plaintiff ($1,076,347.64). The Court thereupon affirmed judgment in favor of the plaintiff in the amount of $818,840.00 after ordering a remittitur of $40,685.20.

Finally, in its third Decision and Journal Entry, the Court of Appeals, realizing that it had failed to credit the defendants the sum of $15,500.00, entered final judgment on February 2, 1982 in the amount of $798,314.80.

ARGUMENT

PROPOSITION OF LAW NO. 1

A new trial, or a remittitur of the full amount of possible excess damages, is required where the extent of prejudicial error in a verdict cannot be determined.

Short of resort to speculation, which the Court of Appeals had specifically rejected in its decision of December 9, 1981 when it determined that a new trial should be granted, it is impossible to determine the precise extent to which the erroneously submitted items of damage totaling $262,532.84 were reflected in the jury's verdict.

Having once determined that the trial court erred to the prejudice of the defendants by submitting to the jury items of damages totaling $262,532.84, the Court of Appeals' choices were either (1) to reverse the judgment of the lower court and order a new trial, or (2) grant a $262,532.84 remittitur from the verdict which, of course, the plaintiff had the option to refuse. Unfortunately, the Court of Appeals did not recognize that its options were so limited.

A remittitur is designed to correct prejudicial error and thereby eliminate the time and the expense involved in a new trial. However, if the amount of the error is determined to be as much as *thirty per cent* (262,532.84/839,000) of the verdict, as in the instant case, how is the error "corrected" if the Court awards only a *four per cent* (40,685.20/839,000) reduction of the verdict? When a remittitur fails of its essential purpose it cannot be deemed to be effectual. To the contrary, a new injustice, an appellate injustice, has been done.

Where the jury verdict was infected by prejudicial error to an unknown degree, it was held that a new trial must be granted in *Powell v. Montgomery*, 27 Ind. App. 2d 112 (Ct. App. Allen County, 1971). *Powell* involved a personal injury action in which the plaintiff recovered a general verdict against the defendant in the amount of $6,500. The defendant appealed on the ground, among others, that the Court erroneously instructed the jury on future medical expenses, future pain and suffering, and impairment of earning capacity. The Court of Appeals determined that there was no evidence to warrant such an instruction and agreed with the appellant that this constituted prejudicial error.

The plaintiff-appellee, while denying the existence of error, urged the Court of Appeals to cure the error by granting a remittitur. The Court of Appeals rejected this offer and held that only a new trial could cure the error created by the erroneous submission of items of damages (viz. future medical expenses, future pain and suffering, future loss of earnings and loss of earning capacity) to the jury, where the jury had returned a general verdict not tested by interrogatories.

> "The verdict in this case was general, and the error is in the charge and not the reception of evidence. We do not know, nor do we have any means of ascertaining, what sum, if any, the jury allowed as to future damages. No doubt exists that this court could order a remittitur if, in our view, the judgment was excessive. We are not prepared to so hold. Without the error, we would have affirmed.

> "Both parties were entitled to a jury verdict based upon proper instruction. The general rule which we believe applicable here, is that where the amount of the remittitur is not clearly ascertainable and such amount can only be reached by speculation and by substituting the judgment of the

court for that of the jury, entry of remittitur is not proper. 5 Am. Jur. 2d 366, Appeal and Error, Section 939, et seq., 4 Ind. Jur. 2d 358, Appellate Review, Section 1036.

"In *Tuttle v. Furi,* 22 C.C. (N.S.) 388, the Sixth Paragraph of the Syllabus provides:

" 'Where the court has erroneously permitted the jury to include certain items of damages in their verdict the error is not cured by a remittitur where there is nothing to show that the amount remitted was the amount which the jury may have awarded because of those items.'

"This court finding error having intervened to the prejudice of the appellee below, the judgment must be reversed and the cause remanded to the trial court." *Powell, supra,* p. 124.

The *Powell* standard, which is the correct rule of law, appears to be widely applied. Courts of other jurisdictions have held, where it is impossible to ascertain the extent of the impact of prejudicial error upon a verdict, that only a new trial will cure the error. Holding that remittitur was an inappropriate remedy where improper testimony as to the value of land was admitted by the trial court, the Supreme Court of Indiana stated:

". . . We are, therefore, at a loss to understand why the Court of Appeals determined that $28,662 of the jury award was motivated by properly admitted evidence and only $16,338 thereof by the improperly admitted evidence, when from all that appears from the record, the entire award may have been based upon the evidence improperly admitted . . . ." *State v. Church of Nazarene of Logansport*, 377 N.E.2d 607 (S. Ct. Ind., 1978).

The Supreme Court of Missouri arrived at the same conclusion where the plaintiff had erroneously introduced the element of punitive damages in a medical malpractice case.

"In the instant case there is no method by which this court can know how much of the verdict represented the jury's response to plaintiff's appeal for a punitive sum. It may be argued that this assumes the jury included a punitive sum in its verdict. The answer to that is that we do assume that the jury did what it was invited to do by plaintiff's argument and included some sum of money in its verdict to deter others from like conduct, but as noted supra, we do not know how much of the verdict represented punitive damages and, therefore, the remittitur solution is not available to correct the error." *Smith v. Courter*, 531 S.W.2d 743, 748 (S. Ct. Mo., 1976).

A remittitur was also held to be an inappropriate remedy in *Vick v. Tisdale*, 324 So. 2d 279 (Ala. App. 1975). There the Court of Appeals determined that the plaintiffs, who had recovered a verdict of $5,090, were not entitled to recover any damages by way of a statutory penalty. Because only $2,500 had been sought by the plaintiffs as compensatory damages, it was determined that, at least, $2,590 of the verdict was allocable to a statutory penalty. The Court of Appeals was then confronted with the issue of whether remittitur would correct the error committed at the trial level. The plaintiff requested that the court affirm the judgment of $2,500—upon their agreeing to a remittitur of $2,590. The Appellate Court, however, rejected this offer because it was unclear as to exactly how much of the verdict was attributable to the penalty vis-a-vis compensatory damages:

> "Able counsel requests this court to order an affirmance conditioned upon a remittitur of damages over $2,500, inasmuch as ample evidence exists to support the jury's finding that the fair market value of the timber cut was $2,500 as prayed for in appellees' Complaint. While we are not unsympathetic to counsel's request, which is based upon considerations of judicial economy and expense to the parties involved, we cannot issue such an order. As our original opinion points out, the evidence was conflicting as to the number of trees actually cut and their fair market value. It therefore cannot be ascertained how to apportion the $5,000 general verdict between compensatory damages and statutory penalty. Accordingly, the remittitur requested by counsel is too speculative to be granted." *Vick, supra,* pp. 283–284.

In *Grand Trunk Western R. Co. v. H.W. Nelson, Inc.,* 118 F.2d 252 (6th Cir. 1941), the plaintiff claimed contract damages of $1,294,307.79. The jury awarded $871,000. However an interest claim of $431,870.39 was improperly submitted at the plaintiff-appellee's request. In rejecting the remedy of remittitur and ordering a new trial the court stated:

> "[3, 4] Appellee urges on us that, excluding the question of interest, all other matters in dispute were settled in its favor by our original opinion and it now offers to remit such portion of the judgment in its favor as is represented by interest. In writing the original opinion we seriously considered whether the error as to interest, although prejudicial, might be cured by permitting appellee to remit a portion of the damages and thereupon affirm the judgment. We recognize the desirability of bringing litigation to an end and the lessening of expenses of retrial, which a remittitur may accomplish, but before such desirable procedure may be resorted to there must be a mathematical basis in the record by which the reduction may be computed or at least closely approximated, otherwise it would be no more than a guess.

New York, C. & St. L.R.P. Company v. Niebel, 6th Cir., 214 F. 952. There is no such basis in this record and therefore appellee's offer must be denied." *Id.,* p. 254.

For the same rule announced in other states, see *Williams v. Safeway Stores, Inc.,* 515 P.2d 223 (S. Ct. Okla., 1973), *Montgomery v. Tufford*, 437 P.2d 36 (S. Ct. Colo., 1968), *Rubner v. Kennedy*, 417 S.W.2d 860 (Tex. App. 1967) and *Chesbrough v. Woodworth*, 195 F. 875 (6th Cir. 1912).

In this case, in its second decision, dated December 23, 1981, in which it ordered a remittitur of $40,685.20, the Marion County Court of Appeals, over the dissent of Judge Bell, cited *Chester Park Co. v. Schulte*, 120 Ind. 273 (1929) and *Larrissey v. Norwalk Truck Lines, Inc.,* 155 Ind. 207 (1951) as providing a legal basis for the granting of a $40,685.20 remittitur. These cases do not provide a legal basis for the action of the Court in ordering a remittitur of only 1/6 of the prejudicial error.

In each case, *Chester Park, supra,* and *Larrissey, supra,* the Supreme Court considered the role of remittitur where it was argued that the verdict was excessive. In each case it was determined that there existed no prejudicial error affecting the verdict (unlike the circumstances of the instant case) and that the verdict was not tainted by passion or prejudice. Under these limited circumstances, the Supreme Court determined that remittitur might properly be used by a Court to reduce the verdict to amounts supported by the evidence:

> "3. If a verdict in an action for unliquidated damages is, in the opinion of the trial court, excessive but not appearing to be influenced by passion or prejudice, the Court may with the assent of plaintiff reduce the verdict by *remittitur* to any amount warranted by the evidence.

> * * * * *

> "5. The Court of Appeals has the same unlimited power and control of verdicts and judgments as the trial court and may weigh the evidence and exercise an independent judgment upon questions of excessive damages and when no passion or prejudice is apparent may modify and affirm the judgment by ordering a *remittitur* with the consent of the prevailing party." (*Chester Park Co., supra*, paragraphs 3 and 5 of syllabus).

In explaining *Chester Park*, this Court in *Larrissey* stated as follows:

> "However, it has long been the rule in Indiana, and it is the majority rule in the nation, that if a verdict in an action for unliquidated damages is excessive, but not appearing to have been influenced by passions or preju-

dice, the court may, with the assent of plaintiff, reduce the verdict by remit-titur to any amount warranted by the evidence." (*Larrissey, supra,* p. 219).

Plaintiff-Appellee has suggested that *Chester Park Co., supra* and *Larrissey, supra,* are authority for the action taken by the Court of Appeals in this case and for the proposition that it is entitled to a "maximum recovery." Because neither of these cases (viz. *Chester Park Co.* and *Larrissey*) concerned the appropriate use of a remittitur where a prejudicial error has intervened, neither is dispositive of the issue now before this Court. Furthermore, these cases do not even support the proposition that the plain-tiff is entitled to the "maximum recovery" allowed by the evidence. In each case the Supreme Court, acknowledging that the Court granting a remittitur substitutes its judg-ment for that of the jury, stated that:

> ". . . the Court may, with the assent of plaintiff, reduce the verdict by re-mittitur to any amount warranted by the evidence." *Larrissey, supra*, p. 219.

Contrary to what has been urged by plaintiff-appellee, this Court did not, either in *Chester Park Co.* or *Larrissey*, provide complete guidance to the lower courts of this state with respect to the use of a remittitur—most specifically it did not provide guid-ance for those cases where prejudicial error has intervened and its full impact upon a verdict is uncertain.

The federal courts, like many of the state courts that have addressed themselves to these issues, approach the use of remittitur differently in situations where a verdict is deemed to be merely excessive and in the situation where prejudicial error has inter-vened. Where there has been *no error* but where it is argued that the verdict is exces-sive, some circuits apply what is known as the "maximum recovery" rule.

> "On the other hand, it has been held that the remitted amount should reduce the verdict only to the maximum that would be upheld by the trial court as not excessive, apparently on the theory that the jury intended to award the plaintiff the maximum legal damages and the court should not in-vade the province of the jury except to reduce the amount of the verdict to that point." 6A Moore's Federal Practice, Par. 59.05[03], pp. 59-56–59-58 (2d ed. 1982).

However, this "maximum recovery" rule has no application where prejudicial er-ror has intervened. In fact, the federal courts apply what may be termed the "maximum effect" rule where error has been found to intervene:

> "Remittitur is not only used by the trial courts, but also by the appel-late courts in two general areas, one particularly applicable to the function of the appellate court, the other quite similar to its use by the district courts.

In the first area, where reversible error is found in proceedings below, such as erroneous admission of evidence or erroneous instructions, and the effect of the error can be reasonably approximated to a definite portion of the amount of the verdict, the appellate court may condition its affirmance on the plaintiff remitting that amount of the verdict which is apparently traceable to the error below. Even when the effect of the error cannot be allocated to a distinct portion of the verdict, remittitur may still be used *if the maximum effect of the error can be established.* In this way, the defendant cannot complain as the maximum effect of the error is avoided; and the plaintiff has his choice of electing to remit or to suffer a new trial." 6A MOORE'S FEDERAL PRACTICE, Par. 59.05[03], pp. 59-64–59-66 (2d ed. 1982). (Emphasis added.)

Hence, remittitur may still be an appropriate remedy where prejudicial error has intervened if it is used in such a way that the "maximum effect" of the error can be purged from the verdict. Applying the "maximum effect" rule to the instant case, the Court of Appeals, if it deemed remittitur appropriate, could have offered the plaintiff-appellee the opportunity to accept a remittitur in the amount of $262,532.84. Instead, the Court of Appeals adopted the plaintiff-appellee's argument that it was entitled to a "maximum recovery" and offered the plaintiff the opportunity to accept a remittitur of $40,685.20. The net result, of course, is that the "maximum effect" of the prejudicial error has not been purged from the verdict, and the plaintiff, after having interjected error into the case, is now permitted to reap the financial fruits of that error. Such a result is intolerable. Such a result frustrates the purpose of a remittitur which is to guarantee both sides a fair trial by eliminating error and at the same time avoiding the expense and time necessarily involved in retrying a case.

State courts from sister jurisdictions which have addressed our issue have uniformly required that the "maximum effect" of the prejudicial error be cured before a verdict infected by error is permitted to stand. As the Texas Supreme Court noted in *Employers' Insurance Ass'n v. Lightfoot*, 139 Tex. 305, 162 S.W.2d 929 (1942):

"It is the law that where the portion of a jury's verdict tainted with misconduct, or improperly arrived at, is capable of definite and accurate ascertainment, and where the jury acted free from prejudice and passion, a remittitur of the portion so tainted or improperly arrived at will cure the error, and the part of the verdict free from the taint of misconduct and properly arrived at will be permitted to stand." *Id.* 162 S.W.2d at 931.

And in *Reserve Life Insurance Company v. Gay*, 213 Ga. 904, 102 S.E.2d 492 (1958) the Georgia Supreme Court, in reversing a Court of Appeals that had improperly used the remedy of remittitur and therefore failed to correct the "maximum effect" of the prejudicial error, stated as follows:

"A verdict which is erroneous may be corrected by the writing off of the illegal part if the illegal part can be determined and is separable from the rest." *Id.* 102 S.E.2d at 493.

Under the facts of this case, it is not the excessive nature of the verdict which mandates reversal, but the presentation of improper items of damages for the jury's consideration. This error requires reversal and a new trial, or in the alternative, a remittitur of $262,532.84, the amount of the prejudicial error, from the verdict. To award plaintiff final judgment for $798,314.80 where as much as $221,847.64 of the amount may well be damages for which it has already been held plaintiff is not legally entitled, is to commit an egregious injustice to defendants and to reward plaintiff hundreds of thousands of dollars in spite of the error plaintiff created.

Had the Court of Appeals ordered a remittitur of the full $262,532.84 from the jury verdict, the plaintiff might have complained, but the plaintiff had a right to refuse to accept the remittitur. Likewise if this Court were to order a remittitur of $262,532.84 the plaintiff would still have the option of accepting such a remittitur or refusing the remittitur and proceeding with a new trial. The defendants, however, have no option of assent; they were simply assigned a remittitur of only $40,685.20 when, in fact a much greater amount of improper damages may well have been included in the verdict. Thus, defendants have been twice wronged: once by plaintiff's prejudicial proofs at trial and again when the Court of Appeals recognized the first wrong, but failed to fashion an adequate remedy.

PROPOSITION OF LAW NO. 2

It is error to reduce a verdict by remittitur to the maximum amount which a jury could have awarded where the jury, as a trier of fact, has not awarded the maximum amount sought by the plaintiff.

For reasons which remain unknown, the Court of Appeals chose to subtract the sum of the erroneously submitted items of damages not from the amount of the verdict ($854,500.00), but rather from the amount of damages claimed ($1,076,347.64).

The procedure adopted by the Court of Appeals in the use of remittitur was erroneous not only because it fails to correct the total error ($262,532.84) but also because it assumes—contrary to what the jury's verdict indicated—that the plaintiff was entitled to a maximum recovery and that all damage issues were resolved in favor of the plaintiff when clearly they were not. Where the jury fixes an award at a maximum level (here $854,500) it is error for a court, in granting a remittitur, to assume that the plaintiff was entitled to more than the maximum sum determined by the jury.

The Court of Appeals' failure to recognize this principle has caused the instant dispute. For if the Court of Appeals had subtracted the $262,532.84 from the jury verdict of $854,500 rather than from the $1,076,347.64 claimed damages, the use of the remittitur would have been appropriate.

Under the facts of this case there is absolutely no way for the Court of Appeals to divine the jury's deliberations with respect to damages. However, by ordering a remittitur of $40,685.30 the Court of Appeals has in essence usurped the jury's function and *sub silentio* ruled as a matter of law that the plaintiff was entitled to a full and complete recovery of all disputed items of damages properly before the jury.

A case which carefully considers this problem is *Hollwedel v. Duffy-Mott Co., Inc.*, 263 N.Y. 95, 188 N.E. 266 (1933). In that case the Court of Appeals of New York had occasion to consider whether the Appellate Division had properly used the remedy of remittitur in a suit for breach of an employment contract.

The verdict of $118,762.53, determined by the trial court to be excessive, was reduced to $113,484.75. The defendant appealed the amount of that judgment to the Appellate Division. The intermediate court determined that a wage loss item ($106,900) should have been discounted to present day values. The intermediate division, however, offered to affirm the judgment in favor of the plaintiff if the plaintiff agreed to accept a remittitur which represented the difference between the future payments reduced to present day value less only the sum of $5,800. New York's highest court, the Court of Appeals, held that the granting of a remittitur in this situation was wrong:

> "The Appellate Division has held that the future payments should be discounted to their value at the time of the breach. From that value they deducted only the amount concededly earned by the plaintiff, and, on condition that the plaintiff stipulate to accept the modification, they affirmed the judgment as modified. In that they erred. The damages thus recovered were, so the Appellate Division said, 'the maximum amount of the damages recoverable under the evidence.' 238 App. Div. 468, 471, 264 N.Y.S. 745, 748. Thus, they eliminated the allowance of $35,000 which the jury might have found, and, as appears did find, upon the evidence represented the probable earnings of the plaintiff during the part of the term which had not expired at the time of trial. *An Appellate Court may correct errors due to erroneous rulings, but it cannot usurp the province of a jury nor upon the consent of the plaintiff reduce a judgment to the 'maximum' amount recoverable by the plaintiff under the evidence, unless the jury verdict has established such amount.*" *Hollwedel, supra*, p. 270. (Emphasis added.)

In the instant case the Court of Appeals failed to recognize that the amount of the recovery set by the jury, $854,500—not $1,076,347.64—represents the maximum the plaintiff was entitled to recover under the evidence produced at trial. By deducting the sum of the erroneously submitted items of damages from the total claim of the plaintiff ($1,076,347.64) the Court of Appeals has failed to properly credit the defendants for the sums which were resolved in their favor by the jury. This prejudiced defendants to the extent of $221,847.46, and constitutes a blatant usurpation of the jury's function by the Court of Appeals and prejudices the defendants. Instead of remedying the error by granting a new trial, the Court of Appeals aggravated an injustice by first finding an error prejudicial to the defendants and then choosing a "remedy" which failed to correct it.

CONCLUSION

In its decision in *Chester Park, supra,* this Court was concerned with offering guidance to lower courts with respect to the permissive use of remittitur:

> "It is likewise very much to be desired that some very definite rules be laid down by this court for the guidance of the trial courts and the courts of appeals, as well as for the bar of the state, in order that there may be uniformity of action in the trial courts and in the Courts of Appeals." *Chester Park Co., supra,* p. 286.

The specific facts of *Chester Park*, however, did not require this Court to address itself to the use of the remittitur where prejudicial error has intervened to contaminate the verdict. It is respectfully submitted that this case now affords the Court of the opportunity to complete its analysis of the permissible use of the remittitur and to provide "very definite rules . . . for the guidance of the trial courts and the Court of Appeals."

Fairness and justice dictate that where error has intervened to the prejudice of the party against whom a verdict has been rendered and where the possible maximum impact upon the verdict is ascertainable, a court should (1) order a new trial or (2) affirm the judgment of the lower court if the plaintiff agrees to accept a verdict reduced by that sum which represents the "maximum effect" of the error. In this case, then, this Court should do what the Court of Appeals failed to do: (1) grant the defendant-appellants a new trial or (2) affirm the judgment if the plaintiff consents to a judgment in the amount of $567,467.16 ($839,000 less $262,532.84). To proceed in this fashion is to ensure a fair verdict, and to eliminate any prejudicial effect of the error upon the verdict. If the plaintiff does not assent to the remittitur the matter should be retried. To do anything less is to deny the defendants-appellants a trial free of prejudicial error and to sanction a verdict which may consist of damages in excess of one quarter of a million dollars which were improperly submitted to the jury.

Respectfully submitted,

How Might That Brief Have Begun?

In the Supreme Court of Indiana

APPEAL FROM THE COURT OF APPEALS
THIRD APPELLATE DISTRICT
MARION COUNTY, INDIANA

PLEBINOL CORPORATION,
Plaintiff-Appellee and Cross-Appellant,

vs.

THE TULL GROUP INC.

and

TULL AEROSPACE,
Defendants-Appellants.

**BRIEF OF DEFENDANTS-APPELLANTS
THE TULL GROUP INC. and
TULL AEROSPACE**

Issue Presented

Plebinol's jury demand was for damages of nearly $1.1 million. But after the jury returned a verdict of $839,000, the intermediate court unanimously decided that $263,000 of the $1.1 million demand had been improperly submitted. Instead of offsetting this amount against the actual verdict, however, the court offset it against the inflated demand, as if the jury somehow knew to reject the improper portion. Shouldn't the improperly submitted amount have been offset against the verdict actually rendered?

Statement of the Case

In August 1985, Plebinol sued the Tull defendants (collectively, "Tull"), alleging that [etc.].

An Unusually Good Example*

**IN THE UNITED STATES DISTRICT COURT
FOR THE SOUTHERN DISTRICT OF TEXAS
HOUSTON DIVISION**

THE FEDERAL DEPOSIT INSURANCE CORPORATION,	§ § §	
Plaintiff,	§ §	
vs.	§ §	CIVIL ACTION NO. 9-7-25R7
FIREMEN'S INSURANCE COMPANY OF NEWARK, NEW JERSEY,	§ § § §	
Defendant.	§	

**Firemen's Reply to
FDIC's Summary-Judgment Brief**

Preliminary Statement

The issue facing this Court boils down to a straightforward question of contractual interpretation:

> Firemen's Insurance Company insured USAT against losses occasioned by real-estate documents that are "defective by reason of the signature thereon of any person having been obtained through trick, artifice, fraud, or false pretenses." Couch engaged in massive fraud when, with valid documentation, he sold USAT grossly undervalued mortgages. Does the mere fact that the mortgages were worth less than USAT thought mean that the sale documents were "defective" by reason of the signatures?

That is the overarching question that swallows all the subissues. In this reply, Firemen's seeks, in light of the FDIC's earlier brief, to develop this major issue and to treat the subissues as succinctly as possible.

Firemen's Reply to FDIC's Summary-Judgment Brief—Page 1

---

* Brief filed by James A. Knox and Karen Kohler Fitzgerald of Vial, Hamilton, Koch & Knox in Dallas. Bryan A. Garner and William M. Coats served as cocounsel.

1. The language of the rider supports coverage only for fraud in the factum.

A. USAT doesn't claim that the instruments are defective by reason of fraudulently obtained signatures.

There are two types of fraud. *Fraud in the factum* is "fraud as to the nature of the writing that one signs"[1]—as when a blind person signs a will when misleadingly told that it's just a letter. *Fraud in the inducement* refers to all other types of common-law fraud—that is, fraud "that induce[s] one to make an agreement,"[2] such as lies that a given piece of land is arable when in fact it's marshland. In mentioning fraud, the rider refers to defective instruments—i.e., "defective by reason of the signature thereon of any person having been obtained through trick, artifice, fraud or false pretenses." No court has ever had any difficulty in deciding which type of fraud this rider refers to.[3]

USAT suffered a loss from fraudulently obtained real-estate loans—loans based on Couch's misrepresentations about lien priority (fraud in the inducement). The

---

[1] DAVID MELLINKOFF, DICTIONARY OF AMERICAN LEGAL USAGE 258 (1992); *see* BLACK'S LAW DICTIONARY 661 (6th ed. 1990).

[2] MELLINKOFF, *supra* note 1, at 258; *see also* BLACK'S LAW DICTIONARY at 661 (defining the term as "[f]raud connected with underlying transaction and not with the nature of the contract or document signed").

[3] *See Jefferson Bank v. Progressive Cas. Ins. Co.*, 1990 WL 180585 (E.D. Pa. 1990), *aff'd*, 965 F.2d 1274 (3d Cir. 1992) (observing that although a claimant argued that "it should collect under the Rider because the mortgage is worthless," even so "[t]he Rider clearly requires that the mortgage be defective by reason of the fraudulent signature"); *Benton State Bank v. Hartford Accident & Indem. Co.*, 338 F. Supp. 674 (E.D. Ark. 1971), *aff'd*, 452 F.2d 5, 7 (8th Cir. 1971) (holding that the rider "deals with induced signatures"—fraud in the factum—but not with fraud in the inducement); *North Jersey Savs. & Loan Ass'n v. Fidelity & Deposit Co.*, 660 A.2d 1287 (N.J. Super. 1993) (distinguishing, for purposes of interpreting the rider, between a fraudulent scheme and a fraudulently induced signature).

Firemen's Reply to FDIC's Summary-Judgment Brief—Page 2

rider purchased by USAT covers only those losses resulting from real-estate loan documents that are defective because the signatures were fraudulently obtained (fraud in the factum). The FDIC stretches the language beyond recognition in claiming that the rider covers USAT's loss.

For three reasons, it is difficult to take seriously the FDIC's view that the rider should have used the phrase "fraud in the factum" in order to "provide clear notice to the policyholder of any limitations the insurer wished to impose."[4] First, few people—few lawyers, even—would know what the phrase "fraud in the factum" means. Second, as a drafting matter, the better practice is to say "in the plainest language, with the simplest, fewest, and fittest words, precisely what it means."[5] Third, the rider itself admirably captures the definition of fraud in the factum—so the Latinism was all the more undesirable.

Although the FDIC argues that the term "defective" should be interpreted broadly, it ignores most of the rider's language: the loss must result from a defective *document,* and the cause of the defect must be a fraudulently obtained *signature.* The FDIC has not pointed—and cannot point—to any such defect.

---

[4] FDIC Brief at 11.

[5] BRYAN A. GARNER, A DICTIONARY OF MODERN LEGAL USAGE 663 (2d ed. 1995) (quoting J.G. Mackay, *Introduction to an Essay on the Art of Legal Composition Commonly Called Drafting,* 3 LAW Q. REV. 326, 326 (1987)).

Firemen's Reply to FDIC's Summary-Judgment Brief—Page 3

B.   The language of the loan exclusion excludes a vast universe of fraud, whereas the rider revives coverage for the narrow, comparatively rare situation in which the fraud concerns the document itself and the signature.

Rather than repealing the exclusion wholesale, the rider merely carves out a minute exception to the exclusion—an exception relating to documents that are defective as a result of fraudulently obtained signatures.

1.   The language isn't parallel: the loan exclusion relates to fraud in an entire loan or transaction, while the rider relates only to fraud in obtaining signatures on documents.

Although the FDIC argues that "[t]he phrase 'trick, artifice, fraud, or false pretenses' in paragraph 1 of the Rider is identical to the phrase appearing in [the loan exclusion]"[6]—as of course it is—the point is entirely irrelevant. Although that part of the phrasing is the same, the critical point is the changes that occur in other words:

The Loan-Exclusion Language	The Rider Language
[L]oss resulting directly or indirectly from the complete or partial non-payment of or default upon any loan or transaction in the nature of a loan or extension of credit, whether involving the Insured as a lender or as a borrower, including the purchase, discounting or other acquisition of false or genuine accounts, invoices, notes, agreements or Evidences of Debt, whether such *loan or transaction* was procured in good faith or through trick, artifice, fraud, or false pretenses	Loss through the Insured's having, in good faith and in the course of business in connection with any loan, accepted or received or acted upon the faith of any real property mortgages, real property deeds of trust or like instruments pertaining to realty or assignments of such mortgages, deeds of trust or *instruments which prove to have been defective by reason of the signature thereon of any person* having been obtained through trick, artifice, fraud, or false pretenses . . . .

---

[6] FDIC Brief at 14.

Firemen's Reply to FDIC's Summary-Judgment Brief—Page 4

The FDIC argues that the trick-artifice phrasing—which has been used to define fraud ever since Samuel Johnson wrote his *Dictionary* in 1755—"should be construed consistently, giving it the broadest possible interpretation to include all types of fraud, not just fraud in the factum."[7] What the FDIC ignores, of course, is the uses to which tricks and artifices may be put: to induce someone to make an agreement (fraud in the inducement) or to deceive someone into signing a document that he or she believes to be something else (fraud in the factum). By its terms, the loan exclusion embraces the former (and more), while the rider embraces the latter.

---

[7] FDIC Brief at 14.

Firemen's Reply to FDIC's Summary-Judgment Brief—Page 5

9

Phrase your issues in separate sentences. Don't start with *whether* or any other interrogative word.

Quotable Quotes

"[The following example] illustrates the problem of how to phrase an issue appealingly . . . .

1

Whether the owner of coupon bonds should include in his gross income the amount of coupons which he detached and gave to his son several months prior to maturity.

2

The taxpayer owned coupon bonds. Several months [before] maturity of the interest coupons he detached them and gave them to his son, retaining the bonds themselves. Is he relieved of income tax with respect to [these] interest coupons?

"Both are well-formulated questions. The second is probably a shade better because it stresses that the taxpayer retained the bonds and then asks on top of that whether he is relieved from tax. . . . Note also the change in the form of the question presented, from the one-sentence 'whether' form to the fact-statement-plus-question form, all in the direction of adding appeal."
   —Frederick B. Wiener, *Briefing and Arguing Federal Appeals* 74–75 (rev. ed. 1967).

"Such a formulation [i.e., the multisentence issue statement] has the advantage of being readable. It is just as concise as the one-sentence format and is much clearer."
   —Girvan Peck, *Writing Persuasive Briefs* 103 (1984).

"The purpose of using separate sentences . . . is to help the reader. A one-sentence issue of 75 or so words is difficult to follow, especially when the interrogative word begins the sentence and the end is merely a succession of *when*-clauses—e.g.:

Can Barndt Insurance deny insurance coverage on grounds of late notice when Fiver's insurance policy required Fiver to give Barndt notice of a claim 'immediately,' and when in May 1994, one of Fiver's offices was damaged by smoke from a fire in another tenant's space, and when 10 months later, Fiver gave notice, and when Barndt investigated the claim for 6 months before denying coverage and did not raise a late-notice defense until 18 months after the claim was filed? [81 words]

"That's a muddle. Readers forget the question by the time they reach the question mark. Part of the reason is that the time is out of joint: we begin with a present question, then back up to what happened, and then, with the question mark, jump back to the present.

"The better strategy is to follow a more or less chronological order, telling a story in miniature. Then, the pointed question—which emerges inevitably from the story—comes at the end:

> Fiver's insurance policy required it to give Barndt Insurance notice of a claim 'immediately.' In May 1994, one of Fiver's offices was damaged by smoke from a fire in another tenant's space. Ten months later, Fiver gave notice. Barndt investigated the claim for 6 months before denying coverage and did not raise a late-notice defense until 18 months after the claim was filed. Can Barndt now deny coverage because of late notice? [73 words]

"Instead of one 81-word-long sentence, we have five sentences with an average length of 15 words. And the information is presented in a way that readers can easily understand."

—Bryan A. Garner, *A Dictionary of Modern Legal Usage* 473 (2d ed. 1995).

Explanation

The one-sentence version of an issue doesn't seem to be required anywhere, but it's a widely followed convention. And it's ghastly in its usual form because it leads to unreadable issues that are deservedly neglected. Either they're surface issues, or else they're meandering, nonchronological statements that can't be understood on fewer than three close readings. Besides, the common "Whether"-version isn't really a sentence at all—much less a question (hence the question mark is odd).

Although Wiener recognized even back in 1967 that the separate sentences had a way of "adding appeal," he didn't seem to recognize that the only way for legal issues to be predictably good is to use the multisentence version.

And my own example quoted above . . . how would most brief-writers state the issue? A sensible writer wouldn't want the 81-word version, but instead might produce something like this:

> Whether Barndt Insurance can deny insurance coverage on grounds of late notice?

That's certainly readable, but it's uninformative. A reader would need to plow through a whole brief to feel comfortable answering that question. It's a classic surface issue.

But if the choice is between that one-sentence version and the 81-

word version quoted above, most would probably take the more reasonable 12-word sentence.

Anyone making that choice, however, ignores the true problem: we've simply started off with a miserably bad premise—that an issue must be cast in a single sentence. Where did we get this premise? It seems to come from a well-intentioned attempt to get issue-writers to be succinct. "By golly," the idea went, "we'll just force them to say it all in one sentence."

There are far better ways to enforce brevity (see #10). We shouldn't choose a method that impairs our ability to convey information clearly. You'll inevitably need to break down the sentences within the issue.

The Solicitor General's Office, which produces some of the best briefs to be found anywhere, often uses the multisentence approach, but not consistently enough. When the SG or any other advocate balls the issue up into one sentence, the facts and the law often get jumbled illogically. And the subject often gets separated from the verb. Here, for example, is an issue statement as the SG presented it to the U.S. Supreme Court in December 2001, with 65 words between subject and verb:

> Whether an order of the National Labor Relations Board directing petitioner to pay back pay to an employee who was discriminatorily laid off for union-organizing activity in violation of Section 8(a)(3) of the National Labor Relations Act (Act), 29 U.S.C. § 158(a)(3), but only up to the date on which petitioner discovered that the employee was an undocumented alien not authorized to be employed in the United States, is a proper exercise of the Board's authority to remedy petitioner's violation of Section 8(a)(3) of the Act.*

Order is the subject; *is* is the verb. With the wide separation, it's hard for even the most tenacious of readers to remember what the subject is by the time the verb comes around. (See #34.) That's mostly a result of the straitjacketing one-sentence format. Notice what happens, though, when the same information is presented in two shorter sentences. It all unfolds more naturally:

> The National Labor Relations Board ordered petitioner to pay backpay to an employee who was discriminatorily laid off for union-organizing activity, but only up to the date when petitioner discovered that the employee was an undocumented alien not authorized to work in the United States. Was this order a proper exercise of the Board's authority to remedy petitioner's violation?

That's an objectively worded issue because it includes only a factual premise and a question, without a legal premise (see #11). Many believe this is the most appropriate way of wording an issue in the Supreme Court—that is, not suggesting the answer. The point of the example, however, is to show how much more appealing—and how much more succinct—the same information is when put into a multisentence format.

---

* See *Hoffman Plastic Compounds, Inc. v. NLRB*, 535 U.S. 137 (2002) (the government lost).

You'll find, quite consistently, that the one-sentence format causes an issue statement to degenerate. Try writing any of the following issues in a single sentence. Either you'll be quite unhappy with the result, or else you'll be satisfying yourself with a statement that's less informative and less readable.

Some Uncommonly Good Examples

- In 1973, Archway manufactured and sold to Feldspar a hoist designed for attachment to a free-swinging trolley system. Thirty years later, without Archway's knowledge, Trubster acquired the hoist, added a new motor, pulley, and cable, and integrated the hoist into a fixed elevator dumbwaiter system. Is Archway liable for injuries resulting from integration of its hoist into a system defectively designed by Trubster? [64 words]

- George Ratliff asks this Court to declare certain provisions of the Campaign Contribution Limits Act of 2003 unconstitutional or inapplicable to him. The Act does not go into effect until January 1, 2004. The Registry of Election Finance, which has the authority to enforce the Act, has not taken any action—or threatened to take any action—against Ratliff for violating the Act. Has Ratliff presented an actual controversy that would make declaratory relief appropriate? [75 words]

- Maryland law prohibits the discharge of effluent to which a permit-holder has added chlorine or chlorine-containing products. Zero Corporation, a permit-holder, is discharging unaltered municipal tap water that contains chlorine added by the city. Are these discharges legal under Maryland law? [44 words]

- The attorney–client privilege protects from disclosure only those communications that are kept confidential within the strict confines of the attorney–client relationship. Eagle Company disclosed communications to a third-party insurance broker after learning of Rush Insurance Company's denial of coverage. Can Eagle Company now refuse to disclose these communications based on a claim of privilege? [57 words]

- Under New York law, a party to a contract may not bring a claim for fraud for unfulfilled promises of future performance made in the agreement. Forsythe Inc. and Stern Corp. entered into a buyout agreement. Forsythe alleges that representatives of Stern committed fraud by promising during negotiations and in the agreement that Stern would refer business to Forsythe after the buyout. May Forsythe recover for fraud in addition to its breach-of-contract claim? [75 words]

- Rule 25 requires a claim to be dismissed if an appropriate party is not substituted for a deceased party within 90 days after a suggestion of death is filed. Christine Black, the plaintiff, died on July 10, 2002.

Western Co. filed a valid suggestion of death ten days later. No party has been substituted for Christine Black, and it has been more than 90 days since July 15. Should Christine Black's claim be dismissed? [75 words]

- In August 2002, the Enclave signed a multiyear lease with Woodhill. Unknown to the Enclave, however, Woodhill had fallen into default on past-due assessments and, after the lease was executed, assigned its interest to the condominium association to avoid foreclosure on the building. Woodhill's successor now wants to cancel the lease even though the Enclave has fully complied with its obligations. May it do so, or is it bound by the lease terms? [74 words]

- Under Louisiana law, a corporation must include all debt in its corporate-franchise-tax base. Louisiana's highest court has long held that an advance is not debt if the borrower is not obligated to repay it. Bayou Boats receives advances on its corporate-owned life-insurance policies, but it has no obligation to repay them. Must Bayou Boats include the advances as debt in its tax base? [67 words]

- In California, a parent may reduce a child-support obligation by showing that the child earned money and that the extra money reduced the child's need for support. Ronald Borden proved that his daughter earned money on her paper route after school, but he did not show that it reduced his daughter's need for support. Is Borden entitled to a reduction in his child-support obligation? [66 words]

- Every Michigan lease inherently imposes a covenant of quiet enjoyment on the owner. Easy Rentals has a ten-year lease on a building owned by James Yost. Under the lease's condemnation clause, the owner is not liable to the lessee if the building is condemned. Yost wants to rebuild on the site and has asked the city to condemn the existing building. Does Yost's request to the city breach the covenant of quiet enjoyment? [74 words]

- U.S. patent law protects only "novel" inventions and expressly bars protection for any invention that is offered for sale more than a year before the inventor applies for the patent. Stephen Phillips developed a prototype of a laser rangefinder and offered to sell it to Largent, Inc. More than a year later, Phillips applied for a U.S. patent on the rangefinder. Is Phillips barred from obtaining the patent? [68 words]

- A criminal defendant has the right to be present whenever prospective jurors are questioned on voir dire. During voir dire in this murder case, a prospective juror was questioned by the judge at the bench. Williams was present and positioned so that he could hear the conversation. He asked to approach the bench while the prospective juror was questioned, but his request was denied. Did that denial violate Williams's right to be present? [73 words]

- Under California and federal law, workplace conversation of a sexual nature is not sexual harassment if the plaintiff invited the interaction. Hannah Ferguson admitted that she routinely confided in Calvin Haskall, the only male among her 12 coworkers, and told him about her sexual activities. She took offense at Haskall's reaction to one story and sued the company for hostile-environment sexual harassment. Is the company liable because of Haskall's conversation? [71 words]

10

Limit your issues to 75 words apiece.

Quotable Quotes

"The way an issue gets to be stated can have fateful consequences. The attention of the judge—catalyzed by the striking written or oral phrase—must be held through to the critical issue. Here concentration and clarity of expression may well become decisive."

—Francis Bergan, *Opinions and Briefs—Lessons from Loughran* 6 (1970).

"It is the rare case indeed—in fact, I have yet to encounter it—in which issues cannot be framed in 75 words. The 75-word limit is the result of experimentation and informal testing: once an issue goes beyond that length, it is likely to be rambling. You lose the rigor of concentrated statement. And you probably lose some readers."

—Bryan A. Garner, *A Dictionary of Modern Legal Usage* 473 (2d ed. 1995).

Explanation

About 98% of the time, if you can't phrase your issue in 75 words, you probably don't know what the issue is. It's that simple.

It takes hard work—I've seen people take a day to frame one question—but it's well worth the effort. Why? You're more likely to spot problems in your logic, and you're more likely to keep the judge's attention. More than that, you'll be satisfying a yearning that almost every judge feels by explaining what the question is in bite-size form.

You'll often be tempted to think that your case turns on issues that are too complex to be reduced to 75 words. Don't kid yourself. Even intellectual-property cases are amenable to this treatment. Consider Bn.com's winning appeal against Amazon.com in the Federal Circuit. In 2000, that court had to decide whether Bn.com had good defenses to Amazon.com's infringement claim on its one-click buying system. Here's how Steven I. Wallach of New York—along with his colleagues William G. Pecau, Jonathan Marshall, Michael N. Rosen, and Mark J. Sugarman, all of New York—framed the four questions using the deep-issue technique:

1. **Consistency of Construction.** Amazon.com's patent claims ordering an item over the Internet with a "single action," such as a mouse click. While

analyzing infringement, the district court construed "single action" as one action taken after descriptions of both the item and the single action are displayed simultaneously. But while analyzing validity, the court construed the claims differently, omitting the item-description requirement when determining whether prior art disclosed a "single action." Was this an error of law?

2. **Prior-Art Disclosures.** The district court granted an injunction, concluding that Bn.com's invalidity defenses lacked substantial merit. But all the claim elements were admittedly old except single-action ordering. And prior-art online ordering systems disclosed:

   - an "instant buy" button;
   - "one-click ordering";
   - a button reading "Chart ($.50)" for one-click ordering; and
   - a Web-page link for one-click ordering.

   Expert testimony that these references invalidated the patent was unrebutted. Did the court err?

3. **Noninfringement Defenses.** The district court also concluded that Bn.com's noninfringement defenses lacked substantial merit. But during its infringement analysis, the court:

   - construed "single action" contrary to the doctrine of claim differentiation, the specification, and the prosecution history; and
   - construed "shopping cart" and "fulfill" by impermissibly relying on extrinsic evidence.

   Under proper constructions of those claim terms, there is no infringement. Did the court err?

4. **Underlying Errors.** The district court's findings on other factors that must be weighed on a preliminary-injunction motion—irreparable harm, balance of hardships, and the public interest—are all based on the assumption that the '411 patent is valid and infringed. Given the legal errors underlying the court's analysis of the merits, did the court's analyses of those other factors themselves include legal errors?

Notice how each successive issue builds on the previous ones. The third issue is probably the most difficult; it requires more background in intellectual-property law than the others. Of course, in this as in all cases, the writer must consider what a generalist reader is likely to know already and avoid repeating it in full. So the phrase *doctrine of claim differentiation* is mentioned but not explained on the principle that any IP generalist— certainly one who sits on the Federal Circuit—knows something about this doctrine. And if not, it's fully explained in the body. The important thing for the writer is to convey as much as possible about each issue within the confines of a 75-word limit. The brief-writers here did that in a hotly contested case. And they won.*

Some advocates make the mistake of thinking they need to put every citation and abbreviation in the issue statement. Doing so typically just clutters the statement and beclouds the thought. Consider this example,

---

* *See Amazon.com, Inc. v. Barnesandnoble.com, Inc.*, 239 F.3d 1343 (Fed. Cir. 2001).

from a brief filed in the U.S. Supreme Court by the Solicitor General's office in December 2001:

> The Food and Drug Administration Modernization Act of 1997 (FDAMA), 21 U.S.C. § 353a (Supp V 1999), provides a limited exemption from the new drug approval (and certain other requirements) of the Federal Food, Drug, and Cosmetic Act (FDCA), 21 U.S.C. § 301 *et seq.* for drugs compounded by pharmacists. The question presented is whether FDAMA's limitation of that exemption to pharmacists who do not solicit prescriptions for or advertise particular compounded drugs, 21 U.S.C. § 353a(a) and (c) (Supp. V 1999), is consistent with the First Amendment.**

The citations need to be readily available in the brief; they just shouldn't be allowed in the issue statement. Even though the whole issue is only 85 words, the thought tends to get lost in all the numbers. Consider how much cleaner that issue is without all the citational volume and section numbers, and with some of the ideas reordered for enhanced readability:

> The Food and Drug Administration Modernization Act (FDAMA) exempts drugs compounded by pharmacists from certain requirements of the Food, Drug, and Cosmetic Act, including requirements for new-drug approval. But the FDAMA limits that exemption to pharmacists who do not solicit pre-scriptions for or advertise particular compounded drugs. Is this limitation consistent with the First Amendment?

Although the revised issue has only 57 words, a deep issue will typically have 60 to 75 words.

But you may well ask, What about a complicated tax case? Is it really possible to do an issue within the 75-word limit? It's certainly easy to exceed the limit, as the Solicitor General showed in an August 2000 brief. Whose eyes wouldn't glaze over when trying to scale this 142-word obe-lisk:

> Petitioners are shareholders in an insolvent Subchapter S corporation. Dur-ing 1991, that corporation obtained a discharge of certain indebtedness. That discharge *would* have been treated as an item of "[i]ncome from dis-charge of indebtedness" (26 U.S.C. § 61(a)(12)) except that, because the dis-charge occurred when the corporation was insolvent, the item is expressly "not include[d] . . . in gross income" under 26 U.S.C. § 108(a)(1)(B). The question presented in this case is whether the amount thus expressly ex-cluded from "income" is nonetheless to be treated as if it *were* an item of "income" which, under 26 U.S.C. § 1366(a)(1)(A), flows through to petition-ers as the shareholders of the Subchapter S corporation, thereby increasing their basis in the stock of the corporation under 26 U.S.C. § 1367(a)(1)(A), and thereby allowing them to deduct losses they were previously unable to deduct because they had exhausted their basis by prior deductions.***

It starts with a fact, then adds another fact. Then it states a legal standard, followed by an exception to that standard. Then it begins to ask a question about that exception, but instead poses the question as if it had to do with

---

** *See Thompson v. Western States Med. Ctr.*, 535 U.S. 357 (2002) (the government lost).
*** *See Gitlitz v. Comm'r of Internal Revenue*, 531 U.S. 206 (2001) (the government lost).

an exception to the exception already mentioned, followed by one new fact and then another. Even if it were tighter, the organization of the issue is all but hopeless. Throw out the unnecessary detail, put it into logical order, and you have a respectable 71-word issue:

> Under § 108(a)(1)(B) of the Internal Revenue Code, the discharge of a Subchapter-S corporation's debt isn't included in gross income if the corporation is insolvent at the time. In 1991, PDW&A, an insolvent Subchapter-S corporation, obtained a discharge of debt. Its shareholders claim that the discharge should be counted as income so that their basis in the stock will increase, thereby allowing them to deduct losses that they otherwise couldn't. Are they right?

Even tax issues, you see, can be stated straightforwardly. Following are several more good examples.

Some Uncommonly Good Examples

- Under Wyoming law, administrative agencies have only those powers provided by statute. No statute gives the Wyoming Natural Resources Commission the authority to impose any sanctions for discovery abuse. May the Commission dismiss a permit application if it finds that the applicant has failed to respond to discovery requests? [49 words]

- Section 305 of the Government Code makes it a crime for a lobbyist to enter into a contingency-fee lobbying contract. Smith has agreed to lobby for water legislation on behalf of the Guernsey Corporation; if the legislation passes, Guernsey will pay Smith $1 million. Has Smith committed a crime? [50 words]

- For over 30 years, Texas courts have held that the term "single-family dwelling" imposes a use restriction unless the term appears in a section of the restrictive covenants solely governing the architectural form of dwellings. The Beautiful Valley covenants contain the term "single-family dwelling" in a section containing both use and architectural restrictions. Do these restrictive covenants prevent Mr. Johnson from running a boarding house in his home? [72 words]

- To decide a parent's request to modify child-support obligations, Virginia law requires a trial court to consider both parents' incomes. Mr. Smith requested a reduction of his child-support obligations. The trial judge refused to hear testimony from Ms. Smith about her income and reduced Mr. Smith's obligation. Should this Court vacate the order and remand for the trial court to consider Ms. Smith's income before setting the amount? [70 words]

- In 1981, Congress directed the HHS to replace the retrospective cost-based method of Medicare payments for kidney dialysis with a prospective payment method. In 1983, the HHS adopted regulations that included a retrospective cost-based limit on the bad-debt component of the payment, providing no valid justification for this departure from the statutory requirement to use the prospective method. Is the HHS authorized to depart from the statutory requirement in this way? [74 words]

- The U.S. Supreme Court has mandated that lower courts must not "accept as true a legal conclusion couched as a factual allegation" in pleadings. Pantheon sued Panathon for trademark infringement but pleaded no facts in its complaint from which a court could determine ownership of the trademark asserted. Should this Court dismiss Pantheon's complaint for failure to state a claim on which relief may be granted? [66 words]

- After Desert Storm, the United States imposed sanctions against Iraq. A regulation implementing those sanctions bars the import of goods in which the Iraqi government has any present, future, or contingent interest. The Iraqi government's interest in oil bought by Paladin Oil Traders ended two years before Paladin tried to import the oil. Acting under the sanctions regulation, the U.S. Customs Service seized Paladin's oil shipment. Was the seizure legal? [70 words]

- Under Utah law, to recover for fraud a plaintiff must prove detrimental reliance on a deliberate misrepresentation. In a meeting with Perkins, Dedman allegedly misrepresented the price of his goods, saying that they were competitively priced when they were not. Perkins sued for fraud. But in his deposition, Perkins testified that he had made no decision based on anything said at that meeting. Can Perkins recover against Dedman for fraud? [70 words]

- The U.S. Supreme Court has held that Title VI of the Civil Rights Act of 1964 does not confer a private right of action under the statute or its implementing regulations. The plaintiffs here are a class of California schoolchildren who allege that the Department of Education has violated Title VI and its implementing regulations. Can these plaintiffs sue the Department of Education for violating Title VI or its implementing regulations? [71 words]

- Relevant evidence makes a fact of consequence more or less probable. In the sentencing phase of Gilkerson's trial, the state offered evidence about the length of Gilkerson's previous sentences. Gilkerson objected, saying that the length of past sentences is not relevant to his culpability for the current conviction; the state argued that the evidence shows that another short sentence would not deter Gilkerson from future crimes. Was the evidence relevant? [70 words]

11

Write fair but persuasive issues that have only one answer. Cast each issue as a syllogism. If you have several issues, give each one a concise, neutral heading.

Quotable Quotes

"In almost all cases . . . , we find that we draw our conclusions from two related statements, the one a general statement covering many cases, which we may call the *major premise*, the other a particular statement of fact, which we may call the *minor premise*."

—Samuel S. Seward, *Rhetoric in Practice* 67 (1906).

"Of course, the first thing that comes up is the issue and the first art is the framing of the issue so that if your framing is accepted the case comes out your way. Got that? Second, you have to capture the issue, because your opponent will be framing an issue very differently. . . . And third, you have to build a technique of phrasing your issue which will not only capture the Court but which will stick your capture into the Court's head so that it can't forget it."

—Karl Llewellyn, *A Lecture on Appellate Advocacy*,
29 U. Chi. L. Rev. 627, 630 (1962).

"[A] good statement of the question or issue involved is fairly complete. It raises an issue of law based upon the concrete facts of the case. It is all inclusive and aids an understanding of the argument."

—Mario Pittoni, *Brief Writing and Argumentation* 51 (1967).

"[T]he issue to be argued must be raised in a way that will establish a point from which the writer can lead his readers to the conclusion he wishes to urge. That is, the introduction must in some fashion lead to a step of the argument by which the writer hopes to secure assent to his thesis."

—William J. Brandt et al., *The Craft of Writing* 48 (1969).

"The rules of formal logic are invaluable to courts, and the fallacies of an argument may sometimes be most effectively exposed by casting it in the form of a syllogism."

—George W. Paton, *A Textbook of Jurisprudence* 200
(G.W. Paton & David P. Derham eds., 4th ed. 1972).

"Questions . . . should be shaped as far as possible to compel a desirable response, or at the very least avoid an undesirable one."

—William A. Rusher, *How to Win Arguments* 118 (1981).

"The way the issues are written will govern the court's first impression on the merits. Whatever the theme, each issue statement should incorporate specific facts and legal principles in a simple, concise, and accurate manner. The briefwriter must try to put the issues persuasively, but must not lose credibility by being strident or overstated."

—Jordan B. Cherrick, "Issues, Facts, and Appellate Strategy,"
in *Appellate Practice Manual* 73, 76 (Priscilla A. Schwab ed., 1992).

"When presented with the properly framed major and minor premises of a syllogism, the human mind seems to produce the conclusion without any additional prompting. Moreover, the mind recognizes the conclusion to be of such compelling force that the conclusion simply cannot be denied. . . . The power of syllogistic argument leads to the only significant rule about crafting legal arguments: *every good legal argument is cast in the form of a syllogism.*"

—James A. Gardner, *Legal Argument* 6, 8 (1993).

Explanation

A good issue statement generally mirrors a syllogism—the basis of all logical thought. You have a major premise stating the law, a minor premise presenting the facts that tie into that major premise, and a conclusion. But when cast as part of an issue statement, the conclusion becomes a question.

Yes, the best issues end with question marks. Why?

Because a bona fide question looks and sounds objective even when it's gently slanted. Rather than pushing your answer, you're putting a question on the table. You're also challenging your opponent to explain how the answer could be other than as you're suggesting. You're seizing the issue—and, as a rule, the side that successfully does that will win (see the Llewellyn quotation above).

In any event, the judge won't accept any answers until he or she figures out the question. If you supply it ready-made, the chances are greater that the judge will see the question as you see it. If you don't supply an explicit question, the judge's formulation is more likely to differ from what you'd like it to be.

And remember: this formulation is inevitable because judges typically want to begin by understanding the questions they're being asked to answer.

There are essentially two types of issue statements: analytical and persuasive. An analytical issue is objectively stated—it doesn't suggest an answer. It's appropriate for a research memo or an opinion letter. A persuasive issue is subtly slanted toward an answer. It's usually intended for a brief (trial or appellate).

Each type has a predictable form, best analyzed by considering the elements of a categorical syllogism:

> All men are mortal. [Major premise]
> Socrates is a man. [Minor premise]
> Therefore, Socrates is mortal. [Conclusion]

These elements should be arranged in legal issues in this way:

Analytical Issue
Minor premise
Conclusion?

Short Answer
Major premise

Persuasive Issue
Major premise
Minor premise
Conclusion?

The major premise is the controlling legal point. The minor premise is the factual point that ties into that legal point. And the conclusion is expressed as a question.

Consider this example:

Analytical Issue	Persuasive Issue
Delaware's blue-sky laws protect investors from various kinds of securities fraud. Ellsmere, a Delaware resident, engaged in various securities transactions with Balancio Securities. Through April 2001, the transactions occurred outside Delaware; beginning in May 2001, most of the transactions occurred in Delaware. Do the blue-sky laws apply to these transactions? Short Answer Delaware courts have consistently held that Delaware's blue-sky laws do not apply to securities transactions that take place out of state. So the transactions that occurred through April 2001 are not subject to the blue-sky laws, and Ellsmere cannot maintain an action in Delaware court for those transactions. But the transactions beginning in May 2001 are subject to the blue-sky laws, and the Delaware courts will assume jurisdiction over a claim that Balancio has violated those laws in transactions that occurred in Delaware.	Delaware courts have consistently held that Delaware's blue-sky laws do not apply to securities transactions that take place out of state. All the transactions between Balancio Securities and Ellsmere before April 2001 occurred outside Delaware—in Kansas, Nebraska, and South Dakota. Should this Court dismiss Ellsmere's claims under the blue-sky laws for the transactions completed before April 2001?

To a clear-headed thinker, the analytical issue precedes the persuasive one. This example shows how to turn a good research memo into a brief: take the short answer, turn it into a major premise (the first sentence of a persuasive issue), trim the minor premise as necessary to get everything within a 75-word compass, and then pose the logical conclusion as a question.

You may wonder whether the elements must appear in this order. The answer is yes—although there may be rare variations from it. Putting the minor premise first, followed by the major premise and then the conclusion, isn't nearly as persuasive. It looks too pat when the answer immediately precedes the question, as here:

> All the transactions between Balancio Securities and Ellsmere before April 2001 occurred outside Delaware—in Kansas, Nebraska, and South Dakota. Delaware courts have consistently held that Delaware's blue-sky laws do not apply to securities transactions that take place out of state. Should this Court dismiss Ellsmere's claims under the blue-sky laws for the transactions completed before April 2001?

Besides, when the issue reads this way, the first sentence has no context. In the syllogistic format, the legal premise supplies the context for the more specific factual premise.

You may also wonder whether the minor premise needs to be so specific. The answer once again is yes: within the 75-word limit, you need to make the minor premise as specific as you reasonably can (see #12). This will enhance your credibility. If you state a conclusory minor premise, readers aren't likely to believe what you're saying. Consider this variation:

> Delaware's blue-sky laws do not apply to securities transactions that take place out of state. All the relevant transactions occurred outside Delaware. Should this Court dismiss the claims?

The writer is asking for a leap of faith. Too much is being held back for the middle part of the writing; instead, the writer can do lots of good here with a greater level of concreteness.

By the way, one of the several shortcomings of a one-sentence *whether*-issue is that it leads to greater vagueness in the facts, as well as to an unchronological presentation. Consider one more variation on our blue-sky-laws issue:

> Whether this Court should dismiss Ellsmere's claims based on Delaware's blue-sky laws when the transactions at issue took place out of state and the Delaware courts have already held that the blue-sky laws do not apply to securities transactions that take place out of state?

That's not horrible, but it's far from great—especially on a first reading. It begins in the present (should this Court dismiss), moves to the transactions (several years ago), and then moves to precedent (many years older). It's harder to get your mind around that sort of long sentence fragment. (Oh, yes, the *whether* makes the issue an ungrammatical sentence fragment.)

Did you know that it's possible for every legal argument to be framed as a syllogism? Not only that. Every legal argument *should* be framed as a syllogism.

There's one other thing about the syllogism. Although you generally want a major premise stating the law, that's true only if the judge needs to be reminded about the law. You don't need a major premise that says, "The First Amendment of the U.S. Constitution protects freedom of speech." Everybody knows that, and you shouldn't waste any of your precious 75 words on something that basic. So in the first example below, you don't need to remind the reader about fundamental fairness in our criminal-justice system. But in all the others, the legal premise needs an explicit statement: it's a helpful reminder.

Some Good Examples

- David Jackson will probably be convicted of capital murder and sentenced to death at next week's trial unless he can present evidence of his mental retardation. Jackson's expert on mental retardation must undergo emergency surgery to remove a cancer that his doctors have just discovered. Should the court grant Jackson's motion for continuance to allow him time to find a new expert? [62 words]

- Under Mississippi discovery rules, computer-stored information is as freely discoverable as tangible, written materials. Even though the defendants' second request for production asked for computer-stored information, the State refuses to search its computers. Given that a search for this computer-stored information would not entail any more effort than searching for tangible, written materials, should this Court compel the State to produce it? [68 words]

- Florida rules allow deposition testimony to be used at trial only if the witness cannot be located after a good-faith attempt to serve a subpoena or if the witness is more than 100 miles from the court. Judge Hand, in Miami, barred the use of the deposition of Jack Throckmorton, an Orlando resident, because the proffering party did not show a good-faith attempt to serve a subpoena. Was Judge Hand's ruling erroneous? [74 words]

- Under Washington law, county commissioners may not appoint a civil servant for a term that is longer than the commissioners' own elective terms. The Skulalia County commissioners, who serve three-year terms, appointed Bartleby as county manager. In a tight labor market, Bartleby was able to negotiate a five-year employment contract. The commissioners accepted and signed the contract. Is Bartleby's contract enforceable? [63 words]

- Under Missouri law, permanent-total-disability benefits are awarded in a workers'-compensation case only if the worker cannot return to any employment in the open labor market. John Shepelwich was injured on the job and applied for permanent-total-disability benefits. Doctors and vocational experts who treated or evaluated him all reported that he could work at available light or sedentary jobs.

Should Shepelwich have been awarded permanent-total-disability benefits? [72 words]

- The Immigration Act lets the Attorney General grant permanent residency to an undocumented alien who has lived in the U.S. continuously for at least ten years and can show that deportation would cause extreme hardship to an immediate relative who is a U.S. citizen. Laura has lived in Texas since 1980 and has a three-year-old U.S.-born daughter who depends on her for support. May the Attorney General grant permanent residency to Laura? [74 words]

- Federal Rule of Evidence 8 requires that a complaint give a "short and concise" statement that puts the defendant on notice of what issues the plaintiff will raise. Erickson filed a 203-page complaint against Brokerage for fraud. The complaint consists largely of multiple-page quotations from Brokerage research reports, followed by generic statements that the reports are fraudulent. Should Erickson's complaint be dismissed for failure to comply with Rule 8? [71 words]

- When a corporate executive communicates with in-house counsel, the attorney–client privilege protects only those communications made for the purpose of obtaining or rendering legal advice. Allan Jones, vice president of Widget Co., had a conversation with Jeannine Meecham, in-house counsel for Widget Co., in which Jones sought both business and legal advice. Are the portions of that conversation pertaining to business advice protected by the attorney–client privilege? [69 words]

- Under California common law, a creditor can obtain an equitable lien on a debtor's property only if the debtor intended to grant the creditor a lien on that specific property. Pat Jones, a creditor of this bankruptcy estate, claims an equitable lien in escrowed funds based on an escrow agreement that does not expressly or implicitly grant Jones a lien on those funds. Does Jones have a lien on the escrowed funds? [72 words]

- The Americans with Disabilities Act protects a disabled employee who can perform the essential functions of the job if the company makes reasonable accommodations. Gail Duval, who became disabled, was terminated by Wyman Corp. and sued under the ADA. In her deposition, she testified that when she was terminated, her disability had rendered her unable to perform her job even with accommodations. Was Duval protected under the ADA? [68 words]

Multiple Issues with Neutral Headings

Scott P. Stolley of Dallas, an accomplished appellate practitioner, has developed a good method for "naming" issues—by providing a neutral label for each one. Both examples below are from his briefs. In the actual briefs, each passage quoted below is followed by the statement of facts.

Example A

Issues

The Borens' appeal presents three main issues:

- **Date of the Breach or Tort.** When the precise date of the breach or tort is ascertainable, a medical-malpractice plaintiff who sends the statutory notice must sue within two years and 75 days after the breach or tort occurs. It is undisputed that Dr. Kellogg examined Mrs. Boren only once and that the Borens did not sue until two years and 76 days later. Are the Borens' claims time-barred?

- **Waiver.** At trial, the Borens argued that the limitations period was extended by a continuous course of treatment. On appeal, the Borens have abandoned this argument and have raised two new arguments—that the state constitution's Open Courts provision saves their claims, and that the limitations period did not begin to run until William Boren was born and became a "patient," four days after Dr. Kellogg saw Mrs. Boren. Have the Borens waived these new arguments?

- **Open Courts.** The Borens' wrongful-death and survival claims are statutory claims not recognized at common law. The Open Courts provision preserves only common-law claims. Does the Borens' Open Courts argument therefore fail?

Example B

Issues

The appeal by the Thompsons and Ms. Taylor-Evans presents three main issues:

- **Applicability of Chapter 38.** Chapter 38 of the Texas Civil Practice and Remedies Code does not permit recovery of attorney's fees from an insurer whose policy is subject to article 21.21 or 21.21-2 of the Texas Insurance Code. State Farm's policy covering the Colby family is subject to both of those articles. Did the trial court therefore properly deny attorney's fees under Chapter 38?

- **"Legal Entitlement."** Attorney's fees are recoverable under chapter 38 only if a defendant fails to pay an amount owed. Uninsured-motorist benefits are not owed until the insured satisfies a condition precedent—namely, that the insured be "legally entitled" to recover from the uninsured motorist. Did the trial court properly deny attorney's fees here, given that the claimants failed—until after judgment was entered—to establish a "legal entitlement" to recover from the Colbys?

- **Presentment.** As a further prerequisite to recovery of attorney's fees under chapter 38, the claimant must also "present" the claim. Here, there is no evidence that Thompson's parents or Ms. Taylor-Evans ever made "presentment," and further, there is no evidence that any claimant ever made "presentment" after belatedly establishing an arguable entitlement to recover from the Colby family. Did the trial court therefore properly deny attorney's fees to the claimants?

12

Weave facts into your issues
to make them concrete.

Quotable Quotes

"[I]n the majority of cases the chief difficulties of the brief writer are not to prove certain legal propositions, but to show that certain legal propositions are applicable and controlling under the specific facts of the case in hand."
—William M. Lile et al., *Brief-Making and the Use of Law Books* 375 (3d ed. 1914).

"An abstract style is always bad. Your sentences should be full of stones, metals, chairs, tables, animals, men, and women."
—Alain de Lille (as quoted in Rudolf Flesch, *The Art of Readable Writing* 83 (1949; repr. 1967)).

"[W]riting should be concrete. It should evoke images and refer to something the reader can identify with particular experiences. A general concept like motion is interesting to a philosopher, but an ordinary reader wants to know what is moving, how fast, whether it is going toward him or away from him, and what effect the motion of this object will have on his income or his likelihood of getting a good night's sleep."
—Sumner Ives, *A New Handbook for Writers* 317 (1960).

"Writing too largely in abstract terms is one of the worst and most widespread of literary faults. It sounds learned; it saves the writer from having to use his eyes and ears; and it makes slovenly thinking possible because it does not require definiteness."
—David Lambuth et al., *The Golden Book on Writing* 32 (1964).

"Not in all, but in most cases, the issues can only be described by reference to the facts as well as the law."
—George W. Paton, *A Textbook of Jurisprudence* 214 (G.W. Paton & David P. Derham eds., 4th ed. 1972).

"The more abstract your argument, the more you should lace it with graphic illustrations, analogies, apt quotations, and concrete details. These are aids not only to your reader's understanding but also to his memory."
—John R. Trimble, *Writing with Style* 79 (1975).

"It is inadequate merely to state the legal issue without any reference to the factual setting in which it arises (e.g., 'Whether the defendant is entitled to judgment notwithstanding the verdict' or 'Whether the trial court's instructions were erroneous and prejudicial')."

> —Girvan Peck, *Writing Persuasive Briefs* 101 (1984).

"The most helpful statement of an issue is in terms of its facts, not as an abstract question of law. The statement should show the precise point of substantive law and its applicability to the facts at hand. Thus, 'was plaintiff guilty of contributory negligence?' does vaguely indicate the general issue; but how much more helpful to the court's concentration and understanding of the issue is: 'Plaintiff's car struck the rear of a vehicle operated by the defendant, who had made an emergency stop without signaling. Where plaintiff admits that he could not have stopped his car within an assured clear distance ahead, is he chargeable with contributory negligence so as to bar his recovery?' "

> —Albert Tate Jr., "The Art of Brief Writing: What a Judge Wants to Read,"
> in *Appellate Practice Manual* 197, 202 (Priscilla A. Schwab ed., 1992).

"I spend a lot of time avoiding conceptual discussions or translating them, where possible, into Joe Six-Pack language. You would be surprised how often abstract concepts conceal a failure to come to grips with the precise issues or facts in the case."

> —Patricia M. Wald, *How I Write*, 4 Scribes J. Legal Writing 55, 59 (1993).

Explanation

Unfortunately, some court rules actually require that advocates write "a concise statement, not exceeding two pages, of the questions involved *without names, dates, amounts or particulars*, with each question numbered, set forth separately and followed immediately by the answer, if any, of the court from which the appeal is taken."*

If you're bound by such an unfortunate rule—which seems like an inarticulate warning against overparticularization (see #27)—follow it. You can still follow most of the advice given here about issue-framing. You'll just be doing it more abstractly.

The better approach is typically to weave concrete facts into your issue statements, so that you tell a story in miniature, with names and all. But remember that you want only the particulars that are important— the ones that help the reader understand the problem.

In fact, when brief-writers try to frame their issues in the syllogistic format outlined in #11, they typically stumble—if they do stumble—on

---

* N.Y. C.P.L.R. 5528(a) (McKinney 1996) (emphasis added). Cf. Pa. R. App. P. 2116(a) ("The statement of the questions involved must state the question or questions in the briefest and most general terms, without names, dates, amounts or particulars of any kind. It [i.e., the *statement of the questions*, presumably, but perhaps a *question*] should not ordinarily exceed 15 lines, must never exceed one page, without any other matter appearing thereon. This rule is to be considered in the highest degree mandatory . . . .").

the middle part of the syllogism. That is, their facts are too abstract or conclusory, or else they're chronologically scrambled. Within your 75-word limit, try to be as concrete as you can helpfully be. And sustain the story line as long as you can before asking a short, punchy question. Try not to bring up new facts in the question, as by including a *when*-clause in the question. Avoid saying, "Is Putnam liable when . . . ?" Instead, say what happened, and then end with "Is Putnam liable?"

For those bound by a don't-give-us-any-particulars rule, it's probably worth citing a couple of winning issues before a state supreme court. William J. Conroy and Robert Toland II of Wayne, Pennsylvania—along with Joseph A. Katarincic of Pittsburgh—used the multiple-sentence approach with success before the Pennsylvania Supreme Court in 2002. In fact, they succeeded in getting the court to reverse on the briefing alone—a rare event in that state. Here are their winning issues, written under the constraint of minimizing particulars:

1. **Waiver.** Rule 227(b) provides that objections to the jury instructions may be made anytime before the jury retires. Here, Defendants objected on the record during the charge conference—well before the jury retired. Yet the Superior Court ruled that Defendants had waived their objections because they had not moved for nonsuit or directed verdict. Does this ruling depart from Rule 227(b) and established caselaw to create a new "waiver rule" without foundation in law?

2. **Crashworthiness.** All the parties tried this case under a crashworthiness theory. Yet the trial court refused to instruct the jury on the elements that this Court and the Superior Court have held must be established for crashworthiness liability; instead, the jury instructions reflected the materially different standards of general strict liability. Did the court err in refusing to instruct the jury on the elements of crashworthiness?

Those issues do a great job of showing syllogistic reasoning. And they passed the ultimate test: they won a reversal.**

Some Good Examples

- At 7:30 one morning last spring, Father Michael Prynne, a Roman Catholic priest, was on his way to buy food for himself at the grocery store when his car collided with Ed Grimley's pickup truck. The Catholic Church neither owned Father Prynne's car nor required its priests to buy groceries as part of their priestly functions. Was Father Prynne acting as an agent for the Church at the time of the accident? [72 words]

** *See Colville v. Crown Equip. Corp.*, 791 A.2d 1168 (Pa. 2002) (per curiam).

- In New York, a person who knowingly purchases used goods cannot bring a claim for breach of implied warranty. Sandra O'Keefe admitted at her deposition that she bought her 2001 Acura—the vehicle that she claims the manufacturer impliedly warranted—with more than 11,000 miles on the odometer. Should O'Keefe's claim for breach of implied warranty be dismissed because the car was used when she bought it? [67 words]

- The Colorado Water Board lowered Cherry Creek's minimum stream flow from 12 cubic feet per second to 7. The Board's decision—reached after four public hearings on the subject—was based on recommendations of both the Colorado Division of Wildlife and three independent aquatic biologists, all of whom concluded that 7 cubic feet per second was the optimal minimum for Cherry Creek. Was the Board's decision arbitrary and capricious under the Administrative Procedure Act? [74 words]

- New York domestic law provides that a maintenance agreement is not binding if it was made under duress or is patently unfair. At the end of her 18-year abusive marriage, Sallie, who has only a ninth-grade education and no financial experience, agreed to a maintenance award so low that she cannot afford food for her children. Should this Court invalidate Sallie's maintenance agreement? [65 words]

- Under Printeen Corp.'s collective-bargaining agreement, the company may fire an employee for good cause. Jane Smith, an employee at Printeen, was temporarily assigned by her immediate supervisor to a position she didn't want to fill. She then left the plant premises without authorization, as a result of which the company had to shut down part of the production line overnight. Did the company have good cause to fire Smith? [70 words]

- Pavemasters, a contractor, agreed to install a masonry surface at Lincoln Hospital. Before the work began, the hospital repeatedly asked about the design's drainage system, but Pavemasters did not answer. Only after installation was well underway did Pavemasters admit that the project included no drainage system. The hospital later sustained water damage because rainwater did not drain properly. Is Pavemasters responsible for the cost of repairing the water damage and installing a drainage system? [74 words]

- State Bar conflict-of-interest rules prohibit an attorney from representing a party in a divorce action if the attorney has previously represented both parties in other litigation. Janie Wilson and her husband Bob hired attorney Ben Bailey when they purchased some property. Two years later, Janie hired Bailey to represent her in her divorce from Bob. Is Bailey barred from representing Janie? [63 words]

- New Hampshire criminal procedure bars a defendant from withdrawing a guilty plea after being sentenced. In 1999, McNair agreed to plead guilty to petty burglary for a probated sentence. Now he has been charged with violating the terms of his probation and faces the probability of a prison sentence. McNair contends that because the sentence may still be changed, he retains the right to withdraw his guilty plea. Is he right? [71 words]

- In Georgia, an out-of-court conversation is admissible as evidence if it explains a person's conduct or state of mind. While visiting the Johnsons on April 2, Marshall watched as (1) Mr. Johnson accused his wife of adultery with his best friend, (2) she confessed, and (3) he slapped her. Two hours later, after Marshall had left, Mrs. Johnson was murdered. Is Marshall's testimony about the conversation admissible in Mr. Johnson's murder trial? [74 words]

- A foreign national who has been "firmly resettled" in a third country is ineligible to apply for asylum in the United States. Before entering the U.S., Marla Simonich, a citizen of Bosnia-Herzegovina, spent 15 months in a refugee camp in the Netherlands. At the camp she was forcibly confined, had no access to education or employment, and was not eligible to apply for residence in the Netherlands. Did Marla firmly resettle in the Netherlands? [75 words]

- Federal jurisdiction under the Alien Tort Statute requires that the plaintiff allege a violation of the law of nations, such as acts of torture committed by government officials acting under color of state authority. Mueller Corp. is a defense contractor. Palmer alleges that Mueller employees, who are all private citizens, harassed, assaulted, and attempted to kidnap him. Has Palmer alleged a claim for torture in violation of the law of nations? [71 words]

- The Supreme Court has held that the Fourth Amendment is not violated when a police officer makes a custodial arrest after seeing the person commit a misdemeanor traffic offense in a public place. A police officer saw John Phillmore driving on Main Street without headlights after dark—a misdemeanor. The officer arrested Phillmore. Did the arrest violate Phillmore's Fourth Amendment rights? [61 words]

- Under New York law, a good-faith purchaser for value cannot acquire valid title to stolen property. In 1939, Nazi troops stole the painting *Portrait of a Woman* from the Bronsky family home in Poland. In 1956, Jane McConnell purchased the painting from a reputable New York gallery. McConnell died in 2002, leaving the painting to her daughter, Maeve. Does Maeve McConnell now have valid title to the painting as against the Bronsky family heirs? [75 words]

- The First Amendment lets school districts regulate student speech only if the speech substantially disrupts school operations. McRae and Barnes were alone in a hallway of Eclipse Middle School. McRae asked to copy Barnes's homework. Barnes refused, and McRae threatened to hit him. A teacher in a nearby classroom overheard the threat and reported McRae, who was suspended. Can the school justify the suspension by asserting that bullying is always and inherently substantially disruptive? [74 words]

- Under Texas law, an attorney who has "committed a crime of moral turpitude" can be suspended from the practice of law. Phyllis Locke, a Texas attorney, was arrested for possession of illicit drugs. While her case was being investigated, but before she was prosecuted (much less convicted), the State Bar of Texas suspended her law license. Is an arrest without a conviction for a crime of moral turpitude sufficient to justify the suspension? [73 words]

- Leonard Slocum Jr., a mentally retarded minor whose father has physically abused him, has become the state's ward and begun a habilitation program that has helped him demonstrably. His father, Slocum Sr., petitioned to become Leonard Jr.'s guardian, but the court found him unfit because of the abuse and because he has sired four illegitimate children by a 25-year-old mentally retarded woman—formerly his ward. Did the court abuse its discretion? [73 words]

13

If you don't open with explicit issue statements, sum up the issues and your theme in a short introduction.

Quotable Quotes

"Almost all reading matter in this country gets off to a false start. This is not an exaggeration; it is a statement of fact [that] I am going to prove.

"Let me first define my terms. What is a false start? It's a beginning that doesn't do what a beginning *ought* to do. Psychologists tell us that an effective piece of writing should start with something that points to its main theme. In other words, you must put your reader in the right frame of mind; you must start by getting him interested in what's going to come.

"Look around you and you'll find that most reading matter doesn't start that way. It usually starts in a routine fashion—with a stale, humdrum opening that does *anything but* whet your appetite for the main dish."

—Rudolf Flesch, *The Art of Readable Writing* 61 (1949; repr. 1967).

"The first thing that a certain Scots professor used to say to his students when they handed in their essays was: 'Did it never occur to you to tear up the first page?' Without reading it, he could guess that it was bad, because beginnings are the most difficult things to manage successfully. 'It is there,' said Chekov, 'that we do most of our lying.' Before we are properly warmed up, we run the risk of being flat and pedantic."

—André Maurois, *The Art of Writing* 21–22 (Gerard Hopkins trans., 1962).

"Judges crave an immediate sense of overview. At the beginning of a brief, they are not interested in hearing all the details of the case. They want to know what kind of case this is and what issues the brief addresses."

—Ruggero J. Aldisert, *Winning on Appeal: Better Briefs and Oral Argument* 182 (1992).

"A thesis statement that leaves readers in doubt about what the writer means will never change their views on an issue. For instance, the thesis that 'The federal government's farm policy must guarantee that economic aid to farmers will achieve desirable results' will hardly change anyone's mind about farm subsidies since it is so vague that few people would disagree with it. A thesis such as 'The federal government must subsidize small farmers to keep family farms from disappearing' is clear, precisely worded, and memorable."

—David I. Daniels & Barbara J. Daniels, *Persuasive Writing* 171 (1993).

"You can usually blame a bad essay on a bad beginning. If your essay falls apart, it probably has no primary idea, no thesis, to hold it together. 'What's the big idea?' we used to ask. The phrase will serve as a reminder that you must find the 'big idea' behind your several smaller thoughts and musings and drafts before you can start to shape your final essay. . . . Thus your thesis is your essay's life and spirit. If it is sufficiently firm, it may tell you immediately how to organize your supporting material. But if you do not find a thesis, your essay will be a tour through the miscellaneous, replete with scaffolds and catwalks—'We have just seen this; now let us turn to this'—an essay with no vital idea."

> —Sheridan Baker, *The Practical Stylist* 17–18 (8th ed. 1998).

"A good opener normally includes a good thesis—bold, fresh, clearly focused. And a good thesis tends to argue itself because it has a built-in thrust."

> —John R. Trimble, *Writing with Style* 26 (2d ed. 2000).

Explanation

Because issues are so very important, you shouldn't depend on a rule to tell you to put them up front. True, the better rules require them at the outset, as Rule 14 of the U.S. Supreme Court does. But many sets of rules—especially for trial courts—don't require them at all. And even on appeal, various state-court rules merely require "Points Relied On" or "Points of Error."

Even so, it's wise to open with an introduction (sometimes called a "preliminary statement") setting out the deep issues. Most of your judicial readers—probably all—will be grateful.

Some years ago, John Morris of New York opposed a plaintiff's motion to compel in a multiparty securities case. The motion began by citing Rule 26 and then droned on for four pages, listing every interrogatory number, every request for production, and every request for admission that was at issue against each defendant—information much better conveyed in a chart (see #70). Even though Morris was opposing the motion, he pointed out that the opener could have been this: "It has been a year since plaintiffs served their first discovery requests. None of the 15 defendants has produced a single document."

Not all such opportunities are missed. Philip S. Beck of Chicago wrote a superb opening paragraph for the preliminary-injunction brief in *Amalgamated Sugar v. NL Industries*, in which his client Harold Simmons (aka Amalgamated) knocked out NL's poison pill and took over the company. Here's how the brief began: "NL Industries is owned by its shareholders. The board of directors works for them. The shareholders want to sell their stock to Harold Simmons. The board won't let them."

Though not always so succinctly, adept brief-writers routinely provide a concrete overview.

Examples A and B are by Stephen M. Shapiro of Chicago, the noted coauthor of *Supreme Court Practice*. Although both of these openers come from briefs to the U.S. Supreme Court, they would fit well into briefs at any level. Notice how Shapiro begins with the larger context and moves quickly to a focused legal question.

Example C is by Scott P. Stolley of Dallas. Notice again how his first sentence is a broad description, followed by a concise story line that moves swiftly to the disputed point. A lesser brief-writer would have been either much more vague in the factual narrative or else much more detailed and much slower in getting to the point.

Examples D and E are by Steven A. Hirsch of San Francisco, who begins with a startling aphorism or simile and then plunges into a well-worded summary of the argument. His openers are more expansive than Examples A, B, and C. Example D comes from a brief to the California Court of Appeal, Example E from a brief to the Board of Immigration Appeals in Falls Church, Virginia. After a dramatic start, they both carefully develop the points to be elaborated more thoroughly in the main body.

Five Uncommonly Good Examples

Example A

Introduction

Like all other states, Pennsylvania requires funds to finance the construction, maintenance, and repair of its roads, bridges, and tunnels. Also like other states, Pennsylvania raises the funds largely through taxes and fees levied on the users of its highways. A substantial proportion of these taxes is paid by interstate motor carriers. Appellant American Trucking Associations, Inc. ("ATA"), as their representative, has brought this suit not because of any objection to the raising of revenues by highway-user charges or to the level of revenues Pennsylvania seeks to raise, but solely because the discriminatory nature of the two highway-use taxes Pennsylvania has adopted—the marker fee and its successor, the axle tax—favors local interests at the expense of interstate commerce.

Example B

Introduction

In their journey from the assembly line to the dealer's showroom, automobiles occasionally experience minor damage requiring repair or refinishing. The question then naturally arises whether, or in what circumstances, the fact of repair or refinishing should be disclosed to the dealer or to the retail purchaser of the automobile. By 1983, several states had answered this question by statute or regulation. BMW canvassed these laws and adopted the strictest disclosure threshold—3% of the manufacturer's suggested retail price ("MSRP")—as its nationwide policy. Since that time, many other states have adopted disclosure thresholds. The vast majority, including Alabama (which enacted its statute after the trial in this case), require disclosure only if any repairs or refinishing cost more than 3% (or some higher percentage) of MSRP. *See, e.g.,* ALA. CODE § 8-19-5(22) (the failure to give notice of repairs or refinishing costing less than 3% of MSRP is not an unfair trade practice and "shall not . . . constitute a material misrepresentation or omission of fact").

In this case, a jury found that BMW's 3% disclosure policy constituted fraud under Alabama common law. It then proceeded to award $4 million in punitive damages (later reduced by the Alabama Supreme Court to $2 million) to plaintiff Dr. Ira Gore, not just for BMW's application of that policy to him but for its application of the policy to hundreds of cars sold outside Alabama—despite the absence of any showing that those sales were unlawful where they occurred.

Example C

Introduction

Wheaton Van Lines, Inc. appeals a $1.3 million judgment holding Wheaton liable for an assault committed by Michael Mullinax, a third party over whom Wheaton had no control. While working for a local mover, David Lux, Mullinax helped move Appellee Kevin Mason to a new apartment in the same apartment complex. Eleven days later, after being fired by Lux for stealing some of Mason's property, Mullinax assaulted Mason in Mason's apartment. The overarching issue is whether Wheaton is liable for Mullinax's criminal conduct, when Wheaton's only connection to Mullinax was a contract under which Lux sometimes acted as Wheaton's agent for interstate moves.

Example D

Introduction

No good deed goes unpunished.

The reason Cellular One now finds itself defending against the harsh accusations made in this lawsuit is that in 1995—alone among Bay Area cellular providers—it voluntarily slashed cellular phone rates for customers with documented disabilities. Had Cellular One not initiated its groundbreaking "Enable-Link" program, it would not now stand accused of deliberately *preventing* disabled customers from obtaining rate discounts.

In this lawsuit, the plaintiffs allege that Cellular One failed to adequately inform some of its disabled customers that they might be eligible for Enable-Link rate discounts. They further allege that Cellular One wrongfully discouraged plaintiff George Eckert and others from applying for the Enable-Link Plan by requiring them to obtain a physician's certification that misrepresented the Plan's eligibility requirements. They also point to similar alleged misrepresentations in an advertising brochure for the program.

What the complaint doesn't say is that this lawsuit represents an ambitious, but deeply flawed, attempt to take Business & Professions Code § 17200 where it has never gone before. Other cases have held that § 17200 "borrows" the substantive provisions of other laws; some have gone so far as to hold that § 17200 can add a private right of action to a statute that does not feature one. But no case ever has held that § 17200 allows a court to step into the shoes of a regulatory agency and promulgate regulations that the agency has declined to issue on its own.

And no case ever should hold that, because it would violate the constitutional separation of powers and thrust courts into a policymaking role they are ill-equipped to handle. This case shows why. The statute plaintiffs rely on to provide a legal standard for their claim, Public Utilities Code ("PUC") § 2896(a), gives *the Public Utilities Commission* the power to impose disclosure requirements on telephone service providers. Plaintiffs claim that the superior court should bypass the Commission and do that job itself. In other words, plaintiffs want the superior court to issue a regulation telling Cellular One exactly what it must disclose to its customers about its special rate program for the disabled, and exactly how the disclosures must be made. Moreover, this court-created regulation would apply only to Cellular One, thus creating the anomalous situation where Cellular One would be the only provider in the state subject to regulation under § 2896(a). This lawsuit therefore invites the superior court to simultaneously usurp legislative power (by rewriting § 2896(a) in a manner contrary to the legislative intent), and executive power (by promulgating regulations within the exclusive jurisdiction of the Commission).

So far, the superior court has declined the invitation. It sustained two successive demurrers, the second one against all remaining causes of action, without leave to amend. This appeal attempts to revive two claims pleaded in the second amended complaint: (1) the count for unlawful and unfair business practices under Business and Professions Code § 17200 *et seq.*, and (2) the count for breach of contract (styled as a "tariff enforcement action").

We will show that the trial court was right and that its judgment dismissing this lawsuit should be affirmed, for four independent reasons:

First, a long line of caselaw holds that the superior court lacks jurisdiction over any civil suit against a regulated utility if that suit asks the court to make factual findings or to grant relief that would conflict with the Commission's orders, policies, or ongoing inquiries. That's exactly what would happen here. In orders issued in 1962 and 1996, the Commission occupied the field of customer-service notification, spelling out exactly what disclosures a telephone company must make and exactly how to make them. In 1996, the Commission launched an ongoing inquiry into whether it should revise those orders in light of changes in technology and markets. The factual findings and relief sought here would conflict with these Commission actions. Accordingly, the superior court lacks any jurisdiction to consider the plaintiffs' claims.

Second, the plaintiffs' § 17200 claim alleges that Cellular One breached duties that do not exist. Their theory is that Cellular One failed to meet disclosure requirements allegedly contained in PUC § 2896(a). But that statute imposes duties only on the Commission. It imposes no duties whatsoever on Cellular One, and certainly not the duties that the plaintiffs claim Cellular One breached. Moreover, the legislative history also shows that § 2896(a) never could have become law had it purported to grant directly enforceable rights to consumers, because the governor would have vetoed it. Lawmakers understood this, and drafted a bill enforceable only by the Commission—indeed, too vague to be enforced by anyone but the Commission.

Third, plaintiffs' § 17200 claim is really an end-run around the state constitution's separation-of-powers clause, which prohibits courts from ordering agencies to promulgate specific regulations. Here, the plaintiffs seek relief that inevitably would require the superior court to specify the customer-service disclosure obligations of California cellular service providers. Granting that order would violate the state constitution and thrust the superior court into a quasi-regulatory role that it is simply not equipped to perform.

Fourth and finally, plaintiffs' breach-of-contract claim fails as a matter of law because Eckert admits that he never applied for the Enable-Link Program; accordingly, he never entered into any contract with Cellular One that could have entitled him to the Plan's benefits. Here, again, plaintiffs allege the breach of non-existent duties.

For all these reasons, this Court should affirm the judgment below.

Example E

Introduction

Khoja Toryali Shujai is a bit like the cosmonauts who were stranded on the Mir space station when the Soviet Union collapsed. When they went up, they were from one sort of nation; when they came down, after a long delay, they belonged to a very different one. The difference is that Shujai cannot safely return to the land he once knew.

During the eight years that Shujai awaited this Board's decision on his appeal from an adverse asylum ruling, his home country of Afghanistan was turned upside down. The Soviet-backed communist government fell.[1] The country disintegrated into violence and brigandry as competing mujahedin groups vied for power while terrorizing the citizenry. A military force led by ethnic Tajiks (a minority to which Shujai belongs) took over the nation's capital and the northeast, gaining international recognition as the country's leaders even as rival warlords carved up the rest of the country.[2]

Beginning in 1994, young peasant men attending primitive religious schools across the border in Pakistan began assembling themselves into a fighting force that vowed to take over all of Afghanistan, suppress the marauding mujahedin groups, and impose an ultraorthodox brand of Islamic fundamentalism on the nation. Calling themselves the Taliban, or "students of Islam,"[3] they belonged to the dominant Pushtun ethnic group that had long ruled the nation. They made rapid inroads and by late 1996 had captured Kabul. Wherever they took power, they imposed an iron-

---

[1] *See generally* Ahmed Rashid, *Taliban: Militant Islam, Oil and Fundamentalism in Central Asia* (Yale University Press 2000) ("*Taliban*"), at 18–21. Excerpts from *Taliban* are attached as Exhibit A to the accompanying Declaration of Elliot R. Peters ("Peters Decl.").

[2] *Id.* at 21.

[3] *Id.* at 22–23.

fisted form of Islam that they believed would restore the social system that prevailed in the time of the Prophet. Other belief systems were crushed; people were forced to convert to Sunni Islam at knifepoint[4]; rival ethnic groups were massacred or forcibly displaced[5]; women were eliminated from public life and placed under virtual house arrest.[6] Everyday life became heavily policed by self-appointed guardians of morality who used stonings, amputations, and severe beatings to enforce a myriad of rules governing everything from marital fidelity to the length of a man's beard to the amount of noise a woman's shoes should make when she walks.[7]

But one obstacle remains to the Taliban's complete takeover of the country. In the Panjshir Valley northeast of Kabul, where Shujai hails from, his Tajik compatriots remain at war with the rapidly consolidating regime. Today, they comprise the last significant pocket of resistance to the Taliban. As a result, ethnic Tajiks like Shujai have been subjected to a campaign of killings, bombardments, forced relocations, detentions without cause, and outright warfare. Families have been divided and entire towns emptied and put to the torch. Not only is Shujai a member of the embattled ethnic group, but two of his brothers have actually fought for the Tajik forces.

Just as his nation has changed, so has Shujai himself. He has now lived in the United States for almost a decade, has largely abandoned his religion, and has become a thoroughly secular and increasingly Westernized man. Unschooled in Islamic religious practice (because his limited education was cut short by war and a war-related head injury) and overtly hostile to the Taliban's beliefs and social program, Shujai will be a marked man if forced to return to Afghanistan. This unreligious man from an embattled ethnic group, who has spent a decade living in the United States, has much to fear upon return to his homeland. He has, in short, a well-founded fear of persecution.

For reasons discussed more fully below, we respectfully urge this Board to reopen Shujai's asylum proceedings to consider all of the evidence set forth here—evidence concerning a brutal, cultish regime that did not even exist when the Immigration Judge denied Shujai asylum in 1991. We note that the Board has previously held that the Taliban's emergence represents a change in country conditions that merits a reopening or remand of asylum and withholding proceedings.[8]

Alternatively, we ask that the Board suspend Shujai's deportation on humanitarian grounds under 8 U.S.C. § 1254(a)(1).

---

[4] *Id.* at 74.

[5] *See* Point V-A, below.

[6] *See* Point V-B, below.

[7] *Taliban*, at 105–06 (Peters Decl., Exh. A).

[8] *See In re A-N-*, Interim Decision 3406, 1999 BIA LEXIS 34 (BIA July 23, 1999); *Matter of N-M-A*, Interim Decision 3368 (BIA 1998).

14

Highlight the reasons for the conclusion you're urging.

Quotable Quotes

"For the writer of argumentation, the *because* clause is apt to be the most difficult element of the whole thesis statement. If the thesis is a good one, it is apt to seem to the writer his ultimate statement upon the subject. To find a *because* clause for that thesis, he must go beyond the ultimate statement. But the step must be taken; he must find the reason that will link him to his audience and make it possible for them to accept the thesis itself. The *because* clause is not an irrational requirement the instructor has invented to make writing difficult; it is an essential connection [that] makes communication persuasive."

—William J. Brandt et al., *The Craft of Writing* 20 (1969).

"One of the temptations you will face in [persuasive] writing, especially if the subject is one you feel strongly about, is to keep repeating your opinion in different words instead of supporting it. Resist that temptation. Remember that you are trying to persuade your readers, not just impress them with your sincerity. And to persuade them, you have to offer them sound reasons for believing as you do."

—James F. Dorrill & Charles W. Harwell, *Read and Write: A Guide to Effective Composition* 284–85 (1987).

"Any argument is only as convincing as the *reasons* that support it. No matter how 'right' you think you are, you have to make your readers agree. And before readers will change their minds, they need to know why. They expect you to complete a version of this statement.

My position is _____ because _____.

"Your reasons follow the 'because.'"

—John M. Lannon, *The Writing Process* 310–11 (1989).

Explanation

If you follow the advice in the preceding tips, writing your conclusion— your statement of what you want the court to do—should be straightfor- ward: it will be the answer to the question posed by your issue.

But when you omit the reason for your conclusion, it appears almost as if you're hiding something. When you give a good reason, on the other hand, you're more likely to seem both thoughtful and sensible. In short, you're more persuasive.

This tip is key to both your opening words and your closing words: succinctly tell the court why it should do what you ask.

You'd be well served to follow the Lannon formula quoted above—except invert it: "Because _____, [my position is] _____." By doing that, you'll move your brief to the top of the stack in terms of clarity and persuasiveness.

Why? Because an appallingly large number of briefs in this country don't clearly state why the court should do what the brief-writer asks. Think of all the briefs you've seen that can be boiled down to something like, "[Proposition 1.] [Citation.] [Proposition 2.] [Citation.] [Proposition 3.] [Citation.] For the foregoing reasons, judgment should be entered for the plaintiff." Or, if a brief does mention reasons, they're often buried somewhere in the middle of a long, jumbled paragraph.

Notice how effectively the examples below highlight the reasons for the conclusions stated. Example A is my revision of a motion to quash. Example B is by Patricia Villareal of Dallas; in her brief, she clarified a difficult problem (notice especially the bulleted points in which her opener culminates).

Two Uncommonly Good Examples

Example A

Corinth's Motion to Quash
Subpoena Duces Tecum

This Court should quash Van Helden's subpoena duces tecum for three reasons:

- The request seeks the personnel files of Corinth's sales and marketing managers—information that is highly confidential and irrelevant to Van Helden's claims.

- The discovery deadline has long since passed, and Van Helden never asked for these materials in discovery.

- Even if Corinth complied with these improper requests, Van Helden would be precluded from using the materials at trial because they aren't included in this Court's pretrial order regarding exhibits.

For these reasons, Corinth moves this Court for an order quashing Van Helden's subpoena.

Respectfully submitted,

[Memorandum in support follows.]

Example B

NO. 91-05637-F

WEATHERFORD ROOFING COMPANY, et al.,	§	IN THE DISTRICT COURT OF
	§	
	§	
Plaintiffs,	§	
	§	
v.	§	DALLAS COUNTY, TEXAS
	§	
EMPLOYERS NATIONAL INSURANCE COMPANY and EMPLOYERS CASUALTY COMPANY, et al.,	§	
	§	
	§	
	§	
Defendants.	§	116TH JUDICIAL DISTRICT

HIGHLANDS' MOTION FOR PARTIAL SUMMARY JUDGMENT

Introduction

In a five-year overhaul of a broken workers' compensation system, the Texas Legislature in 1993 created a statutory safe harbor for any pass-throughs of Assigned Risk Pool deficit assessments. The legislature's judgment was that pass-throughs should be "deemed valid" if consistent with the statute's purpose and if the resulting premium was less than the Rejected Risk Fund premium. The Legislature gave this blanket approval to all pass-throughs except those challenged in a civil proceeding pending on May 1, 1993.

If there were no civil proceeding pending against Highlands on May 1, 1993, has the Texas Legislature preempted the claims McCoy Tree Surgery asserts here against Highlands? Highlands contends the answer must be yes. Hence, Highlands moves for

HIGHLANDS' MOTION FOR PARTIAL SUMMARY JUDGMENT—Page 1

partial summary judgment on McCoy Tree's claims for any pass-throughs of deficit assessments because Section 4.04q expressly authorizes any such assessments:

> The pass-through allowances authorized in Sections (d) and (e) hereof shall be deemed exclusive subsequent to the effective date of this article, but other methods utilized prior to such effective date shall be deemed valid if consistent with the purpose of this article and the premium resulting from their use is less than the premium which would have been charged for a similarly rated risk in the Rejected Risk Fund.

The Legislature wholly removed the question of validity of the pass-throughs from the scrutiny of courts or regulators, with one carefully circumscribed exception:

> The validation made by this amendment shall govern any civil or regulatory proceeding except a civil proceeding pending in a court of competent jurisdiction on May 1, 1993, including civil proceedings filed on or before May 1, 1993, which are seeking class action status, whether or not the plaintiff or defendant classes have been certified.

That exception does not apply to Highlands because:

- On May 1, 1993, Highlands was not named a defendant in *Weatherford*.

- The *Weatherford* defendant class allegations, insufficient in any event to connect Highlands to this proceeding on May 1, 1993, were voluntarily dismissed by plaintiffs, extinguishing any claim against unnamed defendants as if it had never existed.

- On May 1, 1993, no named plaintiff in *Weatherford* had a contractual relationship with Highlands or standing to assert a claim against Highlands.

- On May 1, 1993, the *Weatherford* named plaintiffs, without the defendant class allegations, only assert claims against the named defendants.

- McCoy Tree owes Highlands more than twice the amount of damages it seeks.

Highlands' motion for partial summary judgment should be granted.

15

Make your points as simple as possible, but no simpler.

Quotable Quotes

"When a thought is too weak to be expressed simply, it should be rejected."
—Luc, Marquis de Vauvenargues, *Refléxions et Maximes* no. 3 (1746).

"Order and simplification are the first steps toward the mastery of a subject."
—Thomas Mann, *The Magic Mountain* ch. 5 (1924).

"The desire for simplification is a perennial weakness of the human mind, even the mind of judges."
—Sir Wilfrid Greene M.R., *The Judicial Office* 12 (1938).

"If you know something you can state it clearly. If you have not mastered the thought you are not yet in a position to pass it on to others, although sketching a rough draft for your own further analysis often proves useful."
—George J. Miller, *On Legal Style*, 43 Ky. L.J. 235, 241 (1955).

"[A] simple, clear, and harmonious style does not come easily. It is the product of much mental sweat and a critical evaluation of first efforts."
—Sumner Ives, *A New Handbook for Writers* 275 (1960).

"I prefer the risk of oversimplification to even a whisper of unnecessary complexity."
—John C. Godbold, "Twenty Pages and Twenty Minutes—Effective Advocacy on Appeal," 30 Sw. L.J. 801, 801 (1976).

"[T]he kind of writing instruction most of us have gotten in school is exactly the reverse of what we need. Instead of teaching us how to communicate as clearly as possible, our schooling in English teaches us how to fog things up. It even implants a fear that if we don't make our writing complicated enough, we'll be considered uneducated."
—John L. Beckley, *The Power of Little Words* 8 (1984).

"A lawyer should write the brief at a level a 12th grader could understand. That's a good rule of thumb. It also aids the writer. Working hard to make a brief simple is extremely rewarding because it helps a lawyer to understand the issue. At the same time, it scores points with the court."

> —William Bablitch (as quoted in Mark Rusk, *Mistakes to Avoid on Appeal*, ABA J., Sept. 1988, at 78, 80).

"Simple arguments are winning arguments; convoluted arguments are sleeping pills on paper."

> —Alex Kozinski, *How You Too . . . Can Lose Your Appeal*, 23 Montana Law. 5, 6 (Oct. 1997).

Explanation

This tip itself is a paraphrase of a quotable quote, one by Albert Einstein: "Everything should be made as simple as possible, but not simpler."*

As you'll soon see, simplicity can be achieved by following many of the other tips in this book: striving for shorter sentences, preferring the active voice, breaking up the text with headings, and so on. But perhaps the more important way to achieve simplicity is to think through the issues fully. You'll know you have mastered your points when you can explain them to a nonlawyer in ordinary language.

Of course, that same explanation shouldn't be oversimplified. You can test it on a reasonable colleague, and you probably should. But remember that any old mediocre mind can make things complex: your quest is for simplicity.

A Before-and-After Example

Before   [Final section in a response to a motion for new trial:]

Plaintiff's final point of attack in the timely filed Motion for New Trial is simply the argument that Barkley's presence at trial would have been detrimental to his defense and particularly to the defense of the other insured, Four Star Delivery, and proffers as supporting evidence the fact that separate counsel would have been hired for Barkley due to a conflict of interest between Barkley and Four Star Delivery. Plaintiff references evidence of Barkley's seizure disorder which came out after the underlying trial and which is not before this court in any fashion and argues that Barkley would have hurt his own defense and Four Star Delivery would have had a more difficult time avoiding the cause of action of negligent entrustment. None of this one-sided speculation is relevant to the issues before this court. Plaintiff proffers no evidence to support this speculation. Defense counsel in this case could make similar irrelevant arguments that had Barkley been present and explained his seizure disorder, the defense of unavoidable accident would have been established and,

---

* Reader's Dig., Oct. 1977 (as quoted in *The New International Dictionary of Quotations* 394 (Margaret Miner & Hugh Rawson eds., 2d ed. 1994)).

therefore, not ignored by the jury as it was in the case that was tried, or that Barkley's counsel could have brought in Barkley's physician as a third party defendant and maybe avoided liability. What might or might not have happened, or what might or might not have been successful strategy, is far outside the purview of what is before this court in addressing a motion for new trial on Defendant's Motion for Summary Judgment. [249 words]

After   Finally, Hutchins argues that Barkley's presence at trial would have hurt both his defense and Four Star's. Hutchins speculates that their defenses would have become harder because Barkley—having a conflict of interest with Four Star—would have been represented by separate counsel. Hutchins further speculates that Barkley's seizure disorder, which is not in the record, would not only have hurt Barkley but also have made it more difficult for Four Star to defeat the claim of negligent entrustment.

Defendants could likewise speculate self-servingly about the effect of Barkley's presence, but none of this one-sided, unsupported speculation bears on the issues. What might or might not have happened should not affect this Court in deciding to deny Hutchins a new trial. [123 words]

Marching Forward
Through Sound Paragraphs

16

Begin a paragraph with a topic sentence. Don't end the preceding paragraph with what should be the next paragraph's topic sentence.

Quotable Quotes

"It is customary to indicate the unity of the paragraph, the special nature of the thought it contains, by means of a topic sentence. Although it may occupy any position in the paragraph, and indeed is sometimes omitted altogether, in most paragraphs the topic sentence is placed at the beginning, because this is ordinarily its logical place."

—Norman Foerster & J.M. Steadman, Jr., *Writing and Thinking* 43 (James B. McMillan ed., 5th ed. 1952).

"There are few things more boring than a twenty- or thirty-page paper consisting of page after page of case discussion in which each paragraph begins: 'In *A v. B* . . .'; 'In *C v. D* . . .'; 'In *E v. F* . . . .' By the third one, the reader feels like saying 'who cares?'

"Add a little zip to these paragraphs by a strong lead-in sentence. Use the opening line to give the reader some clue about what's interesting (or whatever) about the case. In other words, what's the point of discussing the case? Tell your reader as you open your discussion of it. Then he or she will work along with you to make the point."

—Paula Samuelson, *Good Legal Writing: Of Orwell and Window Panes*, 46 U. Pitt. L. Rev. 149, 159 (1984).

"A *topic sentence* lets readers know the focus of a paragraph in simple and direct terms. . . . Because paragraphing usually signals a shift in focus, readers expect some kind of reorientation in the opening sentence. They need to know whether the new paragraph is going to introduce another aspect of the topic or develop one already introduced. This need is especially strong when readers are under pressure to read quickly and efficiently."

—Rise B. Axelrod & Charles R. Cooper, *The St. Martin's Guide to Writing* 354 (1985).

"Because the topic sentence, with its controlling idea, is a serviceable guide for achieving unity in the paragraph, you should place it first. Then, as you write, keep it clearly in mind. Allow it to control what you include and exclude. The topic sentence is your general frame of reference; the controlling idea is your specific focus."

—John Ostrom & William Cook, *Paragraph Writing Simplified* 9 (1993).

"Paragraphing is a subtle but important element in writing nonfiction . . . , a road map constantly telling your reader how you have organized your ideas. Study good nonfiction writers to see how they do it. You'll find that most of them think in paragraph units, not sentence units. Each paragraph has its own integrity of content and is rounded off to serve as both an end and a springboard to what's coming next."

—William Zinsser, *On Writing Well* 128 (5th ed. 1994).

Explanation

A good topic sentence—usually the first in the paragraph—centers the paragraph. It announces what the paragraph is about, and the other sentences play supporting roles.

Oddly, though, legal writers frequently make the last sentence in a paragraph what should be the topic sentence in the next paragraph. You see this problem in Example A (corrected, of course, in the revised version).

Example B illustrates a different problem. The first sentence in the second paragraph really should be the final sentence in the preceding one. Why? Because it doesn't really announce the point being developed in the paragraph it begins. It's implicitly a four-part statement, but it opens a paragraph that develops only one of the four points. Also, the fourth paragraph ("Messrs. Nisbet and Morgenthau . . .") lacks a topic sentence.

For ease of reference in seeing the improvements made, the topic sentences are marked in boldface.

Some Before-and-After Examples

Example A

Before   **The attorney–client privilege protects confidential communications between a client and the client's lawyer.** Cal. Evid. Code § 954. Generally, a communication to a third party (i.e., someone other than the client or the client's lawyer) is not privileged. *See* Cal. Evid. Code § 952; *Ver Bryck v. Luby*, 67 Cal. App. 2d 842, 844 (1945). However, Evidence Code section 952 (defining a "confidential communication between client and lawyer") specifies three exceptions to the general rule. *See* Cal. Evid. Code § 952.

The first exception is where the third party is "present to further the interest of the client in consultation." Cal. Evid. Code § 952. The second exception applies when the third party is one "to whom disclosure is reasonably necessary" to transmit the information. *Id.* The third exception applies when a lawyer must disclose information to a third party to accomplish "the purpose for which the lawyer is consulted." *Id.*

After   **The attorney–client privilege protects confidential communications between a client and the client's lawyer.** Cal. Evid. Code § 954. Generally, a communication to a third party (i.e., someone other than the client or the client's lawyer) is not privileged. *See* Cal. Evid. Code § 952; *Ver Bryck v. Luby*, 67 Cal. App. 2d 842, 844 (1945).

But the Evidence Code specifies three exceptions to the general rule, each establishing when a third-party communication *is* privileged. *See* Cal. Evid. Code § 952. The first exception applies when the third party is "present to further the interest of the client in consultation." *Id.* The second exception applies when the third party is one "to whom disclosure is reasonably necessary" to transmit the information. *Id.* The third exception applies when a lawyer must disclose information to a third party to accomplish "the purpose for which the lawyer is consulted." *Id.*

Example B

Before   **To be reliable, scientific testimony must be grounded in the scientific method and must constitute more than subjective belief or unsupported speculation.** *Daubert*, 509 U.S. at 589–90. Factors bearing on reliability include: (1) whether the theory can be tested; (2) whether the theory has been subjected to peer review and publication; (3) the known or potential rate of error; and (4) to some extent, general acceptance in the field. *Id.* at 593.

Burgess's opinion testimony about the Moores' house met the standard for admissibility. First, Messrs. Nisbet and Morgenthau are qualified. They both have master's degrees in engineering and are registered professional engineers with experience in examining house foundations. (SF 808–10; 1007–10.) Even Mr. Moore agreed that they are competent engineers. (SF 741–46.)

Second, their opinion was based in part on a reliable study. Specifically, they relied on the study by the University of Tennessee engineering faculty, reporting on actual tests and observations of many house foundations. (SF 836–37.) One of the Moores' engineers, Fred Hayden, agreed that the Tennessee report is considered reliable. (SF 509–10.) Another of the Moores' engineers testified that the Tennessee staff has done extensive work on this subject. (SF 941.) Even if the Tennessee study was inadmissible, Burgess was entitled to rely on it because the record shows that the report is of the type reasonably relied on by experts in the field. (SF 509–10.)

Messrs. Nisbet and Morgenthau also relied on their inspection of the Moores' house. And contrary to the Moores' assertion, they did examine later-developed information, including the data concerning the size and location of the leak and the moisture content of the soil borings. (SF 764, 816–17, 1015–16.) They even wrote supplemental reports about their additional investigative efforts. (PX 25; DX 14.) Moreover, like any experts, they relied on their general expertise and experience in the field. Before forming its general opinion, Burgess even went so far as to consult with engineers in academia. (SF 813, 833.)

Finally, Burgess's opinion met the last criterion: that the opinion be relevant to the case. Burgess's opinion was germane to a dispositive issue: whether the Moores suffered foundation damage due to an accidental leak from their plumbing system.

Thus, having met all the criteria, Burgess's opinion was admissible. . . .

After   **To be reliable, scientific testimony must be grounded in the scientific method and must constitute more than subjective belief or unsupported speculation.** *Daubert*, 509 U.S. at 589–90. Among the factors bearing on reliability are whether the theory can be tested, whether the theory has been subjected to peer review and publication, the known or potential rate of error, and general acceptance in the field. *Id.* at 593. The testimony of Burgess's two experts met the standard of reliability. Four points demonstrate this.

First, both Mr. Nisbet and Mr. Morgenthau are qualified. They both have master's degrees in engineering and are registered professional engineers with experience in examining house foundations. (SF 808–10; 1007–10.) Even Mr. Moore agreed that they are competent engineers. (SF 741–46.)

Second, their opinion was based in part on a reliable study. Specifically, they relied on the study by the University of Tennessee engineering faculty, reporting on actual tests and observations of many house foundations. (SF 836–37.) One of the Moores' engineers, Fred Hayden, agreed that the Tennessee report is considered reliable. (SF 509–10.) Another of the Moores' engineers testified that the Tennessee staff has done extensive work on this subject. (SF 941.) Even if the Tennessee study was inadmissible, Nisbet and Morgenthau were justified in relying on it because it's the type reasonably relied on by experts in the field. (SF 509–10.)

Third, Nisbet and Morgenthau double-checked their work in two ways: (1) they continued examining data after inspecting the grounds, and (2) they sought second opinions within academia. On the first of these points, they relied not only on their own inspections of the Moores' house, but also on later-developed information. For example, they examined data concerning the size and location of the leak and the moisture content of the soil borings. (SF 764, 816–17, 1015–16.) They even wrote supplemental reports about their additional investigative efforts. (PX 25; DX 14.) On the second point, they went beyond relying on their own general expertise and experience in the field: before forming its general opinion, Burgess even went so far as to consult with engineers in academia. (SF 813, 833.)

Fourth, Nisbet's and Morgenthau's opinions amply met the last criterion: that the opinion be relevant to the case. Their opinions were germane to a dispositive issue: whether the Moores suffered foundation damage due to an accidental leak from their plumbing system.

Thus, having met all the criteria, Burgess's opinion was admissible. . . .

17

Bridge from one paragraph to another.

Quotable Quotes

"[A]s sentences should follow one another in harmonious sequence, so the paragraphs must fit onto one another like the automatic couplings of railway carriages."

—Winston Churchill, *My Early Life: A Roving Commission* 211–12 (1930).

"The topic sentence . . . smooths the way from paragraph to paragraph by binding that which has been said to that which is going to be said. By hooking the previous series of ideas to the coming one, it provides momentum."

—Sherman Kent, *Writing History* 61 (1941).

"Just as transitions can help the reader glide from sentence to sentence within a paragraph, so they can help him or her step easily from paragraph to paragraph. In the usual case, transitions come at the beginning of the paragraph, referring to the thought in the preceding passage and connecting it with the group of sentences to follow. But transitions between paragraphs are usually stronger and longer than transitions and conjunctions between sentences. For one thing, a paragraph presents a new idea or aspect of an idea. For another, it takes the reader longer to find out for himself or herself whether the relationship is one of contrast, amplification, emphasis, or some other nature (whereas in the case of sentences, if there is any doubt, a flick of the eye is all that is needed)."

—David W. Ewing, *Writing for Results in Business, Government, the Sciences and the Professions* 220 (2d ed. 1979).

"If you can't find some way to connect the ideas developed in one paragraph to those being developed in the one that follows, it is likely that you have left out some component of the argument."

—Paula Samuelson, *Good Legal Writing: Of Orwell and Window Panes*, 46 U. Pitt. L. Rev. 149, 159 (1984).

"Transitions between paragraphs connect the unifying idea of one paragraph with the unifying idea of the next. Paragraphs should not be presented as separate from each other; writers need to link these parts to each other and to the thesis."

—Jeanne F. Campanelli & Jonathan L. Price, *Write in Time* 107 (1991).

"Each topic sentence must somehow hook onto the paragraph above it, must include some word or phrase to ease the reader's path: a transition. . . . One brief transitional touch in your topic sentence, your opening sentence, is usually sufficient."

—Sheridan Baker, *The Practical Stylist* 42 (8th ed. 1998).

Explanation

Although it's true that a paragraph should generally have a topic sentence, the more important point—a little-known one—is that it should have a bridge. Ideally, every paragraph (beginning with the second) should connect with the paragraph immediately preceding it—and it should do so explicitly. That's how you create fluent prose, in which the ideas are closely connected. That's how you write a brief that marches forward from one point to the next.

In creating bridges to achieve that effect, you have three options:

- Pointing words (*this*, *that*, *these*, *those*), because they point to something immediately preceding.

- Echo links, which are words that repeat an idea in summary language or otherwise reverberate from what has just preceded.

- Explicit connectives (*further*, *moreover*, *in addition*, *likewise*, *in sum*, etc.), which are obvious transitional words.

Masterly writers use all three devices to establish a continuity from paragraph to paragraph.

In the example that follows, David Fernandez of Newark uses bridges so well that they even work with and through the headings. The result is an unusually tight and readable brief.

An Unusually Good Example

Argument

1. **The motion should be denied because the PUC was not a party to the Essex County litigation, the two matters involve wholly separate facts, the PUC has never raised bidding deficiencies as a defense in this lawsuit, and, in any event, the PUC has waived the right to raise that defense now, on remand.**

Judicial estoppel does not entitle the PUC to summary judgment for a variety of reasons, all rooted in unequivocal caselaw and simple common sense. First, the PUC had no involvement in the Essex County matter and therefore has no standing to assert judicial estoppel here. Second, Roberts cannot be estopped on the basis of positions it took in the Essex County litigation since that matter arose from completely separate facts. Third, Roberts has never expressed any opinion on whether the Local Public Bidding Law applies to the Roberts–PUC contract, and thus has not taken inconsistent positions on this question. And, finally, the PUC long ago waived its right to assert this defense in this litigation. For all these reasons, the Court should deny the motion.

A. **The Court should deny the motion because the PUC was not a party to the Essex County litigation, nor was it in privity with a party in that case.**

Judicial estoppel prevents parties from assuming "inconsistent or mutually contradictory positions with respect to the same matter in the same or a successive series of suits." *Scarano v. Central R.R. Co.*, 203 F.2d 510, 513 (3d Cir. 1953). Unlike equitable estoppel, which concerns the relationship between the parties, "[j]udicial estoppel looks to the connection between the litigant and the judicial system." *Oneida Motor Freight, Inc. v. United Jersey Bank*, 848 F.2d 414, 419 (3d Cir.), *cert. denied*, 488 U.S. 967 (1988). The central purpose of judicial estoppel is to preserve the integrity of the judicial system "by preventing parties from 'playing fast and loose with the courts.'" *Fleck v. KDI Sylvan Pools, Inc.*, 981 F.2d 107, 121 (3d Cir. 1992) (citations omitted), *cert. denied sub nom., Doughboy Recreational, Inc., Div. of Hoffinger Ind., Inc. v. Fleck*, 507 U.S. 1005 (1993).

At least one important boundary limits this doctrine in a way that is dispositive here. Simply put, a party may not assert judicial estoppel if he had no involvement in the earlier matter. The Third Circuit has held that judicial estoppel is appropriate only "where the same parties are involved." *Gleason v. United States*, 458 F.2d 171, 175 (3d Cir. 1972). This limitation arises from the Third Circuit's earliest and most significant cases on judicial estoppel. In the seminal *Scarano* case, for example, the Third Circuit built this important limitation into the basic rule itself: a plaintiff who successfully asserts a position in one case may not contradict himself "in an effort to establish *against the same adversary* a second claim inconsistent with his earlier contention." 203 F.2d at 513 (emphasis added).

The Western District of Pennsylvania—speaking through Judge D. Brooks Valentino—recently reaffirmed this limitation in the recent case of *Mellon Bank, N.A. v. Ma-*

koroff, 153 B.R. 155 (W.D. Pa. 1993). In that bankruptcy case, a debtor argued in an adversary proceeding brought against a business partner that an agreement structured as an employment contract was actually for the sale of assets, entitling him to a full payout. The debtor received $124,000 in settlement of this action, but promptly found himself defending against the Mellon Bank's efforts to collect these funds under a security agreement covering the debtor's business proceeds. The bank argued that the debtor could not deny that these funds were for the sale of assets, given the debtor's position in the earlier action against the business partner.

On appeal from the Bankruptcy Court, Judge Valentino held that the debtor was free to oppose the banks' efforts to collect these proceeds because judicial estoppel did not apply. In reaching this decision, Judge Valentino held that judicial estoppel does not empower a litigant to hold an adversary to a previous position unless that litigant played some role in the earlier action:

> This circuit . . . has endorsed a restrictive approach to judicial estoppel which allows judicial estoppel to be invoked *only by a party to the prior proceeding or someone in privity with that party.* Accordingly, although C & J Travel [the adversary in the earlier matter] might in the appropriate case be able to invoke judicial estoppel, Mellon cannot. [*Id.* at 158–59 (citations omitted).]

If judicial estoppel is limited in the way that Judge Valentino held in *Mellon Bank*, then the upshot for the PUC is clear: it may not attempt to hold Roberts to positions Roberts took in the Essex County matter. The PUC played no role in the Essex County litigation. It was not a party to that case. It was not in privity with any party to that case. It made no appearances in that case. The PUC's only connection with the ECUA litigation, in fact, is that these two entities share the same attorneys—a circumstance that certainly explains the origins of this motion, but does not create a sufficient connection to assert judicial estoppel here. In short, because the PUC was neither a party to nor in privity with a party to the Essex County matter, the PUC may not invoke judicial estoppel.

B.   The motion should be denied because the two litigation matters involve wholly unrelated facts.

A larger and more serious flaw in the PUC's position is that it would radically expand judicial estoppel far beyond its accepted contours. The PUC is attempting to capitalize on a legal position Roberts took in the ECUA litigation in order to restrict the legal positions Roberts may articulate here. Setting aside for the moment the obvious fact that Roberts has never taken any position in this litigation on the issue of public bidding, the central weakness with the PUC's argument is that these two lawsuits arise from *completely separate facts.* This litigation involves Roberts' claim that the PUC breached a long-term disposal contract that Roberts and the PUC entered into in 1987. The Essex County lawsuit, by contrast, involved a contract that the ECUA and Waste Management entered into in 1994. These lawsuits thus involve separate contracts, awarded to different entities, at different times, and by different government agencies. There is, in short, no factual overlap between these two cases.

The PUC nevertheless suggests that judicial estoppel applies, even though these lawsuits are factually unrelated. The PUC does this by quoting out of context from the *Oneida Motor Freight* case, in which the court articulated the rule broadly, as follows: judicial estoppel "applies to preclude a party from assuming a position in a legal proceeding inconsistent with one previously asserted." 848 F.2d at 419 (quoted at p. 12 of PUC's Brf.). The PUC does not bother to observe, of course, that the *Oneida* case involved legal positions taken in two lawsuits arising from the identical facts. The PUC forges ahead anyway, making the enormous leap from this isolated expression of the rule to the breathtaking proposition that judicial estoppel applies to positions taken in completely unrelated lawsuits. PUC Brf. at 14–16.

This theory of judicial estoppel is flat wrong. The PUC has furnished no authority for the extraordinary proposition that litigants are encumbered by the legal positions they took in earlier, factually unconnected cases. To the contrary, this doctrine only prevents litigants from taking inconsistent positions in the *same* litigation or in successive cases arising from the *same* core set of facts. *See Himel v. Continental Ill. Nat'l Bank & Trust Co.*, 596 F.2d 205, 210 (7th Cir. 1979) (rejecting judicial estoppel argument on the grounds that "the facts here are not 'the same facts' in the first suit") (citation omitted). As one court recently observed, in order for a litigant to assert judicial estoppel, "the facts at issue should be the same in both cases." *Levinson v. United States*, 969 F.2d 260, 264 (7th Cir.), *cert. denied*, 506 U.S. 989 (1992).

The PUC proves this point in its own brief. Not only does the PUC fail to furnish a single case holding that judicial estoppel applies across factually unrelated lawsuits, but *every* case it relies on involves two lawsuits arising from the same facts. In some of these cases, a litigant asserts judicial estoppel to prevent an adversary from taking diametrically opposite factual positions in two matters arising from the same factual scenario. For example, in *Lewandowski v. Nat'l R.R. Passenger Corp. (Amtrak)*, the court barred a former railroad employee from claiming in a reinstatement lawsuit that he was physically fit, because in an earlier lawsuit against the railroad, the plaintiff claimed that he had suffered injuries that rendered him incapable of working. 882 F.2d 815, 819 (3d Cir. 1989).

In other cases, as the PUC points out, the courts have used judicial estoppel to prohibit contradictory *legal* positions as well. PUC Brf. at 13. But these cases, too, all involve positions advanced in the same lawsuit, or in successive lawsuits arising from the same facts. A classic example of this is *Levin v. Robinson, Wayne & LaSala*, in which a lawyer claimed in his divorce action that his partnership agreement entitled him to a certain distribution, but then took the position in a later lawsuit against his law firm that the same agreement entitled him to a higher amount. 246 N.J. Super. 167

(Law Div. 1990). The court held that judicial estoppel barred the plaintiff from asserting such diametrically opposite readings of the identical agreement.

The PUC's overbroad theory of judicial estoppel not only contradicts settled caselaw, it also lacks common sense. The PUC argues that Roberts may not sue for breach because of a legal position that it took in a lawsuit arising from wholly separate facts. But imagine the consequences of holding litigants to legal positions successfully taken in earlier, unrelated matters. By the PUC's logic, a litigant would be stuck—presumably forever—with whatever legal positions he or she successfully asserts in any single case. Not only would a litigant's claim or defense depend on legal consistency *within* a lawsuit, but it would now depend on legal consistency across *all other* lawsuits in which that litigant or anyone in privity with that litigant ever successfully participated. Indeed, if the PUC is correct, then Roberts is entitled to rifle through the PUC's own litigation history, catalogue all legal positions the PUC has ever successfully advanced, and hold the PUC to those positions in *this* lawsuit. Surely the PUC does not believe that positions of law it has taken in other unrelated lawsuits hamper its ability to take legal positions in this case.

The caselaw provides no support for such a radical transformation of the doctrine of judicial estoppel. The courts in this Circuit have consistently adopted a "restrictive" approach to judicial estoppel, reminding litigants that this doctrine is meant to apply only when contradictory positions taken in the same or related matters "threaten the integrity of the court." *Mellon Bank*, 153 B.R. at 158; *Sim Kar Lighting Fixture Co. v. Genlyte, Inc.*, 906 F. Supp. 967, 975 (D.N.J. 1995). In the absence of any authority that taking inconsistent legal positions in factually unconnected matters "threaten[s] the integrity of the court[s]," the Court should reject this motion.

C.   Roberts has not taken any position in this litigation on whether the local public bidding law applies to the Roberts–PUC contract.

The Court should deny the PUC's motion for yet another important reason. For judicial estoppel to apply, the two offending positions must truly be "diametrically opposed." *Unum Corp. v. United States*, 886 F. Supp. 150, 159 (D. Me. 1995) (quoting *United States v. Levasseur*, 846 F.2d 786, 794 (1st Cir.), *cert. denied*, 488 U.S. 894 (1988)). If there is any way to reconcile the two positions, judicial estoppel does not warrant summary judgment. *See Levinson*, 969 F.2d at 264 (in order for judicial estoppel to apply, "the later position must be clearly inconsistent with the earlier position").

Here, the PUC claims that Roberts has taken contradictory positions on whether New Jersey law requires long-term disposal contracts to be publicly bid. But one will search the pleadings, the briefs, and, indeed, the entire record in this case in vain for any mention of this issue anywhere, by either Roberts or the PUC. Roberts has never raised this issue because the PUC has never asserted it as a defense. And one can certainly understand the PUC's reluctance to raise it. The PUC, after all, took full advantage of the Roberts contract for almost six years. Then, when it was convenient to do so, the PUC replaced that agreement with a cheaper Empire contract that it *also* awarded without public bidding. Hence, attacking the manner in which it awarded this contract to Roberts would have the embarrassing result of asserting that the Empire contract, too, is "void for illegality." More broadly, the PUC cannot bring itself to assert this defense because by doing so it would be expressly stating in a forum open to full public scrutiny that it is legally obligated to publicly bid all such contracts in the future. Apparently the PUC wishes to refrain from making such a statement in this setting.

Whatever the reason for the PUC's skittishness, the blunt truth is that the PUC has never asserted that it ought to have publicly bid the Roberts contract. As a result, Roberts has never once taken any position on this issue. Because the PUC cannot point to two instances in which Roberts has taken a position on whether contracts of this kind should be publicly bid—much less that these two positions are "diametrically opposed"—judicial estoppel does not apply. *Unum Corp.*, 886 F. Supp. at 159.

The PUC's response to this state of affairs is to strike a precarious, even disingenuous, legal posture. Although the PUC cannot bring itself to assert illegality as a defense, it argues that Roberts "is estopped from *denying* that the contract it seeks to enforce here is void for illegality." PUC Brf. at 1 (emphasis added). Clever though it may be, this argument begs the question of how a party can deny a defense that the other party has never asserted. Even if it were true that Roberts may not "deny" that the Roberts–PUC contract is "void for illegality," doesn't the PUC have to affirmatively maintain that the contract is illegal before Roberts can be prevented from opposing that defense?

More to the point, even if the PUC attempted to assert this defense, Roberts would be free to oppose it without fear of contradicting its position in the ECUA litigation. If the PUC were to advance this defense now, Roberts' position would be simple. By failing until now to complain even once about the manner in which it awarded the contract to Roberts, the PUC either waived this defense or is estopped from asserting it. *See* Section I.D., *infra*. This argument is not "diametrically opposed" to anything Roberts stated in the ECUA matter. For in the ECUA matter, Roberts took a position on the merits of the public bidding issue. Here, Roberts' position would enable the Court to dispose of the PUC's defense *without* reaching the merits. In this way, there is no threat that the Court's conclusion here would in any way conflict with the conclusion reached by the court in the ECUA lawsuit.

In short, permitting Roberts to proceed in this litigation does not threaten the integrity of the courts. As a result, judicial estoppel does not prevent Roberts from advancing its claim for breach of contract. *See Linan-Faye Constr. Co. v. Housing Auth. of Camden*, 49 F.3d 915, 933 (3d Cir. 1995).

18

Connect your sentences smoothly to one another. Avoid "bumps" in the prose.

Quotable Quotes

"One aspect of organization that seems to have eluded practically all graduate students is that involved in the making of transitions. Even those who have been taught how to lay beads in a row have not been taught how to string them. . . . The ability to move from one sentence or paragraph or chapter to the next, in such a way as to blend them into a unified whole, is largely dependent upon an understanding of the reasons for going from one to the next . . . ."
—Wendell Johnson, "You Can't Write Writing," in *20th Century English* 229, 235–36 (William S. Knickerbocker ed., 1946).

"[A] first draft is rather like a road under construction. A reader, like a motorist, would have to go slow and watch for obstructions. A writer, like a builder, must smooth out the bumps and fill in the holes."
—Sumner Ives, *A New Handbook for Writers* 275 (1960).

"In whatever paragraphs . . . you write, verify the sequence of ideas and take out or transpose everything that interrupts the march of thought and feeling."
—Jacques Barzun, *Simple & Direct* 176 (1975).

"One of the differences between inexperienced writers and mature writers is that mature writers know how to make connections between ideas. Inexperienced writers have lots of ideas, but they jot them down as independent units, sometimes single sentences that, like items on the evening news, have little to do with what comes before and after them. Sometimes, in fact, inexperienced writers make an assertion in one sentence and contradict it in the next . . . ."
—James C. Raymond, *Writing (Is an Unnatural Act)* 112 (1980).

"Transition is the technique of drawing sentences together, dovetailing them, making them overlap so that the reader's journey from one sentence to the next is not a series of jerks and lunges but a smooth ride . . . ."
—Thomas Whissen, *A Way with Words* 111 (1982).

"Experienced readers are on the lookout for . . . transitional phrases because they mark out an interpretive path through a paper. Needless to say, clear marking helps the reader cooperate with you, while clumsy marking or none at all forces the reader to guess at the relationship between one sentence and the next."

—Peter Richardson, *Style: A Pragmatic Approach* 45 (1998).

"Good writers are sticklers for continuity. They won't let themselves write a sentence that isn't clearly connected to the ones immediately preceding and following it. They want their prose to flow, and they know that this is the only way to achieve that beautiful effect."

—John R. Trimble, *Writing with Style* 45 (2d ed. 2000).

Explanation

If it's true that connections should exist at the paragraph level, it's equally true at the sentence level: every sentence should relate directly to the ones next to it. For example, in a follow-up sentence you might amplify, qualify, modify, or exemplify the preceding sentence.

But if you ever find yourself darting off in a new direction, you'll create a "bump" in the narrative line unless you include a contrasting connective—usually a word such as *but*, *however*, or *even so*. Avoid bumps.

A Before-and-After Example

Before

Introduction

Spelce has filed a motion to compel her own treating chiropractor, Dr. Baxter, to appear on her behalf and testify personally in court on May 11, 1992, the original trial date. In her motion to compel, Spelce attacks the constitutionality of Idaho Code Ann. § 101–24. [*Bump.*] Dr. Baxter has appeared for the limited purpose of filing a motion to quash the subpoena to testify in court. [*Bump.*] According to Spelce's motion to compel, Dr. Baxter has offered to give a video deposition on Spelce's behalf. [*Bump.*] Spelce has asked the Court to "waive the statutory immunity" granted by the Legislature in Idaho Code § 101–24 and to "exercise the Court's discretion." [*Bump.*] The State of Idaho appears to defend the constitutionality of the statute.

After

Introduction

Spelce has filed a motion to compel her own chiropractor, Dr. Baxter, to appear on her behalf and testify at trial. Although he has offered to give a video deposition, Dr. Baxter does not wish to appear in court and has sought to quash the subpoena to testify. In her motion, Spelce attacks Idaho Code Ann. § 101–24—which exempts practicing chiropractors from trial subpoenas—as unconstitutional. Spelce thus asks the Court to exercise its discretion, waive this statutory immunity, and compel Dr. Baxter to appear at trial.

In defense of the statute's constitutionality, the State of Idaho files this brief and asks the Court to deny Spelce's motion.

19

Ease your readers' way by providing signposts.

Quotable Quotes

"The secret ambition of every brief should be to spare the judge the necessity of engaging in any work, mental or physical."
—Mortimer Levitan, *Confidential Chat on the Craft of Briefing*, 1957 Wis. L. Rev. 59, 63.

"Think of a piece of writing as a trip from a definite starting point to a definite destination. At the very start we look for a signpost pointing the way and naming the place we are headed for. At every fork of the road we need directions—legible and understandable directions. From time to time we glance back over the road we have already come, in order to remind ourselves of our position and direction. At the end we want to know that we have arrived at the point we set out for. Reminders of this sort are just as necessary in writing as they are in posting a road."
—David Lambuth et al., *The Golden Book on Writing* 6–7 (1964).

"Signpost your argument every step of the way. If you have three important pieces of evidence to support a particular contention, *tell* your reader so she can understand precisely where you're going. For instance: 'Three examples will bear this out. First, the original treaty of 1923 . . . . ' "
—John R. Trimble, *Writing with Style* 47 (2d ed. 2000).

"Headings . . . are signposts, of course, but you'll also need textual signposts in all but the most elementary writing. If there are three issues you're going to discuss, state them explicitly on page one. If there are four advantages to your recommended course of action, say so when introducing the list. And be specific: don't say that there are 'several' advantages. If there are four, say so. This shows that you've thought through the problem."
—Bryan A. Garner, *Legal Writing in Plain English* § 27, at 75 (2001).

Explanation

Picture yourself as a passenger in a car, going somewhere but not knowing where because the driver won't tell you. If you're like most people, you'd probably feel uneasy—even if you know the driver, but more so if you don't. You'd probably like to know something about where you're going and how you're going to get there. In that way, a written argument is analogous to a car journey.

This means, of course, that the effective writer must orient the reader at the outset and place signposts along the way as the analytical journey proceeds. Even as you approach little bends in the road, it's helpful to know that they're coming up. Hence, you need to supply signposts both for the brief as a whole and for individual paragraphs as well. In Example A, notice how much easier it is to follow the argument when a simple sentence—"That allegation is meritless for two reasons"—is added. And in Example B, notice what a big difference two additional words (and three parenthetical numerals) make.

Some Before-and-After Examples

Example A

Before   To the extent that Defendants' laches argument rests on the allegation that Boorland acted inequitably by allowing Defendants to build up sizable damages over many years, it must be rejected because Boorland could not and did not recover monetary damages for the vast majority of Defendants' sales of plastic-encapsulated products before February 23, 1989, which was when the Process Patent Amendments Act added 35 U.S.C. § 271(g), making Defendants' importation of products made by an infringing process abroad compensable in monetary damages, and after receiving notice of infringement, Defendants failed to mitigate their damages and, in fact, increased their sales of infringing products.

After   Defendants' sole allegation on laches is that Boorland acted inequitably by allowing Defendants to build up sizable damages over many years. **That allegation is meritless for two reasons. First,** Boorland could not and did not recover monetary damages for the vast majority of Defendants' sales of plastic-encapsulated products before February 23, 1989, the date when the Process Patent Amendments Act first made Defendants' importation of products manufactured by an infringing process abroad compensable in monetary damages. **Second,** after receiving notice of infringement, Defendants failed to mitigate their damages. In fact, they increased their sales of infringing products.

Example B

Before   Since a court looks to the surrounding circumstances to determine "reasonable assurance," it is important to examine the progress and state of PSI's negotiations with Park Central, Park Central's satisfaction with PSI and the previous contract, and whether Park Central was seeking alternatives to PSI.

After   Since a court looks to the surrounding circumstances to determine "reasonable assurance," the court should examine **three things:** (1) the progress and state of PSI's negotiations with Park Central; (2) Park Central's satisfaction with the parties' earlier contract; and (3) whether Park Central was seeking alternatives to PSI.

20

Break up long, complex sentences. Shoot for an average sentence length of 20 words.

Quotable Quotes

"Whenever you can shorten a sentence, do. And one always can. The best sentence? The shortest."

—Gustave Flaubert (as quoted in Rudolf Flesch, *The Art of Readable Writing* 119 (1949; repr. 1967)).

"Highly complex sentences are increasingly difficult to justify as business and professional readers grow more demanding, even when the readers are scientific, engineering, and legal people. In this category fall sentences that contain long series of modifying phrases and clauses piled one on top of the other, like driblets of sand on a sand castle."

—David W. Ewing, *Writing for Results in Business, Government, and the Professions* 337–38 (1974).

"Most long sentences are not totally bewildering. Usually you can get some sense out of them. But they do make the meaning foggier and the reading less enjoyable."

—John L. Beckley, *The Power of Little Words* 32 (1984).

"All readers find continuous reading of long sentences a strain. The writer continually makes maximum, and sometimes unreasonable, demands on their short-term memories; gradually they get tired, and concentration lapses. The writer of long sentences risks making readers inattentive."

—Christopher Turk & John Kirkman, *Effective Writing: Improving Scientific, Technical, and Business Communication* 94 (2d ed. 1989).

"Short sentences are better. One of the easiest ways to write short sentences is to give each sentence just one job."

—James W. McElhaney, *Writing to the Ear*, ABA J., Dec. 1995, at 74, 76.

Explanation

Lawyers are afraid of periods. They fear simplicity. Yet a brief *should* be as simple as possible—that is, simple to read. Even if your arguments are technical or complex, your sentences never should be. And the best way to keep your sentences simple is to keep them short. In a 2001 survey of a California appellate court, 91% of the respondents agreed with this statement: "Sometimes long sentences are distracting or confusing even if they are grammatically correct."*

Readability experts agree that the average sentence length for most expository prose should be something fewer than 20 words. But note that the goal of 20 words is only an average. If all your sentences are short, your prose will seem clipped and choppy. You should vary your sentence length to give your prose some rhythm.

Of course, it's rare to see a choppy brief. More likely, the style could be characterized as suffocating. And the most common cause of this literary asphyxia is the overlong sentence.

Some Before-and-After Examples

Example A

Before   It was the understanding of the parties and the Court at the time the divorce agreement was entered that Mr. Montgomery would take all necessary steps to relieve Ms. Priddy of mortgage debt on the property, which was to become his alone, even if it required refinancing on the property. To the extent that Ms. Priddy is compelled to continue to carry this mortgage obligation, she will not be able to obtain any credit to assist her in getting back on her feet financially. Accordingly, this factor should be taken into consideration as an additional extenuating circumstance requiring deviation from the child-support guidelines. [104 words; avg. sentence length: 34 words]

After   The parties and the Court understood at the time of the divorce agreement that Mr. Montgomery would take all necessary steps to relieve Ms. Priddy of the mortgage debt. The property was to become his alone. He knew he might have to refinance it. To the extent that Ms. Priddy continues to carry this mortgage obligation, she will not be able to obtain any credit. The Court should consider this extenuating circumstance in deciding whether to deviate from the child-support guidelines. [82 words; avg. sentence length: 16 words]

Example B

Before   The fact that the attorney was not a party to the probate action necessarily means that he did not have a "full and fair" opportunity to litigate the issue of negligence, and he therefore should not be precluded from denying negligence in the later malpractice action despite the fact that the issue of his negligence may have been decided as an issue integral to the

---

* *California Appellate Practice Handbook* 237 (7th ed. 2001).

outcome of the will-construction action. [71 words; avg. sentence length: 71 words]

After   Because Smithweck was not a party to the probate action, he could not have had a full and fair opportunity to litigate the issue of negligence. Therefore, he cannot now be precluded from denying negligence, regardless of what the probate court decided. [42 words; avg. sentence length: 21 words]

21

Avoid tiresome repetitions that hurt the mind's ear.

Quotable Quotes

"To repeat the identical word over and over produces a very crude and awkward effect."
—John F. Genung, *Outlines of Rhetoric* 160 (1894).

"The alert editor will . . . pick up the inadvertent repetition of a word. The author, concentrating on what he is trying to say, may not notice such a repetition. To the editorial eye, not clouded by the original pressure of thought, a word used, say, five times in five successive sentences, will stand out sharply. The editor will then find some way to get rid of the repetition—perhaps by introducing synonyms, or perhaps by recasting the sentence."
—Lester S. King, *Why Not Say It Clearly* 92 (1978).

"[R]epetitiveness is nowadays considered a sign of pauperdom in oratory, and of feeble-mindedness in narrative."
—Robert Graves & Alan Hodge, *The Reader over Your Shoulder* 103 (2d ed. 1979).

"My file contains another striking example of how not to say it short and plain. The case was complex, and the brief-writer had used up all allowable pages after being denied permission to file an overlength brief. One of the major parties was United States Fidelity & Guaranty Company, known to everyone who has done much trial practice, and surely to the brief-writer, as USF&G. In every instance from the beginning of the brief to the end—more than 200 times—USF&G is referred to as 'defendant-appellant United States Fidelity & Guaranty Company, a Maryland Corporation.' Similarly, in every instance the trial judge is described not as 'the judge,' 'the court,' 'the trial judge,' 'Judge Roe,' or even 'he,' but as 'Honorable Richard R. Roe, United States District Judge for the _____ District of _____' . . . .

"Motivated by frustration and curiosity, I made a word count of the excess baggage consisting of the description of USF&G and of the trial judge. (Of course there was more flab than that.) This verbiage alone used up 16 pages, space precious to both the writer and the court."
—John C. Godbold, "Twenty Pages and Twenty Minutes," in *Appellate Practice Manual* 84, 91 (Priscilla A. Schwab ed., 1992).

"Avoid frequent repetition of a character's name; identify him or her with a pronoun or descriptive phrase. Few things are more annoying than the overuse of a name."

—David L. Carroll, *A Manual of Writer's Tricks* 55 (2d ed. 1995).

Explanation

If a word or phrase appears in sentence after sentence, the droning effect will annoy readers. For some reason, this is a common problem among legal writers. Why might that be?

Well, there seem to be two convergent reasons. First, some legal writers fear pronouns. They have decided, because pronouns are sometimes ambiguous, to stop using them. Sometimes, though, you need them.

Second, some writers are simply tone-deaf. They haven't attuned themselves to the melodies of language. When you edit, try reading your sentences aloud, one after the other. This exercise helps you hear repetitions that you might not otherwise notice. You've probably heard this advice before. If so, have you acted on it? It's a suggestion meant to be followed—not merely to sound good.

One other thing: find a good thesaurus and use it. Most word processors these days have one built in. Or try J.I. Rodale's *Synonym Finder* or *Roget's Thesaurus*.

Some Before-and-After Examples

Example A

Before   **The district court correctly recognized that it was bound by the jury's findings.**

After remand, both Hartnett and Woodcrest **requested** the **district court** to enter judgment on Hartnett's **Title VII** claim. (Record, Vol. 3, at pp. 572–85, 586–90.) Plaintiff **requested** judgment based on his assertion that he had shown a prima facie case of **Title VII** discrimination. (Record, Vol. 3, at pp. 572–85.) Woodcrest filed a motion for summary judgment, **requesting** the **district court** to enter judgment against Hartnett because the jury's findings of no discrimination on Hartnett's § 1981 claim precluded a finding of discrimination on his remaining **Title VII** claim. (Record, Vol. 3, at pp. 586–90.)

On September 8, 1994, the **district court** issued a memorandum order and entered a judgment against Hartnett and for Woodcrest on Hartnett's **Title VII** claim. (Record, Vol. 3, at pp. 777–91, 792; Exhibit 2 to Appellant's Record Excerpts.) In making this determination, the **district court** did not **request** additional evidence from the parties, as allowed by the remand. In the **district court's** memorandum order, the **district court** found that Plaintiff failed to make out a prima facie case of discrimination under **Title VII** because he was not qualified for the job positions for which he applied. (Record, Vol. 3, at p. 783.) The **district court** also expressly found that Woodcrest did not discriminate against Hartnett on the basis of race or national origin. (Record, Vol. 3, at p. 784.) It is from the **district court's** judgment, along with the accompanying memorandum order, that Hartnett has taken this appeal. [261 words]

After **The district court correctly recognized that it was bound by the jury's findings.**

After remand, both Hartnett and Woodcrest asked the district court to enter judgment on Hartnett's Title VII claim. (3:572–85, 586–90.) Hartnett requested judgment based on his claim that he had shown a prima facie case of discrimination. (3:572–85.) Woodcrest filed a motion for summary judgment because the jury's findings of no discrimination on Hartnett's § 1981 claim precluded a finding of discrimination on his remaining claim. (3:586–90.)

On September 8, 1994, the court issued a memorandum order and entered a judgment against Hartnett and for Woodcrest on Hartnett's discrimination claim. (3:777–91, 792; Appellant's Ex. 2.) In ruling, the court did not request additional evidence from the parties, as allowed by the remand. In its order, the court found that Hartnett failed to make out a prima facie case of discrimination under Title VII because he was not qualified for the job positions for which he applied. (3:783.) The court also expressly found that Woodcrest did not discriminate against Hartnett on the basis of race or national origin. (3:784.) Hartnett now appeals. [188 words]

Example B

Before Plaintiff alleges that **Great American** violated **Article 21.21 of the Texas Insurance Code**. A plaintiff suing under **Article 21.21** must give proper notice at least 30 days prior to filing suit. Because Plaintiff has not sent proper notice to **Great American**, **Great American** respectfully requests that the Court abate all proceedings in this case until 30 days after receipt of proper notice under **Article 21.21 of the Texas Insurance Code**. [70 words]

After Washburn alleges that Great American violated Article 21.21 of the Texas Insurance Code. That statute, however, requires a plaintiff to give proper notice at least 30 days before filing suit. Because Washburn did not do this, Great American respectfully requests that the Court abate all proceedings in this case until 30 days after Washburn meets its notice obligations. [58 words]

Example C

Before **Dynasty Mutual** has apparently abandoned and waived a series of other arguments that **Dynasty Mutual** had been vigorously pursuing up to the date **Dynasty Mutual** filed its Motion for Summary Judgment. These defenses had previously been the primary focus of **Dynasty Mutual's** attempts to avoid its defense obligation to Courtland. **Dynasty Mutual's** Motion for Summary Judgment addresses several of these issues. Most of the legal arguments of **Dynasty Mutual** were the subject of **Dynasty Mutual's** Motion to Dismiss and were rejected by Judge Pointer in his Order dated January 24, 1996. However, Judge Pointer reserved ruling on whether **Dynasty Mutual** had a duty to defend to allow **Dynasty Mutual** to conduct discovery on **Dynasty Mutual's** purported defenses. [117 words]

After   Dynasty Mutual has apparently abandoned and waived a series of other arguments that it had vigorously pursued before moving for summary judgment. These defenses—several of which are addressed in the motion—had previously been the primary focus of Dynasty Mutual's motion to dismiss, which Judge Pointer denied in January 1996. But Judge Pointer reserved ruling on the duty to defend until the parties conducted further discovery. [67 words]

22

Put all your citations in footnotes, while saying in the text what authority you're relying on. But ban substantive footnotes.

Quotable Quotes

References in footnotes:

"I don't know what we are going to do with the briefs, but it does seem to me . . . that it is a wearisome thing to have these long citations."
> —Almet F. Jenks [presiding justice of the Appellate Division of the N.Y. Supreme Court], lecture before the Ass'n of the Bar of the City of New York, 1 Mar. 1923 (as quoted in Mario Pittoni, *Brief Writing and Argumentation* 44 (1967)).

"[W]here a brief is written with the hope of presenting an argument [that] will be interesting as well as instructive, footnotes may advantageously be used for the incorporation of necessary reference material, the inclusion of which in the text would interrupt the otherwise smooth-flowing chain of argument."
> —Frank E. Cooper, *Writing in Law Practice* 266 (2d ed. 1963).

"[T]he system used for citing references should be designed to give minimum interruption to readers' progress through the text. It should allow them to concentrate on primary information."
> —Christopher Turk & John Kirkman, *Effective Writing: Improving Scientific, Technical, and Business Communication* 69–70 (2d ed. 1989).

"Many brief writers suffer chronic cases of literary hiccups. They insert citations as often as possible, three or four in a simple declaratory sentence, irrespective of how these interfere with the flow of the prose, the rhythm of the presentations or the order of argument."
> —Ruggero J. Aldisert, *Winning on Appeal: Better Briefs and Oral Argument* 202 (1992).

"Only the hardiest of stylists will own up to this difficult fact: in many types of legal writing—in briefs and memos, for example—the only sensible place for citations is in footnotes. Putting them in the body clutters the text, slows the reader, and hampers the writer's ability to construct a coherent paragraph. Few writing reforms would benefit the legal world more than adopting the following rules: (1) put all citations in footnotes; and (2) ban footnotes for all purposes other than providing citations."

—Bryan A. Garner, *A Dictionary of Modern Legal Usage* 156 (2d ed. 1995).

"As lawyers, we often forget how much cites break up the flow of a narrative, even for a lawyer who is used to reading them. . . . [Y]our readers don't absorb cites; they jump over them. Once they start jumping, it's hard to get them to stop so they don't miss subsequent text."

—Steven D. Stark, *Writing to Win* 232–33 (2000).

"Citations belong in footnotes. You will be amazed at the increased readability. The clutter of letters and numbers in the middle of a paragraph is gone. The sentences flow into each other, instead of being isolated islands in a sea of citations."

—Judge Mark P. Painter, *The Legal Writer* 47 (2d ed. 2003).

No substantive footnotes:

"Perhaps no single implement of all the vast apparatus of scholarship is so thoroughly misused in the law as the footnote. There may be some justification in the manifold areas of the academic world for that formidable display of learning and industry, the thin stream of text meandering in a vale of footnotes, but such a technique is quite self-defeating in the law: it makes the writer's thoughts more difficult to follow—and hence far less likely to persuade the judicial reader."

—Frederick B. Wiener, *Briefing and Arguing Federal Appeals* 245 (rev. ed. 1967).

"Avoid footnotes. . . . [T]hey are nuisances in the field of argumentation. They impede readability and understanding, and they break up the continuity of argument. True, at times, they are unavoidable. But generally, if the 'pearl' cannot be worked into the main part of the brief it is either unimportant or is part of muddled thinking; and the note is used to cover muddiness of thought."

—Mario Pittoni, *Brief Writing and Argumentation* 39 (1967).

"If your point is important, it belongs in the text; if it is not important, it does not belong in the brief. Like all rules, this one may have exceptions, and occasionally a particular case may necessitate the use of footnotes; but, as a rule of thumb, work with the presumption that they will not be utilized. You are not writing a scholarly law review article that is expected to be filled with long, tortuous footnotes."

—Harvey C. Couch, *Writing the Appellate Brief*, 17 Prac. Law. 27, 30 (1971).

"If footnotes were a rational form of communication, Darwinian selection would have resulted in the eyes being set vertically rather than on an inefficient horizontal plane."

—Abner J. Mikva, *Goodbye to Footnotes*, 56 U. Colo. L. Rev. 647, 648 (1985).

"Footnotes . . . are usually a sign that the writer has not thought out carefully what he or she wanted to say, or what importance to attach to each piece of information."

—Christopher Turk & John Kirkman, *Effective Writing: Improving Scientific, Technical, and Business Communication* 71 (2d ed. 1989).

Explanation

Put Citations in Footnotes

Of all the tips in this book, this one is the most controversial. Its inclusion in the first edition resulted in a minor furor in which I was called a "Rasputin" who was misleading lawyers and judges into undermining the doctrine of precedent.[1] *The New York Times* ran a front-page article on the brouhaha,[2] and soon after Judge Richard A. Posner debated me on the point in an exchange that deserves greater attention than it has gotten.[3] Justice Rodney Davis of California weighed in on my side of the dispute.[4] Despite the occasionally raucous objections, as well as the calmer ones raised by Judge Posner, the power of the tip remains undiminished, and it continues to make headway in the profession. The trend is slow but steady.

Here, essentially, are the pros and the cons:

---

[1] *See* William Glaberson, *Legal Citations on Trial in Innovation v. Tradition*, N.Y. Times, 8 July 2001, at 1, 16.

[2] *Id.*

[3] *See* Bryan A. Garner, *Clearing the Cobwebs from Judicial Opinions*, 38 Court Rev. 4 (Summer 2001); Richard A. Posner, *Against Footnotes*, 38 Court Rev. 24 (Summer 2001); Bryan A. Garner, *Afterword*, 38 Court Rev. 28 (Summer 2001). These articles are archived in PDF files on Court Review's website at http://aja.ncsc.dni.us/courtrv/review.html. *See also* Bryan A. Garner, *Footnoted Citations Can Make Memos and Briefs Easier to Comprehend*, 32 Student Law. 11 (Sept. 2003).

[4] Rodney Davis, *No Longer Speaking in Code*, 38 Court Rev. 26 (Summer 2001).

Footnoted Citations
(Without Substantive Footnotes)

Pros	Cons
1. They shorten the average sentence length.	1. Legal readers have already learned one system: textual citations. [Yes, but legal writers have proved unable to handle the convention. Besides, readers see citation-free text everywhere *except* in legal writing.]
2. They make paragraphs more coherent and forceful.	
3. They lead readers to focus on ideas, not numbers.	2. Citations often contain important information about precedents. [All that important stuff should be woven into the text.]
4. They eliminate the sinfulness of string citations.	
5. They expose poor writing and poor thinking in the text, thereby promoting clearer writing and thinking.	3. Readers shouldn't have to glance at the bottom of the page. [Right: they shouldn't ever have to read footnotes. All that's down there is volume numbers and page numbers—and optional parentheticals.]
6. They result in fuller discussions of controlling caselaw.	
7. They result in much greater efficiency in conveying ideas.	4. Writers can more easily fudge what authorities say. [That's silly: too many fudge in the text right now.]
8. They make legal writing accessible to far more people.	5. Garner's suggestion results in a confusion of literary genres: scholarship vs. practical writing. [But the absence of substantive footnotes signals that this isn't scholarship.]
	6. You can't retrain yourself to read past superscripts. [If you can retrain yourself to read past two lines of citational numbers, you can retrain yourself to read past a tiny superscript.]
	7. It requires more effort: you can't simply paste quotations and citations into your writing. [If it results in greater accessibility for all readers, surely it's worth the effort.]

Whereas the pros are hard to answer—often unanswerable—the cons are mostly easy to counter.

Why, you may wonder, have briefs always had citations in the text? That's never been so of law reviews and treatises, but there must be a good reason why briefs are different. Right? Wrong. The reason is quite simple: the traditional method of preparing briefs involved scribes and (after the 1880s) typewriters. It was all but impossible to get citations in footnotes and to make the lines work out right on the page. That's why citations were in the text in 1900, and that's why they were still there in the late 20th century.

Today, things have gotten worse. With computer research and the proliferation of caselaw, it has become easier than ever to find a passel of cases to support almost every sentence in a brief. So, over time, the pages of briefs have become increasingly cluttered. Some have become virtually unreadable. Others are readable, but only by a reader who is mentally capable of dealing with lots of underbrush.

Meanwhile, in the late 1980s, technology gave us word processors with the ability to rid the text of citations. The computer automatically finds where to break pages, how to place footnotes—even keeping track of changing footnote numbers.

Of course, it's not that simple for the writer. You must rewrite in a way that cues the reader to what your authority is. It's just that you put this into prose; you work it into your paragraph, while ridding the text of volume numbers and page numbers—and thereby make life easier for the judge who reads your brief.

Citations have posed a major problem not just for readers, but also for writers. Many lawyers have gotten in the habit of putting a citation or two between sentences. That weakens the connection between consecutive sentences. So distrusting the reader to make a connection, they repeat the relevant part of the preceding sentence in the one that follows. The sentences get longer and longer and more and more repetitive. All this is anathema to a good writing style.

So you see, even if readers think they can handle citations in the text, the fact is that most legal writers can't.

Although writers continue to experiment with possible solutions—such as putting citations in smaller type or in colored ink, both of which would violate the Federal Rules of Appellate Procedure—the sensible solution is to use reference notes. That is, put citations (and only citations) in footnotes. And write in such a way that no reader would ever have to look at your footnotes: give the name of the court you're quoting, the year in which it wrote, and (if necessary) the name of the case up in the text. Just get the numbers out of the way.

"Why not endnotes?" you might ask. Well, endnotes simply aren't handy. For the reader who really wants to see the citation, it's annoying to have to flip back and find the relevant note. You've probably tried to read articles or books that annoyed you in this very way.

If you think that footnoting citations is an off-the-wall idea, ask yourself why you've never seen a biography written like this:

> Hand's assumption that judges are likely to impose their class predilections if they are involved in determination of the fundamental issues of society, Learned Hand, "Mr. Justice Holmes at Eighty-Five," *N.Y. World*, Mar. 8, 1926 (repr. in Learned Hand, *The Spirit of Liberty* 24 (Irving Dillard ed., 1952) (hereinafter *Spirit of Liberty*) (stating that "[j]udges are usually taken from that part of the bar which has distinguished itself in the field of action," and adding: "They are likely to be men of strong will, set beliefs and conventional ideals")), seems to be more speculative, and Hand himself insisted that some people are free from such bias, *see, e.g.,* Learned Hand, "The Speech of Justice," 29 *Harv. L. Rev.* 617, 619 (1916) (noting that some members of the American bench "could utter justice without misgiving or constraint"); *cf.* Kathryn Griffith, *Judge Learned Hand and the Role of the Federal Judiciary* 93 (1973) (analogous point for the receipt as well as the meting out of justice). He was not as much concerned with the grosser economic or material interests of judges, *Southern Transp. Co. v. Dauntless Towing Line*, 140 F.2d 215 (2d Cir. 1944) (evincing characteristic disinterestedness

in a case involving the collision of barges), as with their more basic understanding of what constitutes the good life, *see* Learned Hand, "How Far Is a Judge Free in Rendering a Decision?" (CBS nationwide radio broadcast) (repr. in Learned Hand, *Spirit of Liberty* at 103). Hand believed that most judges did not use their power for personal gain but that it was often difficult for them to maintain an open mind to ideas which challenge their basic faith and most profound assumptions. *See* Learned Hand, "The Commodities Clause of the Fifth Amendment," 22 *Harv. L. Rev.* 250, 252 (1909); Learned Hand, "Due Process of Law and the Eight-Hour Day," 21 *Harv. L. Rev.* 495, 497 (1908); *but see* Jerome Frank, "Some Reflections on Judge Learned Hand," 24 *Chi. L. Rev.* 666, 668 (1957) (throwing into question, by implication, Hand's point about basic faith and profound assumptions) (citing *U.S. v. Kirschenblatt*, 16 F.2d 202, 203 (2d Cir. 1926)). He felt that these fundamental predispositions would almost invariably be part of a decision in which a judge sought to interpret vague and ill-defined pronouncements of the public will. Learned Hand, "Is There a Common Will?" in *Spirit of Liberty* at 47, 50. He did not argue that judges can or should divest themselves of their basic beliefs or make their own beliefs the criteria of the basic values of society. *See id.* According to Hand's understanding of the American system, *see, e.g., U.S. v. Coplon*, 185 F.2d 629, 631 (2d Cir. 1950) (illustrating same); *U.S. v. Cotter*, 60 F.2d 689, 690 (2d Cir. 1932) (same), the court was not the proper forum for a confrontation of fundamental "interests" in either the material or the ideological sense, *see* Learned Hand, "Mr. Justice Holmes at Eighty-Five," *N.Y. World*, Mar. 8, 1926 (repr. in Learned Hand, *Spirit of Liberty* at 24, 26 (noting that the court is not the proper forum for a confrontation of ideological and material interests)); *see also* Felix Frankfurter, "Learned Hand," in *Of Law and Life & Other Things That Matter* 224, 229 (Philip B. Kurland ed., 1965) (noting that "[t]he individual contribution of judges is absorbed in the anonymity of the coral reef by which the judicial process shapes the law").

A historian would be insane to ruin a good story that way. But brief-writers commonly do something like it.

Besides improving readability, putting citations in footnotes allows you to strip down an argument and focus on what you're really saying. In Example A, for instance, you'll see a lack of coherence once the citations have been removed. This type of incoherence is commonplace, but textual citations help mask it.

Three other points.

First, you generally shouldn't just footnote naked propositions of law. Instead, say something like "New Jersey courts have held . . ." or "Section 28.007 of the Probate Code requires . . ." so that the reader can get the gist of your authority without having to glance down at the bottom of the page.

Second, even when citing cases in footnotes, some writers think they should put record references in the text if they're uniformly short. That's the method in the three model fact statements in tip #80. My own preference is to put even the record references in footnotes (see pp. 378–85). The prose gains continuity if it's not interrupted by little parentheticals.

Third, know your audience. Some judges say they don't like citations in footnotes. I happen to believe that they haven't fully thought through the point or seen good examples. Why do I think that? Because every time I teach a seminar on judicial writing, a vast majority of the judges finally conclude that they think it makes sense to put citations in footnotes. A few others, however, think otherwise. And if you know that's what a judge thinks, heed the judge's preference. Just don't let your temporary heed become your regular habit.

Ban Substantive Footnotes

In substantive footnotes—as distinguished from footnotes limited to citations—a writer argues or explains points related to those in the text. Although some judges defend substantive footnotes,[5] the safer bet is that your judicial reader will react to them with revulsion. It's a common feeling among judges these days because so many brief-writers abuse footnotes. Sometimes the writer wants to seem more scholarly; sometimes the purpose is to squeeze more words into the brief.

There's surely much to be said for substantive footnotes in scholarship. But in purely persuasive writing, you'll find them pretty easy to do without. My rule of thumb allows one or two substantive footnotes in a year of busy brief-writing.

Adopt an up-or-out policy: if it's not important enough to say up in the text, then take it out of the brief altogether.

Some Before-and-After Examples

Example A

Before   Nor is the due-process requirement satisfied. "Due process requires that a defendant have sufficient contact with the forum state so that an exercise of long-arm jurisdiction will not offend 'traditional conceptions of fair play and substantial justice,' . . . 'and so that a defendant should reasonably anticipate being haled into court there.'" *Tidgewell*, 820 F. Supp. at 632 (quoting *International Shoe Co. v. Washington*, 326 U.S. 310, 320, 66 S.Ct. 154, 160, 90 L.Ed. 95 (1945) and *World-Wide Volkswagen Corp. v. Woodson*, 444 U.S. 286, 297, 100 S.Ct. 559, 567, 62 L.Ed.2d 490 (1980)). "The Court has identified five relevant criteria: (1) the defendant's burden of appearing, (2) the forum state's interest in adjudicating the dispute, (3) the plaintiff's interest in obtaining convenient and effective relief, (4) the judicial system's interest in obtaining the most effective resolution of the controversy, and (5) the common interests of all sovereigns in promoting substantive social policies." *United Elec. Radio & Mach. Workers*, 960 F.2d at 1088 (citing *Burger King v. Rudzewicz*, 471 U.S. 462, 477, 105 S.Ct. 2174, 2184, 85 L.Ed.2d 528 (1985)).

After   Nor is the due-process requirement satisfied: "[A] defendant [must] have sufficient contact with the forum state so that an exercise of long-arm

---

[5] *See* Edward J. Becker, *In Praise of Footnotes*, 74 Wash. U. L.Q. 1 (1996).

jurisdiction will not offend 'traditional conceptions of fair play and substantial justice,' . . . 'and so that a defendant should reasonably anticipate being haled into court there.' "[32] In gauging this standard, the Supreme Court has named five relevant criteria:

- the defendant's burden of appearing;

- the forum state's interest in adjudicating the dispute;

- the plaintiff's interest in obtaining convenient and effective relief;

- the judicial system's interest in obtaining the most effective resolution of the controversy; and

- the common interests of all sovereigns in promoting substantive social policies.[33]

Example B

Before   In order for a family of trademarks to be protected, the common characteristic must have developed secondary meaning. *Spraying Sys. Co. v. Delavan, Inc.*, 975 F.2d 387, 393 (7th Cir. 1992); *see also Traffix Devices, Inc. v. Marketing Displays, Inc.*, 532 U.S. 23, 27–29, 121 S. Ct. 1255, 1259, 149 L. Ed. 2d 164 (2001) ("The design or packaging of a product may acquire a distinctiveness which serves to identify the product with its manufacturer or source; and a design or package which acquires this secondary meaning, assuming other requisites are met, is a trade dress which may not be used in a manner likely to cause confusion as to the origin, sponsorship, or approval of the goods."). In other words, the family characteristic must be such as to inform the consumer of the product's source, not simply of its nature, *Ft. Howard Paper Co. v. Nice-Pak Prods., Inc.*, 127 U.S.P.Q. 431 (T.T.A.B. 1960) ("-NAP" suffixes told public that products were used in connection with napkins, not that they came from the same source), so as to prompt the consumer who sees an article of merchandise to say, "That's the article I want because I know its source," not "Who makes that article?" *Ferrari S.P.A. v. Roberts*, 944 F.2d 1235, 1239 (6th Cir. 1991) (citing *West Point Mfg. Co. v. Detroit Stamping Co.*, 222 F.2d 581, 595 (6th Cir. 1955)). Whether a family of marks exists is an issue of fact based on the common formative component's distinctiveness, the family's use, advertising, promotion, and inclusion in related marks. *McDonald's Corp. v. McBagel's, Inc.*, 649 F. Supp. 1268, 1271 (S.D.N.Y. 1986). Whether the party claiming a family of marks has used joint advertising and promotion in a manner designed to create an association of common origin may be pertinent. *Champion Int'l Corp. v. Plexowood, Inc.*, 191 U.S.P.Q. 160 (T.T.A.B. 1976).

After   For a family of trademarks to be protected, the common characteristic must have developed secondary meaning—a distinctiveness that serves to identify the product with its source.[1] This characteristic must be something that consumers associate with the *source*, not just the nature, of the goods or services.[2] But once consumers rely on that association, competitors and others may not use the same characteristic in a way that creates confusion about the source.[3] As the Sixth Circuit has put it, the distinctive characteristic must prompt the consumer who sees it to say, "That's the article I want because I know its source," not "Who makes that article?"[4] Whether a family of marks exists is an issue of fact based not just on the common component's distinctiveness, but also on the family's use, advertising, promotion, and inclusion in related marks.[5] The use of joint advertising and promotion to create an association of common origin may also be pertinent.[6]

1. *Spraying Sys. Co. v. Delavan, Inc.*, 975 F.2d 387, 393 (7th Cir. 1992).

2. *Traffix Devices, Inc. v. Marketing Displays, Inc.*, 532 U.S. 23, 27–29, 121 S.Ct. 1255, 1259, 149 L.Ed.2d 164 (2001).

3. *Ft. Howard Paper Co. v. Nice-Pak Prods., Inc.*, 127 U.S.P.Q. 431 (T.T.A.B. 1960).

4. *Ferrari S.P.A. v. Roberts*, 944 F.2d 1235, 1239 (6th Cir. 1991).

5. *McDonald's Corp. v. McBagel's, Inc.*, 649 F. Supp. 1268, 1271 (S.D.N.Y. 1986).

6. *Champion Int'l Corp. v. Plexowood, Inc.*, 191 U.S.P.Q. 160 (T.T.A.B. 1976).

Substantive Footnotes: An Example of What Judges Detest

APPLICANT INTERVENOR may be impaired in civil prosecution sui juris of federal law allegation of "prohibited activities" under a pattern of racketeering, inclusive of the intervening state court judgment[10] as a component artifice, capable of proof by a preponderance of the evidence[11] as contradistinguished from the accelerated "clear and convincing" standard required to establish both vacation of the state

---

[10] Judicial review of the pending vacation petition weights heavily the correct analysis of the issues interposed and dispositioned in Civil Action No. CJ-49-87-96 (Okl. Co. Okl. 1986) and interpretation of the character and effect to be accorded such. By its own terms, 12 Okla. Stat. § 1031 applies only to "judgments" or "orders." The Oklahoma statute is therefore distinguishable from its federal counterpart, Rule 60(b), Fed. R. Civ. Proc. which applies only to "final" judgments or orders. The question of "finality" is critical to the underpinnings of procedural and substantive analysis in review of the petition. In ruling on the § 1031 petition is it error for the Court to inferentially hold the apparent stipulated judgment to be a final one? It does not appear from the record that the stipulated compromise and settlement of claims and "judgment" were contingent upon further judicial proceedings. If that were true, the "judgment" would not be final. The stated test for "finality" is whether the "judgment" is appealable. The entry into the compromise and settlement agreement appears to have rendered the disposition of the matter a consent judgment. While a consent judgment may become a final judgment of a court, it is not "appealable" in the usual sense. Consent judgments are therefore indistinguishable from litigated judgments for purposes of § 1031 analysis. *Zimmerman v. Quinn*, 744 F.2d 81, 82 (10th Cir. 1984). Once concluded, a settlement is as binding, conclusive and final as if it had been incorporated into a judgment. So read, the stipulation and judgment are final.

[11] "The Supreme Court strongly suggests that the proper burden of proof of predicate acts in RICO litigation is by a preponderance of the evidence. *Sedima*, 105 S.Ct. at 3282–83 (no indication that Congress sought to depart from preponderance standard); *Armco Indus. Credit Corp. v. SLT Warehouse Co.*, 782 F.2d 475, 481 (5th Cir. 1986) (noting that Supreme Court "strongly suggested" that preponderance standard applies). Post-*Sedima* appellate decisions hold that a plaintiff in a civil RICO action bears a "preponderance of the evidence standard" of proof. *E.g., Cullen v. Margiotta*, 811 F.2d 698, 731 (2d Cir. 1987); *United States v. Local 560, Int'l Brotherhood of Teamsters*, 780 F.2d 267, 279–80 n.12 (3rd Cir. 1985), *cert. denied*, 476 U.S. 1140, 106 S.Ct. 2247, 90 L.Ed.2d 693 (1986). We have found no civil RICO cases applying the clear and convincing standard of proof for predicate acts. Conversely, district courts have uniformly applied the preponderance standard. [citations omitted]. ("Third Circuit and the Supreme Court have concluded that the proper standard of proving predicate acts is by a preponderance of the evidence"). We conclude that the preponderance of evidence standard applies to proof of predicate acts in civil RICO litigation." *Wilcox v. First Interstate Bank of Oregon, N.A.*, 815 F.2d 522, 531 (9th Cir. 1987).

court proceeding[12] and proof of any underlying state law questions which substantively devolve to common law fraud.

The critical component of the impairment theory devolves to a judgment analysis of whether § 1031 (¶ IV) review sub judice actually metastasizes federal law issue preclusion under the Full Faith and Credit Act, 28 U.S.C. § 1738 (1982). The metastasis would occur not only as to pure state law issues of common law fraud justiciable under pendent jurisdiction, but also as to heretofore pristine federal law issues. Academic scrutiny finds impairment to be more than conjecture.

---

[12] At the postjudgment vacation stage, the burden is upon the movant to overcome the presumption of correctness that attaches to the trial court's decision and to the proceedings by "clear, cogent, and convincing" evidence. Therefore, the presumption of prima facie fraud inuring to the "confidential relation" between fiduciary and cestui que trust [fn. 13, infra.] at the prejudgment stage does not continue under the § 1031 burden of proof. "The principle governing a movant's burden of proof for postjudgment vacation relief is vastly different from that which applies to the allocation of onus probandi and of the pleading burden in prejudgment stages." *Davidson v. Gregory et al.*, No. 65,146 (Okl. S. Ct. May 31, 1989) Vol. 60 Okla. B.J. 1464, 1467 at Note 19. Every fact not negatived by the record must be presumed to support the trial court's judgment or order. Intervention by the trial court under authority of 60 Okla. Stat. § 175.23(A) in Civil No. CJ-86-5861 is by equitable cognizance. Consent judgments are indistinguishable from litigated judgments for purposes of § 1031 analysis. "While an appellate court may and will examine and weigh the evidence, the findings and decree of the trial court cannot be disturbed unless found to be clearly against the weight of the evidence. Whenever possible, an appellate court must render, or cause to be rendered, that judgment which in its opinion the trial court should have rendered. If the result is correct the judgment is not vulnerable to reversal because the wrong reason was ascribed as a basis for the decision or because the trial court considered an immaterial issue or made an erroneous finding of fact. We are bound neither by the reasoning nor by the findings of the trial court. Whenever the law and facts so warrant, an equity decree may be affirmed if it is sustainable on any rational theory and the ultimate conclusion reached below is legally correct. Once invoked in a proper proceeding, equity will administer complete relief on all issues formed by the evidence regardless of whether the pleadings specifically tendered them for resolution." *Matter of Estate of Bartlett*, 680 P.2d 369, 374 (Okl. 1984). Resolution of the vacation petition under § 1031 analysis rests upon criteria of (1) against the clear weight of evidence, and (2) clear abuse of discretion. *Brown v. Batt*, 631 P.2d 1346, 1348 (Okl. App. 1981). A strong showing is required with respect to a stipulated judgment by consent.

A Model Example of Citations in Footnotes

Beverly Ray Burlingame of Dallas is a master at writing readable briefs with citations in footnotes. What follows is a brief for an evidentiary hearing in federal court. Notice how clean the pages look in comparison with those in most briefs.

IN THE UNITED STATES DISTRICT COURT
FOR THE NORTHERN DISTRICT OF TEXAS
DALLAS DIVISION

Johnson Electronics, Inc.,	§	
	§	
Plaintiff,	§	
	§	
v.	§	Civil Action No. 97 CV 126
	§	
SemPro Corporation,	§	
	§	
Defendant.	§	

Johnson's Brief on the
Use of Extrinsic Evidence in Claims Construction

This brief addresses SemPro's objections to the exhibits that Johnson intends to offer at the upcoming *Markman* hearing.[1] These objections are apparently based on two errors by SemPro: (1) it has misinterpreted the purpose of some of the exhibits; and (2) it has overlooked recent Federal Circuit law, including the *Markman* case itself, explaining the proper role of extrinsic evidence in construing patent claims.

---

[1] *See* Letter from John Reynolds, dated April 24, 1998 ("Reynolds Letter"), attached to this brief as Exhibit A.

JOHNSON'S BRIEF ON THE USE OF EXTRINSIC EVIDENCE—Page 1

Argument

A.   **Extrinsic evidence can properly be used in claim construction as long as it does not vary the unambiguous meaning of the claim.**

As the Federal Circuit has observed, "In determining the proper construction of a claim, the court has numerous sources that it may properly utilize for guidance."[2] When the court is unfamiliar with technical terms or the underlying technology of a patent, "the testimony of witnesses may be received upon these subjects, and any other means of information [may] be employed."[3]

In construing a claim, a district court should look first to the intrinsic evidence of record, including the claim, the specification, and, if in evidence, the prosecution history.[4] If this public record "unambiguously describes the scope of the patented invention," then reliance on extrinsic evidence is improper.[5] But if the meaning of a disputed claim cannot be determined from the public record, then extrinsic evidence may be helpful, particularly if a critical technical aspect of the invention was neither discussed in the specification nor commented on during patent prosecution.[6]

Under such circumstances, extrinsic evidence—including expert testimony, inventor testimony, dictionaries, technical treatises, and articles—may be useful to the

---

[2]   *Vitronics Corp. v. Conceptronic, Inc.*, 90 F.3d 1576, 1582 (Fed. Cir. 1996).

[3]   *Markman v. Westview Instruments, Inc.*, 116 S. Ct. 1384, 1394–95 (1996) (quoting 2 W. Robinson, *Law of Patents* § 732, at 481–83 (1890)).

[4]   *Markman v. Westview Instruments, Inc.*, 52 F.3d 967, 984–85 (Fed. Cir. 1995) (in banc), *aff'd*, 116 S. Ct. 1384 (1996).

[5]   *Vitronics*, 90 F.3d at 1583.

[6]   *Fromson v. Anitec Printing Plates, Inc.*, 132 F.3d 1437, 1444 (Fed. Cir. 1997) (approving the use of "extrinsic evidence derived from expert testimony, demonstrative evidence, and scientific tests").

JOHNSON'S BRIEF ON THE USE OF EXTRINSIC EVIDENCE—Page 2

court in reaching a proper understanding of the patent and of the claim languages.[7] The only pertinent limit on using such evidence is that the court should not rely on it to vary or contradict unambiguous claim language.[8]

B.   SemPro has no valid objection to the extrinsic evidence that may be offered by Johnson.

1.   Evidence concerning prior art—both cited and uncited—is relevant in construing the asserted claims.

As SemPro apparently recognizes, some of Johnson's exhibits relate to prior products and patents that were not cited in the prosecution histories of the patents-in-suit.[9] From this fact, SemPro leaps to the incorrect conclusion these exhibits will be offered at the *Markman* hearing to prove that some of the asserted claims are invalid.[10] Although for some claims, Johnson has asserted the defense of invalidity based on prior art, the issue of invalidity is not the subject of this proceeding. Indeed, Johnson intends to offer prior art at the *Markman* hearing to show that to the extent that any claim may be found ambiguous, it must be construed narrowly to *uphold* its validity.

Under well-established law, patent claims "are generally construed so as to sustain their validity, if possible."[11] As Johnson's previously filed brief makes clear, the

---

[7]   *See Vitronics*, 90 F.3d at 1584; *Markman*, 52 F.3d at 979–81.

[8]   *Vitronics*, 90 F.3d at 1584–85 (extrinsic evidence cannot be used "to vary or contradict the manifest meaning of the claims").

[9]   *See* Reynolds Letter at 1.

[10]   *See id.*

[11]   *Whittaker Corp. v. UNR Indus., Inc.*, 911 F.2d 709, 712 (Fed. Cir. 1990); *see Modine Mfg. Co. v. U.S. Int'l Trade Comm'n*, 75 F.3d 1545, 1557 (Fed. Cir. 1996) (when "reasonably possible," claims should "be interpreted so as to preserve their validity"); *ACS Hosp. Sys., Inc. v. Montefiore Hosp.*, 732 F.2d 1572, 1577 (Fed. Cir. 1984).

JOHNSON'S BRIEF ON THE USE OF EXTRINSIC EVIDENCE—Page 3

relevant prior art—both cited and uncited—is being offered by Johnson so that the claims can be properly, and narrowly, construed to avoid their being invalidated by the prior art.[12]

In *Amhil Enterprises*, the Federal Circuit construed a claim to sustain its validity over several instances of prior art.[13] There, the court addressed the proper meaning of "substantially vertical" in describing the faces and side edges of a cup lid. The court first considered the prior art Zabner and Davis patents, which were cited by the examiner in initially rejecting the claim under section 103.[14] As the court explained, the patentee distinguished its invention from the cited prior art "based in part on the slope of the projection faces."[15] Thus, the term "substantially vertical" was construed to mean "vertical," or "not including lids with sloping faces like those of Zabner '645."[16]

As the Federal Circuit explained, the claim had to be construed narrowly to avoid the prior art:

> Finally, it is apparent from our review of the prior art of record that lids of the general construction claimed in the '244 patent were common in the industry. Several prior art lids depict outwardly extending projections with variously sloped outward faces as may be seen in the figures from some prior art lid patents reproduced in the attached appendix. In order for claim 1 of the '244 patent to "avoid" these prior art lids, "substantially vertical face" must be construed as the same as or very close to "vertical face." . . . Any other construction of claim 1 would render it invalid.[17]

---

[12] *See* Johnson's Pre-*Markman*-Hearing Brief on Claim Construction at 5, 10, 42–45, 55–59.

[13] *Amhil Enterprises Ltd. v. Wawa, Inc.*, 81 F.3d 1554, 1559–62 (Fed. Cir. 1996).

[14] *Id.* at 1560–61.

[15] *Id.* at 1561.

[16] *Id.*

[17] *Id.* at 1562; *see id.* at 1565.

JOHNSON'S BRIEF ON THE USE OF EXTRINSIC EVIDENCE—Page 4

Exactly the same type of analysis will be required for some of the claims asserted in the present case. These claims must be construed so that they avoid the prior art. Otherwise, as in *Amhil Enterprises*, the claims would be rendered invalid.

SemPro suggests that while prior art that was actually cited in the prosecution history might be relevant, the Court should ignore any prior art that was not cited.[18] But in *Vitronics*, the Federal Circuit expressly authorized considering both cited and uncited prior art in construing patent claims: "a court in its discretion may admit and rely on prior art proffered by one of the parties, *whether or not cited in the specification or the file history*."[19]

Consistent with *Vitronics*, a Michigan federal court recently used extrinsic prior art in construing a claim to sustain its validity.[20] As the district court explained, the "Chudov prior art reference serves as extrinsic evidence, i.e., evidence external to the patent and prosecution history, that demonstrates the state of the art at the time of the invention."[21] Quoting *Markman*, the court observed that this extrinsic prior art was "useful 'to show what was then old, to distinguish what was new, and to aid the court in the construction of the patent.' "[22]

The *Renishaw* court then construed the claim to sustain its validity over the uncited prior-art Chudov reference: "Using [plaintiff's] proposed construction, these

---

[18] *See* Reynolds Letter at 1.

[19] *Vitronics,* 90 F.3d at 1584 (emphasis added).

[20] *See Renishaw v. Marposs Societa' Per Azioni*, 974 F. Supp. 1056, 1088–89 (E.D. Mich. 1997).

[21] *Id.* (citing *Markman*, 52 F.3d at 980).

[22] *Id.* at 1089 (quoting *Markman*, 52 F.3d at 980, and *Brown v. Piper*, 91 U.S. 37, 23 L. Ed. 200 (1875)).

limitations, along with the rest of claim 51, literally read on the Chudov reference. . . . To avoid rendering claim 51 invalid, these limitations would have to be construed so as to exclude the Chudov reference . . . ."[23] In the same way, some of the asserted claims in this case should be construed to avoid rendering them invalid based on extrinsic prior art that will be proffered by Johnson at the *Markman* hearing.

Despite SemPro's objections, both cited and uncited prior art may properly be considered and used by this Court in construing the asserted claims. Such evidence will plainly be helpful "to show what was then old, to distinguish what was new, and to aid the court in the construction of the patent."[24]

2. There is no support for the notion that extrinsic evidence must be limited to evidence that is dated *before* the filing date of the patents.

SemPro's second objection to Johnson's extrinsic evidence is that some of the exhibits are "dated after the filing of the various patents-in-suit to which [the exhibits] relate."[25] Without citing any authority, SemPro asserts that such exhibits are irrelevant and "can never have any bearing" on claim construction.[26] But recent Federal Circuit caselaw makes this assertion insupportable.

In *Vitronics*—a case in which the sole issue was claim construction—the plaintiff brought suit in November 1991 for infringement of its '502 patent.[27] The district

---

[23] *Id.*

[24] *Markman*, 52 F.3d at 980 (quoting *Brown v. Piper*, 91 U.S. 37, 23 L. Ed. 200 (1875)).

[25] Reynolds Letter at 1.

[26] *Id.*

[27] *See Vitronics*, 90 F.3d at 1579 (suit brought in 1991); *id.* at 1582 (claim construction is the only issue on appeal).

JOHNSON'S BRIEF ON THE USE OF EXTRINSIC EVIDENCE—Page 6

court considered a wide array of extrinsic evidence, including expert testimony, live testimony of one of the plaintiff's engineers, deposition testimony, technical articles, and a paper by one of the plaintiff's employees.[28] This employee paper had been written in 1994—which was plainly several years after the filing date of the patent.[29] And all the testimony considered by the court, including the deposition testimony, was clearly taken after that filing date.

The Federal Circuit ultimately concluded that because there was no ambiguity in the phrase "solder reflow temperature," as used in the claims, the district court should not have relied on extrinsic evidence "to vary or contradict the manifest meaning of the claims."[30] As explained in *Vitronics*, a district court should use extrinsic evidence in claims construction only if there is "some genuine ambiguity in the claims, after consideration of all available intrinsic evidence."[31]

But the Federal Circuit expressly approved of a trial court's hearing *all possible evidence* before construing the claim: "even if the judge permissibly decided to hear all the possible evidence before construing the claim, the expert testimony, which was inconsistent with the specification and file history, should have been accorded no weight."[32] As the court noted, if the district court had, instead, used "the expert testi-

---

[28] *Id.* at 1581.

[29] *Id.*

[30] *Id.* at 1585.

[31] *Id.* at 1584.

[32] *Id.; see Tanabe Seiyaku Co.,* 109 F.3d 729, 732 (Fed. Cir. 1997) (extrinsic evidence may be considered "when appropriate as an inherent part of the process of claim construction and as an aid in arriving at the proper construction of the claim").

JOHNSON'S BRIEF ON THE USE OF EXTRINSIC EVIDENCE—Page 7

mony and other extrinsic evidence to help it understand the underlying technology, we could not say the district court was in error."[33]

Similarly, the *Markman* court concluded that a district court can properly admit extrinsic evidence and then later reject such evidence to the extent that it contradicts the construction required by the public record: "We conclude that (1) the trial court did not abuse its discretion when it admitted the extrinsic evidence offered by Markman—Markman's testimony and the testimony of Markman's 'patent expert'—on the issue of claim construction, and that (2) the trial court properly rejected this extrinsic evidence to the extent it contradicted the court's construction of the claims based on the specification and prosecution history."[34] As one Pennsylvania federal court recently recognized, a district court may properly "consider extrinsic evidence when helpful, such as expert testimony, learned treatises, and even sales literature."[35]

Moreover, the *Vitronics* court recognized that in some cases, district courts can go beyond merely considering such evidence. In construing ambiguous claims, they can properly rely on exactly the types of extrinsic evidence discussed in *Vitronics*, including the paper written by the patentee's employee several years after the patent issued:

> Here, the trial judge considered not only the specification, but also
> expert testimony and other extrinsic evidence, such as the paper written by

---

[33] *Vitronics*, 90 F.3d at 1585.

[34] *Markman*, 52 F.3d at 981.

[35] *Applied Telematics, Inc. v. Sprint Commun. Co.*, No. 94-CV-4603, 1996 WL 421920, at *5 (E.D. Pa. 1996) (citing *Markman*, 52 F.3d at 979, 980).

JOHNSON'S BRIEF ON THE USE OF EXTRINSIC EVIDENCE—Page 8

the former Vitronics employee. No doubt there will be instances in which intrinsic evidence is insufficient to enable the court to determine the meaning of the asserted claims, and in those instances, *extrinsic evidence, such as that relied on by the district court, may also properly be relied on to understand the technology and to construe the claims.*[36]

This 1996 opinion from the Federal Circuit thus directly contradicts SemPro's argument that documents created after the patent's filing date "can never have any bearing on claim construction."[37]

By its very nature, most extrinsic evidence—including all expert testimony—will have been created **after** the date the patent was filed. Contrary to SemPro's view, that sequence of events provides no reason for excluding such evidence.

Conclusion

Vitronics authorizes this Court to hear all possible evidence—including extrinsic evidence—before construing the claims at issue. This method promotes efficiency because it allows the Court to hear all the evidence that might possibly be useful and relevant, instead of: (1) hearing solely the intrinsic evidence; (2) deciding whether each claim is ambiguous; and (3) then possibly having to hear additional evidence to resolve any ambiguities in the claims.

Johnson therefore respectfully asks this Court to overrule SemPro's objections to Johnson's extrinsic evidence and to grant Johnson any further relief to which it is justly entitled.

---

[36] *Vitronics*, 90 F.3d at 1584 (emphasis added) (citing *Markman*, 52 F.3d at 979).

[37] Reynolds Letter at 1.

JOHNSON'S BRIEF ON THE USE OF EXTRINSIC EVIDENCE—Page 9

23

If you must cite in text, make the citations unobtrusive.

Quotable Quotes

"[B]y any measure, the attorneys did a poor job of restricting their presentations of authority to those [cases] the judges considered useful. This is one of the major points made in the judges' writings on appellate advocacy. A substantial number ask counsel to limit themselves to the more relevant authority; especially galling to the judges is the long string of case citations to support a proposition, rather than a few apposite ones."
> —Thomas B. Marvell, *Appellate Courts and Lawyers* 133 (1978).

"Use authorities sparingly and only to the extent necessary to support a well-thought-out theory of your case."
> —Nathan S. Hefferman (as quoted in Ruggero J. Aldisert, *Winning on Appeal: Better Briefs and Oral Argument* 198 (1992)).

"About citations: A lawyer should include as few as practical, mainly those of the leading or more recent cases."
> —Albert Tate Jr., "The Art of Brief Writing: What a Judge Wants to Read,"
> in *Appellate Practice Manual* 197, 205 (Priscilla A. Schwab ed., 1992).

"[P]lace citations so as to have them available but out of the way. Always subordinate citations to the statements they support. Never begin a sentence with a citation. By the time your readers get to the first parallel citation in the second line of your 'sentence' and realize that no thoughts have yet filtered through, they will decide that you're a writer who deserves, at the very most, a quick scan."
> —Bryan A. Garner, *The Elements of Legal Style* 90 (2d ed. 2002).

Explanation

If you're nervous about following the advice of #22—or if court rules prohibit you from doing so—then, when citing in text, avoid four bad conventions.

First, don't begin a sentence with a citation. Nobody gets excited about reading a sentence that begins, "The Voting Rights Act of 1965,

Pub. L. No. 89–110, 79 Stat. 445 (codified at 42 U.S.C. §§ 1971, 1973 to 1973bb-1 (1988)), provides . . . ."

Second, don't put a citation in midsentence. Instead, always arrange for the citation to fall at the end of the sentence, even if you mention the case in the text. Here's an example of what not to do:

> While Name Plaintiffs' lack of standing also precludes them from meeting Fed. R. Civ. P. 23(a)'s "typicality" requirement for class certification, *see LaMar v. H & B Novelty & Loan Co.*, 489 F.2d 461, 465–66 (9th Cir. 1973) ("In brief, typicality is lacking when the representative plaintiff's cause of action is against a defendant unrelated to the defendants against whom the cause of action of the members of the class lies . . . . [W]e assert that a plaintiff who has no cause of action against the defendant cannot 'fairly and adequately protect the interests' of those who do have such causes of action."), standing is a threshold requirement that must be met before any inquiry into class representation under Rule 23 is made, *see Weiner v. Bank of King of Prussia*, 358 F. Supp. at 694 ("It must be noted that the question of standing is totally separate and distinct from the question of plaintiff's right to represent a purported class under Rule 23 . . . . Standing to sue is an essential threshold which must be crossed before any determination as to class representation under Rule 23 can be made.").

Is that a 187-word-long sentence? Or a 41-word-long sentence with citations stuck in it?

Less horrific examples abound in briefs. Here's a typical one:

> In *Fitzpatrick v. Illinois Human Rights Comm'n*, 267 Ill. App. 3d 386, 642 N.E.2d 486 (4th Dist. 1994), the plaintiff alleged that the employer discriminated on the basis of physical handicap when it failed to accommodate the plaintiff, who had been diagnosed with a sleeping disorder, by simply transferring her from the day shift to the night shift. 267 Ill. App. 3d at 387, 642 N.E.2d at 487. The court held that . . . .

Even assuming that this is the first passage where the case has been cited, you could handle the citation in this way:

> In *Fitzpatrick v. Illinois Human Rights Comm'n*, the plaintiff alleged that the employer discriminated on the basis of physical handicap when it failed to accommodate the plaintiff, who had been diagnosed with a sleeping disorder, by simply transferring her from the day shift to the night shift. 267 Ill. App. 3d 386, 387, 642 N.E.2d 486, 487 (4th Dist. 1994). The court held that . . . .

Of course, you'd be better off following tip #22.

Third, don't put the citation flush left after a block quotation. Example A shows how misleading it can be to end a block quotation and put the citation at the left margin, where the text is meant to resume. The sentence after the quotation is all but lost. Instead, the better practice—regardless of what the *Bluebook* says—is to tuck the bracketed citation under the quoted matter.

Fourth, don't use string citations. This warning has become something of a cliché, yet lawyers everywhere continue to use string citations. They're a bad habit. And like many other bad habits in legal writing, string citations often betray a lack of confidence.

Once again, tip #22 eliminates the problem. But if you're citing in text, and you can support a proposition with just one case, do it. There's no need to cite every case on point. Simply pick the most recent case from the court of last resort in your jurisdiction. Generally, that case will serve as ample authority.

If, however, you're convinced of the need to highlight the cases in your string—when, for example, the development of the law is important to understanding the argument you're making—then put them in a list, preferably with holdings before citations. The whole problem of textual citations is one of emphasis and subordination. Most relevant to the authority of a citation are the court, the holding, and the date of the holding—all the information that appears at the end of the citation, with the holding further buried in parentheses. Least important are the name of the case (typically), the volume number, and the page numbers. So traditional modes of textual citation emphasize the least important things and subordinate the most important, as here:

> New York courts have held that several types of activities by a defendant are evidence of doing business in the state. *W. Lowenthal Co. v. Colonial Wooden Mills, Inc.*, 38 A.D.2d 775, 776, 327 N.Y.S.2d 899, 901 (3d Dep't 1972) (holding that maintenance of an office in New York is doing business); *Dunn v. Southern Charters, Inc.*, 506 F. Supp. 564, 567 (E.D.N.Y. 1981) (holding that solicitation of business in New York is doing business); *Masonite Corp. v. Hellenic Lines, Ltd.*, 412 F. Supp. 434, 438 (S.D.N.Y. 1976) (holding that having a New York bank account is doing business); *Kazlow & Kazlow v. A. Goodman & Co.*, 92 Misc. 2d 1084, 1086, 402 N.Y.S.2d 98, 99 (1st Dep't 1977) (holding that making use of New York courts is doing business).

It would be hard, without getting quite far-fetched, to devise a more inefficient way of delivering the message contained in that passage. But consider what happens when the parentheticals are highlighted in a list and the rest is subordinated in parentheses:

> New York courts have held that the following types of activities by a defendant are evidence of doing business in the state:
> - maintaining an office in New York (*W. Lowenthal Co. v. Colonial Wooden Mills, Inc.*, 38 A.D.2d 775, 776, 327 N.Y.S.2d 899, 901 (3d Dep't 1972));
> - soliciting business in New York (*Dunn v. Southern Charters, Inc.*, 506 F. Supp. 564, 567 (E.D.N.Y. 1981));
> - having a New York bank account (*Masonite Corp. v. Hellenic Lines, Ltd.*, 412 F. Supp. 434, 438 (S.D.N.Y. 1976));
> - making use of New York courts (*Kazlow & Kazlow v. A. Goodman & Co.*, 92 Misc. 2d 1084, 1086, 402 N.Y.S.2d 98, 99 (1st Dep't 1977)).

Example B illustrates a variation on this technique: the case names come first, before substantial quotations, to show the development of the law during the 20th century. Either way of doing a string citation—the one just above or the one in the revised version of Example B—is much stronger than run-in strings with parentheticals.

Example A: The Problem of the Flush-Left Citation

Before   At least two current or former Navpro employees have confirmed in their depositions that Mr. Riley had no involvement in the Maplewood One development. Richard Shipman, who was vice president of property management in Navpro's New York office when Riley worked there, adamantly declared that Riley had nothing to do with Maplewood One:

> Q: Are you aware of what Michael Riley's responsibilities were at the time that you had responsibilities in the New York office for Maplewood One?
>
> Mr. Conyers: Objection.
>
> The Witness: Michael Riley had responsibility for developing new properties. Therefore, he had no responsibility on Maplewood One . . . .
>
> . . .
>
> Q: Do you recall if Mr. Riley would have had any involvement with either the decision to remove asbestos from Maplewood One or the actual removal of asbestos from Maplewood One?
>
> Mr. Conyers: Objection.
>
> The Witness: Absolutely not.
>
> Q: Would Mr. Riley have had any management responsibilities for the Maplewood One building?
>
> Mr. Conyers: Objection.
>
> The Witness: Absolutely not.

(*See* the transcript of the deposition of Richard Shipman, dated December 14, 1995, at 83:18, 84:14, attached as Exhibit A to the Certification of Counsel.) Matthew Brooks, who was the asset manager for Maplewood One while Riley worked in the New York office, also confirmed this fact. (*See* the transcript of the deposition of Matthew Brooks, dated December 20, 1995, at 76:20–23, attached as Exhibit B to the Certification of Counsel.)

After   At least two current or former Navpro employees have confirmed in their depositions that Mr. Riley had no involvement in the Maplewood One development. Richard Shipman, who was vice president of property management in Navpro's New York office when Riley worked there, adamantly declared that Riley had nothing to do with Maplewood One:

> Q: Are you aware of what Michael Riley's responsibilities were at the time that you had responsibilities in the New York office for Maplewood One?
>
> Mr. Conyers: Objection.
>
> The Witness: Michael Riley had responsibility for developing new properties. Therefore, he had no responsibility on Maplewood One . . . .
>
> . . .
>
> Q: Do you recall if Mr. Riley would have had any involvement with either the decision to remove asbestos from Maplewood One or the actual removal of asbestos from Maplewood One?
>
> Mr. Conyers: Objection.
>
> The Witness: Absolutely not.

Q: Would Mr. Riley have had any management responsibilities for the Maplewood One building?

Mr. Conyers: Objection.

The Witness: Absolutely not.

[Shipman dep., 83:18, 84:14, Ex. A to Counsel Cert.]

Matthew Brooks, the asset manager for Maplewood One while Riley worked in the New York office, also confirmed this fact. (*See* Brooks dep., 76:20–23, Ex. B to Counsel Cert.)

Example B: A String Citation in a Bulleted List

Still, the case is not unique. A long and unbroken line of Texas cases establishes that an insurer who unqualifiedly defends without a reservation of rights is estopped to disclaim liability for an adverse judgment. These cases began with this Court's holding in *Automobile Underwriters' Ins. Co. v. Murrah*, in which the Court concluded that "when [the insurer], with full knowledge of the issues to be tried in the suit against Adair [the insured], took exclusive control and management of Adair's defense in such suit, introduced all of the evidence that was before the court on such defense, filed all of the pleadings that were filed for Adair, examined and cross-examined all witnesses, it thereby waived the defensive clauses in the policy of insurance and admitted an unconditional indebtedness . . . in favor of Adair . . . ." 40 S.W.2d 233, 234 (Tex. Civ. App.—Dallas 1931, writ ref'd). The more recent cases in this line of authority follow *Murrah*'s lead:

- *Pacific Indem. Co. v. Acel Delivery Serv., Inc.*, 485 F.2d 1169, 1175 (5th Cir. 1973) (applying Texas law), *cert. denied*, 415 U.S. 921 (1974): "[F]or estoppel to be effective against a defense of noncoverage even where the insurer has assumed the defense, prejudice must be shown to have been suffered by the party contending estoppel. . . . Pacific's untimely withdrawal less than one month prior to trial of the . . . suit, however, certainly does not preclude a finding of prejudice, but compels it."

- *Western Casualty & Sur. Co. v. Newell Mfg. Co.*, 566 S.W.2d 74, 77 (Tex. Civ. App.—San Antonio 1978, writ ref'd n.r.e.): "Insurer undertook the defense, its attorneys selected a jury, and an offer of settlement was received with no indication to the insured defendant that a determination of breach of the policy had been made and that insurer had elected to withdraw. It certainly would have been grossly unfair, at that time, to notify defendant that it had decided to withdraw from the defense."

- *Farmers Texas County Mut. Ins. Co. v. Wilkerson*, 601 S.W.2d 520, 521–22 (Tex. Civ. App.—Austin 1980, writ ref'd n.r.e.): "[I]f an insurer assumes the insured's defense without obtaining a reservation of rights or a non-waiver agreement and with knowledge of the facts indicating noncoverage, all policy defenses, *including those of non-coverage*, are waived, or the insurer may be estopped from raising them."

- *Arkwright-Boston Mfrs. Mut. Ins. Co. v. Aries Marine Corp.*, 932 F.2d 442, 445 (5th Cir. 1991): "The paradigm estoppel situation occurs when the insurer assumes the insured's defense of a claim arguably not covered by the policy without reserving its right to deny coverage. After losing the litigation, the insurer refuses to pay the claimant on the ground of non-coverage and suggests that the claimant collect from the insured. Estoppel is predicated upon the insurer's conflict of interest: it is too likely to be defending the insured in the lawsuit while at the same time formulating policy defenses to deny coverage."

Guardian can point to no contrary line of authority. Even so, it is mildly surprising that Guardian could file with this Court a 49-page brief without citing (much less distinguishing) any of these controlling cases, several of which the Court relied on in its earlier opinion.

24

Say something about
the critical cases you cite:
show how and why they apply.
For other cases, be satisfied
with a simple citation.

Quotable Quotes

"Only when a case is being cited for a blackletter rule of law is it sufficient to merely cite the case. All other authorities, especially less well-known cases, deserve a minimum of one or two sentences explaining how the facts in that case or its reasoning apply to your case. If you think back to the research, there were reasons why you chose to make a note about that case as opposed to others; that reason was probably a similarity of facts or clarity of reasoning, which should be highlighted in your brief."
> —Richardson R. Lynn, *Appellate Litigation* § 9.8, at 188 (1985).

"In most instances, the purpose of a citation should be explained. A case may be important for its facts, its holding, its reasoning, its approval of other authority, or for an observation that is dictum. It is essential to tell the court exactly how a case is being used."
> —E. Norman Veasey, Chief Justice of Delaware (as quoted in *Judges on Briefing* 17 (Bryan A. Garner ed., 2001)).

Explanation

Make sure to give the context for the important cases you cite. Unless you're stating a well-known or routine point of law, briefly explain how the facts and holding of the cited case apply to your point.

The following example—again from Beverly Ray Burlingame of Dallas—contains a caselaw discussion that typifies truly excellent legal writing.

An Unusually Good Example

B. The Supreme Court has broadly interpreted section 1305 to preempt state-law claims.

In *Morales v. Trans World Airlines, Inc.*, the Supreme Court construed the scope of section 1305 preemption broadly, concluding that state deceptive-advertising rules could not be enforced against the airlines because they are laws "relating to rates, routes, or services of an air carrier."[42] The *Morales* Court interpreted the phrase "relating to" expansively:

> The ordinary meaning of ["relating to"] is a broad one—"to stand in some relation; to have bearing or concern; to pertain; refer; to bring into association with or connection with," *Black's Law Dictionary* 1158 (5th ed. 1979)— and the words thus express a broad pre-emptive purpose.[43]

Relying on its interpretation of a similarly worded preemption provision in ERISA, the Court noted that such a provision has a "broad scope" and an "expansive sweep."[44]

In *Morales*, the Supreme Court made clear that a state rule or law may be preempted even if: (1) it is not specifically addressed to the airline industry; (2) its effect is only indirect; and (3) it is not inconsistent with federal law.[45] As this Court characterized the *Morales* rule: "Laws of general applicability, even those consistent with federal law, are preempted if they have the 'forbidden significant effect' on rates, routes or services."[46] *Morales* "leaves little doubt that a claim based on com-

---

[42] *Morales v. Trans World Airlines, Inc.*, 504 U.S. 374, 112 S. Ct. 2031, 2037 (1992).

[43] *Id.*

[44] *Id.*

[45] *Id.* at 2038; *see Hodges*, 44 F.3d at 336.

[46] *Hodges*, 44 F.3d at 336 (citing *Morales*, 112 S. Ct. at 2039); *see Morales*, 112 S. Ct. at 2038 (noting that common-law tort and contract claims may be preempted) (citing *Pilot Life Ins. Co. v. Dedeaux*, 481 U.S. 41, 47–48, 107 S. Ct. 1549, 1552–53 (1987); *Mackey v. Lanier Collection Agency & Service, Inc.*, 486 U.S. 825, 829, 108 S. Ct. 2182, 2185 (1998)).

mon law tort or contract is as subject to § 1305 preemption as any other claim, if it can be demonstrated that it 'relates to' airline 'rates, routes, or services.' "[47]

As the *Morales* Court explained, some state actions may affect airline rates, routes, or services "in too tenuous, remote, or peripheral a manner" to be pre-empted.[48] But as this Court recognized in *Hodges*, the *Morales* Court did not state exactly where the line should be drawn.[49] Like the claims in *Morales*, the claims in this case do not present a borderline question.[50] Instead, enforcing these state-law claims would create direct and profound effects on airline services.

C. The Ninth Circuit has correctly recognized that state-law claims relating to alcohol service are preempted.

Relying extensively on *Morales*, the Ninth Circuit has recently recognized that state-law claims related to an airline's service of alcohol are completely preempted.[51] *Harris v. American Airlines*, which addresses a similar issue to the one raised in this case, was decided after this Court's en banc opinions in *Hodges* and *Smith*.[52]

In *Harris*, the plaintiff filed an action in state court, alleging negligence and other causes of action.[53] As in the present case, American Airlines removed the case to federal court and filed a summary-judgment motion, arguing that the state-law

---

[47] *Williams v. Express Airlines I, Inc.*, 825 F. Supp. 831, 833 (W.D. Tenn. 1993).

[48] *Morales*, 112 S. Ct. at 2040; *see Williams*, 825 F. Supp. at 833.

[49] *Hodges*, 44 F.3d at 336; *see Williams*, 825 F. Supp. at 833.

[50] *See Morales*, 112 S. Ct. at 2040.

[51] *See Harris v. American Airlines*, 55 F.3d 1472, 1476 (9th Cir. 1995).

[52] *Compare Harris*, 55 F.3d at 1472 (decided June 1, 1995) *with Hodges*, 44 F.3d at 334 (decided Feb. 15, 1995) *and Smith*, 44 F.3d at 344 (decided Feb. 15, 1995).

[53] *Harris*, 55 F.3d at 1473.

claims were preempted and alternatively that no genuine fact issue existed.[54] The trial court ruled that Harris's state claims were not preempted, but granted American Airlines' summary-judgment motion on the merits.[55]

On appeal, the Ninth Circuit affirmed on grounds of preemption, declining to reach the merits of the state-law claims.[56] As the Ninth Circuit concluded, because these claims related directly to the service of an airline, they were preempted:

> [Harris] is complaining directly about the service of alcoholic beverages that she claims caused John Doe's reprehensible conduct . . . . These allegations pertain directly to a "service" the airlines render: the provision of drink.[57]

The issue before the Ninth Circuit was identical to the issue in this case: "whether § 1305(a)(1) of the Federal Aviation Act . . . preempts state-law claims against an airline for negligence."[58] As the court correctly concluded, all the plaintiff's state-tort claims, including negligence, were completely preempted because they related to an airline's services.[59]

The *Harris* court considered facts similar to those in this case and concluded that an airline cannot be sued under state law for harm caused by a passenger who has allegedly become intoxicated during a flight.[60] Harris sued American Airlines for events that occurred during a flight from Dallas to Portland in 1990.[61] Harris, a pas-

---

[54] *Id.*

[55] *Id.*

[56] *Id.*

[57] *Id.* at 1476.

[58] *Id.* at 1473.

[59] *Id.* at 1476–77.

[60] *See id.*

[61] *Id.* at 1473.

senger in the first-class cabin, claimed that during the flight, American Airlines served four drinks to a fellow passenger, whom she believed to be intoxicated.[62] The passenger uttered racial slurs that upset Harris, an African-American.[63]

The Ninth Circuit's decision in *Harris* is directly on point. The Millers complain specifically of American Airlines' alleged failure to honor its duty as an alcoholic beverage server and to properly control the conduct of an intoxicated passenger.[64] Consistent with *Harris*, the Ninth Circuit would almost certainly hold that the state-law claims in this case "relate to" airline services and are therefore completely preempted by section 1305(a)(1) of the Airline Deregulation Act.

Even the dissenting opinion in *Harris* supports the preemption of the Millers' state-law claims.[65] While concluding that preemption was improper, the dissenting judge based his opinion on his belief that the claims were related not to the service of alcohol, but to the airline's failure to ensure the safety of a passenger by protecting her from the abusive conduct of another passenger.[66] In contrast, the Millers' claims cannot be viewed as related to the safety of a passenger because the Millers were not passengers on the flight. Instead, the claims are directly and solely related to the service of alcohol to Barber. Under both the majority and dissenting opinions in *Harris*, the Millers' state-law claims are preempted.

---

[62] *Id.*

[63] *Id.*

[64] 1 R. 25 (R.E. Tab F).

[65] *Harris*, 55 F.3d at 1477 (Norris, J., dissenting).

[66] *Id.* at 1477–78.

25

Use parenthetical case explanations merely to show why you're citing the cases—not to present your argument.

Quotable Quotes

"Subordination provides the means of distinguishing major points from minor points or bringing in supporting context or details."
—Andrea Lunsford & Robert Connors, *The St. Martin's Handbook* 310 (1989).

"Parentheticals are for the facts of unimportant cases. Don't put the facts of an important case in parentheses. Parentheses signal the reader that what's inside them is incidental."
—Alan L. Dworsky, *The Little Book on Legal Writing* 96 (2d ed. 1992).

"Parenthetical information is generally recommended when the relevance of a cited authority might not otherwise be clear to the reader . . . ."
—*The Bluebook* § 1.5, at 28 (17th ed. 2000).

Explanation

If citations in the text cause problems (see #22), then parentheticals in the text cause even greater ones. Although citation parentheticals are terrific in footnotes, they are horrendous in text. Why? Because they drive an even bigger wedge between your sentences.

Brief-writers often present major chunks of their argument in parentheticals. These case explanations, they often tell me, are important. But the phrase "important parenthetical" is surely an oxymoron.

Instead of appearing in parentheticals, the important information ought to be elevated to the text, and the citations should be subordinated—preferably in footnotes.

A Typically Bad Example

I. <u>Acquiescence</u>

Acquiescence involves one party's implicit or explicit assurances to another party that induce reliance by the latter party, *Conan Properties, Inc. v. Conan's Pizza, Inc.*, 752 F.2d 145, 153 (5th Cir. 1985) (acquiescence found where defendant was in business for five years and during that time plaintiff visited defendants' restaurant, congratulated them on their venture, and later sent a signed photograph wishing them success); while laches is defined as an unreasonable delay in filing suit that results in prejudice to the defendant, *id.* But drawing a distinction between the two terms can be difficult because they are frequently referred to interchangeably by different courts. *See, e.g., University of Pittsburgh v. Champion Prods., Inc.*, 686 F.2d 1040, 1045 (3d Cir.), *cert. denied*, 459 U.S. 1087 (1982) (university's forty-year delay in filing suit against Champion was a "silent acquiescence" that barred monetary relief); *Saratoga Vichy Spring Co., Inc. v. Lehman*, 625 F.2d 1037, 1041 (2d Cir. 1980) (in discussion of a laches defense, court held that the Saratoga Vichy Spring Co. had acquiesced in the state's use of its mark by failing to make any objection to defendant's use over a period of seven years); *Pflugh v. Eagle White Lead Co.*, 185 F. 769, 772 (3d Cir.) (plaintiff "acquiesced" in defendant's use by its silence where defendant had rejected two of plaintiff's cease-and-desist letters, asserted its own adverse rights to the mark and plaintiff took no legal action over a period of 14 years), *cert. denied*, 220 U.S. 615 (1911).

Other courts have enunciated a clear distinction between acquiescence and laches. *See, e.g., Dial-A-Mattress Operating Corp. v. Mattress Madness, Inc.*, 841 F. Supp. 1339, 1356 (E.D.N.Y. 1994) (distinguishing acquiescence from laches in that acquiescence requires active encouragement of defendant's use whereas laches results from prolonged negligence or inaction); *Chase Fed. Savs. & Loan Ass'n v. Chase Manhattan Fin. Servs., Inc.*, 681 F. Supp. 771, 783 (S.D. Fla. 1987) (distinguishing acquiescence from laches); *Carl Zeiss Stiftung v. V.E.B. Carl Zeiss, Jena*, 293 F. Supp. 892, 917 (S.D.N.Y. 1968) ("As distinguished from laches, acquiescence constitutes a ground for denial of relief only upon a finding of conduct on the plaintiff's part that amounted to an assurance to the defendant, express or implied, that the plaintiff would not assert his trademark rights against the defendant."), *aff'd as modified*, 433 F.2d 686 (2d Cir. 1970), *cert. denied*, 403 U.S. 905 (1971).

Part D

Editing for Brisk, Uncluttered Sentences

26

Relax the tone: eliminate the jargon known as "legalese."

Quotable Quotes

"Simple English is no one's mother tongue. It has to be worked for."
—Jacques Barzun, *Teacher in America* 47 (1945).

"I am the last one to suppose that a piece about the law could be made to read like a juicy sex novel or a detective story, but I cannot see why it has to resemble a cross between a nineteenth century sermon and a treatise on higher mathematics."
—Fred Rodell, *Goodbye to Law Reviews—Revisited*, 48 Va. L. Rev. 279, 282 (1962).

"In jargon nobody ever does anything, feels anything, or causes anything; nobody has an opinion. Opinions are had; causes result in; factors affect. Everything is reduced to vague abstraction. The writer can even abolish himself, for jargon never sounds as though anybody had written it; it seems simply to come about, as from a machine, and it talks mechanically of things that come about, through some indistinct interaction of forces."
—Robert Waddell, "Formal Prose and Jargon," in *Modern Essays on Writing and Style* 84, 89 (Paul C. Wermuth ed., 1964).

"The major fault in modern prose generally is Stuffiness. . . . For most people . . . in most situations, in the writing of everyday serious expository prose, it is the Stuffy voice that gets in the way. The reason it gets in the way, I submit, is that the writer is scared. If this is an age of anxiety, one way we react to our anxiety is to withdraw into omniscient and multisyllabic detachment where nobody can get us."
—Walker Gibson, *Tough, Sweet & Stuffy* 107 (1966).

"I'm no English professor, and I don't expect my literary preferences in argumentative writing to coincide with those of others. I can only repeat that good, clear, forceful English is essential."
—Frederick B. Wiener, *Briefing and Arguing Federal Appeals* 67 (rev. ed. 1967).

"[L]egalese is worse than smoking cigarettes. To kick the habit is extremely hard. So don't kid yourself. If you want to write plain English, you'll have to learn how. You'll have to study it as if it were Spanish or French. It'll take much work and lots of practice until you've mastered the skill."

—Rudolf Flesch, *How to Write Plain English:*
A Book for Lawyers and Consumers 2 (1979).

"Attitudes need to change more than rules of composition need to be memorized. Lawyers must be convinced that there is no purpose, or value, in sounding archaic. This is a tall order. It will take an emotional, almost psychological, pitch to teach many attorneys that there is nothing wrong with sounding like a citizen of the second half of the 20th century. You are no less a lawyer for being understandable."

—Christopher T. Lutz, "Why Can't Lawyers Write?" in *Appellate*
Practice Manual 167, 177 (Priscilla A. Schwab ed., 1992).

"Play a game with yourself . . . . : see how long a list you can make of lawyers' words we could perfectly well do without. Examine your language from this day on. Strip out *anything* that sounds lawyerish. Find some other way of saying what you want to say. Work hard at it because it really matters. The Golden Rule is clear: *Do not sound like a lawyer any more than is absolutely necessary.*"

—Keith Evans, *The Golden Rules of Advocacy* 17 (1993).

"[If] you have fallen under the spell of 'legalese,' . . . words take on a certain institutional stiffness. When words such as *whereby, thereby, heretofore,* and *wherein* creep into your vocabulary, put down your pen, take a few deep breaths, and read your work aloud. Your ear will soon tell you just how awkward and antiquated these phrases are."

—Gary Blake & Robert W. Bly, *The Elements of Technical Writing* 73 (1993).

"I am particularly careful to avoid jargon, and to write simply and clearly. For certain types of writing a high level of technicality is unavoidable; but in general it is the second-rate intellect that cultivates a pretentious vocabulary and a solemn and portentous style."

—Richard A. Posner, *How I Write,* 4 Scribes J. Legal Writing 45, 49 (1993).

"For a hundred years, good lawyers have been writing without all the garbage and in a simple, direct style."

—Lynn N. Hughes (as quoted in Bryan A. Garner, *Judges on Effective Writing:*
The Importance of Plain Language, 73 Mich. B.J. 326, 326 (1994)).

"The idea is to avoid any word that does not command instant understanding. Your words should be transparent vehicles that let the reader see your ideas without straining to grasp the meaning. . . . Most of the concepts you struggled to master in law school can be grasped by the average 12-year-old. It is the vocabulary training that makes it such a drudgery."

—James W. McElhaney, *Writing to the Ear,* ABA J., Dec. 1995, at 74, 76.

"When it comes to plain talk, lawyers are the worst. Most speak and write as if they live in a repository for dead bodies. When they write briefs that some poor trapped judge must read, they fill them with heavy, gray, lifeless, disgustingly boring word gravel—piles of it, tons of it. When I read most briefs I want to scream. I want to throw the brief out the window and jump. If I could find the author, and had the power, I would make the villain eat the thing a page at a time without salt or catsup."

—Gerry Spence, *How to Argue and Win Every Time* 105 (1995).

Explanation

Pursuant to the above-referenced quotations, and each and all of the ideas embodied therein, notwithstanding anything to the contrary herein contained . . . .

Did you know that in every state in which judges have been polled, they've overwhelmingly said that they'd like lawyers to stop using legalese? Did you know that they consider lawyers who use legalese to have little prestige, to be less smart, and to be lower in their academic rankings?

Any phrase that smells like jargon should be immediately suspect.

This means that you might have to let go of some cherished phrases. What you'll find, though, is that you'll not only communicate better, but also think more clearly.

Some Before-and-After Examples

Example A

Before   TO THE HONORABLE JUDGE OF SAID COURT:

COMES NOW Guy Walt Williams, Plaintiff in the above styled and numbered cause, and files this his response to Defendant's Motion for Summary Judgment and would respectfully show unto the court as follows:

After   In response to Mitsubishi's summary-judgment motion, Guy Walt Williams will show that there remain no fewer than 17 genuine issues of material fact in this case. One of the principal factual issues is . . . .

Example B

Before   Pursuant to leave of Court granted on March 4, 1992, General Golf Inc. has, contemporaneously with the filing of this letter brief, supplemented the summary judgment evidence before this Honorable Court with an additional affidavit from Lynn Presbee dated March 8, 1992 (hereinafter the "Presbee Affidavit").

After   With the Court's permission, General Golf has today supplemented the summary-judgment evidence with Lynn Presbee's affidavit.

Example C

Before   WHEREFORE, PREMISES CONSIDERED, Defendant requests that final judgment be entered against Plaintiffs on the matters set forth herein, that Defendant recover from Plaintiffs all of Defendant's reasonable and necessary attorney's fees and costs and postjudgment interest at the highest rate allowed by law, and such other and further relief to which Defendant may show itself to be justly entitled.

After   Defendant therefore requests final judgment against Plaintiffs, together with attorney's fees and costs, plus postjudgment interest at the highest lawful rate, and any other relief to which it may be entitled.

27

Avoid overparticularization.

Quotable Quotes

"True brevity of expression consists in everywhere saying only what is worth saying, and in avoiding tedious detail about things that everyone can supply for himself. This involves correct discrimination between what is necessary and what is superfluous."

—Arthur Schopenhauer, "On Style" (1851), in *Theories of Style in Literature* 251, 263 (Lane Cooper ed., 1923).

"A great deal of good advice is given about the need for detail in writing, but one should not add so many details that the main line of discussion is buried under them."

—Sumner Ives, *A New Handbook for Writers* 316 (1960).

"[Y]ou must state the facts of the case in your brief as you yourself would wish to read them—the introductory summary first, the details later—in order to get a clear, consecutive, understandable picture of what the case is really about."

—Frederick B. Wiener, *Briefing and Arguing Federal Appeals* 45 (rev. ed. 1967).

"Being precise doesn't mean compiling details; it means selecting details."

—Michael Alley, *The Craft of Scientific Writing* 35 (1987).

"[A] reader should not be forced to confront details before the writer has provided a framework for understanding."

—William A. Bablitch, *Writing to Win*, Compleat Law., Winter 1988, at 11.

"I like a brief that shows the signs of an organizing and discriminating mind: no swamping with unnecessary facts . . . a brief so written that I can quickly scan it in preparation for oral argument but can find further riches if I have been assigned the opinion to write."

—Frank M. Coffin, *On Appeal: Courts, Lawyering, and Judging* 120 (1994).

"People who lavish unnecessary information on their conversational partners are known as bores. They can be recognized by their detailed accounts of summer vacations and longwinded descriptions of common experiences . . . .

[T]he basic challenges of writing resemble those of conversation; in both, the trick is to keep things moving forward without skipping anything important."
—Peter Richardson, *Style: A Pragmatic Approach* 2–3 (1998).

Explanation

Judge Thomas Gibbs Gee, the great Fifth Circuit judge, gave this vice its name. In his judicial style sheet, he wrote: "No overparticularization, which can throw your reader off by causing him to try to keep track of things that do not matter."* Judge Gee had diagnosed the most common literary disease from which legal writers suffer: the progressive inability to winnow important from unimportant facts.

Here's my test: if it isn't necessary to understanding the issues, or if it doesn't add human interest, then leave it out.

A Before-and-After Example

Before: [What follows begins a "Procedural History" section of a motion for summary judgment, but the history has nothing to do with why summary judgment is appropriate. And the dates have nothing to do with anything in the motion.]

Procedural History

Plaintiff, Robin B. Sorter, Administratrix of the Estate of Walter E. Sorter ("Sorter"), commenced this action against the defendant, Chudon Mutual Insurance Company ("Chudon"), by filing a Complaint in the Superior Court of Connecticut on or about June 22, 1994. Chudon was served on or about July 12, 1994. On August 3, 1994, Chudon removed to this Court. On September 24, 1994, Chudon filed its Answer and Affirmative Defenses. *See* the Affidavit of John T. Green, Jr. ("Green Affidavit"), ¶ 2. Chudon now seeks summary judgment pursuant to Fed. R. Civ. P. 56 with respect to Count One of Sorter's Complaint and seeks dismissal pursuant to Fed. R. Civ. P. 12(b)(6) of Counts Two through Five for failure to state a claim upon which relief can be granted.

After: [The better strategy would be to begin with the deep issues.]

Introduction

In deciding Chudon's summary-judgment motion, the court faces two issues:

1. [Statement–Statement–Question.]

2. [Statement–Statement–Question.]

---

* *A Few of Wisdom's Idiosyncrasies and a Few of Ignorance's,* 1 Scribes J. Legal Writing 55, 57 (1990).

28

Populate your sentences.
Use real names (not procedural labels) for parties.

Quotable Quotes

"[N]othing adds more realism to a story than names; nothing is as unrealistic as anonymity. Imagine a story whose hero has no name! If you ever read Franz Kafka's nightmarish novels about 'K.', you will know what namelessness does to a story. So name your characters."
—Rudolf Flesch, The Art of Readable Writing 80 (1949; repr. 1967).

"It is easier for us, or at least me, to remember the parties by *name* . . . . I have difficulty in remembering who is petitioner, respondent, appellant, relator, and the like."
—Joe R. Greenhill, Advocacy in the Texas Supreme Court, Tex. B.J.,
June 1981, at 624, 628.

"Whenever you can, write about people. In fact, adding people to your sentences may do more to make them clear than any other writing habit you could develop."
—Maxine Hairston, Successful Writing 115 (2d ed. 1986).

"[S]peak of real people, not of categories. The plaintiff, defendant, and witnesses have names. Use them."
—Michael Tigar, Federal Appeals: Jurisdiction and Practice 333 (2d ed. 1993).

"The idea was to refer to people as 'plaintiffs' and 'defendants,' or 'petitioners' and 'respondents,' instead of using their real names. That way, we lawyers could drain all the humanity out of the case and focus on pure questions of rights and duties. But it makes the whole story harder for anyone to follow— even lawyers and judges who have been doing it for years. Use the real names whenever you can."
—James W. McElhaney, Writing to the Ear, ABA J., Dec. 1995, at 74, 77.

"Imagine a world in which all novelists used the terms 'Protagonist' and 'Antagonist' as the names of their principal characters. Assume that playwrights

181

and screenwriters did the same. The stories would grow tedious, wouldn't they?

"Legal writers have traditionally spoiled their stories by calling people 'Plaintiff' and 'Defendant,' 'Appellant' and 'Appellee,' or 'Lessor' and 'Lessee.' It's a noxious habit that violates the principles of good writing."
—Bryan A. Garner, *Legal Writing in Plain English* 44 (2001).

Explanation

By putting people in your sentences, you'll make your briefs clearer and more memorable. Even in a dispute between, say, two insurance companies, it's better to refer to "Allstate" and "CNA" than to "Plaintiff" and "Defendant" or "Appellant" and "Appellee."

And don't try to personalize your client and dehumanize your adversaries by using the real name for the client and a procedural label for the adversaries. Instead, use real names for both parties and let your arguments do the talking. (See Example A.)

That helps judges keep track of who's who. There's a reason, after all, why Rule 28(d) of the Federal Rules of Appellate Procedure enacts this principle:

> **References to Parties.** In briefs and at oral argument, counsel should minimize use of the terms "appellant" and "appellee." To make briefs clear, counsel should use the parties' actual names or the designations used in the lower court or agency proceeding, or such descriptive terms as "the employee," "the injured person," "the taxpayer," "the ship," "the stevedore."*

The same is true at the trial-court level.

But the tip does have two exceptions. First, if an opponent is extremely sympathetic, you may wish not to remind the court repeatedly just who that person is. Second, if multiple parties are aligned in such a way that a single name is inaccurate—that is, the defendants are banks, insurance companies, and individuals as well—then you may have to say "Defendants." But do it as a last resort.

Some Before-and-After Examples

Example A

Before   Prior to October of 1992, Plaintiff became addicted to narcotics and had purchased cocaine on Company premises for a number of years. Also prior to October of 1992, Plaintiff claims that the Company denied his requests for substance-abuse treatment in breach of their agreement. On October 2, 1992, a co-employee promised to share cocaine with Plaintiff, if Plaintiff would obtain and deliver the cocaine to the co-employee. Plaintiff maintains that had he received the substance-abuse treatment that

---

* Fed. R. App. P. 28(d).

had been refused, Plaintiff would not have obtained the cocaine as requested. Plaintiff was discharged effective October 3, 1992, for selling narcotics on Company premises.

After Sometime before October 1992, Kent Smith became addicted to narcotics and had started buying cocaine while at work for Wheelock, Inc.—on company premises. He did this for several years. Although Smith was an at-will employee, he now claims that Wheelock breached an "employment agreement" by denying his requests for substance-abuse treatment. On October 2, a coworker suggested that if Smith would get some cocaine, the two could share it. The next day, Smith got the cocaine, was discovered, and was promptly fired. He now claims that if he had gone through a substance-abuse program, he wouldn't have gotten the cocaine as requested. And, of course, Smith says he wouldn't have been fired.

Example B

> *The brief-writer represents the City of Amarillo, the defendant in a § 1983 civil-rights action. The statement of facts is drawn from an appellate brief assigning as error the omission of a requested charge. Record citations are omitted. Instead of repeatedly referring to "Plaintiff," the writer should have called the opponent "Burton." "Plaintiff" is a Teflon name—bad facts don't stick to "Plaintiff" the way they do to "Burton."*

Before ## NATURE OF THE ACTION

This is a civil action brought pursuant to 42 U.S.C. § 1983 by Plaintiff against (1) the City of Amarillo; (2) Dory L. Fiske, Director of the Department of Public Safety; and (3) three individual police officers. In his Complaint, Plaintiff claims he was (1) falsely arrested; (2) exposed to excessive force (handcuffing); (3) falsely imprisoned; (4) deprived of due process; and (5) deprived of rights secured to him under 42 U.S.C. § 1983. Plaintiff also asserts state-law claims for (1) assault and battery; (2) malicious prosecution; (3) intentional infliction of emotional distress; (4) defamation; and (5) common-law conspiracy.

SUMMARY OF FACTS

This case arises out of the Plaintiff being arrested for Driving While Intoxicated ("DWI") at approximately 2:20 a.m. on Saturday, November 20, 1996, by Officer Gibson. Officer Gibson observed Plaintiff's vehicle coming westbound in the 3700 block of Paramount Avenue in Amarillo toward the four-way stop sign at the corner of Paramount and St. John's. Plaintiff did, in fact, stop at the stop sign and then remained stopped there for what Officer Gibson felt was a rather lengthy period of time. Officer Gibson then observed Plaintiff proceed one block to the next four-way stop sign and also stop there for a rather long period of time. Officer Gibson also noticed that when Plaintiff was stopped at the stop sign, Plaintiff opened the driver's side door of his pickup truck and was leaning out of the vehicle. This leaning out of the vehicle at this hour of the morning concerned Officer Gibson that Plaintiff was possibly intoxicated and he followed Plaintiff. Officer Gibson observed that as Plaintiff left the second stop sign, at Lakeside Drive and Marlowe, Plaintiff was driving straddling the line with his wheels, straddling the center line or the center stripe indicator of the roadway. Officer Gibson observed that Plaintiff would periodically get back into the correct lane of traffic and then a little bit later, he would tend to weave off and steer down the center line again.

Officer Gibson also observed that as Plaintiff began going south-bound on Marlowe, after he crossed the intersection of Stanton Avenue and Marlowe, Plaintiff was in the center lane at this time and there was a vehicle in front of Plaintiff in the center lane. Plaintiff changed lanes to the right-hand lane without signaling and cut back in front of the car and proceeded across the three lanes on this three-lane, one-way street into the left-hand lane of traffic. From there, Plaintiff crossed Hillcrest, continuing to periodically leave his lane of traffic. As he crossed Hillcrest, Officer Gibson made the decision to attempt to stop him. Officer Gibson activated the strobe lights and the alternating flashing high beams on his vehicle and radioed in that he was attempting to stop Plaintiff's vehicle. Rather than immediately pulling over, Plaintiff continued driving for another five blocks, at which time Officer Gibson decided Plaintiff was not aware of the patrol vehicle with all its lights activated, and Officer Gibson turned on his siren. When the sirens went on, Plaintiff pulled over in the parking lot of a medical clinic at the intersection of Marlowe and Iberville.

Officer Gibson approached the Plaintiff's vehicle and asked him where he had come from. Plaintiff told him that . . . . [549 words]

After
Nature of the Case

In this § 1983 action, Randall Burton has sued the City of Amarillo; Dory L. Fiske, Director of the Department of Public Safety; and three police officers (Gibson, Pyle, and McAllister). In his Complaint, Burton has stated claims for:

- false arrest;
- excessive force;
- false imprisonment;
- deprivation of due process;
- violations of 42 U.S.C. § 1983;
- assault and battery;
- malicious prosecution;
- intentional infliction of emotional distress;
- defamation; and
- common-law conspiracy.

Summary of Facts
This case arises out of Burton's arrest by Officer Brent Gibson for driving while intoxicated at about 2:20 a.m. on Saturday, November 20, 1996, in

Amarillo. Officer Gibson first saw Burton's pickup truck coming westbound on Paramount Avenue toward the four-way stop sign at the corner of Paramount and St. John's. Burton stopped at the stop sign, but then remained there for what Officer Gibson felt was an unusually long time. Officer Gibson then watched Burton proceed one block to the next stop sign and stop there for an unusually long time as well. Officer Gibson also noticed that while Burton was stopped, he opened the door of his truck and leaned outside. This caused Officer Gibson to suspect that Burton might be intoxicated, so he followed Burton.

Burton continued driving, but quite erratically. After he crossed the center line several times, Officer Gibson decided to stop him. Gibson turned on his patrol car's strobe lights, flashed his high beams, and radioed in that he was stopping Burton's truck. But instead of pulling over immediately, Burton continued driving for another five blocks. Officer Gibson then decided that Burton was unaware of the patrol car with all its lights activated, so he turned on his siren. When the siren went on, Burton pulled over into the parking lot of a medical clinic at the intersection of Marlowe and Iberville.

Officer Gibson approached Burton's truck and asked him where he had come from. Burton replied that . . . . [321 words]

29

Work hard to replace *be*-verbs with action verbs.

Quotable Quotes

"If you go through any newspaper or magazine and look for active, kicking verbs in the sentences, you will realize that this lack of well-used verbs is the main trouble with modern English writing. Almost all nonfiction nowadays is written in a sort of pale, colorless sauce of passives and infinitives, motionless and flat as paper."

—Rudolf Flesch, *The Art of Plain Talk* 67 (1946).

"*Is* so besets us—we are willing to sit back on our *is*es—that we not only replace active with passive voice, but active verbs with sedentary ones."

—Sheridan Baker, "Scholarly Style, or the Lack Thereof" (1956), in *Perspectives on Style* 64, 68 (Frederick Candelaria ed., 1968).

"[T]he stronger the verb the better the sentence. No generalization is wholly true, as Disraeli reminds us, including this one, but you will find it of great practical use to husband verbs. They will repay attention a hundredfold, for they flash pictures across the mind, reduce our craving for adjectives if they do not deliver us from it entirely, and force us to reckon with structure."

—Charles W. Ferguson, *Say It with Words* 117 (1959).

"For those persons willing to make a substantial effort to improve their writing, I suggest the following exercise. Choose eight to ten consecutive sentences from any random text and count the total number of verbs. Record this as the denominator of a fraction. Then count the copulas [*be*-verbs] or passives and record that number as the numerator. If the fraction exceeds ⅓, consider the number of copulas as excessive."

—Lester S. King, *Why Not Say It Clearly* 27 (1978).

"Verbs act. Verbs move. Verbs do. Verbs strike, soothe, grin, cry, exasperate, decline, fly, hurt, and heal. Verbs make writing go, and they matter more to our language than any other part of speech."

—Donald Hall, *Writing Well* 83 (4th ed. 1982).

"Although the verb *to be* in all its forms (*is, am, was, were, will be, have been,* and so on) remains the central verb in our language, careful writers use it sparingly."

—Maxine Hairston, *Successful Writing* 118 (2d ed. 1986).

"[R]esort to forms of *to be* only when an arduous search turns up no alternative. In nine sentences out of ten, a better verb can be found, and the entire shape and structure of the sentence will immediately improve once an *is* or *was* or *has been* has made its exit."

—Christopher Lasch, *Plain Style* 76 (Stewart Weaver ed., 2002).

Explanation

Be-verbs lack muscle. When you overuse them, your writing becomes flaccid—even inert.

As an editorial exercise, try highlighting every *be*-verb and converting it into a stronger verb. I did it with this book; perhaps I missed opportunities to replace still more *be*-verbs than I did, but the text certainly improved with the changes I made.

A Before-and-After Example

Before   There **is** no classification in the savings clause, other than the deadline for filing cases that **are** excepted from the amendment. Such a deadline **is** reasonable. Every statute typically has a date upon which it **is** effective, and therefore automatically distinguishes between those it affects and those it does not. The deadline in the savings clause **is** analogous to an effective date of a statute. Certainly it cannot **be** argued that such a deadline **is** a classification in violation of Art. 3, section 56 of the Texas Constitution. Moreover, even if the deadline can **be** characterized as a classification, it operates equally on all within the class. Any and all such cases throughout the state that **were** on file prior to May 1, 1993, **were** "saved" from the amendment.

[129 words; 10 *be*-verbs; 4 passive-voice constructions]

After   The savings clause contains no classification other than the deadline for filing cases to which the amendment does not apply. This deadline operates as an effective date, much like the effective date that every statute contains to distinguish between persons it affects and those it does not. Certainly the deadline does not amount to a classification that violates article 3, section 56 of the Texas Constitution. Even if the deadline did classify, though, the classification operates equally on all class members: by virtue of the savings clause, all cases filed before May 1, 1993 fall outside the amendment.

[98 words; no *be*-verbs; no passive-voice constructions]

30

Know what the passive voice is, and minimize it.

Quotable Quotes

"In its modern uses the passive fails to present an impression of swift action or vividness. It is the staple of the report, the research monograph, and the catalogue."
—Margaret M. Bryant & Janet Rankin Aiken, *The Psychology of English* 144 (1940).

"The difference between an active-verb style and a passive-verb style—in clarity and vigor—is the difference between life and death for a writer."
—William Zinsser, *On Writing Well* 111 (5th ed. 1994).

"[A]lthough the passive voice has its occasional legitimate uses—usually, when the actor is either unimportant or unknown—its frequent use makes a piece of writing much less interesting and readable."
—Bryan A. Garner, *A Dictionary of Modern Legal Usage* 643 (2d ed. 1995).

Explanation

Many lawyers talk about passive voice without knowing exactly what it is. In fact, many think that any *be*-verb signals passive voice, as in:

> The doctrine is applicable to this case.

But that sentence is actually in active voice—even though it's badly in need of editing. Most professional editors would change *is applicable* to *applies*, but they wouldn't call it "passive" because it's not. It's just a flabby *be*-verb.

The point about passive voice is that the subject of the clause doesn't perform the action of the verb. Instead, you back into the sentence:

> Passive: The deadline was missed by defense counsel.

> Active: Defense counsel missed the deadline.

And, of course, in the passive form, it's possible to omit the actor altogether—a prime source of unclarity. Sometimes it amounts to responsibility-dodging:

Passive: The deadline was missed.

As anyone who follows political discourse knows, the passive voice is a staple of politicians.

The unfailing test for passive voice is this: you must have a *be*-verb (or *get*) plus a past participle (usually a verb ending in *-ed*). Thus, constructions such as these are passive:

is	dismissed
are	docketed
was	vacated
were	reversed
been	filed
being	affirmed
be	sanctioned
am	honored
got	paid

Sometimes, though, the *be*-verb won't appear. It's simply an implied word in the context. For example:

> Recently I heard it suggested by a client that national insurance should cover all legal fees.

Grammatically speaking, that sentence contains the implied verb *being* after the word *it*, so it's in the passive voice. To make it active, you'd write:

> Recently I heard a client suggest that national insurance should cover all legal fees.

What's the real problem with using passive voice? There are three. First, passive voice usually adds a couple of unnecessary words. Second, even if it doesn't add those unnecessary words, it fails to say squarely who has done what. That is, a *by*-phrase is necessary to show the actor (*The brief was filed* vs. *The brief was filed by LoriVon, Inc.*). Third, the passive subverts the normal word order for an English sentence, thereby making it harder for readers to process the information.

The opposite of each of those liabilities appears as a gain in the active voice: it saves words, says directly who has done what, and meets the reader's expectation of an actor–verb–object order.

Sometimes, of course, you'll be justified in using the passive voice. There's no absolute prohibition against it—and anyone who tried to follow such a prohibition would spoil a piece of writing. In his fine book *Mightier Than the Sword*, Ed Good identifies eight situations in which you'll sometimes need the passive:

- When the actor is unimportant.

- When the actor is unknown.

- When you need to put the punch word at the end of the sentence (see #36).

- When you want to hide the actor's identity.

- When you want to avoid sexist language (see #56).

- When the focus of the passage is on the thing being acted upon.

- When you need to generalize without using *one* as the subject.
- When the passive simply sounds better.*

Still, professional editors find that these eight situations don't account for more than about 15 to 20% of the contexts in which the passive appears.

That means you ought to have a presumption against the passive, unless it falls into one of the categories just listed. The following examples typify what you'll see in many briefs.

Some Before-and-After Examples

Example A

Before   Commercial success *is considered* relevant to the question whether an invention was obvious under the rationale that competitors would have *been* economically *motivated* to make the invention sooner if it had been truly obvious.

After   Commercial success is relevant to the question whether an invention was obvious, because competitors would have had an economic incentive to make the invention sooner if it had been truly obvious.

Example B

Before   To support a trespass action when the injurious acts [that are] *complained* of *were* not actually *committed* by the defendant himself, the person who committed the acts must *be* either *employed, paid,* or *controlled* by the defendant in order to hold him liable.

After   For the defendant to be liable in a trespass action when the defendant did not personally commit the acts complained of, the defendant must have employed, paid, or controlled the person who did commit them.

Example C

Before   Whether the Burgdorfs' gift to the Library must *be returned* because the Burgdorf Lecture Hall has *been renamed* is an entirely different matter that in no way addresses the actions [that were] *taken* by the Defendants prior to the time when the complaint *was filed*.

After   Whether the Library must return the Burgdorfs' gift because it has renamed the Burgdorf Lecture Hall is an entirely separate matter from the Defendants' actions before the filing of this lawsuit.

---

* C. Edward Good, *Mightier Than the Sword* 126–28 (1989) (I've paraphrased and re-ordered his points).

31

Uncover buried verbs—especially words ending in *-tion*.

Quotable Quotes

"Turgid flabby English is full of abstract nouns; the commonest ending of abstract nouns is *-tion*, and to count the *-ion* words in what one has written, or, better, to cultivate an ear that without special orders challenges them as they come, is one of the simplest and most effective means of making oneself less unreadable. It is as an unfailing sign of a nouny abstract style that a cluster of *-ion* words is chiefly to be dreaded."

—H.W. Fowler, *A Dictionary of Modern English Usage* 640
(Ernest Gowers ed., 2d ed. 1965).

"Wordy writing not only droops from weak verbs but sags under bulky nouns—especially long Latinate ones with endings like *tion* and *ment* and *ence*."

—Claire K. Cook, *Line by Line: How to Improve Your Own Writing* 6 (1985).

"To Michelangelo, every piece of marble had a form hidden in it. He had only to chisel through to reveal a Pietà or a Moses. So it is with verbs hidden in and weighted down by noun forms like these:

negotiation
administration
documentation
utilization
transmittal

" 'Mr. Jones had the company's authorization' is correct, but 'The company authorized Mr. Jones' is better. 'They made a determination of' is correct, but 'They determined' is better."

—Miriam Kass, "The Ba Theory of Persuasive Writing," in *Appellate Practice Manual*
179, 180–81 (Priscilla A. Schwab ed., 1992).

"Why uncover buried verbs? Three reasons are detectable to the naked eye: first, you generally eliminate prepositions in the process; second, you often eliminate *be*-verbs by replacing them with so-called 'action' verbs; and third, you humanize the text by saying who does what (an idea often obscured by buried verbs). The fourth reason is not detectable to the naked eye: in fact, it is the sum of the three reasons already mentioned. By uncovering buried verbs, you make your writing much less abstract—it becomes easier for readers to visualize what you're talking about."

—Bryan A. Garner, *A Dictionary of Modern Legal Usage* 123 (2d ed. 1995).

Explanation

A "buried verb" isn't really a verb at all. It's a noun created by a verb—the verb has been buried in the longer noun. Usually, a buried verb ends in one of the following suffixes: *-tion, -sion, -ment, -ence, -ance, -ity.* Whenever the true verb will work in context, the better choice is to use it instead of the buried verb. Thus:

The Verb Buried	*The Verb Uncovered*
allegation	allege
assistance	assist
compulsion	compel
conformity	conform
enforcement	enforce
examination	examine
indemnification	indemnify
knowledge	know
litigation	litigate
obligation	obligate, oblige
opposition	oppose
performance	perform
preference	prefer
settlement	settle
transportation	transport

Why do lawyers like buried verbs so much? It might have something to do with Jeremy Bentham, who wrote about what he dubbed the "noun-preferring principle." Bentham thought that you should always choose a noun over a verb.

But there's no reason to think that Bentham carried any particular weight on this point: he was probably describing an age-old lawyerly bias. As a group, we've historically preferred writing about static things—abstract static things—over people's actions. And that should tell you something about why so much legal writing is as dull as it is.

If you want to be fresh and punchy and memorable, though, you'll have to try the "verb-preferring principle." Given the choice between a noun and a verb, choose the verb. Given the choice between a *-ion* word and an *-ing* word, choose the *-ing* word. Almost every time you do it, you'll eliminate a prepositional phrase; you'll avoid *be*-verbs; and you'll force yourself to be more concrete about people performing actions (not, mind you, *about the performance of actions*).

Some Before-and-After Examples

Example A

Before   Zelman alleges that the Caswell Company's actions are in *violation* of the Americans with Disabilities Act.

After   Zelman alleges that the Caswell Company's actions violate the Americans with Disabilities Act.

Example B

Before   The court placed principal *reliance* on its findings that the *existence* of official signs and state and national flags on the building gave the *appearance* of a government stamp of *approval* on discriminatory conduct and that the city, through its lease, derived a financial *benefit* from the restaurant's *discrimination*.

After   The court relied principally on its findings that signs, as well as state and national flags, hung from the building, making it appear that the government approved discriminatory conduct and that the city, through its lease, benefited financially from the restaurant's *discrimination*.

Example C

Before   Plaintiff's lawsuit is predicated on her *dissatisfaction* with the Company's *response* to her *complaint* regarding her former supervisor, Monty Crump.

After   Moore sued because she was dissatisfied with how the Company responded when she complained about her former supervisor, Monty Crump.

Example D

Before   The IRS has suspended the *issuance* of *determination* letters with respect to the *qualification* of an ESOP under the Tax Reform Act of 1986.

After   The IRS has stopped issuing *determination* letters on whether an ESOP qualifies under the Tax Reform Act of 1986.

Example E

Before   Those *allegations* include *violations* of failing to provide *documentation* specifically required by the Act, failing to provide proper *identification* showing the name of a professional solicitor during *solicitation* campaigns, failing to sign required *documentation* prior to filing same, and entering into contracts with professional solicitors without the benefit of *registration*.

After   In particular, the Burber Club failed to provide documents specifically required by the Act, failed to identify the professional solicitor properly while soliciting, failed to sign required papers before filing them, and contracted with unregistered solicitors.

32

When given the choice between a passive-voice verb and a buried verb, choose the passive voice.

Quotable Quote

"[T]he language is overrun by a plague of nouns, most of them ending in 'ion,' with the result that formal writing (reports, public speaking, scholarship, even fiction) becomes a string of nouns weakly tied together by prepositions and connective phrases of the type 'as far as . . . is concerned' and 'in terms of.' This sort of writing, easy to write and dull to read, is the surest protection against the critical analysis of thought."

—Jacques Barzun, *The House of Intellect* 233 (1959).

"Though long neglected in books about writing, buried verbs ought to be a sworn enemy of every serious writer. In legal writing, they constitute a more serious problem even than passive voice—whether in analytical writing, persuasive writing, or drafting."

—Bryan A. Garner, *A Dictionary of Modern Legal Usage* 123 (2d ed. 1995).

Explanation

We hear a lot about passive voice. For the most part, it deserves its bad press. But we don't hear much about buried verbs (or "nominalizations," to use the English teacher's jargon).

This is a curious state of affairs because every observant editor notices the frequency with which you must choose either the buried verb or the passive-voice construction. And 90% of the time when you're faced with this dilemma, the better choice is passive voice. See for yourself in the examples below.

Some Before-and-After Examples

Example A

Before   The Internal Revenue Code provides rules governing *the taxation of* ESOPs.

After   The Internal Revenue Code provides rules governing how ESOPs *are taxed*.

Example B

Before   Abraham's transfer took place on July 18, 1995, prior to *the announcement of* any layoffs.

After   Abraham's transfer took place on July 18, 1995, before any layoffs *were announced*.

Example C

Before   Prior to *the promotion of* Ms. Hall to the position of Laboratory Assistant Administrator, she worked as a Medical Technologist in the lab.

After   Before Ms. Hall *was promoted* to laboratory assistant administrator, she worked as a medical technologist in the lab.

Example D

Before   Horne alleges that the commissioner did not inform Horne that, six months after the *completion of* the audit, the General Assembly revised the revenue statutes.

After   Horne alleges that the commissioner did not inform him that, six months after the audit *was completed*, the General Assembly revised the revenue statutes.

Example E

Before   Wholesale Silks asks the Arbitrator to issue an order denying Brogna's motion to dismiss and requiring Brogna to serve an answer within seven days after *service of* the Arbitrator's ruling.

After   Wholesale Silks asks the Arbitrator to deny Brogna's motion to dismiss and require Brogna to serve an answer within seven days after *being served with* the Arbitrator's ruling.

33

Eliminate unnecessary prepositional phrases—especially those beginning with *of*.

Quotable Quotes

"[I]t is certain that our sentences can easily sound like a stick being drawn along railings; we could condone our clusters of little prepositions if they firmly surrounded and placed their nouns in an indisputable context, but they have multiple meanings, and when used irresponsibly they jam the traffic of their sentences. 'For me, for example, for years the question has been as to whether in the event of . . .' is the kind of rambling that constitutes the real menace of the preposition—not whether it is used to end a sentence with."
—Basil Cottle, *The Plight of English* 13 (1975).

"The overuse of prepositions is a severe and extremely common fault. Indeed, if I wanted to offer a single rule for improving the quality of writing, I would unhesitatingly say, Reduce the number of prepositions."
—Lester S. King, *Why Not Say It Clearly* 34 (1978).

"However innocuous it may appear, the word *of* is, in anything other than small doses, among the surest indicators of flabby writing. . . . The only suitable vaccination is to cultivate a hardy skepticism about its utility in any given context. If it proves itself, fine. Often, though, it will fail to do so."
—Bryan A. Garner, *A Dictionary of Modern Legal Usage* 612 (2d ed. 1995).

Explanation

When Dr. John R. Trimble—the great editing maven at the University of Texas—first told me that we should encourage legal writers to focus on eliminating as many *of*-phrases as possible, I scoffed. The advice seemed simplistic.

The amazing thing is that it works quite well, in passage after passage. When I was working on the Federal Rules of Appellate Procedure in 1995, I encountered the phrase *the principal office of the clerk of the court of appeals*. In the revision adopted in 1998, that phrase became *the circuit clerk's principal office*. It went from 11 words to 5.

You won't always cut more than half the words in a phrase, but your savings will usually be significant. And once you sensitize yourself to the flabbiness that *of* signals, you'll achieve a much leaner style.

Other prepositions help propagate clutter, to be sure, but *of* is the prime offender. Scrutinize its every appearance.

Some Before-and-After Examples

Example A

Before   Defendant is contending that delays **on** the part **of** Penney have resulted **in** delays **by** Defendant. [16 words: 4 prepositions]

After   Kosko claims that Penney's delays have caused Kosko's delays. [9 words: no prepositions]

Example B

Before   The facts **of** this case indicate that the Penate Corporation, **of** which Burgos was the CEO, allegedly bribed certain officials **of** the State Department **of** Taxation and Finance to resolve some tax problems **of** the Corporation. During the course **of** the investigation **into** the alleged illegal activity, the SEC alleged **in** its indictment **of** Burgos that he failed to disclose **in** the proxy statement **of** the corporation that he was a member **of** a conspiracy to bribe said officials. [79 words: 12 prepositions]

After   The facts show that the Penate Corporation, **of** which Burgos was the CEO, allegedly bribed certain state officials to resolve some corporate tax problems. While investigating the alleged illegal activity, the SEC indicted Burgos, alleging that he failed to disclose **in** the Penate Corporation's proxy statement that he had conspired to bribe those state officials. [55 words: 2 prepositions]

Example C

Before   In this case, there is a substantial risk that the current collection arrangement **with** Woolverton will be deemed a violation **of** the FDCPA. Many courts have found that the use **of** another party's letterhead, **without** actual participation **by** that party **in** the collection **of** the debt, is a deceptive practice **in** violation **of** Sections 1692e and 1692j, subjecting both the creditor and the flat-rater **to** liability. [67 words: 10 prepositions]

After   The current collection arrangement **with** Woolverton may well be found to violate the FDCPA. Many courts have found that using another party's letterhead, **without** that party's actually helping to collect the debt, is a deceptive practice that violates §§ 1692e and 1692j, subjecting both the creditor and the flat-rater **to** liability. [52 words: 3 prepositions]

34

Don't separate a short subject from its verb with a modifying phrase. Instead, start the sentence with the modifier.

Quotable Quotes

"Be compact; do not put a strain on your reader's memory by widely separating parts of a sentence that are closely related to one another."
—Sir Ernest Gowers, *The Complete Plain Words* 37 (1954; repr. 1964).

"Don't *interrupt* subject and verb with intervening subordinate constructions and modifiers."
—Walker Gibson, *Tough, Sweet & Stuffy* 108 (1966).

"Whenever you write a long sentence, . . . be sure that you have not so separated the subject and the verb that the reader forgets who before learning what."
—Miriam Kass, "The Ba Theory of Persuasive Writing," in *Appellate Practice Manual* 179, 183 (Priscilla A. Schwab ed., 1992).

Explanation

The core words in a sentence are the subject and the verb. They are related both in sense and in grammar. And related words should go together. If you separate them very much, the sentence goes asunder.

Although it's sometimes necessary to modify a subject with an interruptive phrase—and to highlight the phrase by doing so (see #57)—writers too often lump words between the subject and verb with no special purpose in mind. Look at the first example below. Notice how long it takes to get from each subject to its corresponding verb—all the qualifiers get in the way. Indeed, the writer had the same problem matching parts of speech.

Try putting any modifying phrases at the beginning of the sentence, so that the subject and verb can remain together. Amateur writers consider the move counterintuitive, but it works.

A Typically Bad Example

Consideration of the legal and factual elements of their claims and the corresponding defenses, as well as the language of the insurance policies at issue, *reveals* that Plaintiffs' *knowledge* of the extent, if any, to which its activities and operations resulted in, or were likely to result in, environmental contamination, as well as the knowledge of when, if ever, such contamination occurred and when Plaintiffs first had knowledge of such contamination, *are* [read *is*] of central relevance.

Some Before-and-After Examples

Example A

Before   *Defendant*, in his motion, *has represented* to the Court that he has complied with all outstanding discovery requests.

After   In his motion, Fowlkes has represented to the Court that he has complied with all outstanding discovery requests.

Example B

Before   *The court*, in reaching this conclusion, first *discussed O'Neil v. Quilter*, in which the Texas Supreme Court had found a three-room house, built by a tenant, to be removable.

After   In reaching this conclusion, the court first discussed *O'Neil v. Quilter*, in which the Texas Supreme Court had found a three-room house, built by a tenant, to be removable.

Example C

Before   *The cases* on which Nikka Corporation relies, dealing with the narrow question of whether state statutes of frauds can bar 10b-5 claims predicated on otherwise valid contracts, *do not dictate* a contrary result.

After   Nikka Corporation relies on cases dealing with the narrow question whether state statutes of frauds can bar 10b-5 claims predicated on otherwise valid contracts. These cases do not dictate a contrary result.

Example D

Before   In *Barber v. SMH (US), Inc.*, 9 I.E.R. Cases 244 (1993), the Michigan Court of Appeals held that the plaintiff's *reliance* on a statement made by defendant that "as long as [he] was profitable and doing the job for Defendant, [he] would be Defendant's exclusive representative" as establishing an oral contract for just-cause employment *was* misplaced.

After   In *Barber v. SMH (US), Inc.,*[7] the plaintiff claimed reliance on the defendant's statement that "as long as [he] was profitable and doing the job for Defendant, [he] would be Defendant's exclusive representative." According to the plaintiff, this statement established an oral contract for just-cause employment. But the Michigan Court of Appeals rejected this claim.

Example E

Before   *The interests* of Fizell's children, who have been hanging in temporary-care limbo since 2001, *are* paramount.

After   The interests of Fizell's children are paramount. They have been hanging in temporary-care limbo since 2001.

35

Don't separate a verb from its object.

Quotable Quotes

"[A] frequent offence against ease [is] that caused by the separation of words [that] belong together in meaning, such as subject and verb, verb and object . . . ."

—Adams Sherman Hill, *The Principles of Rhetoric* 203 (rev. ed. 1896).

"[R]emember to keep the object of a verb close to the verb. In the negative, do not let a gap disrupt the natural relationship a transitive verb has with its object."

—C. Edward Good, *Mightier Than the Sword* 29 (1989).

"In seeking to understand a sentence, the reader's mind searches for the subject, the verb, and the object. If those three elements are set out in that order and close together in the sentence, then the reader will understand quickly."

—Richard C. Wydick, *Plain English for Lawyers* 43 (4th ed. 1998).

Explanation

The rationale for the previous tip applies here as well. After encountering a verb, the reader naturally expects the verb's object to follow close behind. Put any modifying phrases before the subject or after the object.

Some Before-and-After Examples

Example A

Before   Bradley *testified* in his February 8, 1995 deposition *that* he did not know the law had changed and *that* he thought the plaintiff was paying the bills correctly.

After   In his February 1995 deposition, Bradley testified that he did not know the law had changed and that he thought Adams was paying the bills correctly.

Example B

Before   After the Supreme Court's decision, this Court *granted*, over the United States' vehement objection, *plaintiffs' motion* for leave to amend their complaint.

After   After the Supreme Court's decision—and over the United States' vehement objection—this Court granted the Rittenberrys' motion for leave to amend their complaint.

36

To write forcefully, end your sentences with punch.

Quotable Quotes

"The emphatic position in a sentence is the end; the beginning is also an emphatic position, although to a less degree."
  —Margaret M. Bryant & Janet Rankin Aiken, *The Psychology of English* 172 (1940).

"[T]he most emphatic place in clause or sentence is the end. This is the climax; and, during the momentary pause that follows, that last word continues, as it were, to reverberate in the reader's mind. It has, in fact, the last word. One should therefore think twice about what one puts at a sentence-end."
  —F.L. Lucas, *Style* 39–40 (1955).

"A sentence must be so written that the punch word comes at the end."
  —Karl Llewellyn, *A Lecture on Appellate Advocacy*, 29 U. Chi. L. Rev. 627, 628 (1962).

"[A] word or phrase gains importance by being placed at the beginning or the end of a sentence. The end is the more important position of the two, for the sentence that trails off in a string of modifiers runs downhill in interest. By saving an important part of the predicate till the end, you emphasize the main idea."
  —Alan H. Vrooman, *Good Writing: An Informal Manual of Style* 131 (1967).

"The strongest stress falls naturally at the beginning and at the end, and it is at these points that the important words or ideas are properly placed. Of the two positions, the last is most emphatic. (If I had said, 'The last is the most emphatic of the two positions,' the sentence would have been less forceful, since it would have ended with an unimportant word.)"
  —Ellsworth Barnard, *English for Everybody* 110 (1979).

"A writer who wants a sentence with punch will generally avoid putting flabby elements at the end, and will prefer . . . having the main accent at the end."
  —Dwight Bolinger, *Language: The Loaded Weapon* 178 (1980).

"Because the end of a sentence is the last thing a reader sees, it is a position of emphasis. Don't use it to express minor thoughts or casual information. Don't write 'Both candidates will appear here in July, if we can believe the reports.' (This is correct only if you want to stress the doubtfulness of the reports.) Don't write 'Pray for the repose of the soul of John Bowler, who died last week in Cleveland.' (Your reader will start wondering what he was doing in Cleveland.)"

—Daniel McDonald, *The Language of Argument* 219 (5th ed. 1986).

"Make your sentences rise to a climax: let them reveal their most significant information at the end."

—David L. Carroll, *A Manual of Writer's Tricks* 63 (2d ed. 1995).

"Try to arrange sentences so that the most important words or ideas come at the end."

—Christopher Lasch, *Plain Style* 81 (Stewart Weaver ed., 2002).

Explanation

Every sentence is a crescendo. The point eludes many people: the primary position of emphasis in an English sentence is not at the beginning, but at the end. Whatever you put there will get special attention.

This means that we can deduce the following general rules:

- Don't end a sentence with a date unless the date is critical.

- Don't end with a citation unless the case name is critical.

- Don't end with a client's name unless it comes as a surprise.

- Don't end with a qualifying phrase such as *in many circumstances*, *generally speaking*, or the like.

One way of testing how effective your sentence-ends are is to read aloud, exaggerating the last word in each sentence. If the reading sounds foolish, then the sentence probably needs to be recast.

Some Before-and-After Examples

Example A

Before   Significantly, Gutierrez did not identify his ex-girlfriend, her brother, or LouAnne Burger as persons with knowledge of relevant facts in his Routine Discovery submitted pursuant to Local Rule 26.

After   Significantly, in his discovery under Local Rule 26, Gutierrez did not identify his ex-girlfriend, her brother, or LouAnne Burger as persons with knowledge of relevant facts.

Example B

Before   At the time when Paul's plane hit the ground, Paul's wife Betty was helping a friend with a garage sale. Shortly after the accident, Betty received a call from Billy Nugent. He came by and drove Betty to her parents' house, where she was told of the death of her husband about thirty minutes earlier.

After   Betty, Paul's wife, was helping a friend with a garage sale when Paul's plane crashed. Shortly after the accident, Betty received a call from Billy Nugent, a family friend, who came by and drove her to her parents' house. There she learned that Paul had just died.

Example C

Before   For example, in *Steenbergen*, defendants produced numerous documents in response to plaintiffs' request for production. 814 S.W.2d at 759. Several documents were created by others or could not be verified as accurate or authentic. *Id.* The court indicated that "[p]roduction of these documents expressed nothing more than Ford's belief that they contained information on passive restraints as described in [plaintiffs'] request." *Id.* at 760. Thus, the documents were properly excluded since no authenticating testimony was given. *Id.*

After   For example, in *Steenbergen*, defendants produced many documents at plaintiffs' request. 814 S.W.2d at 759. Several either were created by others or could not be verified as accurate or authentic. *Id.* The court said that "[p]roduction of these documents expressed nothing more than Ford's belief that they contained information on passive restraints as described in [plaintiffs'] request." *Id.* at 760. But since no witness could authenticate the documents, they were properly excluded. *Id.*

Example D

Before   The Buick being operated by Mr. Warren was owned by Neva Chowning and was being operated with the consent and permission of Ms. Chowning.

After   Warren was driving the Buick with the owner's permission.

Example E

Before   This action was filed in the state district courts of Dallas County, Texas by Data Security on May 22, 1995. In addition to seeking damages under various business-tort causes of action, Data Security sought injunctive relief against Nautica International. In the three weeks that followed, Data Security pursued discovery at breakneck speed in the course of obtaining temporary injunctive relief against Nautica International.

After   Data Security filed this action in the state district courts of Dallas County in May 1995. Besides seeking damages under various business-tort theories, Data Security sought an injunction. And in the three weeks that followed, Data Security pursued discovery at breakneck speed.

Example F

Before   It is undisputed that Deckard had no role in the decision whether to rehire Plaintiff in 1993.

After   It is undisputed that Deckard had no role in deciding whether to rehire Kirkland.

Example G

Before   **BRIEF OF KLUWER MUTUAL INSURANCE COMPANY IN OPPOSITION TO FIVEASH'S MOTION FOR SUMMARY JUDGMENT**

I. The Manifestation Rule Governs This Case.

After Kluwer briefed its Motion for Summary Judgment, a Georgia court issued a highly significant "trigger" ruling. *See Plantation Pipeline Co. v. Lumbermans Mut. Casualty Co.*, No. D-92719 (Ga. Super. Ct., Fulton Cty., Oct. 7, 1994) (Ex. 67). *Plantation Pipeline* is the first and only Georgia authority to trigger coverage for environmental-property-damage cases. The court for Fulton County, Georgia, ruled that the manifestation rule governed an environmental-property-damage case. *Plantation Pipeline* involved petroleum contamination.

Contrary to Fiveash's assertion, the manifestation rule is hardly a "dead letter." The *Plantation Pipeline* case shows that courts continue to adopt the manifestation rule for environmental-property-damage cases. *See also New Hampshire Ball Bearings v. Aetna Casualty*, 848 F. Supp. 1082 (D.N.H. 1994) (holding that the date on which coverage is triggered is the time when the contamination of the groundwater was reasonably capable of discovery). Fiveash refers to a section of an article published by the Defense Research Institute ("DRI"), which Fiveash identifies as "Whither Manifestation?" This one-and-a-half page tract does not state that an overwhelming number of courts reject the manifestation rule. The article notes that California has already adopted manifestation as the trigger rule for first-party property-damage cases. *See Prudential-LMI Commercial Ins. Co. v. Superior Court*, 51 Cal. 3d 674 (1990). The article also cites North Carolina and South Carolina cases, a Fourth Circuit case, and others that adopt the manifestation rule.

After   **Kluwer's Brief in Opposition to Fiveash's Motion for Summary Judgment**

1. The manifestation rule governs because Georgia courts have adopted it.

Fiveash brought its bad-faith claim merely because Kluwer has relied on the manifestation rule in this environmental-property-damage case. Although Fiveash claims that this rule is insupportable and baseless, the only Georgia case on point—*Plantation Pipeline*,[1] which was decided only last month—adopts this very rule. In light of this precedent, Fiveash's motion for summary judgment on the bad-faith claim should fail.

37

Cut filler phrases such as *there is* and *there are.*

Quotable Quotes

"The habit of beginning statements with the impersonal and usually vague *there is* or *there are* shoves the really significant verb into a subordinate place instead of letting it stand vigorously on its own feet."
—David Lambuth et al., *The Golden Book on Writing* 19 (1964).

"The trouble with 'there' has nothing to do with grammar or with 'correctness' of any kind. It's a perfectly proper word, and it moves in the best circles; you will find it in abundance in the work of the most distinguished writers. But the fact remains that it is one of the most insidious enemies a beginning writer faces in his search for style. It is the enemy of style because it seldom adds anything but clutter to a sentence. And nothing saps the vitality of language as quickly as meaningless clutter."
—Lucile Vaughan Payne, *The Lively Art of Writing* 64–65 (1965).

Explanation

When you need to talk about the existence of something, you'll need *there is* or *there are*. For example:

> Despite what Jackson claims, there is a good reason for this rule.

> There are several possible objections to this question.

But most of the time when you see one of these phrases, you'd be better off cutting it. By doing that, you'll almost certainly supply the sentence with a stronger verb, and you'll eliminate some unnecessary words.

Some Before-and-After Examples

Example A

Before   *There are* three reasons why the Court should overrule that case.

After   The Court should overrule that case for three reasons.

Example B

Before   *There is* no medical evidence to contradict Dr. Goodman's opinion that an award should be apportioned 50% to the special fund and 50% to the employer.

After   No medical evidence refutes Dr. Goodman's opinion that an award should be apportioned 50% to the special fund and 50% to the employer.

Example C

Before   To date, *there have been no such third-party actions* in the Hunt County suit.

After   To date, no third-party actions have been filed in the Hunt County suit.

Example D

Before   *It is* apparent that the parties to the agreement did not intend that Fortas Inc. could sue for its breach.

After   The parties did not intend that Fortas Inc. could sue for breach of the agreement.

38

Eliminate throat-clearing phrases.

Quotable Quotes

" 'I might add,' 'It should be pointed out,' 'It is interesting to note that'—how many sentences begin with these dreary clauses announcing what the writer is going to do next? If you might add, add it. If it should be pointed out, point it out. If it is interesting to note, *make* it interesting. Being told that something is interesting is the surest way of tempting the reader to find it dull . . . ."
—William Zinsser, *On Writing Well* 16–17 (5th ed. 1994).

"Make every word tell. Rooting out verbiage isn't easy; verbosity often results from quick, facile writing. Watch out for recurrent phrases that are the verbal equivalent of throat-clearing; for example:

> In my considered opinion, ...
> May I respectfully suggest that . . . .
> I should note here that it would be helpful to remember the fact that . . . .
> It should not be forgotten that . . . .
> It is also of importance to bear in mind the following considerations . . . .
> Consideration should be given to the possibility of carrying into effect . . . .

"These needless buildups wrap the reader's mind in wool before the point can be made. Forget the opening flourish and say what you mean."
—Bryan A. Garner, *The Elements of Legal Style* 53–54 (2d ed. 2002).

Explanation

The English language is full of phrases that allow you to make noises as you prepare to say something. For example:

> It is important to remember that . . . .
> It is noteworthy that . . . .
> It is not unworthy of mention in this regard to note that . . . .
> It must also be borne in mind that . . . .

These may have a place in speech, which is almost always wordier than good writing. They can warm up the speaker's sentence.

    But in writing they take up precious space. They're symptomatic of a verbal tic with which some writers are afflicted. The good news is that if you can recognize the tic, it's easy enough to rid yourself of it.

Some Before-and-After Examples

Example A

Before   *It is respectfully submitted that* genuine issues of material fact remain such that defendant's motion for summary judgment must be denied.

After   Because genuine issues of material fact remain, this court should deny Taylor's motion for summary judgment.

Example B

Before   *It should be noted that* a vast majority of the value of the sale proceeds came from the Historical Society's collection of European paintings and decorative arts—the maintenance of which was contributing very little to the study of the history of New York.

After   The sale proceeds came mostly from the Historical Society's collection of European paintings and decorative arts—the maintenance of which was contributing little to the study of New York history.

Example C

Before   *It is important to note that* the exclusive-benefit and prudence rules outlined in ERISA § 404(a)(1) apply also to ESOPs.

After   The exclusive-benefit and prudence rules outlined in ERISA § 404(a)(1) apply also to ESOPs.

Other Typical Examples

- *It should be noted that* the Second Circuit in *Flickinger* went on to hold that plaintiff failed to show the required element of "deceitful intent" on the part of the fiduciary; therefore, the claim was properly rejected.

- *It is beyond dispute that* an employee's personnel file is confidential and that production of such a file in litigation involving third parties invades the employee's privacy rights.

- The court reasoned that *there is no doubt that* the four-year statute of limitations applies to a written contract for the sale of goods.

39

Ruthlessly cut unnecessary words.

Quotable Quotes

"It is an amiable maxim that words which add nothing to the sense or to the clearness must diminish the force of the expression."
—George Campbell, *Philosophy of Rhetoric* (1776) (as quoted in Alfred Ayres, *The Verbalist* vi (rev. ed. 1911)).

"The great vice in the style of almost all our modern philosophers and anti-philosophers is prolixity. A noteworthy example is the *System of Nature*. In this obscure book there are four times too many words; and it is in part on this account that it is so obscure."
—Voltaire, "Style," in *Theories of Style in Literature* 180, 185 (Lane Cooper ed., 1923).

"Wherever we can make twenty-five words do the work of fifty, we halve the area in which looseness and disorganization can flourish, and by reducing the span of attention required we increase the force of the thought. To make our words count for as much as possible is surely the simplest as well as the hardest secret of style."
—Wilson Follett, *Modern American Usage* 14 (1966).

"Unnecessary words waste space and the reader's time, and they make strong writing weak."
—Gary Blake & Robert W. Bly, *The Elements of Technical Writing* 65 (1993).

"Once you develop a distaste for surplus words, you will find many word-wasting idioms that can be trimmed from your sentences with no loss of meaning."
—Richard C. Wydick, *Plain English for Lawyers* 14 (4th ed. 1998).

Explanation

When you use fewer words to express an idea, you enhance your writing's speed, clarity, and impact. Conversely, when you use more words than necessary, you make the writing slower, less clear, and less emphatic.

That's why you should take it seriously whenever someone points out a shorter way of saying something. You save here and there, and soon your savings will grow into something quite valuable.

Some Before-and-After Examples

Example A

Before   Inferentially, the decision of the *Champlin* court can be read to stand for the proposition that mere ownership of property in a county does not establish venue where employees operate out of that property only on a sporadic basis. [39 words]

After   *Champlin* suggests that a company's merely owning property in a county does not establish venue if employees work there only sporadically. [21 words: a 46% saving]

Example B

Before   Since December 2, 1995, certain of Plaintiff's experts have promulgated a new theory regarding the case that had not been expressed by them at the time Defendants were determining which of Plaintiff's experts would be deposed or at the time Defendants deposed Plaintiff's experts. [44 words]

After   Some of Miles's experts have recently expressed a new theory that was unknown to Pantor when deposing Miles's experts. [19 words: a 57% saving]

Example C (from the same brief as the passage in Example B)

Before   This theory is a drastic departure from that put forth by Plaintiff at the time his experts were deposed by Defendants. [21 words]

After   This theory differs radically from Miles's earlier one. [8 words: a 62% saving]

Example D

Before   Mr. Sutherlin wholly fails to plead Alger Life Insurance's knowledge of any alleged falsity nor does Mr. Sutherlin plead any intent on the part of Alger Life to defraud. [29 words]

After   Sutherlin does not plead that Alger Life knew about an alleged falsity or intended to defraud. [16 words: a 45% saving]

Example E

Before   If there was any doubt on this issue, it is eliminated by observing Defendants' conduct after they actually received formal notice from Edgerton. The evidence is clear that they did not convert to an allegedly noninfringing alternative in a timely manner, but rather continued to invest in infringing molds and converted only when forced to by an exclusion order issued by the ITC. From the objective evidence, it is apparent that Defendants would have followed the same course of conduct regardless of what Edgerton did or did not do. Thus, Defendants cannot show that they acted to their detriment because of any delay by Edgerton, thereby precluding a finding of material prejudice necessary to prevail on a laches defense. [119 words]

After   Most telling, though, is Defendants' conduct after they received formal notice from Edgerton. Instead of timely converting to a noninfringing alternative, they continued to invest in infringing molds and converted only when forced to by an ITC exclusion order. Thus, Defendants would have followed the same course of conduct regardless of what Edgerton did or did not do. Since they cannot show that they acted to their detriment because of any delay by Edgerton, they are precluded from showing the material prejudice necessary to prevail on a laches defense. [89 words: a 25% saving]

Example F

Before   But assuming arguendo that plaintiff and defendant are parties to the unilateral contract plaintiff alleges in the second breach-of-contract cause of action, and assuming arguendo that in this cause Mr. Swanson's form of pleading is legally sufficient, the cause is nonetheless foreclosed and must be dismissed because this is fundamentally a dispute in the employee-employer relationship, governed by the employment agreement alone. [65 words]

After   But even if Swanson and Bognar were somehow parties to a unilateral contract, and even if Swanson had pleaded adequately, the case would still be foreclosed because the employment agreement alone governs. [32 words: a 51% saving]

Example G

Before   With respect to matters not covered by the provisions of the Uniform Rules for the Court of Claims (the "Uniform Rules"), the Court of Claims adheres to the rules set forth in the Civil Practice Law and Rules (the "CPLR"). Ct. Cl. R. § 206.1(c). Because the Uniform Rules do not discuss disclosure of expert witnesses, it follows that the Court of Claims' rules on the subject are governed by the CPLR. [72 words]

After   On matters not covered by its Uniform Rules, the Court of Claims follows the Civil Practice Law and Rules ("CPLR"). And because the Uniform Rules do not discuss the disclosure of expert witnesses, the CPLR governs. [36 words: a 50% saving]

Example H

Before   Courts have addressed the scope of the attorney's duty to preserve client confidences in cases where the attorney's duty of confidentiality to a former client potentially conflicts with the duty of confidentiality to a present client. In such a case, ... [36 words]

After   Sometimes a lawyer owes conflicting duties of confidentiality to former and present clients. In such a case, ... [13 words: a 64% saving]

40

Keep your sentences to one main thought, but combine related sentences if doing so will minimize choppiness.

Quotable Quotes

"When several short sentences, each of which is a unit in itself, are so closely connected in thought as to form parts of a larger unit, they may be put into one sentence."
—Adams Sherman Hill, *The Principles of Rhetoric* 212 (rev. ed. 1896).

"It is . . . necessary to avoid putting each idea into a separate sentence. Study to see which is the main thought; then group within one sentence the ideas naturally belonging with it."
—Helen J. Robins & Agnes F. Perkins, *An Introduction to the Study of Rhetoric* 232 (2d ed. 1921).

"Embedding [clauses and phrases] . . . is an effective way of combining complicated units of meaning into a single sentence. This operation allows you to squeeze an entire sentence or phrase into one of the noun slots of a main clause."
—Gary A. Olson et al., *Style and Readability in Business Writing* 63 (1985).

"Good writers avoid the choppy style caused by using too many short, subject-first sentences. . . . As you combine short, choppy sentences . . . , you will be learning to achieve a more fluent style, richer in variety and interest."
—John E. Warriner, *English Composition and Grammar* 386–87 (1988).

"In my own editing, I'm guided by the following principle: '*If a sentence carries too little information to warrant grammatical independence, treat it as a scrap.*' When I find such a starveling, I convert it into a subordinate clause and embed it in a neighboring sentence. Do this and you'll see it yields five advantages: it saves words, reduces choppiness, makes your sentences meatier, finds you a home for details not worth a separate statement, and shows the reader which of two ideas you count the more important."
—John R. Trimble, *Editing Your Own Prose* (forthcoming).

Explanation

One idea to a sentence: that's what you commonly hear. But in fact, if you were to try to hold to that advice, it would spoil your style. No longer would you be able to capitalize on one of the most important devices known to writers: subordination. You want one *main* thought, but there might be some well-chosen minor points as well.

As Trimble suggests, convert a "starveling"—a short sentence that says little—into a subordinate clause and merge it with another sentence. The examples below illustrate this method.

Also, of course, you can minimize unfavorable facts in this way. For example, "Although Dulgar was a confessed felon, ..."

Some Before-and-After Examples

Example A

Before   Section 5(A)(2) prohibits an employer from discharging an employee "during a period of temporary total disability." However, Section 5(A)(2) did not become effective until September 1, 1992.

After   Although § 5(A)(2) prohibits an employer from discharging an employee "during a period of temporary total disability," this provision did not become effective until September 1, 1992.

Example B

Before   Third, there are no extraordinary circumstances to support setting aside the court's judgment. Consequently, there is no basis either to reconsider the Court's decision or to grant Reynolds leave to amend his complaint.

After   Third, in the absence of extraordinary circumstances, the Court should not reconsider its decision or grant Reynolds leave to amend his complaint.

Example C

Before   During her employment, Eisenstadt never saw any writing that placed any restriction on MOX's right to terminate her employment. Further, no oral statements were ever made to Eisenstadt restricting MOX's right to terminate her employment.

After   During her employment, Eisenstadt never saw any writing—and no one ever told her anything—that restricted MOX's right to terminate her employment.

Example D

Before   True, Eisenstadt was employed by MOX for more than ten years and received certain promotions and pay increases. However, promotions and salary increases are common occurrences for an employee who remains with an employer for very long.

After   Although Eisenstadt was employed by MOX for more than ten years and received promotions and pay increases, these rewards are common occurrences for an employee who remains with an employer for very long.

41

Use parallel constructions whenever you can—but make sure the ideas are really parallel.

Quotable Quotes

"One of the first requisites for the writing of good clean sentences is to have acquired the art of enumeration, that is, of stringing together three or four words or phrases of identical grammatical value without going wrong."
—H.W. Fowler, *A Dictionary of Modern English Usage* 142 (1926).

"Everyone who tries to write—at least, everyone not afflicted with what is sometimes called a tin ear—has a degree of natural instinct for putting like thoughts into like constructions. Some have the instinct *in excelsis*. . . . [But] most of us possess the instinct for matching parts in no more than a variable and inferior degree and must strengthen it by self-discipline and taking thought."
—Wilson Follett, *Modern American Usage* 211 (1966).

"Of all the major structural blunders, the fault in parallelism is the most tenacious. It hangs on even in rather sophisticated styles, long after the writer has ceased to commit such barbarities as dangling modifiers, agreement errors, reference errors, and case-form errors."
—Bertrand Evans, "Grammar and Writing," in *A Linguistics Reader* 111, 122 (Graham Wilson ed., 1967).

"[W]hen one reads a sentence in which two or more elements are compared, contrasted, joined, listed, or in any way presented to the mind as parallels, comprehension is quicker and smoother if the verbal forms presenting those elements to our view are also parallel. . . . Matching serves the reader's convenience by enabling him to anticipate intelligently."
—Jacques Barzun, *Simple & Direct* 131 (1975).

"How do you make ideas parallel? In a series, all the items should be alike, whether all nouns, all gerunds, all infinitives, all phrases or all clauses. If a series of verbs is used, they should all be in the same tense, voice and mood. Subjects of parallel clauses should be in the same person and number. When

two phrasal prepositions or conjunctions are used together, both need to be present in their entirety."
> —Brian S. Brooks & James L. Pinson, *Working with Words* 73 (2d ed. 1993).

"No long complex sentence will hold up without parallel construction. Paralleling can be very simple. Any word will seek its own kind, noun to noun, adjective to adjective, infinitive to infinitive."
> —Sheridan Baker, *The Practical Stylist* 101 (8th ed. 1998).

Explanation

A parallel construction is a phrase or clause that grammatically mirrors another phrase or clause. In a list, for example, you put noun–noun–noun, or verb–verb–verb, or adjective–adjective–adjective. You shouldn't vary the grammatical constructions in a listing. Grammar reflects logic.

Parallelism helps satisfy every reader's innate craving for order and rhythm. By phrasing parallel ideas in parallel grammatical constructions, you show the reader how one idea relates to another. You supply correspondences.

Parallel construction is especially important when you enumerate items. Only a sloppy thinker breaks up ideas illogically, disrupting both the grammatical and the commonsense relationships:

> There are four elements in fraud: (1) a knowing misrepresentation or concealment of (2) the truth or a material fact (3) to induce another (4) to his or her injury.

Why four and not six:

> There are six elements in fraud: (1) a knowing (2) misrepresentation or concealment of (3) the truth or a material fact (4) to induce (5) another (6) to his or her injury.

And if there are in fact four, the orderly way to present them is in a parallel fashion. This may require a few more words, but now form follows content, and the breakdown becomes more logical:

> Fraud has four elements:
>
> (1) misrepresentation of the truth, or concealment of a material fact;
> (2) knowledge by the person who misrepresents or conceals;
> (3) reliance on the misrepresentation or concealment;
> (4) injury to the person who relies.

The corollary to the tip is this: "Avoid unparallel constructions at all costs." Skewed sentences, like those in the examples below, betray a small ineptitude in handling words and ideas. They often result from mismatching sentence-parts framed by correlative conjunctions, as in Examples A and B; from using so many words that the writer loses track of the structure, as in Example C; from simply mixing up items in a list, as in Example D; or from trying to put too much into one sentence, as in Example E.

Some Before-and-After Examples

Example A

Before   The rule appears both in state and federal statutes.

After   The rule appears in both state and federal statutes.

Example B

Before   The judge was not only young but also was inexperienced.

After   The judge was not only young but also inexperienced.

Example C

Before   With respect to collateral estoppel, Trezail argues again that (1) federal law and state law with respect to the discovery rule are substantially different, and (2) that the dismissal of a federal action for failure to state a claim under Rule 12(b)(6) is not a dismissal on the merits, and therefore collateral estoppel cannot apply.

After   As for collateral estoppel, Trezail once again argues that (1) federal law differs substantially from state law on the discovery rule, and (2) a dismissal under Federal Rule 12(b)(6) is not a dismissal on the merits, so collateral estoppel cannot apply.

Example D

Before   Plaintiff must also establish that the City had notice of the defect. Notice may be shown in three ways: (1) actual notice; (2) notice will be conclusively presumed if Plaintiff can prove that the defect existed for more than 30 days before the incident; or (3) notice will be imputed to the City if the defect is of such a nature that the City should have discovered and repaired the defect in the exercise of reasonable diligence.

After   Brewster must also establish that the City had notice of the defect. She can do this by proving that: (1) the City had actual notice of it; (2) the defect existed for more than 30 days before the incident, in which case notice is conclusively presumed; or (3) the City should have discovered and repaired this type of defect in exercising reasonable diligence, in which case notice is imputed.

Example E

Before   The house was inadequately constructed, leaked badly, and construction specialists had to be called in to fix the problem. [Here, the listing is unparallel because the items don't really belong in a list.]

After   Because the house was poorly built, water continually leaked through the roof and walls. The owners had to call in construction specialists to fix the problem.

Part E

Choosing the Best Words

42

Replace humdrum phrases with snappy ones that spark interest.

Quotable Quotes

"Nearly always the things a writer says are less striking than the way he puts them; for people in general have much the same ideas about the matters that form the stock in trade of all. It is the expression, the style, that makes all the difference."

—Voltaire, "Style," in *Theories of Style in Literature* 180, 184
(Lane Cooper ed., 1923).

"[M]ake your briefs clear, concise, honest, balanced, buttressed, convincing, and interesting. The last is not least. A dull brief may be good law. An interesting one will make the judge aware of this."
—Wiley B. Rutledge, "The Appellate Brief" (1942), in *Advocacy and the King's English* 429, 438–39 (George Rossman ed., 1960).

"You are constrained only by the salutary fear of being a bore."
—Gorham Munson, *The Written Word* 98 (rev. ed. 1949).

"[Y]ou need to interest [the judges] in that brief. You've got to make them feel that when they come to the brief, 'Oh, baby; is it going to be hot.' And they've got to approach the brief with that favorable atmosphere you need."
—Karl Llewellyn, *A Lecture on Appellate Advocacy*, 29 U. Chi. L. Rev. 627, 630 (1962).

"[I]f the attorney is to write an outstanding rather than a routine brief, he must pay attention to such details as will capture the court's attention and imagination."

—Jean Appleman, *The Written Argument on Appeal*,
41 Notre Dame Law. 40, 41 (1965).

"Writing memoranda can be creative. It can be satisfying, even enjoyable. But if you wish what you have written to be read, write for the reader. As the first obligation of a politician is to be elected, the first obligation of a writer is to be read."

—Harold G. Christensen, *How to Write for the Judge*,
Litigation, Spring 1983, at 25, 63.

"Think of how many dreary briefs a judge has to read in a judicial lifetime. What can you do to make your work sparkle, so that your judge actually looks forward to reading what you have to say?"

—James W. McElhaney, *The Art of Persuasive Legal Writing*,
ABA J., Jan. 1996, at 76, 78.

Explanation

How many briefs do you suppose a judge or law clerk reads in a given day? The answer, as you might have guessed, is *a lot*. And like anyone else, the judicial reader gets bored reading briefs; after four or five in an afternoon, the mind becomes a little numb.

So when you edit a brief, look for opportunities to make it more interesting, especially by choosing slightly offbeat words that will precisely convey your meanings. Take pen to paper and follow this book's editing tips. But more than that, tweak your wordings. Aim for distinctive word choices—words that, although judges don't routinely see them, are well within their vocabulary. The result will be a brief that livens an afternoon of reading.

Some Before-and-After Examples

Example A

Before   Plaintiff merely *takes two paragraphs out of context* from the Swartz publication 2348, which is the manual dealing with career opportunities.

After   Cottam merely *plucks* two isolated paragraphs from Swartz's career-opportunities manual.

Example B

Before   The trial court made a finding of fact that *the abrupt manner in which Houseman made his departure from* the firm and his subsequent solicitation of the firm's employees interfered with the firm's existing contracts with clients and the firm's prospective business.

After   The trial court found that *the way Houseman bolted* from the firm and then raided its staff interfered with the firm's existing contracts and prospective business.

Example C

Before   Because Dr. Rader *has failed to include a discussion of* the standard of care and breach of the standard with respect to the performance of surgery, plaintiff's confusing allegation that Dr. Howe was negligent in the performance of the surgery *is not sufficient to meet the statutory requirements*.

After   Because Dr. Rader *ducked* the issue of the standard of care and how it
               was supposedly breached, Findlay's confusing allegation that Dr. Howe
               negligently performed the surgery *does not pass statutory muster.*

Example D

Before   Plaintiffs' request for an injunction in this case *is in reality nothing more
               than a restatement of* their claim for money damages.

After   The Isaacs' request for an injunction *just rehashes* their claim for money
               damages.

Example E

Before   Plaintiffs have *repeatedly refused* Defendants' requests to interview Francis
               Stevenson. On July 29 and December 9, 1995, Defendants requested the
               opportunity to meet with Stevenson; each time, Plaintiffs refused. Ste-
               venson has been listed by Plaintiffs as a fact witness at trial.

After   The Stevensons have *stymied* the Montgomerys' attempts to interview
               Francis Stevenson. On July 29 and again on December 9, 1995, the Mont-
               gomerys asked to meet with Francis; both times, the Stevensons refused,
               even though they list him as a fact witness at trial.

An Unusually Good Example

Dengler's *scant* legal analysis of factual *minutiae* fails to rebut Steeldust's
motion in limine. Dengler tries to *squeeze* implications out of collateral
agreements that contradict the parties' written contract. At the same time,
though, Dengler confuses, rather than corrects, Steeldust's exposition of
the law—which prohibits contradictory evidence, no matter how persuasive. Not surprisingly, Dengler does not try to apply any law to its so-
called wealth of evidence to avoid the inevitable outcome: inadmissibility.
Instead, Dengler recites a *revisionist* history that *belies* the straightforward
application of the parol-evidence and contract-modification rules. This
court should ignore Dengler's strategy to *dodge* the legal standards that
make her evidence inadmissible.

43

State your ideas freshly; use clichés only when you can turn them to good advantage.

Quotable Quotes

"[M]odern writing at its worst does not consist in picking out words for the sake of their meaning and inventing images in order to make the meaning clearer. It consists in gumming together long strips of words [that] have already been set in order by someone else, and making the results presentable by sheer humbug."
—George Orwell, "Politics and the English Language," in *Modern Essays on Writing and Style* 98, 103–04 (Paul C. Wermuth ed., 1964).

"[P]ut away the sugar bowl, the saccharine pills, the purple crayon, the cliché mill, and the metaphor gun. Sickly sweet, sophomoric, cliché-ridden writing, studded with inapt metaphors, is unpersuasive. The quiet force of facts, arrayed in active declarative sentences, will bear the argument along."
—Michael Tigar, *Federal Appeals: Jurisdiction and Practice* 334 (2d ed. 1993).

"Don't use [clichés] unwittingly. But they can be effective. There are two kinds: (1) the rhetorical—*tried and true, the not-too-distant future, sadder but wiser, in the style to which she had become accustomed*; (2) the proverbial—*apple of his eye, skin of your teeth, sharp as a tack, quick as a flash, twinkling of an eye*. The rhetorical ones are clinched by sound alone; the proverbial are metaphors caught in the popular fancy. Proverbial clichés can lighten a dull passage. You may even revitalize them because they are frequently dead metaphors . . . . Avoid the rhetorical clichés unless you turn them to your advantage: *tried and untrue, gladder and wiser, a future not too distant*."
—Sheridan Baker, *The Practical Stylist* 243–44 (8th ed. 1998).

"The best way to handle clichés is not to avoid them altogether, but to use them warily. Usually a cliché (*comparing apples and oranges*) is better than a circumlocution invented merely to displace it (*comparing plums and pomegranates*). But avoid the prepared wads of verbiage that displace thought."
—Bryan A. Garner, *The Elements of Legal Style* 203 (2d ed. 2002).

Explanation

Actually the commonplace advice to avoid all clichés is overdrawn. Sometimes they're just the ticket, but only when there's no other phrase to fit the bill. Despite that standard, though, you'll find more clichés in modern briefs than you could shake a stick at.

Many clichés are almost exclusively legal. Consider the phrase *it is well settled that*—a phrase that many practitioners will defend by saying that it aptly introduces an idea for which there is much precedential support. In fact, it's a lame phrase because it's so worn out. A better phrasing is tailored to the situation: *In a series of seven cases decided over the past decade, the New Mexico Supreme Court has consistently held that . . . .* Or this: *Since 1938, the rule of this Circuit has been that . . . .*

When you start *strenuously objecting* about *foregone conclusions* and *open-and-shut cases*, ask yourself whether you're not just using a tired expression that would immediately occur to every other legal writer. Try to find a bold new expression for the idea, or try putting some spin on the cliché (*Although Durham has cited a good many reasons why the Court might create a new rule, there are a bad many more reasons why it shouldn't do so*—in which *a good many* gets a new antonym [*a bad many*]). But avoid the rote, unconscious use of clichés.

Some Clichés to Avoid

a bird in the hand is worth two in the bush
a chain is only as strong as its weakest link
a day late and a dollar short
a dime a dozen
a happy camper
a pound of flesh
a rose by any other name
a rose is a rose is a rose
a snail's pace
a thorn in my side
a word to the wise
above and beyond (the call of duty)
airing your dirty laundry
all that glitters is not gold
always a bridesmaid, never a bride
an accident waiting to happen
an eye for an eye, a tooth for a tooth
as old as the hills
as slow as molasses
as smooth as silk
as straight as an arrow
as stubborn as a mule
as tough as nails
at death's door

at the drop of a hat/dime
barking up the wrong tree
beating a dead horse
bed of roses
beggars can't be choosers
better late than never
better safe than sorry
between a rock and a hard place
bit off more than you could chew
blind ambition
blood from a turnip
blood is thicker than water
blue in the face
bone of contention
cakewalk
can't see the forest for the trees
catch as catch can
Cheat/fool me once, shame on you. Cheat/fool me twice, shame on
    me!
chip on his (or her) shoulder
clash of Titans
close the barn door after the horse gets out
come hell or high water
cried all the way to the bank
cross the Rubicon
cross to bear
cut off your nose to spite your face
damned if you do, damned if you don't
dead in the water
dead letter
dead on arrival
dead to rights
digging his (or her) own grave
dodged the bullet
dollars to doughnuts
don't bite the hand that feeds you
don't count your chickens before they hatch
don't look a gift horse in the mouth
don't make a mountain out of a molehill
don't put all your eggs in one basket
don't put the cart before the horse
don't throw the baby out with the bathwater
doubting Thomas
easy come, easy go
easy (or slim) pickin's
every dog has its day
fast track
feast or famine
fight tooth and nail
fit to be tied

fools rush in where angels fear to tread
game plan
gild the lily
go with the flow
greatest thing since sliced bread
green with envy
grin and bear it
half-baked idea
hard-and-fast rule
haste makes waste
hindsight is 20–20
holier than thou
hot under the collar
hour of need
if at first you don't succeed, try, try again
if it ain't broke, don't fix it
if it walks like a duck, quacks like a duck, and flies like a duck, it's
    probably a duck
if you can't beat 'em, join 'em
if you can't take the heat, get out of the kitchen
if you can't walk the walk, don't talk the talk
if you're not part of the solution, you're part of the problem
in for a penny, in for a pound
in one ear and out the other
in the bag
in the ballpark
in the fast lane
it ain't over till it's over
it ain't over till the fat lady sings
it's not rocket science/brain surgery
jump on the bandwagon
keep the pot boiling
kill two birds with one stone
knee-jerk reaction
law and order
lay down the law
leave no stone unturned
lesser of two evils
let her hair down
let sleeping dogs lie
let the cat out of the bag
like a bat out of hell
like shooting fish in a barrel
like there's no tomorrow
make ends meet
monkey see, monkey do
more than meets the eye
more than one way to skin a cat
more than you bargained for
music to my ears

net result
never look a gift horse in the mouth
never say never
no use crying over spilled milk
on a roll
on his (or her) high horse
on the ropes
on top of the world
once bitten, twice shy
one in a million
one man's trash is another man's treasure
only the strong survive
out in left field
out of sight, out of mind
out of the frying pan and into the fire
pass the buck
penny-wise and pound-foolish
people who live in glass houses shouldn't throw stones
play possum
play with fire
plumb the depths
possession is nine-tenths of the law
pot calling the kettle black
pull strings
pull yourself up by the bootstraps
rats abandon a sinking ship
read between the lines
read me like a book
receive his (or her) just deserts
road to Damascus
rode hard and put up wet
rule with an iron hand
sell like hotcakes
shape up or ship out
shoe is on the other foot
shoot first, ask questions later
shooting from the hip
shooting yourself in the foot
shot in the dark
sick and tired
six of one, half a dozen of the other
skeletons in the closet
slippery slope
so close, yet so far away
something is rotten in Denmark
sorely lacking
sound and fury
sour grapes
spur of the moment
start from scratch

steal his (or her) thunder
still wet behind the ears
straight from the horse's mouth
straw that broke the camel's back (or last straw)
string along
stuck in your craw
survival of the fittest
sweep it under the rug
take him (or her) down a peg
that dog won't hunt
that takes the cake
the apple doesn't fall far from the tree
the blind leading the blind
the buck stops here
the die is cast
the emperor wears no clothes
the end justifies the means
the grass is always greener on the other side
the prodigal son returns
the squeaky wheel gets the grease
the writing's on the wall
think outside the box
thorn in the side
throw in the towel
time is of the essence
time is ripe
to hesitate is to lose
to the victor belong the spoils
too close for comfort
too little too late
train of thought
turn over a new leaf
two heads are better than one
up a creek without a paddle
up one side and down the other
wait with bated breath
walk a mile in his (or her) shoes
walking on eggshells/thin ice
wear his (or her) heart on his (or her) sleeve
what doesn't kill us makes us stronger
what goes around comes around
what goes up must come down
what's done is done
what's sauce for the goose is sauce for the gander
when hell freezes over
when in Rome, do as the Romans do
when pigs fly
when the cat's away, the mice will play
where there's smoke there's fire
whistle in the dark

whole new can of worms
wolves (or foxes) guarding the henhouse
worth his (or her) salt
you can catch more flies with honey than you can with vinegar
you can lead a horse to water, but you can't make it drink
you can't judge a book by its cover
you can't make a silk purse out of a sow's ear
you can't teach an old dog new tricks
you do the math
you made your bed, now you've got to lie in it

Some Typically Poor Examples

- Thus, it is crystal clear that the brochure was describing a liability insurance policy.

- At best, Bortley played fast and loose with the truth.

- At first blush, one might think that the plaintiffs would be happier in blissful ignorance.

- It goes without saying that the Defendants pulled no punches.

- But when the moment of truth came, and the trials and tribulations ceased, the wheels of justice were in perfect working order.

44

Strive for distinctive nouns and verbs—minimizing adjectives and adverbs.

Quotable Quotes

"In writing, as in life, when we try to add strength, we often betray weakness. The man who asks you to feel his muscles makes you suspect that he really doesn't believe in his virility. Likewise, the writer who must emphasize every noun with an adjective makes us suspect that his nouns don't carry enough weight. An excessive display of adjectives, like an excessive flexing of muscles, usually indicates some inner doubt of strength."
—Sydney J. Harris, *Last Things First* 269–70 (1961).

"Write with nouns and verbs, not with adjectives and adverbs. The adjective hasn't been built that can pull a weak or inaccurate noun out of a tight place."
—William Strunk, Jr. & E.B. White, *The Elements of Style* 71 (3d ed. 1979).

"Minimize your adjectives. Try to let nouns—especially *accurate* nouns—work alone. This will simplify your style *and* give it more point. Voltaire, who knew something about style, wasn't overstating the case much when he said, 'The adjective is the enemy of the noun.' Twain echoed him: 'As to the Adjective: when in doubt, strike it out.' "
—John R. Trimble, *Writing with Style* 76–77 (2d ed. 2000).

Explanation

Strong nouns don't need adjectives. Likewise, strong verbs don't need adverbs. When editing, try to bolster the nouns and verbs so that you can make their modifiers superfluous and thus delete them. Consider the following examples:

Adverb and Verb	*Better Verb*
briskly walked	marched, strode
abruptly stated	snapped
cried loudly	bawled, wailed

quickly went	ran, rushed
read carefully	pored over
loudly stated	yelled, shouted

Adjective and Noun	***Better Noun***
famous people	celebrities
famous places	landmarks
big, heavy book	tome
rude person	boor

Because a good brief should tell a story, you'll want to focus on the words that evoke a picture in the reader's mind. Vivid verbs, especially, will enliven your prose. And as they animate what might otherwise seem to be dull ideas, they'll spare you the many qualifiers that so often clutter legal writing.

Listed below are some picturesque verbs. These are words that we all know but are likely to overlook in our own sentences. Supplement this list with one of your own. Then think of opportunities to use these verbs—and others like them—when they fit.

Examples of Picturesque Verbs

ambush	dance	hammer	pilfer	smother
becloud	dangle	harangue	pillage	snatch
bleach	dredge	hurl	plague	spew
block	drench	infect	plod	sprinkle
blossom	drift	inflame	plow	stain
blunder	drone	jar	pluck	stampede
bluster	drown	leap	plunder	stumble
bombard	dupe	linger	plunge	stymie
bridle	echo	loiter	pulverize	swagger
broadside	eclipse	lunge	purge	swell
bungle	engulf	mar	ramble	tackle
burden	ensnare	mask	raze	teem
burst	flail	masquerade	rend	teeter
chant	fling	meander	repel	thrust
chastise	flit	mirror	rumble	thwart
choke	float	mock	rummage	trudge
clamor	flock	mold	scorn	waffle
clash	flounder	muddy	scramble	waver
clench	flout	paint	shave	wither
cling	fluster	pale	shower	wobble
cloak	fumble	parade	shroud	wrangle
clutch	fuse	pare	sling	wreak
corrupt	gallop	parry	slither	wrestle
crack	glimmer	peel	smolder	wring

Some Before-and-After Examples

Example A

Before　Despite its content-neutrality, § 533(b) fails to meet the standard of *O'Brien* and related cases.

After　Despite its content-neutrality, § 533(b) wilts under *O'Brien* and its progeny.

Example B

Before　Jackson vehemently states that the plaintiffs' theory is wholly unsupported.

After　Jackson insists [clamors? swears?] that the plaintiffs' theory is flawed [wrong? bogus?].

Example C

Before　The problem with that methodology is that the data provide absolutely no guidance as to the actual percentage of time when the calls were uninterrupted.

After　That approach shrouds [beclouds?] the percentage of time when the calls went uninterrupted. [*Or:* That approach doesn't reveal how often the calls succeeded.]

45

Save syllables.
Shoot for one-syllable words
when possible; failing that,
aim for two-syllable words.

Quotable Quotes

"If it [is] an advantage to express an idea in the smallest number of words, then it must be an advantage to express it in the smallest number of syllables."
—Herbert Spencer, "The Philosophy of Style" (1871), in
Essays on Rhetoric 147, 149 (Dudley Bailey ed., 1965).

"There is a tendency, almost an instinct in the American, to use and prefer high-sounding words. The American, as such, likes to be unsimple and grandiloquent when it comes to his manner of expression."
—Richard Burton, *Why Do You Talk Like That?* 124 (1929).

"It is a habit, amounting almost to mania, among inexperienced and ignorant writers to shun simple words. They wrack their brains and wear out their dictionaries searching for high-sounding words and phrases to express ideas that can be conveyed in simple terms."
—Edward Frank Allen, *How to Write and Speak Effective English* 57 (1938).

"Those who run to long words are mainly the unskillful and tasteless; they confuse pomposity with dignity, flaccidity with ease, and bulk with force."
—H.W. Fowler, *A Dictionary of Modern English Usage* 342
(Ernest Gowers ed., 2d ed. 1965).

"Make about two-thirds of your total vocabulary monosyllabic; keep words of three syllables or more down under 20 percent."
—Walker Gibson, *Tough, Sweet & Stuffy* 108 (1966).

"Communication is most complete when it proceeds from the smallest number of words—and indeed of syllables."
—Jacques Barzun, *Simple and Direct* 196 (1975).

"[T]he more you surrender to the temptation to use big words . . . , the further you are apt to stray from your true feelings and the more you will tend to write a style designed to impress rather than to serve the reader."
—John R. Trimble, *Writing with Style* 80 (1975).

Explanation

This is an odd point. On the one hand, you want a big vocabulary. (That's as a reader.) On the other hand, you want to abstain from using it too much. (That's as a writer.) In fact, you should develop your vocabulary of small words (*spate, blight, stench, dross, funk,* and the like).

But if you engage in the chthonic practice of lexiphanicism, you'll venenate or obelize your gongorism. Nothing will be ben trovato—you'll be inviting furibund readers to objurgate your caliginous style. Only a polyhistor will refrain from billingsgate. And who might blame your readers' cyclopean renitency? It results naturally from your nodus.

One irony of writing—I learned it a little late—is that you need to cultivate your vocabulary of small words. If you save syllables, you gain in clarity and force. You're no longer writing to impress, but to express. And that is the prerequisite to persuasion.

Look for every chance to save a syllable or two.

Some Before-and-After Examples

Example A

Before   Defendants' special exceptions are a disguised attempt to obtain the functional equivalent of a partial summary judgment in their favor on a number of causes of action.

After   The Blodgetts' special exceptions are a ploy to win what amounts to a partial summary judgment on several claims.

Example B

Before   While it is true that the contract of employment between attorney and client may be implied by the conduct of the parties, it is a constituent element of the relationship that the parties explicitly or by their conduct manifest an intention to create the attorney–client relationship.

After   Though the attorney–client relationship may be implied, the parties must show that they intend to create that relationship.

Example C

Before   Plaintiff made no assurances to Defendant that this matter would not be litigated in a judicial forum if settlement could not be effected.

After   Turner never told Carlisle that this matter would not go to trial if the parties failed to settle.

46

Avoid heavy connectors.

Quotable Quotes

"Long conjunctions are to be avoided. Such are the words *nevertheless, notwithstanding, furthermore, forasmuch*. The improvement of our language has caused most of these conjunctions to give place to others, which are shorter; and as such words are but secondary parts of sentences, it is desirable that they should not occupy more room, and become more conspicuous, than is absolutely necessary."

—Samuel Phillips Newman, *Practical System of Rhetoric* 151 (5th ed. 1835).

"As for the words that need to be made more rapid, as for instance connectives cut down to shorter ones, and the like, the writer must learn to determine . . . where a change will improve the expression."

—John F. Genung, *Outlines of Rhetoric* 137 (1894).

"*Consequently* is a four-syllable word meaning *so*."

—Rudolf Flesch, *The ABC of Style* 71 (1964).

"*Inasmuch as* sounds formal and stilted. Say *since*."

—*Id.* at 152.

"*Notwithstanding* is much too ponderous for everyday life. Say *in spite of* or *despite*."

—*Id.* at 207.

Explanation

Transitions are critical to a clean analytical line. But big, heavy connectors will counteract the purpose of transitions. What's a "heavy" connector? A word or phrase such as *consequently, notwithstanding,* or *inasmuch as*. Instead of smoothly pushing the reader forward through sentences and paragraphs, heavy connectors slow the reader down. They contribute to the molasses-like style common in legal writing.

So try replacing heavy connectors with faster, more conversational ones:

Heavy	*Light*
accordingly	so, thus
consequently	so, thus
for the reason that	because
for this reason	so, thus
furthermore	further
inasmuch as	because, since
nevertheless	still, even so, but, however, yet
notwithstanding	despite
notwithstanding the fact that	although
subsequently	later

By making these replacements, you'll gain some momentum in your sentences.

Some Before-and-After Examples

Example A

Before   Zybel has never argued that there is a mistake in the Hybrid Contract. *Therefore,* Zybel should be disallowed from offering evidence that the Contract mistakenly refers to the wrong part, the wrong source-control drawing, or the wrong specifications. *Accordingly,* the Court should preclude Zybel from introducing evidence that Harrison had an obligation to deliver any part other than the specific part identified in the Hybrid Contract. *Similarly,* the Court should preclude Zybel from introducing evidence or argument that Harrison had an obligation to meet specifications that are not in Source Control Drawing CV90-3488-3.

After   *Because* Zybel has never argued that the Hybrid Contract contains a mistake, Zybel should be disallowed from offering evidence that the Contract mistakenly refers to the wrong part, the wrong source-control drawing, or the wrong specifications. *So* the Court should exclude any evidence that Harrison was obliged to deliver any part other than the specific part identified in the Hybrid Contract. *And* the Court should bar Zybel from introducing evidence or argument that Harrison was obliged to meet specifications that are not in the source-control drawing.

Example B

Before   *Notwithstanding* the Court's decision granting leave to amend, the United States now challenges whether the four original plaintiffs—and only those plaintiffs—have standing to participate in the suit.

After   *Despite* the Court's decision granting leave to amend, the United States now challenges whether the four original plaintiffs—and only those plaintiffs—have standing to participate in the suit.

Example C

Before   Defendant admits that *subsequently* it enrolled in a one-year service commitment with Pantego Enterprises, commencing in December of 1994. *See* Counterclaim at 8, ¶ 19. *However,* defendant alleges that *inasmuch as* Pantego Enterprises delayed in posting a promotional credit to defendant's account, defendant became dissatisfied with Pantego and terminated its service eight months early. *See* Counterclaim at 11, ¶¶ 34–35.

After   Sequoia admits that it *later* enrolled in a one-year service commitment with Pantego Enterprises, beginning in December 1994. (CC ¶ 19.) *Yet* Sequoia alleges that *because* Pantego delayed in posting a promotional credit to its account, Sequoia became dissatisfied with Pantego and terminated its service eight months early. (CC ¶¶ 34–35.)

47

Simplify wordy prepositions:
with respect to, as to,
in order to, in connection with, etc.

Quotable Quotes

"Train your suspicions to bristle up whenever you come upon 'as regards,' 'with regard to,' 'in respect of,' 'in connection with,' 'according as to whether,' and the like. They are all dodges of jargon, circumlocutions for evading this or that simple statement; and I say that it is not enough to avoid them nine times out of ten, or nine-and-ninety times out of a hundred. You should never use them."

—Arthur Quiller-Couch, *On the Art of Writing* 114 (1916; repr. 1961).

"[S]ome [compound prepositions] are much worse in their effects upon English style than others, *in order that* being perhaps at one end of the scale, and *in the case of* or *as to* at the other; but, taken as a whole, they are almost the worst element in modern English, stuffing up what is written with a compost of nouny abstractions."

—H.W. Fowler, *A Dictionary of Modern English Usage* 102
(Ernest Gowers ed., 2d ed. 1965).

Explanation

If you're trying to sound like a bureaucrat, you'll have much need for multiword prepositions. If you're trying to communicate—and to show your reader that you're a plain, down-to-earth talker—you'll have little need for them. It's just about that simple.

Some Before-and-After Examples

Example A

Before   The Health Center's motion is not clear *as to* whether the Health Center ("the Center") seeks a severance or a separate trial of Dixon's counterclaims.

After   The Health Center's motion is not clear *about* whether the Center seeks a severance or a separate trial of Dixon's counterclaims.

Example B

Before   The requirements for a stock-bonus plan are similar to those of a profit-sharing plan, except that *with regard to* a stock-bonus plan, benefits are distributable in the employer's stock, not in cash.

After   The requirements for a stock-bonus plan are similar to those of a profit-sharing plan, except that *with* a stock-bonus plan, benefits are distributable in the employer's stock, not in cash.

Example C

Before   *Subsequent to* the commencement of the administrative hearings, the U.S. Supreme Court decided *Carbone v. Town of Clarkstown*, declaring unconstitutional a New York municipal waste-flow ordinance.

After   *After* the administrative hearings began, the U.S. Supreme Court decided *Carbone v. Town of Clarkstown*, declaring unconstitutional a New York municipal waste-flow ordinance.

48

Don't use *However* to start a sentence: use *But* instead, move *however* inside the sentence, or collapse the preceding sentence into an *Although*-clause.

Quotable Quotes

"The group of Adversative conjunctions represented by BUT (called Arrestive) very often fulfil the office of relating consecutive sentences. . . . An entire paragraph is not unfrequently devoted to arresting or preventing a seeming inference from one preceding, and is therefore appropriate opened by But, Still, Nevertheless, &c."
—Alexander Bain, *English Composition and Rhetoric* 110 (4th ed. 1877).

"The notion that it is not 'good style' to stick your conjunction at the front of your sentence is of moonshine all compact."
—*The Casual Essays of "The Sun"* 234, 236 (1905).

"A student writer will almost invariably give *however* first position in a sentence . . . . But [this word] works best if it is inside the sentence. Just exactly why this position is best is one of those stylistic mysteries that can't really be explained. It simply sounds better that way. And the importance of sound can't be dismissed, even in silent reading.

. . .

"Occasionally you will find yourself with a *however* that simply refuses to be tucked into a sentence comfortably. In that case, change it to *but* and put it in first position . . . ."
—Lucile Vaughan Payne, *The Lively Art of Writing* 85–86 (1965).

"*But* (not followed by a comma) always heads its turning sentence; *Nevertheless* usually does (followed by a comma). I am sure, however, that *however* is always better buried in the sentence between commas: *But* for the quick turn; the inlaid *however* for the more elegant sweep."
—Sheridan Baker, *The Complete Stylist* 55–56 (2d ed. 1972).

"*But* works especially well as the opening word of a paragraph . . . ."
—Maxine Hairston, *Successful Writing* 97 (2d ed. 1986).

" 'However, . . . ' induces sleep. Your reader will miss the fireworks. . . . If you do use 'however,' do not serve it as the appetizer. Stick it in the middle of your sentence."
—D. Alexander Fardon, *Writing to Persuade*, Barrister Mag., Summer 1994, at 14, 14.

"I can't overstate how much easier it is for readers to process a sentence if you start with 'but' when you're shifting direction."
—William Zinsser, *On Writing Well* 74 (6th ed. 1998).

"When you begin a sentence with *And* or *But* (and you most definitely should now and then), don't, for heaven's sake, put a comma after it. You want to quicken your prose with those words, and the comma would just kill any gain."
—John R. Trimble, *Writing with Style* 79 (2d ed. 2000).

"If you want to begin a sentence by contradicting the last, use *but* instead of *however*."
—Christopher Lasch, *Plain Style* 101 (Stewart Weaver ed., 2002).

" 'Though' outperforms 'however' 75% of the time. It's quicker, smoother, and far less bookish. And if you place it at the front of two sentences you're contrasting, you can (a) combine those sentences, (b) eliminate a comma or two, and (c) instantly cue your reader to the contrast ahead."
—John R. Trimble, *Editing Your Own Prose* (forthcoming).

Explanation

When indicating contrast, *However* can—and should—be replaced in one of the ways listed in the tip. (Of course, *However* is okay as a sentence-starter when used in the sense "in whatever way" or "to whatever extent.") If you're worried that using *But* will make the contrast too stark, move *however* to midsentence—between commas, not as a conjunction—or rephrase with *Although* or *Though*.

But don't be afraid of starting a sentence with *But*. Follow the long-established practice of good legal writers:

- **U.S. Constitution:** "But neither the United States nor any State shall assume or pay any debt or obligation incurred in aid of insurrection . . . ." Amend. XIV, § 4.

- **Alexander Hamilton:** "But let it be admitted, for argument's sake, that mere wantonness and lust of domination would be sufficient to beget that disposition. . . ." *The Federalist* No. 17, at 119 (Clinton Rossiter ed., 1961).

- **John Henry Wigmore:** "I believe in democracy. And I would rather emigrate or die than see the American people Prussianized. But I do not believe that democracy has to be synonymous with incompetency." *Problems of Law* 101 (1920).

- **Oliver Wendell Holmes:** "But to many people the superfluous is necessary, and it seems to me that Government does not go beyond its sphere in attempting to make life livable for them." *Tyson & Brother v. Banton*, 273 U.S. 418, 447 (1927) (Holmes, J., dissenting).

- **Max Radin:** "But it will be an error to suppose that the most carefully drafted statute will be immune from the process of interpretation." *The Law and Mr. Smith* 188 (1938).

- **Fred Rodell:** "But some such concept—of justice, of humanitarianism, of democracy with a small 'd'—was rampant in the land by the time Marshall died." *Nine Men* 109 (1955).

- **Learned Hand:** "But when once his [Cardozo's] mind came to rest, he was as inflexible as he had been uncertain before." *The Spirit of Liberty* 131 (3d ed. 1960).

- **H.L.A. Hart:** "But these are theories requiring the support of empirical facts, and there is very little evidence to support the idea that morality is best taught by fear of legal punishment." *Law, Liberty, and Morality* 58 (1963).

- **Charles E. Wyzanski, Jr.:** "But if Judge Hand scored his fellows' foibles, he also underscored their virtues." *Whereas—A Judge's Premises* 75 (1965).

- **Lon L. Fuller:** "When a vessel at sea begins to founder there comes a time when it must be given up as lost. But we do not give the order to abandon ship as soon as, let us say, a fuel pump begins to function erratically." *Anatomy of Law* 21 (1968).

- **William O. Douglas:** "Retailers who may receive food stamps and turn them in to the local bank for cash have prescribed remedies if they are discriminated against. But the faceless, voiceless poor have no such recourse." *Points of Rebellion* 73–74 (1969).

- **Grant Gilmore:** "But if parties who pay are to be discharged for something less than 'objective impossibility,' then, it would seem to follow, parties who do should equally be discharged for something less. And so they were." *The Death of Contract* 81 (1974).

- **Geoffrey C. Hazard, Jr.:** "We can have a system that does not charge user fees, lets everyone play, seeks both law and common justice, and is subject to few inhibitions in style. We can also have a system in which a trial is a serious search for the truth or at least a ceremony whose essential virtue is solemnity. But we probably cannot have both." *Ethics in the Practice of Law* 135 (1978).

- **Susan Estrich:** "People are more afraid of stranger crime because they assume, often wrongly, that no one they know would victimize them. But once it happens, betrayal by someone you know may be every bit as terrifying, or more so, than random violence." *Real Rape* 25 (1987).

- **William H. Rehnquist:** "Hay and Wirt, urged on by Jefferson, insisted that a court had no right to require the attendance of the president at a trial, or even to subpoena documents from him. But Marshall ruled to the contrary, holding that the court did have the authority to require Jefferson to produce the documents in question." *Grand Inquests* 117 (1992).

- **Ronald Dworkin:** "But though the presumption that a fetus has no rights or interests of its own is *necessary* to explain the paradigm liberal view, it is not sufficient because it cannot, alone, explain why abortion is ever morally wrong." *Life's Dominion* 34 (1993).

- **Patricia M. Wald:** "But more basically, I have selected the priorities among the subjects and arguments discussed, described how broadly or narrowly the principles will be stated, edited the piece for style, and put my tonal mark on it." *How I Write*, 4 Scribes J. Legal Writing 55, 60 (1993).

- **Charles Alan Wright:** "But what if the parties fail to raise any jurisdictional question?" *Law of Federal Courts* 28 (5th ed. 1994).

- **Peter M. Tiersma:** "[T]his simple—almost austere—style is much harder to maintain when wading through the morass of legal doctrine, as opposed to merely reciting facts. But it is surely worth striving for." *Legal Language* 218 (1999).

- **Lawrence M. Friedman:** "President Truman vetoed this law [putting an absurdly low quota on Asian immigrants]; it passed over his veto. But the racist twist of the law was becoming an anachronism." *American Law in the 20th Century* 342 (2002).

Some years ago, a researcher found that 8.75% of the sentences in the work of first-rate writers—including H.L. Mencken, Lionel Trilling, and Edmund Wilson—began with coordinating conjunctions (i.e., *And* or *But*).* In *The New York Times* (front page during the 1990s) and *U.S. News & World Report* (in 1997)—according to my own informal survey—the average is closer to 10%. To the professional rhetorician, these figures aren't at all surprising.

Some Before-and-After Examples

Example A

Before   Anderson argues that NedFys waived its right of removal by taking various actions in the state court prior to removal. *However,* the caselaw clearly mandates that NedFys's actions prior to removal do not constitute a waiver of this right. As the following decisions demonstrate, not a single one of the actions listed in Anderson's litany of NedFys's pre-removal activity has been held to constitute a waiver of the right to removal.

---

* Francis Christensen, *Notes Toward a New Rhetoric*, 25 College English 9 (1963) (as reported in Edward P.J. Corbett, *Classical Rhetoric for the Modern Student* 442–43 (2d ed. 1971)).

After   Anderson argues that NedFys waived its right of removal by taking various actions in the state court before removal. *But* as the following decisions show, not one action listed in Anderson's litany of NedFys's pre-
removal activity has been held to constitute a waiver of the right to
removal.

Example B

Before   In his "Statement of Disputed Material Facts," Plaintiff lists numerous
"facts" he presumably believes show a retaliatory intent. *However,* Plaintiff never attempts to explain how these facts show retaliatory intent.

After   *Although* Kautz's "Statement of Disputed Material Facts" lists many
"facts," he never tries to explain how they show any retaliatory intent.

Example C

Before   Plaintiff also presents no evidence that he is "disabled" under the ADA.
Rather, as in his retaliation claim, Plaintiff spends several pages rambling
on about the legal standards for determining disability under the ADA.
(Pl. Br. at 26–28.) *However,* Plaintiff never applies these standards to the
facts of this case.

After   Nor does Webber present any evidence that he is "disabled" under the
ADA. Rather, as in his retaliation claim, Webber merely discusses the legal
standards for determining disability. (Pl. Br. at 26–28.) *But* he never applies these standards to the facts of this case.

49

Strike *pursuant to* from your vocabulary.

Quotable Quotes

"*Pursuant to* . . . is an expression we are so used to seeing that we barely notice we are using it. Yet to most nonlawyers, it is one of the hallmarks of legalese. Ordinary people say *under* . . . or *according to* . . . . There is no reason why lawyers cannot do the same."

> —Michele M. Asprey, *Plain Language for Lawyers* 128 (1991).

"Because the phrase [*pursuant to*] means so many things, it is rarely—if ever—useful. Lawyers are nearly the only ones who use the phrase, and they often use it imprecisely."

> —Bryan A. Garner, *A Dictionary of Modern Legal Usage* 721 (2d ed. 1995).

"*Same, pursuant to, said*, and *herein* are commonly used by lawyers but do not have unique legal meanings. . . . [Y]ou can replace all of them with common terms."

> —Wayne Schiess, *Waiting for the Legal Audience* 47–48 (2003).

Explanation

This phrase—*pursuant to*—is dangerously addictive. You'll find it teeming in mediocre legal writing. And you'll search in vain for it in masterly legal writing. That probably says it all.

Some Before-and-After Examples

Example A

Before   The Court affirmed a dismissal of the action on defendant's motion for summary judgment, holding that the action was time-barred *pursuant to* Ohio Code § 1302.98.

After   The Court affirmed a dismissal of the action on Campbell's motion for summary judgment, holding that Ohio Code § 1302.98 barred the claim as untimely.

Example B

Before Because defendant's services were provided *pursuant to* the terms of AT&T's tariff, the tariff and its provisions dictate the rights and liabilities of the parties.

After Because Allen's services were provided *under* AT&T's tariff, the tariff and its provisions dictate the rights and liabilities of the parties. [Depending on the meaning, the best term might be *in accordance with* or *by virtue of*. But any of the three suggested phrases would be clearer than *pursuant to*.]

Example C

Before On February 7, 1995, Defendant Holmes was evicted from his apartment *pursuant to* a court order.

After On February 7, 1995, Holmes was evicted from his apartment *by* court order.

50

Use *that* restrictively,
which nonrestrictively.

Quotable Quotes

"What most people don't realize is that one 'which' leads to another. . . . Your inveterate whicher . . . is not welcome in the best company."
> —James Thurber, "Ladies' and Gentlemen's Guide to Modern English Usage," in *The Ways of Language: A Reader* 142, 143 (Raymond J. Pflug ed., 1967).

"The careful writer, watchful for small conveniences, goes *which*-hunting, removes the defining *whiches*, and by so doing improves his work."
> —William Strunk, Jr. & E.B. White, *The Elements of Style* 59 (3d ed. 1979).

"Just think what happens in the mind of the person who knows the difference between restrictive and nonrestrictive clauses. Anyone who understands that distinction is on the brink of seeing the difference between simple fact and elaborative detail and may well begin to make judgments about the logic of such relationships. He may start bothering his head about the difference between things essential and things accidental, a disorder that often leads to the discovery of tautologies. Furthermore, anyone who sees the difference between restrictive and nonrestrictive clauses is likely to understand *why* modifiers should be close to the things they modify and thus begin to develop a sense of the way in which ideas grow from one another. From that, it's not a long way to detecting non sequiturs and unstated premises and even false analogies."
> —Richard Mitchell, *Less Than Words Can Say* 154 (1979).

"The words *which* and *that* have distinct meanings. If you are familiar with those meanings, you can convey information precisely; if you are not, you risk confusing your reader. There are several ways to understand the difference between these two words. *That* identifies the objects about which you are speaking, whereas *which* merely provides further information about those objects . . . . A *that* clause picks out one among many, whereas a *which* clause often implies that there is only one . . . . If we remove a *that* clause from a sentence, we destroy the original meaning; if we remove a *which* clause, we leave the meaning intact."
> —Lyn Dupré, *Bugs in Writing: A Guide to Debugging Your Prose* 67–68 (rev. ed. 1998).

Explanation

More than any other habit of language, the handling of this distinction has become the acid test for the careful legal writer. And despite what some occasionally say, it's important because meaning often depends on it. Take this example:

> All the cases that were decided before the 1995 legislation support this argument.

> All the cases, which were decided before the 1995 legislation, support this argument.

The first sentence implies that some cases decided after the 1995 legislation don't support the argument. The second implies that no cases were decided after the 1995 legislation.

That's a big difference. In the first sentence, the phrase *that were decided before the 1995 legislation* is essential information. But in the second sentence, the phrase between commas, *which were decided before the 1995 legislation*, is inessential; you could cut it without harming the basic meaning of the sentence.

Here's the easiest statement of the rule: If you see a *which* without a comma or preposition before it, 90% of the time it needs to be a *that*. About 10% of the time, it will need a comma. So get in the habit of thinking comma-*which*.

Beyond that, think about *which*-clauses and *that*-clauses. If omitting the clause changes the basic meaning of the sentence, you'll need *that*. If omitting the clause doesn't change the basic meaning, you'll need a comma-*which*.

What could be simpler? (Don't answer that.)

Examples of Ambiguous Constructions

- The legislative validation is expressly inapplicable to pass-through charges *which* are the subject of any litigation before May 1, 1993.

- The company developed a new program for the northeastern divisions *which* had lost money for three consecutive quarters.

Some Before-and-After Examples

Example A

Before   The vessel's master was unsure of the plastic-disposal procedures and made statements *which* he felt would prevent Coast Guard action but later learned those statements were incorrect.

After   The vessel's master was unsure of the plastic-disposal procedures and made statements *that* he felt would prevent Coast Guard action but later learned those statements were incorrect.

Example B

Before   While to date no consensus has emerged on what body of law applies to determine the validity of an antitrust assignment, the courts consider the factors *which* are discussed below.

After   While to date no consensus has emerged on what body of law applies to determine the validity of an antitrust assignment, the courts consider the factors *that* are discussed below.

or

After   While to date no consensus has emerged on what body of law applies to determine the validity of an antitrust assignment, the courts consider the factors discussed below.

Example C

Before   In the matter at hand, Rule 166b is in direct conflict with § 552 of Title 5 of the United States Code *which* is often referred to as the Freedom of Information Act.

After   In the matter at hand, Rule 166b directly conflicts with 5 U.S.C. § 552, *which* is often referred to as the Freedom of Information Act.

51

Fix every remote relative pronoun—that is, ensure that *that* or *which* immediately follows the noun it refers to.

Quotable Quotes

"The following passage in Bishop Sherlock's Sermons is . . . censurable: 'It is folly to pretend to arm ourselves against the accidents of life, by heaping up treasures, which nothing can protect us against, but the good providence of our Heavenly Father.' *Which* always refers grammatically to the immediately preceding [noun], which is here 'treasures.' The sentence ought to have stood thus: 'It is folly to pretend, by heaping up treasures, to arm ourselves against the accidents of life, which nothing can protect us against but the good providence of our Heavenly Father.'"
——Hugh Blair, *Lectures on Rhetoric* 63 (1783; Grenville Kleiser cond., 1911).

"Relatives should be so placed as to prevent all ambiguity in regard to the words that they are intended to represent. The following sentence is therefore objectionable: 'He is unworthy of the confidence of a fellow-being *that* disregards the laws of his Maker.' Corrected: 'He *that* disregards the law of his Maker is unworthy of the confidence of a fellow-being.'"
——*Live and Learn: A Guide for All Who Wish to Speak and Write Correctly* 52 (1856).

"Be cautious about separating a relative clause from its antecedent."
——John F. Genung, *Outlines of Rhetoric* 201 (1894).

"The ambiguous sentence caused by a word or words put between a relative and the word it refers to is very common . . . . If relatives cannot conveniently be placed next to the words they refer to, they are better removed altogether."
——R.G. Ralph, *Put It Plainly* 37 (1952).

Explanation

The remote relative—a *that* or comma-*which* that doesn't immediately follow the noun it modifies—is a prime indicator of a sloppy sentence. It causes ambiguity, as in *the man living down the street that I was talking about last night*. What was I talking about last night? The man or the street?

The main problem is *which* when not preceded by a comma, as in the following glorious example from William Walsh's book on equity. The question is what word the *which* modifies:

> This work required a law court in the modern sense made up of a small number of judges of education and ability skilled in the law which sat regularly term after term, generally at Westminster, often at the Exchequer.*

In fact, as you might have gathered, *which* is supposed to jump back 21 words—over 6 nouns—and refer to *court*. The syntax is unacceptable.

The problem is less common with *that*, but it does occur:

> Section 219 contains an exception for the sale of partnerships that is not applicable to this fact pattern.

This example is particularly bad because of the seeming disagreement between *partnerships* and the singular verb *is*.

Here's the remedy: whether you're using the restrictive *that* or the nonrestrictive comma-*which*, always be sure that it comes right after the noun it refers to.

Some Before-and-After Examples

Example A

Before   Defendants knowingly conspired to bring securities onto the market *that* could not be legally marketed.

After   Inman and Marcus knowingly conspired to bring onto the market securities that could not be legally marketed.

Example B

Before   There is an outstanding warrant against Mr. Erutu in Ethiopia, *which* on its face declares that he is to be arrested for expressing his political beliefs.

After   There is an outstanding warrant against Mr. Erutu in Ethiopia; the warrant declares that he is to be arrested for expressing his political beliefs.

Example C

Before   Defendant Mutual Life Insurance Company of Boston ("Mutual Life") respectfully submits this motion for partial summary judgment on all claims brought against it by plaintiff Nippondenso of San Francisco Inc. ("Nippondenso") *which* are barred on grounds other than statute of limitations.

---

* William F. Walsh, *A Treatise on Equity* 3 (1930).

After   Defendant Mutual Life moves for partial summary judgment on all of Nippondenso's claims *that* are barred on grounds other than statute of limitations.

Example D

Before   Recent discovery has revealed significant new facts in the case *that* must be investigated in order for Mockley to prepare its defense.

After   Recent discovery has revealed significant new facts that must be investigated in order for Mockley to prepare its defense.

Example E

Before   If Chubb wants to attempt to avoid its defense obligation, then Chubb must meet its burden of establishing facts outside the pleadings *which* demonstrate that the claims against Crown fall outside coverage under the Chubb policy.

After   If Chubb wants to try to avoid its defense obligation, it must establish facts outside the pleadings to demonstrate that the claims against Crown fall outside coverage under the Chubb policy.

52

Resist rabid deletions of *that*.
Even so, prefer [verb + *-ing*]
over *that* [+ verb].

Quotable Quotes

"The omission of the conjunctive *that* sometimes causes a momentary confusion. In Milton Propper's *The Great Insurance Murders* (an American 'thriller'), we find: 'There were no marks or scratches that indicated the lock had been forced' and 'Rankin ushered her to a chair and learned her name was Mrs. Emily Reilly.' 'Indicated the lock' and 'learned her name' might possibly have been independent, self-contained statements: but with something of a jar, one finds that the sentences continue.—This defect is much commoner in American than in English writers."

—Eric Partridge, *Usage and Abusage* 330 (1947; repr. 1963).

"Omitting a word such as *that* is often a power move, but that word is not always dispensable. Take the sentence that begins a science fiction film: 'Many Americans believed visitors from outer space had actually landed.' Without *that*, it is possible to misread it momentarily as 'Many Americans believed visitors from outer space'; with *that*, there can be no misreading: 'Many Americans believed that visitors from outer space had actually landed.' "

—Jeffrey McQuain, *Power Language: Getting the Most Out of Your Words* 66 (1996).

Explanation

That is the most wrongly persecuted word in the English language. Some people want to murder it wherever it appears.

But the word is quite useful and even necessary. We need it as a restrictive relative pronoun (*the books that are on the shelf*—see #50). We need it as a demonstrative adjective (*that idea is sound*—see #53). We need it as a conjunction (*he remarked that all the documents were accounted for*).

True, you can sometimes advantageously cut the word—*the documents she offered* rather than *the documents that she offered*—but the cuts often create gross miscues, as here:

- In *Cox*, the court held a contract indemnifying a casualty company for all liability under the Structural Work Act was void as against public policy. [Insert *that* after *held.*]

- The court pointed out an executor cannot appeal for the protection of the interests of a particular devisee or legatee who is able to take an appeal. [Insert *that* after *out.*]

- The court decided the question did not need to be addressed. [Insert *that* after *decided.*]

If a noun follows *that*, as in the examples above, you'll almost always need to keep it. If a verb follows *that*, you can often change the verb to an *-ing* word: *decision that reversed a judgment* becomes *decision reversing a judgment*. In carrying out this edit, you'll prevent such awkward constructions as *the statute that provides that . . . .* You see this technique in the last three examples below.

In examples A and B, you'll see the havoc that a writer can wreak by omitting necessary *that*s. In each example, the sentence seems to have a typographical error until you read further into it and see that the writer has ill-advisedly omitted the word *that*.

Some Before-and-After Examples

Example A

Before   Plaintiff's counsel has informed Defendants the media, and possibly others, will attend the deposition.

After   Hammond's counsel has informed Safeco *that* the media, and possibly others, will attend the deposition.

Example B

Before   Dr. Moore disagreed these diagnoses are directly and proximately caused by the alleged industrial injury. Dr. Moore concluded Ginsburg had a permanent partial medical impairment of 3–4%, half of which is due to arousal of the preexisting dormant condition. Dr. Moore also testified Ginsburg could lift no more than ten pounds.

After   Dr. Moore disagreed *that* these diagnoses are directly and proximately caused by the alleged industrial injury. Dr. Moore concluded *that* Ginsburg had a permanent partial medical impairment of 3–4%, half of which is due to arousal of the preexisting dormant condition. Dr. Moore also testified *that* Ginsburg could lift no more than ten pounds.

Example C

Before   More important, Weiss has not presented any authority *that holds* that this Court may acquire jurisdiction over this matter by estopping the defendant from raising subject-matter jurisdiction as a defense.

After　　More important, Weiss has not presented any authority *holding* that this Court may acquire jurisdiction over this matter by estopping Floydell from raising subject-matter jurisdiction as a defense.

Example D

Before　　The statute *that provides* that ESOPs are not taxable in this circumstance has now been amended.

After　　The statute *providing* that ESOPs are not taxable in this circumstance has now been amended.

Example E

Before　　The Tunney letter is a seven-page document *that describes* Korbel and *explains* the enhanced special mobile radio services that Korbel provides.

After　　The Tunney letter is a seven-page document *describing* Korbel and *explaining* the enhanced special mobile radio services that Korbel provides.

53

Don't use *such* as a pronoun <rejected such> or demonstrative adjective <such property>.

Quotable Quotes

"As a pronoun, *such* is best avoided in at least two kinds of contexts. One is the kind in which *same* would be the word chosen in legalistic or business English: 'For those who fancy such, the tripe is first-rate.' *Same* and *such* are equally nondescript when used in this manner. The other context is one in which *such* means *the like*: 'The party feasted on hot dogs, hamburgers, and such.' Both must be classed as casualisms, to be used only with semi-humorous intent."
—Theodore M. Bernstein, *The Careful Writer* 432 (1965).

"*Such* used in place of a regular pronoun is not acceptable to careful writers. It is as common and unattractive as its shabby mates, *said* and *same*."
—Karen Larsen, *The Miss Grammar Guidebook* 108 (1994).

"Properly used to mean 'of this kind' <such an appeal>, *such* is deplorable as a substitute for *this* or *these* or *the* <such appeal>. Sir Frederick Pollock tried unsuccessfully to 'choke off' this bit of legalese during the last century; may we finally succeed where he failed."
—Bryan A. Garner, *The Elements of Legal Style* 141 (2d ed. 2002).

Explanation

The point about the demonstrative adjective needs some amplification. If you use *such* to mean "of this kind" or "of that type," you're within the mainstream of English: *My sister doesn't particularly enjoy talking with such people*. Snobbish mainstream English, on occasion. Or if you use *such* in the phrase *such a* (*Where did you get such an idea?*), once again you're in the mainstream.

But if you mean "the very one I just mentioned," you're engaging in arrant legalese. Not only is it poor usage (Fowler called it "illiterate"*); it's also inherently unclear. That is, by *such property* do you mean "the property I just referred to" or "property of that type"?

The easy solution is to use ordinary words, such as *this, that, these, those,* and *the.* They're every bit as precise—often more so.

Some Before-and-After Examples

Example A

Before   The statute places three stringent requirements on the moving party, that there be newly discovered evidence, that *such* evidence be material to the outcome of the case, and the moving party establishes reasonable diligence to discover and produce the evidence at trial.

After   The statute requires the movant to show that (1) there is newly discovered evidence, (2) the evidence is material to the outcome of the case, and (3) reasonable diligence was used to discover and produce the evidence at trial.

Example B

Before   In his motion for new trial, Plaintiff asserts that *such* motion is based on "newly discovered evidence."

After   McDuff bases his motion for new trial on "newly discovered evidence."

Example C

Before   The SEC has historically applied a broad test and held an adviser to have "custody" of client assets if *such* adviser has any direct or indirect access to them.

After   The SEC has historically applied a broad test and held that an adviser has "custody" of client assets if the adviser has any direct or indirect access to them.

Example D

Before   *Such* cause of action, if any *such* there was, survived her death.

After   The claim, if there was any, survived her death.

---

* H.W. Fowler, *A Dictionary of Modern English Usage* 602 (Ernest Gowers ed., 2d ed. 1965).

54

Use well-recognized symbols and abbreviations, but avoid uncommon ones.

Quotable Quotes

"As long as your reader understands, use the shortest possible symbol."
—Rudolf Flesch, *How to Write, Speak, and Think More Effectively* 299 (1960).

"The current practice of using initial letters of lengthy titles as a shorthand reference can become extremely confusing. Use of NLRB for the National Labor Relations Board presents no problems. But it is not unusual to read a sentence such as this in a brief:

> The Port Association of Freight Forwarders (PAFF) entered into an Agreement Covering Loading Practices in the Inner Harbor (ACLPIH) with the Seattle Chapter of the Union of Warehousemen and Stevedores (SCUWS).

"Two pages later the following appears:

> Under the ACLPIH, SCUWS was required to consult with PAFF before taking that action.

"This problem could be avoided if, instead of using these initials, the writer employed shorthand terms, such as 'Association,' 'Agreement,' and 'Union.' In place of the gibberish just quoted, the sentence would be fully comprehensible and succinct:

> Under the Agreement, the Union was required to consult with the Association before taking that action."

—Daniel M. Friedman, "Winning on Appeal," in
Appellate Practice Manual 129, 134 (Priscilla A. Schwab ed., 1992).

Explanation

There's nothing wrong with abbreviations. Indeed, the reader will frown if you repeatedly spell out such well-known initialisms as FBI, IRS, and NAACP. So if an abbreviation is readily understood and will save space, use it. And if your specific audience will understand some less-common abbreviations, then use those as well.

Symbols, too, can save space and lessen distraction. One of many examples is the percent sign: *54%* is faster than *54 percent* (much less *fifty-four percent*). Two others that can come in especially handy for brief-writers are the section symbol (§) and the paragraph sign (¶). Remember a couple of tips about these two. First, there should always be a space between the symbol and the number it designates (e.g., 42 U.S.C. § 1983). Second, if you're referring to multiple sections or paragraphs, use two symbols with no space between them (e.g., ¶¶ 5–8).

As for other abbreviated forms, consult a good dictionary to see whether they're included. If an abbreviation isn't listed, think twice about using it unless you're dealing with specialists who are well familiar with it. Examples in this category are terms such as FELA and CERCLA.

Unfortunately, in some fields—especially environmental law—it has become commonplace to see briefs with glossaries such as this:

GLOSSARY

ADC	Arkadelphia Development Company
ARC	Arkadelphia Research Corporation
AWQC	Ambient Water Quality Criteria
CCC	Colomber Chemical Corporation
CERCLA	Comprehensive Environmental Response, Compensation, and Liability Act
CERCLIS	Comprehensive Environmental Response, Compensation, and Liability Information System
CPI	Consolidated Preadapters, Inc.
CS	Consolidated Sources
DOI	United States Department of the Interior
HRDD	Hotspur Road Drum Dump
HRS	Hazard Ranking System
HWQF	Hazardous Waste Quantity Factor
HWQV	Hazardous Waste Quantity Value
IRC	International Recharging Corporation
NCP	National Oil and Hazardous Substance Pollution Contingency Plan
NJDEP	New Jersey Department of Environmental Protection
NPL	National Priorities List
NWI	National Wetlands Inventory
OSC	On-Scene Coordinator
POLREP	Pollution Report
PRP	Potentially Responsible Party
RI/FS	Remedial Investigation and Feasibility Study
SARA	Superfund Amendments and Reauthorization Act of 1986
SPD	Seagoville Pesticide Dump
TDL	Target Distance Limits
USEPA	United States Environmental Protection Agency

Then, the text that follows reads like this:

According to the NJDEP, IRC occupied the same property at which ARC subsequently conducted its operations, and USEPA claims that the operations at ARC were the same as IRC without any supporting evidence linking ARC to IRC's operations. Moreover, in its investigation to identify the owners and tenants of the ADC and ARC sites, NJDEP was unable to find any indication of a formal tie between ARC and ADC. And USEPA can point to no evidence suggesting that the owners/operators of these facilities were related. See ADC POLREPS [D.A. 419]; ADC OSC Rep. [D.A. 694]; HRDD POLREPS [D.A. 142]; SPD Action Memo [D.A. 1649].

All of this suggests that the writer is concerned not with the reader's convenience, but with the writer's own convenience. Or else the writer has simply assumed that readers are just as familiar with these "hieroglyphs" as the writer is. (Also, of course, "USEPA" is quirky in place of "EPA"—the only initialism worth using in that passage.) The priorities are badly misplaced.

Avoid dishing out prose with an alphabet-soup flavor. Instead, follow the advice in the second quotable quote: use shorthand terms made up of real words.

Some Before-and-After Examples

Example A

Before   On April 30, 1994, Plaintiff, Power Data ("PD"), filed its complaint against Defendant seeking damages for breach of contract, specific performance, and damages for tortious interference with contractual relations.

After   On April 30, 1994, Power Data filed its complaint against Penntech seeking breach-of-contract damages, specific performance, and damages for tortious interference with contractual relations.

["PD" is a poor initialism. Stick with the fairly concise "Power Data."]

Example B

Before   Defendant served Plaintiff with an RFP, an RFA, and a request for an IME.

After   Fishburn served Haynes with a request for production, a request for admissions, and a request for an independent medical examination.

Example C

Before   The first exception applies when the third party is "present to further the interest of the client in the consultation." Law Revision Commission Comment to Evidence Code section 952 (West's Annotated 1966 and Supplement 1995).

After   The first exception applies when the third party is "present to further the interest of the client in the consultation." Cal. Evid. Code § 952 cmt. (West 1966 & Supp. 1995).

55

Generally, dispense with *Mr.*, *Mrs.*, and *Ms.*; use last names alone after the first mention of a party's or witness's name.

Quotable Quotes

"Use *Mr.*, *Mrs.* and *Miss* only in obituaries, in reference to couples, in direct quotations and where essential for effect, as in editorials and critiques. In particular, do not use the terms with surnames after the first reference."
—Robert A. Webb, *The Washington Post Desk-Book on Style* 33 (1978).

"Do not use *Mr.* in any reference unless it is combined with *Mrs.*: *Mr. and Mrs. John Smith, Mr. and Mrs. Smith.*"
—*The Associated Press Stylebook and Libel Manual* 53 (1987).

Explanation

Legal writers seem to fear that, when referring to parties, they're being impolite if they don't consistently use *Mr.*, *Ms.*, or some other courtesy title. Actually, though, they're simply creating a brisker, more matter-of-fact style. Journalists aren't being rude when they do this, and neither are you.

But titles are desirable in four situations. First, if you're representing a criminal defendant, you may want to dignify your client with a *Mr.* or *Ms.* Second, if Mr. and Mrs. Smith are both involved in the case—and their roles differ—you'll probably need to use titles to distinguish them. Third, earned degrees aren't governed by the same rules as courtesy titles: where you're referring to an expert witness, you'll want to say "Dr. Heimlitz," not "Heimlitz." Still that shorter form might do nicely if Heimlitz is your opponent's expert and has only questionable credentials. Fourth, "Mr." can be useful when sex discrimination is an issue; for a good example, see example A in tip #84.

A Before-and-After Example

Before   Notwithstanding **Mr.** Patterson's assertion of the existence of a "unilateral contract" between **Mr.** Patterson and Mutual Life, **Mr.** Patterson's second (breach of contract) count fails because (a) there is no "unilateral contract" between **Mr.** Patterson and Mutual Life because there was no offer of a unilateral contract by Mutual Life and (b) the employment agreement between **Mr.** Patterson and Mutual Life, which has been ignored and hidden from the court by **Mr.** Patterson, is the sole writing governing the employer–employee relationship between **Mr.** Patterson and Mutual Life. The employment agreement is an integrated instrument completely reflecting the intentions of the parties. That **Mr.** Patterson did not bring any claim for breach of contract under the employment agreement means that **Mr.** Patterson has no breach of contract claim and that **Mr.** Patterson knows that.

After   Even though Patterson asserts the existence of a "unilateral contract" between himself and Mutual Life, his second (breach-of-contract) count fails for two reasons. First, there is no unilateral contract between Patterson and Mutual Life because Mutual Life never made an offer. Second, the employment agreement—which Patterson has ignored and kept hidden from the court—is the sole writing governing the employer–employee relationship between the parties. This employment agreement is an integrated instrument completely reflecting the parties' intentions. Because Patterson did not bring any claim under this agreement, he must realize that he has no breach-of-contract claim at all.

56

Shun sexist language,
but do it invisibly.

Quotable Quotes

"[W]ith the radical changes today [that] have resulted in no less than a revolution in woman's status in every conceivable relation of human life, it has become evident that she no longer plays second fiddle, as of old, and that therefore an idiom invented when man was ranked as her superior, and resulting in the clumsiness and inconsistency I speak of, is more objectionable than it was once held to be; and is likely, sooner or later, to be got around in some way."

—Richard Burton, *Why Do You Talk Like That?* 204–05 (1929).

"When you're troubled by a word that carries sexist connotations, don't automatically substitute *person* for *man*, or the effect will more than likely be clumsy, attention-getting, and distracting. Words like *henchperson* make people smile no matter how serious the context. A good way to avoid mutant words is to consult your thesaurus. There you'll find nonsexist synonyms like *gilly, goon, lackey, flunky, stooge,* and *sycophant*."

—Judi Kesselman-Turkel & Franklynn Peterson, *Good Writing* 100 (1981).

"There are other, subtler forms of sexist language. One is to refer to prominent men by their title or last name but to prominent women by their full name or married name: for instance, designating the United States president as 'President Reagan' but the British prime minister as 'Mrs. Thatcher' or referring to the American male writer as 'Hemingway' but the American female writer as 'Eudora Welty.' Another is to mention specifically the appearance or marital status of women but not of men. For instance, it would be sexist to mention in a report that a woman employee is 'an attractive blonde' or 'a divorcee' but not to indicate whether a man employee is married or divorced or whether he is attractive or homely."

—Maxine Hairston, *Successful Writing* 125 (2d ed. 1986).

"Just as lawyers omit irrelevant facts that may detract from the focus of the argument, they should avoid language that may distract readers with intended or unintended messages about pronouns, sexism, or society."

—Beverly Ray Burlingame, *Reaction and Distraction: The Pronoun Problem in Legal Persuasion*, 1 Scribes J. Legal Writing 87, 88 (1990).

"I believe that gendered writing . . . will one day be immediately recognized as archaic and ludicrous. My only message to brief-writers is that, to many brief-readers today, it already is."

—Judith S. Kaye, *A Brief for Gender-Neutral Brief-Writing,*
N.Y.L.J., 21 Mar. 1991, at 2.

Explanation

Forget the social issues—if you must—and think about your credibility. That's the question here: how do you maintain your credibility?

With a diverse or unknown readership, the best approach is to write in such a way that no one would ever consider either sexist or awkwardly nonsexist. Then the question of sexism doesn't even occur to the reader, who can concentrate without distraction on the ideas themselves.

Among the useful techniques for avoiding sexist language are these:

- Use *someone, anyone, person, people, human,* etc. for nouns like *man* and *woman.*

- Use gender-neutral occupational titles like *mail carrier, police officer, flight attendant,* etc. for gender-specific ones like *mailman, police-man, stewardess,* etc.

- Use plural pronouns (*they, them, their*) for singular ones (*he, she, his, her*).

- Substitute, in moderation, *he or she*—but not the clumsy and distracting *he/she* or *s/he*—for the traditionally generic *he.*

- Substitute a plural antecedent (e.g., *doctors* for *doctor*) so that you can later use the plural pronoun *they* instead of *he.*

- Delete the personal pronoun when possible. Instead of writing, say, "conferences between a lawyer and his client," write "conferences between lawyer and client" or "lawyer–client conferences."

- Repeat the noun instead of using the generic *he.*

- Use an article (*a, an, the*) instead of the possessive masculine pronoun (*his*).

- Reword the sentence in some other way.

Some Before-and-After Examples

Example A

Before   Under California law, an employee must exhaust *his* administrative remedies under the Fair Employment Housing Act before *he* sues *his* employer under the Act.

After   Under California law, an employee must exhaust any administrative remedies under the Fair Employment Housing Act before suing the employer under the Act.

Example B

Before   To permit or require a landlord to wait until *she* finds a new tenant willing to bind *herself* to the terms of the original tenancy agreement would render the duty to mitigate meaningless.

After   To permit or require a landlord to find a new tenant willing to accept the terms of the original tenancy agreement would render the duty to mitigate meaningless.

Example C

Before   Federal Civil Rule 54(d)(2) permits a plaintiff to recover an attorneys' fee only if *he* establishes that *he* was a prevailing party.

After   Under Rule 54(d)(2), plaintiffs can recover attorney's fees only by establishing that they were prevailing parties.

Example D

Before   California statutes exempt an individual from licensing as an agent when (s)he is an employee of a life insurer, only gives technical assistance to a licensed person, and receives no commission. The GFR representative meets two of these criteria, but (s)he is not employed by a life insurer. Even though (s)he works indirectly for the insurer during all presentations, (s)he would not qualify for exemption.

After   California statutes have an exemption from agent licensing for anyone who (1) is an employee of a life insurer, (2) gives only technical assistance to a licensed person, and (3) receives no commission. Although the GFR representative meets the second and third criteria, she is not employed by a life insurer. And even though she works indirectly for the insurer, she is not "an employee" and would not qualify for exemption.

[This example is discussing a particular person—not some abstraction.]

Part F

Punctuating for Clarity and Impact

57

Use dashes—not parentheses—
to highlight interruptive phrases.

Quotable Quotes

"The best stop for the normal parenthesis, which, though it is an 'aside' or digression, still fits into the general sentence pattern, is the dash."
—G.H. Vallins, *Good English: How to Write It* 109 (1951).

"[T]he dash is a handy stop for use, either in pairs or singly, with somewhat abrupt interjections or 'asides' sandwiched into, or tacked on to, a main sentence."
—G.V. Carey, *Mind the Stop* 73 (rev. ed. 1958).

"In general, parentheses are used with numerals, short identifications and illustrations, and definitions. Dashes are used with explanations and with qualifications of what is in the main text."
—Sumner Ives, *A New Handbook for Writers* 181 (1960).

"[W]e are sure that most business writers can use dashes considerably more often than they now do without 'overusing' them."
—Scott R. Pancoast & Lance M. White,
The Business Grammar Handbook 104 (1992).

"The dash is often a good choice for lightening the overload of commas, while adding emphasis."
—Martha Kolln, *Rhetorical Grammar* 92 (3d ed. 1999).

"[W]hen the dash errs, it's a victim, not a culprit, and nothing can quite replace it. In fact, of all the punctuation marks, it's the most indispensable for brightening our prose."
—John R. Trimble, *Writing with Style* 120 (2d ed. 2000).

Explanation

Strangely, many writers harbor a prejudice against dashes. But they are genuinely useful—even indispensable—to the writer who cares about rhythm and emphasis.

Next time you want to insert an interruptive phrase in a sentence—
and, though that may sound bad, you'll sometimes need to do it—put it
within a pair of long dashes. Em-dashes, that is.

You'll probably want a macro for this, perhaps activated by Alt-M.
Put a hard space before the dash and a soft space after (the hard space
will ensure that it won't begin a line). Then you'll have a quick keystroke
that you can use whenever you need an em-dash.

This tip may sound nitpicky, but if you learn how to use dashes well,
without overdoing them, you'll wonder how you ever did without them.

Some Before-and-After Examples

Example A

Before   The Court should deny those requests because neither Embrie nor Sea-
grams makes the showing required by Rule 56(f) that knowledge of the
relevant facts is outside its control. [See tip #51 on remote relatives.]

After   The Court should deny those requests because neither Embrie nor Sea-
grams makes the showing—required by Rule 56(f)—that knowledge of
the relevant facts is outside its control.

Example B

Before   Now that Mr. Utley has refused to settle and trial is imminent, even
though the case has been pending only six months, it is important that
the facts be fully developed before trial so that justice may be served.

After   Now that Utley has refused to settle and trial is imminent—even though
the case has been pending only six months—the parties must fully develop
the facts before trial so that justice may be served.

Example C

Before   The evidence of all these efforts to protect confidentiality, combined with
the fact that for all the firm's years of existence there had never been an
instance of misappropriation, amply shows that the firm made reasonable
efforts to protect its trade secrets.

After   The evidence of all these efforts to protect confidentiality—combined with
the fact that the firm had never had a trade secret misappropriated—
amply shows that the firm tried to protect its trade secrets.

Example D

Before   Ning alleged that Sunstrom, who was not an executive officer, director,
stockholder, or partner, engaged in an intentional course of conduct that
caused Ning mental distress and other injuries.

After   Ning alleged that Sunstrom—who was not an executive officer, director, stockholder, or partner—engaged in an intentional course of conduct that caused Ning mental distress and other injuries.

Example E

Before   In *McCarthy*, a case involving the alleged third-party-beneficiary status of a contracting party's agent, the First Circuit identified the following indicators: mention of this particular agent in the contract, mention of agents or employees generally, and some basis for the agent's inclusion by necessary implication.

After   In *McCarthy*—a case involving the alleged third-party-beneficiary status of a contracting party's agent—the First Circuit identified three indicators: (1) mention of this particular agent in the contract; (2) mention of agents or employees generally; and (3) some basis for the agent's inclusion by necessary implication.

58

Hyphenate your phrasal adjectives.

Quotable Quotes

"The hyphen is useful. We can string nouns together to make a complex name for what is almost indescribable in a single word, and we can use the hyphen to make the relationship clear when mere juxtaposition does not do so."
—Edward N. Teall, *Putting Words to Work* 15 (1940).

"In general, writers, editors, and proof-readers need to be more alive to the *double entendre* that may result from omission of a hyphen."
—G.V. Carey, *Mind the Stop* 119 (rev. ed. 1958).

"The first and by far the greatest help to reading is the compulsory hyphening that makes a single adjective out of two words before a noun: *eighteenth-century painting / fleet-footed Achilles / tumbled-down shack / Morse-code noises / single-stick expert*. Nothing gives away the incompetent amateur more quickly than the typescript that neglects this mark of punctuation . . . ."
—Wilson Follett, *Modern American Usage* 428 (1966).

"How prevalent is the omission of the hyphen? Out of curiosity I counted the number of missing hyphens in a 7,600-word article on steel production I had just edited. It came to 226, or about seven missing hyphens per typewritten page. This, I believe, is about par for the course, at least as far as metallurgical literature is concerned. A dull headache is the least of the evils caused by the reading of such writing."
—H. George Classen, *Better Business English* 69 (1966).

"Hyphens are particularly necessary to make sense of the noun clusters that occur in technical writing. An engineer may refer to 'polyethylene coated milk carton stock smoothness test results.' What does that mean? It becomes clearer with hyphens: 'polyethylene-coated milk-carton-stock smoothness-test results.' But it is always best to keep the hyphens and rewrite the phrase: 'the results of smoothness tests conducted on polyethylene-coated milk-carton stock.' "
—Daniel McDonald, *The Language of Argument* 226 (5th ed. 1986).

"When uncertain whether or not to use a hyphen to join two words, refer to the following when-in-doubt rule: *Use a hyphen to join two or more words to form a compound adjective when there is any doubt as to the meaning or when*

providing a hyphen makes the reader's task easier. The only common exception to this rule is when the first word of the adjective phrase is an adverb ending in '-ly' (e.g., 'a completely clear conscience')."
—Scott R. Pancoast & Lance M. White, *The Business Grammar Handbook* 107 (1992).

"When a phrase functions as an adjective—an increasingly frequent phenomenon in late-20th-century English—the phrase should ordinarily be hyphenated. Seemingly everyone in the literary world knows this except lawyers. For some unfathomable reason—perhaps because they are accustomed to slow, dull, heavy reading—lawyers resist these hyphens."
—Bryan A. Garner, *A Dictionary of Modern Legal Usage* 657 (2d ed. 1995).

"The most important use of the hyphen is to tie together two words that modify a third, when the third word follows the first two. If you learn how to use hyphens in such compound adjectives, you will be able to tell your reader what you intend to modify what, and that is useful information. Without the hyphens, compound adjectives are ambiguous."
—Lyn Dupré, *Bugs in Writing: A Guide to Debugging Your Prose* 134 (rev. ed. 1998).

"*Middle class* . . . should be written without a hyphen when it appears as a noun, but it should be hyphenated when it appears as an adjective."
—Christopher Lasch, *Plain Style* 61 (Stewart Weaver ed., 2002).

"The hyphen is helpful to quick understanding even in some frequently used compound modifiers: *high-school students, real-estate dealers, stock-market rally, federal-funds rate.*"
—Paul R. Martin, *Wall Street Journal Guide to Business Style and Usage* 118 (2002).

Explanation

Invariably, lawyers are skeptical of this point, as if it were something newfangled or alien. But professional editors learn this lesson early and learn it well: you need to hyphenate your phrasal adjectives.

Here's the rule: if two or more consecutive words make sense only when understood together as an adjective modifying a noun that follows, those words (excluding the noun) should be hyphenated. For example, you should hyphenate *summary-judgment hearing*, but only because *hearing* is a part of the phrase; if you were referring merely to a *summary judgment*, a hyphen would be wrong. Thus:

bench trial		bench-trial strategy
joint venture		joint-venture issues
law of the case	**but**	law-of-the-case doctrine
legal writing		legal-writing instructor
mutual mistake		mutual-mistake doctrine

But you should not hyphenate when one of three exceptions applies:

(1) when a two-word phrasal adjective contains an adverb ending in *-ly* followed by a past-participial adjective (*firmly held opinion*);

(2) when the phrase follows, rather than precedes, whatever it's modifying (*he was well trained*); and

(3) when the phrase consists of a proper noun or foreign words (*several United States officers*; *ad hoc committee*).

Yet in working on briefs, I've had to contend with colleagues who wanted everything to be an exception. They have wanted to write *the no waiver of royalty clause*, and write it repeatedly. Meanwhile, others have wanted to refer to *the law of the case doctrine*. Unhyphenated, these phrases cause a slow style, full of double takes. And we lawyers ought to be doing better.

Examples from *The New York Times* and *The Wall Street Journal*

advance-free loan
air-conditioned tent
anti-Iraq coalition
bankruptcy-law protection
big-spending Texan
bikini-clad blondes
birds-and-bees metaphor
blue-jeans-and-T-shirt crowd
boom-to-bust story
business-related lawsuits
call-in television show
career-damaging scandal
cease-fire agreement
civil-rights suit
commercial-free television
commodities-law violations
credit-card applications
cut-rate prices
day-care center
Democratic-stronghold states
dirty-tricks operative
disk-drive maker
dog-eat-dog, man-eat-man, cat-
    eat-bird beastliness
draft-choice compensation
electoral-college strategies
equal-protection clause
failure-to-warn claim
five-day trip
flat-panel computer screens
forest-products stocks
fourth-quarter earnings
free-agent compensation
full-time officials
gay-rights groups

general-election attack
get-out-the-vote activities
guns-and-butter policy
hard-bitten it's-just-another-
    audition Scarletts
health-care products
highest-ranking naval officers
high-frequency sounds
high-profit pharmacy
high-tech oblivion
in-stock LP's
junk-bond rating
late-afternoon buying surge
Latin-stock strategist
lead-paint makers
limited-liability company
loan-loss provisions
long-term, job-intensive projects
low-power pocket phones
mail-order products
man-eat-man business
minimum-height requirement
modern-dance festival
money-market rates
much-talked-about strategies
mutual-fund company
net-interest margins
non-capital-intensive service
    sector
nuclear-power plant
off-the-shelf operation
100-share index
one-time dissident
one-time emergency sale
open-air market

pay-in-kind preferred stock
per-share earnings
price-earnings multiple
private-car perks
racial-discrimination suit
remote-control methods
satellite-TV equipment
Scarlett-is-my-life Scarletts
second-quarter operating profits
short-term debt
six-day, eight-state bus tour
small-business arena
special-interest money
sports-utility vehicles
state-enterprise boards
state-of-the-art semiconductor
state-owned public housing
stronger-than-expected second-
    quarter profit
subchapter-S corporation
take-it-or-leave-it shot
tax-and-spend Democrat
tax-law risk
third-largest steelmaker
30-second sound bites
tit-for-tat accusations
top-line growth
turkey-calling champion
two-year sentence
U.S.-built cars
used-record stores
weaker-than-usual results
white-collar workers
wood-products segment
year-to-year rise

Examples of Common Phrasal Adjectives in Legal Writing

20-ounce glass
20-year-old sister
30-day deadline
30-day time limit
120-hour notice requirement
305-paragraph complaint
above-the-line deduction
abuse-of-discretion standard
acceptance-of-responsibility
  reduction
accident-reconstruction expert
accord-and-satisfaction
  agreement
accrual-basis taxpayer
actual-cash-value insurance
adequate-assurances doctrine
administrative-agency
  determination
administrative-compliance
  proceeding
advance-fee scheme
adverse-splits policy
affirmative-action policy
after-the-fact objections
age-discrimination claim
age-discrimination law
agreed-upon market-share level
aiding-and-abetting provision
air-courier company
air-pollution-control
  requirements
air-rights-restriction issues
alarm-system dealers
alter-ego claim
alter-ego theory
alternative-dispute-resolution
  clause
amount-in-controversy threshold
annuity-payment date
antitrust-enforcement practices
asbestos-related claims
asset-purchase agreement
as-yet-unaddressed problem
attorney-client-relationship
  threshold
attorney-corporate-client
  privilege
attorney-work-product privilege
attorneys'-fee award
at-will employment

automatic-stay period
aviation-fueling liability
  insurance
bad-faith case
bad-faith claim
bad-faith conduct
bad-faith enforcement
bad-faith refusal
bad-faith tactics
balance-sheet requirement
bar-code reader
below-the-line deduction
benefit-of-the-bargain damages
big-six accounting firm
birth-control device
bodily-injury claims
brain-cancer patients
breach-of-contract action
breach-of-contract claim
breach-of-contract count
breach-of-duty-of-loyalty claim
breach-of-employment-contract
  action
breach-of-fiduciary-duty case
breach-of-fiduciary-duty claim
breach-of-implied-covenant
  claim
breach-of-loyalty claim
breach-of-settlement-agreement
  counterclaim
breach-of-warranty claim
breast-implant cases
business-combination laws
business-income coverage
business-judgment standard
business-management
  consultant
business-meal policy
business-necessity defense
business-outreach program
business-records exception
campaign-finance law
capital-gains tax
case-management order
case-or-controversy requirement
case-specific application
cease-and-desist order
certificate-of-need application
change-in-control compensation
change-of-address form

charitable-gift-annuity
  agreement
child-abuse laws
child-care expenses
child-molestation incident
child-support obligation
child-support program
child-welfare services
choice-of-forum clause
choice-of-law clause
choice-of-law principles
civil-enforcement provision
civil-rights action
civil-rights violations
class-action complaint
class-action decision
class-action lawsuit
class-action mechanism
class-action plaintiffs
class-action settlement
class-certification discovery
clearly-erroneous standard of
  review
code-upgrade coverage
collateral-estoppel doctrine
collateral-estoppel effect
collateral-impeachment rule
collective-bargaining agreement
commercial-arbitration rules
commercial-liability defense
  costs
common-fund cases
common-law claims
common-law jurisprudence
common-law liability
common-law-liability promise
common-law negligence
community-property
  presumption
competitive-pay programs
complete-diversity rule
complete-preemption doctrine
compulsory-attendance law
computer-repair industry
computer-science principles
computer-security measures
computer-software packages
conflict-of-interest grounds
conflict-of-laws issue
conspiracy-law dispute

conspiracy-to-infringe claims
consumer-credit reporting
  agency
consumer-dispute verification
  form
contract-formation issues
contract-modification rule
copyright-infringement claim
corporate-shield doctrine
cost-allocation agreement
cost-conscious management
cost-management services
cost-recovery action
customer-handling process
customer-related activities
cutting-edge fuel-injector
  technology
danger-creation theory
dangerous-condition-of-public-
  property case
data-entry operator
dealer-only auction
death-compensation form
debt-limitation statute
declaratory-judgment action
declaratory-relief action
declining-interest-rate scenario
deliberate-indifference standard
desert-tortoise habitat
design-defect case
direct-action statute
direct-mail promotion
direct-recognition program
direct-trunked transport-pricing
  relationships
discounted-cash-flow valuation
  mistrade
disparate-impact analysis
diversity-jurisdiction statute
document-production process
document-request responses
domain-name registration
domestic-violence case
domestic-violence counseling
drinking-water-quality
  regulations
drug-tax stamp
dual-agency relationship
due-diligence issues
due-diligence review
due-process concerns
due-process rights
duty-to-develop cases
duty-to-warn claims

emotional-distress damages
employee-benefit plans
employee-conduct matter
employer-relations ordinance
employment-discrimination
  laws
employment-discrimination suit
environmental-cleanup cases
environmental-exposure
  litigation
environmental-impact report
environment-contamination
  cases
equal-protection rights
exclusive employee-grievance
  remedies
executive-level employees
expense-management strategies
expert-affidavit requirements
expert-disclosure requirements
expert-witness designation
fact-finding conference
fact-intensive exercise
fact-specific question
fair-use defense
fair-use doctrine
false-imprisonment claim
family-preservation services
fax-filing requirements
federal-question jurisdiction
federal-question-jurisdiction
  statute
fee-shifting provisions
field-representative support
filed-tariff doctrine
firm-commitment basis
first-to-file rule
first-use date
fitness-for-duty evaluation
five-part test
five-year effort
fixed-term deposit
fixed-term employment contract
flood-control district
floor-care equipment
follow-up care
food-concession-fixture business
foreign-relations expert
forum-selection clause
four-inch-thick case file
four-year limitations period
fraud-on-the-market claim
free-speech rights
frivolous-action statute

fruit-of-the-poisonous-tree
  doctrine
fundamental-analysis approach
garden-variety business dispute
garden-variety grievance
general-obligation municipal
  bond
generic-parts lawsuit
geographic-market definition
going-concern value
golden-parachute provisions
good-cause requirement
good-faith argument
good-faith attempt
good-faith doctrine
good-faith effort
good-faith-reliance defense
good-faith requirement
government-contracts attorney
gross-population data
group-published-information
  presumption
growth-inducing effects
hair-replacement clients
harmless-error rule
hazardous-waste-disposal plans
health-benefit plan
health-care benefits
health-care costs
health-care district
health-care expenditures
health-care management
health-insurance plan
highest-ranking companies
hit-and-run accident
home-of-parent order
hostile-work-environment
  sexual-harassment suit
human-rights organization
implied-consent statute
incentive-bonus agreement
incidental-take authorizations
income-tax withholding
indirect-effects analysis
indirect-purchaser action
indispensable-party inquiry
industrial-park bonds
inequitable-conduct claims
inequitable-conduct defense
information-and-belief
  allegations
innocent-landowner defense
insurance-coverage case
insurance-law commentator

intellectual-property law
intellectual-property rights
intentional-act exclusion
interest-sensitive whole-life
  policy
interstate-commerce provisions
investment-management
  company
invited-error doctrine
issue-preclusion doctrine
joint-replacement surgery
joint-venture relationship
judicial-admission exception
judicial-restraint philosophy
jury-demand requirement
jury-selection strategy
key-number system
knock-and-announce rule
known-risk defense
lack-of-relevance argument
last-chance warning
last-minute attempt
last-straw job-performance
  discharge
law-enforcement agency
law-review article
learned-intermediary doctrine
legal-defense costs
legal-justification defense
legal-liability policy
legal-malpractice claim
legislative-veto provision
life-insurance-fraud scheme
life-insurance trust
life-or-death situations
likelihood-of-confusion issues
limitation-of-damages clause
limitation-of-liability clause
limited-liability company
limited-partnership interests
limited-purpose agency
liquidated-damages clause
long-distance
  telecommunications
long-distance telephone service
long-term foster care
long-term growth
long-term primary-care
  physicians
long-term prospects
long-term service contracts
loss-causation requirement
loss-of-rent claim
lost-profit damages

lump-sum award
mail-fraud case
mandatory learner-outcome
  standards
marital-status discrimination
market-efficiency information
market-manipulation case
market-share agreement
market-share calculations
measure-of-damages rule
medical-causation opinion
medical-malpractice claim
medical-malpractice insurance
meet-and-confer letter
meet-and-confer process
mental-anguish damages
mental-health professional
merger-and-acquisition activity
minimum-contacts prong
money-market funds
mortgage-loan funds
motion-picture-production
  rights
motion-to-compel hearing
motion-to-dismiss standard
motion-to-transfer factors
motor-vehicle records
multiple-employer welfare
  arrangements
multiple-fatality motor-vehicle
  accident
municipal-bond business
name-brand parts
national-origin discrimination
natural-gas liquids
natural-resource damage claim
necessary-party analysis
negligence-per-se theory
negligence-related damages
negligent-repair charges
new-car dealers
newly-discovered-evidence
  argument
nine-step walk-and-turn test
no-action clause
no-contest plea
no-further-obligation clause
non-interest-bearing account
non-sports-related cases
notice-hearing procedure
nude-dancing cases
officer-and-director bar
one-year statute of limitations
on-the-job inquiry

open-door policy
open-market repurchase
  program
open-meeting requirements
opt-out provisions
order-flow payments
out-of-context quotations
out-of-pocket expenses
out-of-state class members
owned-property exclusion
paid-in capital
paper-recycling plant
parking-space density
parol-evidence rule
partial-waiver doctrine
past-due accounts
patent-infringement action
patent-infringement claim
patent-law expert
patent-licensing agreement
peak-demand times
performance-monitoring
  services
periodic-reporting obligations
per-person limits
personal-consumption expenses
personal-injury claims
personal-injury lawyer
pilot-program results
plain-view doctrine
plan-document obligations
point-of-service products
police-pursuit case
political-question doctrine
pollution-coverage insurance
  policy
pollution-exclusion clause
post-office box
preexisting-condition exclusion
preliminary-injunction relief
price-fixing agreement
primary-violator argument
private-letter rulings
private-party funding source
private-securities litigation
probable-cause affidavit
probable-cause charge
products-liability action
professional-malpractice action
profit-sharing plans
progressive-loss case
promissory-fraud exception
property-damage claimant
property-tax appeals

prosecution-history estoppel
prosecutorial-misconduct case
prudent-investor rule
public-interest considerations
public-policy exceptions
public-policy issues
public-record requirements
public-works contract
punitive-damages award
punitive-damages phase
pure-agency theory
qualified-immunity defense
quality-assurance measures
quality-control requirements
question-and-answer session
race-car driver
race-discrimination case
railroad right-of-way law
ready-to-drink form
real-estate agent
real-estate development
real-estate lien
real-estate listings
real-estate loan
real-party claimants
real-party-in-interest rule
record-keeping duties
recreational-land-use statute
regular-course-of-business
    foundational requirement
remote-analysis technology
repair-history standpoint
replacement-cost insurance
reservation-record databases
residential-mortgage service
response-action costs
retail-ground-floor space
revenue-adjustment alteration
reverse-confusion context
right-of-privacy objection
right-to-sue letter
risk-allocation provisions
risk-of-loss issue
rule-of-reason analysis
rule-of-reason defense
rule-of-reason proceeding
safe-harbor argument
safe-harbor rules
sale-of-goods context
sales-prize calculations
school-desegregation case
second-degree robbery
securities-fraud actions
securities-fraud claim

securities-law claims
securities-law violations
security-alarm dealers
seizure-alert dog
selective-enforcement defense
self-insured employee-welfare
    benefit plan
separation-of-powers doctrine
separation-of-powers issue
service-of-process clause
settlement-approval hearings
settlement-conference statement
severance-pay plan
sex-discrimination award
sex-reassignment surgery
sexual-abuse problems
sexual-deviancy evaluation
sexual-harassment claim
shifting-burden-of-proof
    analysis
short-swing profits
short-term cash
single-vehicle accident
sister-state judgment
six-day period
six-month exception
slander-of-title action
slip-and-fall accident
small-business owner
social-security benefits
soft-dollar arrangements
solid-waste-management
    facilities
special-purpose entity
special-relationship
    requirement
special-verdict form
spinal-fusion surgery
split-limit insurance policy
standard-form fire-insurance
    policy
state-court disciplinary action
state-court proceeding
state-law cases
state-law claims
state-law contribution action
state-law prohibition
state-law wrongful-discharge
    claim
state-promulgated forums
state-tax immunity
statute-of-limitations defense
statute-of-limitations grounds
statute-of-limitations period

statutory-interpretation
    argument
stipulated-judgment case
stock-appreciation rights
stock-option agreement
stock-option holders
stock-option plan
stock-purchase agreement
stop-and-frisk procedures
straight-line method
stream-of-commerce theory
street-level operations
strict-liability standard
strict-scrutiny test
subject-matter jurisdiction
substance-abuse treatment
suit-limitation provision
summary-judgment evidence
summary-judgment motion
summary-judgment phase
summary-judgment procedure
summary-judgment ruling
summary-judgment standard
supervised-visitation services
surface-water ponds
switched-access rates
system-enhancement fees
tax-deficiency determination
tax-liability questions
tax-return position
teacher-internship programs
team-building meetings
ten-day filing period
tender-offer statutes
termination-of-officer severance
    agreement
terms-of-service agreement
thermal-energy recovery
third-degree assault
third-party action
third-party-beneficiary standing
third-party claim
third-party debt collector
third-party obligor
third-party property-damage
    claims
third-party witnesses
three-count indictment
three-part test
three-step analysis
three-year statute of limitations
tire-storage sites
title-insurance company
tortious-interference claim

total-disability compensation
trade-dress case
trade-dress protection
trademark-infringement claims
trademark-infringement context
trademark-infringement suit
trade-secret analysis
trade-secret documents
trade-secret misappropriations
trade-secret protection
trade-secret status
trial-court proceedings
truck-maintenance contracts
two-count declaratory-judgment-
    act claim
two-party check
two-year period
unborn-widow rule
unconscionable-contract claim
undue-burden test
unemployment-insurance
    benefits
unfair-business-practice claim

unfair-competition claim
unjust-enrichment claim
unlawful-detainer action
unlawful-use-of-a-weapon
    charge
value-added tax
vending-machine company
vendor-registration form
venue-hearing requirements
victim-impact statement
Virginia-based company
void-for-vagueness doctrine
wage-and-hour laws
wait-and-see principle
waiting-period requirements
waiver-of-privilege issues
waste-disposal practices
waste-disposal services
water-resource development
water-rights scheme
water-supply contracts
welfare-benefit plan
welfare-fraud charges

well-pleaded complaint
willful-and-malicious-acts
    exclusion
willful-infringement allegations
witness-statement rule
work-product privilege
worst-case scenario
written-description
    requirement
wrongful-death action
wrongful-death beneficiaries
wrongful-death claim
wrongful-death statute
wrongful-discharge claims
wrongful-liquidation case
XYY-chromosome defense
year-and-a-day rule
year-to-year lease
yellow-dog contract
zero-coupon bond
zone-density pricing
zone-of-danger rule

59

Otherwise, be stingy with hyphens—especially after prefixes.

Quotable Quotes

"For some years now, the trend in spelling compound words has been away from the use of hyphens. There seems to be a tendency to spell compounds solid as soon as acceptance warrants their being considered permanent compounds, and otherwise to spell them open. This is a trend, not a rule, but it is sometimes helpful . . . ."

—*The Chicago Manual of Style* § 6.38, at 203 (14th ed. 1993).

"Phrasal adjectives aside, the American branch of the English language has become more and more inhospitable to hyphens. Professional writers and editors today prefer that prefixes and their bases be written as solids 99% of the time—that is, as *un*hyphenated single words, whatever the word class of the base may be (adjective, noun, adverb, or verb)."

—Bryan A. Garner, *The Elements of Legal Style* 26 (2d ed. 2002).

Explanation

In American English, most prefixes aren't hyphenated. They make solid words, as in *coworker*, *pretrial*, and *nonstatutory*. If you write *co-worker*, *pre-trial*, or *non-statutory*, you're running against the grain of well-edited writing.

There are several exceptions, however. Use a hyphen in the following circumstances:

- If the solid form might lead the reader to mistake the syllables (as in *anti-inflammatory*, *co-occurrence*, *post-sentencing*).

- If the main word is a proper name (as in *non-Darwinian*).

- If the prefix is part of a noun phrase (as in *non-high-school athletics*).

- If there might be any confusion in meaning (as in *re-lease* when referring to leasing again, not letting go).

But remember: the general rule is no hyphens with prefixes.

Examples of Solid Prefixed Words

coauthor	postelection
coconspirator	postjudgment
cocounsel	postmarital
codefendant	postmortem
coexecutor	postpetition
coheir	posttrial
coplaintiff	postverdict
cotenant	
	prebankruptcy
nonadmission	predate
nonappealable	predeceased
nonassertion	prediscovery
noncancelable	preemployment
noncertified	preemption
nonconstitutional	preexisting
noncontractual	prefiling
noncriminal	prejudgment
nonforfeiture	premortgage
nongovernmental	presentencing
noninjury	prestatutory
nonjury	pretrial
nonjusticiable	preverdict
nonlawyer	prewriting
nonnegligent	
nonnegotiable	semiannual
nonobvious	semiautomatic
nonpracticing	semicommercial
nonresident	semimonthly
nonreversible	semiofficial
nonsubstantive	semipermanent
nontransferable	semiretirement

60

Avoid gratuitous quotation marks and other typographic oddities.

Quotable Quotes

"To the do-it-yourself sign painter and poster letterer, quotation marks are a fascinating and irresistible mystery. There is no accounting for the way in which these artists reach for quotation marks at the slightest, even at no, provocation: 'Special "Mother's Day" Dinner'; 'Prices Slashed for Our "Fire Sale" '; ' "No Trespassing." ' And the card that graces (or graced) the knick-knack shop in Palm Beach: 'Brow "z" ers Always Welcome.' Somebody had something cute in mind, but what?"

— Theodore M. Bernstein, *The Careful Writer* 372 (1965).

"Sometimes quotation marks are used by writers to disown words: to show the reader that the writer knows they're slang, or are used unconventionally, or express ideas with which the writer doesn't agree. Readers faced with this use of quotes seldom know why the word or phrase is being disowned, and the attention-getting device generally ends up looking sophomoric."

— Judi Kesselman-Turkel & Franklynn Peterson, *Good Writing* 128 (1981).

"[W]riters who find themselves underlining frequently for emphasis might consider whether many of the italics are not superfluous, the emphasis being apparent from the context, or whether, if the emphasis is not apparent, it cannot be achieved more gracefully by recasting the sentence. The same reservations apply to frequent use of quotation marks to suggest irony or special usage."

— *The Chicago Manual of Style* § 6.63, at 210 (14th ed. 1993).

"Some writers melt together words by using quotation marks around them. For us, using these marks becomes a guilt-ridden, I-know-this-word-does-not-really-exist signal from the writer to the reader."

— Gary Hoffman & Glynis Hoffman, *Adios, Strunk and White* 40 (1999).

"Academic writers too easily become addicted to the use of quotation marks, whether to signify irony and sarcasm, to establish a certain lofty distance from the commonplace facts of everyday life, to imply that ordinary terms are being used in an unfamiliar and esoteric way, or perhaps also to confess the writer's inability to say anything in a straightforward way."

— Christopher Lasch, *Plain Style* 66 (Stewart Weaver ed., 2002).

Explanation

Quotation marks are, if I may say so, the most "misused" punctuation mark in the English language. Well, perhaps not "English," but more accurately "American."

If you know what I mean.

Reserve quotation marks for three situations: (1) when you're quoting someone; (2) when you're referring to a word as a word (*the word "that"*); and (3) when you mean so-called-but-not-really (*If this is a "fixture," it certainly doesn't fit any definition in the caselaw*).

Don't use them for phrasal adjectives (see #58), don't use them to be cute, and don't use them to suggest that the marked word or phrase is somehow informal or slangy. If you mean what you say, say it without hesitation. If you don't, say something else.

Likewise, don't experiment with funky fonts or unusual typefaces. Using these devices will suggest that you're desperately trying to jazz up an otherwise dull brief. Notice in Example C below how the first version distracts with its frilly title, its sans-serif typeface, and its use of boldface for emphasis. The second version cleans up the text—and makes the arguments clearer by putting them into a numbered list.

Some Before-and-After Examples

Example A

Before   To do this, Gateway turned to the "take or pay" provisions most commonly found in oil-and-gas leases.

After   To do this, Gateway turned to the take-or-pay provisions most commonly found in oil-and-gas leases.

Example B

Before   According to the "fraud on the market" theory, if the market itself is "defrauded" by misrepresentations, then plaintiffs who relied on the "integrity" of the market price when purchasing securities have presumptively relied for the purposes of a Rule 10b-5 claim.

After   According to the fraud-on-the-market theory, if the market itself is defrauded by misrepresentations, then plaintiffs who relied on the integrity of the market price when purchasing securities have presumptively relied for the purposes of a Rule 10b-5 claim.

Example C

Before   *Defendants' Response to Plaintiffs' Trial Brief*

Defendants, Alpha Corporation and Alpha Plus Corporation (collectively, "Alpha"), respectfully respond to address the issue of which state's law applies in this case. Contrary to plaintiffs' suggestions, Alpha's position on the choice of law for the construction of the written Alpha employment contracts and the 2003 Alpha Deferred Compensation Plan has always been and remains consistent. **First,** **New York** law applies to issues relating to the construction, interpretation and enforceability of plaintiffs' written Alpha contracts, as well as any alleged oral amendment of the contracts pursuant to § 8.7 of the March 1, 2001 employment contracts. **Second,** to the extent that plaintiffs' alleged claim of bad faith refers to plaintiffs' written Alpha contracts, **New York law** applies. To the extent that plaintiffs' alleged claim of bad faith refers to plaintiffs' Deferred Compensation Plan, **federal law** applies because ERISA preempts all state law claims. However, apart from the ERISA preemption, it does not matter whether New York or Oklahoma law applies since neither New York nor Oklahoma recognizes an independent cause of action for the implied covenant of good faith and fair dealing. **Finally,** plaintiffs worked in Oklahoma for a corporation with its headquarters in Oklahoma. Consequently, substantive New York labor law does not apply.

After
Alpha's Response to Plaintiffs' Trial Brief

Despite Major's suggestions to the contrary, Alpha Corporation and Alpha Plus Corporation (collectively, "Alpha") have maintained a consistent position on the choice-of-law issues in this case. But in an effort to clarify any possible misunderstanding, Alpha will reiterate its arguments:

1. New York law applies to issues involving the construction and enforceability of plaintiffs' written employment contracts, as well as to any alleged oral amendment of these contracts under § 8.7 of the March 2001 employment agreements.

2. Major's bad-faith claims are subject to New York law and federal law. New York law applies to the claims involving plaintiffs' written employment contracts; federal law (by preemption under ERISA) applies to the claims involving plaintiffs' deferred-compensation plan. Apart from the ERISA preemption, however, it does not matter whether New York or Oklahoma law applies because neither state recognizes an independent claim for bad faith.

3. Because Major worked in Oklahoma—and for a corporation with its headquarters in Oklahoma—substantive New York labor law does not apply.

61

Use bullets for lists.

Quotable Quotes

"I consider the bullet a magical device, a wonderful way to help untangle ideas and show readers the organization within paragraphs."
—Edward P. Bailey, Jr., *The Plain English Approach to Business Writing* 77 (1990).

"When you don't mean to imply that one thing in a list is any more important than another—that is, when you're not signaling that there is a rank order—and there is little likelihood that the list will need to be cited, you might use bullet dots. They draw the eye immediately to the salient points and thereby enhance readability."
—Bryan A. Garner, *A Dictionary of Modern Legal Usage* 290 (2d ed. 1995).

Explanation

Although legal writers seem to fear that bullets characterize the breezy journalist's style, in fact they help convey information quickly. That's why journalists use them, and it's why you should consider using them.

You'll need some guidelines:

- Ensure that the size of your bullets is proportional with the size of your type. You don't want overpowering bullets; the best bullets are typically just smaller than a lowercase "o" filled in with ink.

- Adjust your tab settings so that you'll have a small tab between the bullet and the text. Space them about the way you see them throughout this book—about .15 inch from the text that follows. Use a larger space for a paragraph indent.

- Always use a hanging indent. That is, don't allow the text to wrap under the bullet; instead, leave the bullet hanging out to the left. Learn what keystroke to use with your software.

- Single-space the bulleted text. If you have longish points, though, double-space between them. But don't ever make your bulleted items too long: you don't want to raise suspicions that you're playing with the text to sidestep page limits.

- Capitalize the first word in each bulleted item if that item ends with a period. Otherwise, lowercase the first word and put a semicolon at the end of each one (except the last, which should end with a period).

- Keep your items grammatically parallel (see #41).

- End your introduction to the bulleted list with a colon. It serves as a bridge.

- Resist the temptation to play with computer-generated boxes, arrows, check marks, and other eye-catchers. Nothing else works quite as well as a bullet.

It's not that bullets will invariably replace numerals (which more strongly suggest that you're ranking the items). In a given context, you can choose whether to use bullets as a visual device or numerals as a ranking device. The point is that you'll need bullets as one of your enumerative tools.

Some Before-and-After Examples

Example A

Before   Defendants' conduct from the date they first learned that Boorland had patents relating to plastic encapsulation in 1986 up through the time of the jury's verdict has been egregious. A detailed discussion of Defendants' egregious conduct is set forth in Boorland's Brief in Support of Its Motion for Entry of Judgment After Jury Verdict, sections III and IV, filed on June 14, 1995. Examples of Defendants' failure to act equitably include: (1) burying their heads in the sand so as to avoid learning the specifics of the patents when they started their operations and even after they learned of the BERN proceeding and its application to many of the largest microchip manufacturers in the world, (2) failing to proceed with due care after receiving formal notice of infringement from Boorland, (3) wasting judicial resources by trying the same case before the jury that they lost before the ITC, and (4) presenting testimony at trial that was inconsistent with prior sworn testimony. The evidence before the Court and the jury's findings that each of the Defendants are willful infringers demonstrate that they have unclean hands and therefore are precluded from raising in the first instance a defense of laches.

After   Smithfield's conduct has been egregious ever since 1986, when they first learned that Boorland had patents relating to plastic encapsulation, and up until the jury's verdict. (For a detailed discussion, see Boorland's post-verdict brief in support of its motion for entry of judgment.) Examples of Smithfield's inequitable conduct include:

- purposely avoiding learning the specifics of the patents, not only when they started their operations but even after they learned of the BERN proceeding and its application to many of the largest microchip manufacturers in the world;

- failing to proceed with due care after receiving formal notice of infringement from Boorland;

- wasting judicial resources by asking the jury to consider the same evidence they had used when losing before the ITC; and

- presenting testimony that contradicted prior sworn testimony.

The evidence before the Court and the jury's findings that Smithfield is a willful infringer demonstrate that the company has unclean hands. It is therefore precluded from raising a defense of laches.

Example B

Before

CONCLUSION

WHEREFORE, PREMISES CONSIDERED, the named plaintiffs pray that they be granted partial summary judgment that the savings clause is not a special law in violation of article III, section 56 of the Texas Constitution; that the amendment is unconstitutional in violation of article I, section 16 of the Texas Constitution; that the defendant insurers were not entitled to charge their insureds a charge, or rate of premium, that was not promulgated by the State Board of Insurance for use with Workers' Compensation and Employers' Liability and related casualty policies covering risks in Texas; that the defendants were not entitled to use forms, including premium agreements, that were not approved by the State Board of Insurance for use with Workers' Compensation and Employers' Liability and related casualty policies covering risks in Texas; that the defendants were not entitled to employ a higher premium tax multiplier than approved by the State Board of Insurance to govern the taxes collected under the retrospectively-rated casualty policies issued in Texas; that the defendants were not entitled to employ factors that were not approved by the State Board of Insurance in determining the premiums due under retrospectively-rated workers' compensation and related casualty policies issued in Texas; and that the named plaintiffs are entitled to summary judgment on the affirmative defenses of waiver, estoppel, laches, unclean hands, ratification, and illegality as pled by the defendants, and for such other and further relief to which they may show themselves to be justly entitled.

After

Conclusion

The named plaintiffs ask the Court to grant partial summary judgment that the following points are correct:

- The savings clause is not a special law that violates article III, section 56 of the Texas Constitution.

- The amendment is an unconstitutional violation of article I, section 16 of the Texas Constitution.

- The defendant insurers were not entitled to charge their insureds a fee or premium rate that was not promulgated by the State Board of Insurance for use with workers'-compensation, employers'-liability, and related casualty policies covering risks in Texas.

- The defendants were not entitled to use forms—including premium agreements—that were not approved by the State Board of Insurance for use with workers'-compensation, employers'-liability, and related casualty policies covering risks in Texas.

- The defendants were not entitled to use a higher premium-tax multiplier than that approved by the State Board of Insurance to govern the taxes collected under the retrospectively rated casualty policies issued in Texas.

- The defendants were not entitled to use factors that were not approved by the State Board of Insurance in determining the premiums due under retrospectively rated workers'-compensation and related casualty policies issued in Texas.

The named plaintiffs also ask the Court to grant summary judgment rejecting the following affirmative defenses pleaded by the defendants:

- waiver;

- estoppel;

- laches;

- unclean hands;

- ratification; and

- illegality.

The named plaintiffs also ask the Court for general relief.

62

Use the serial comma.

Quotable Quotes

"If *and* occurs with the last member of the series, the comma should precede it just the same."
—John F. Genung, *Outlines of Rhetoric* 190 (1894).

"What . . . are the arguments for omitting the last comma? Only one is cogent—the saving of space. In the narrow width of a newspaper column this saving counts for more than elsewhere, which is why the omission is so nearly universal in journalism.

. . .

"The recommendation here is that [the writer] use the comma between *all* members of a series, including the last two, on the common-sense ground that to do so will preclude ambiguities and annoyances at a negligible cost."
—Wilson Follett, *Modern American Usage* 398, 401 (1966).

"In a series of the form *a, b, and c* or *red, white, and blue* most publishers prefer a comma (sometimes called the serial comma) before the conjunction, whether the items of the series are words, phrases, or clauses. The consistent use of this comma is recommended, for in many sentences it is essential for clarity."
—*Words into Type* 187 (3d ed. 1974).

"Three or more elements in a series are separated by commas. When the last two elements (words, phrases, or clauses) in a series are joined by a conjunction, a comma comes before the conjunction—unless you're a journalist."
—Karen Elizabeth Gordon, *The New Well-Tempered Sentence* 46 (rev. ed. 1993).

"Use a comma before the last item in a series. This practice is now almost universally preferred."
—Christopher Lasch, *Plain Style* 55 (Stewart Weaver ed., 2002).

Explanation

Although journalists omit the serial comma to save space, virtually all writing authorities outside journalism recommend consistently using it to prevent ambiguities. When it comes to legal writing, is it even a close call?

Consider this sentence: "As soon as Jones recognized that he had a potential conflict of interest, he placed calls to Standard Oil, Fidelity Bank, Thompson and Lee and Baines." Did Jones make four calls or five? Probably four, assuming that in calling "Thompson and Lee and Baines," he didn't call three separate persons. Two of these names probably go together (as a firm name, perhaps), but which two? Is it *Thompson and Lee*, and *Baines*; or is it *Thompson*, and *Lee and Baines*? Without the serial comma, you can't tell. That's only one of several contexts in which ambiguity can result from omitting the serial comma.

Many people, including many lawyers, mistakenly believe that the serial comma is incorrect. Yet no authority calls the serial comma wrong. It's true that the *AP Stylebook* says not to use it in simple series (as in *red, white and blue*—but see the Nurnberg quotation below).* Yet omitting the serial comma is a matter of style, not a rule of punctuation. No such rule has ever existed. No such rule *could* exist, because as series get more complex the need for the serial comma grows stronger.

Apart from the *AP Stylebook*, the authorities line up pretty solidly in favor of the serial comma. So when a colleague tries to tell you that a comma shouldn't precede the *and* or *or* introducing the last item in a list, ask for authority on the point. Your colleague probably can't cite one. You, on the other hand, will have an impressive array of authorities to support your position. Here's just a smattering of what you can use:

- Edgar A. Alward & Jean A. Alward, *Punctuation Plain and Simple* 36 (1997): "A comma is preferred after the next-to-last item."

- *Chicago Manual of Style* § 6.19, at 245 (15th ed. 2003): "Chicago strongly recommends this widely practiced usage, blessed by Fowler and other authorities, since it prevents ambiguity."

- H. W. Fowler, *A Dictionary of Modern English Usage* 24 (1926): "The only rule that will obviate . . . uncertainties is that after every item, including the last unless a heavier stop is needed for independent reasons, the comma should be used."

- Joseph Gibaldi, *MLA Style Manual* § 3.4.2b, at 67 (2d ed. 1998): "Use a comma to separate words, phrases, and clauses in a series."

- Andrea Lunsford & Robert Connors, *The St. Martin's Handbook* § 27d, at 427 (1989): "You may often see a series with no comma after the next-to-last item, particularly in newspaper writing, as in *The day was cold, dark and dreary*. Occasionally, however, omitting the comma can cause confusion, and you will never be wrong to include it."

- Joan I. Miller & Bruce J. Taylor, *The Punctuation Handbook* 21 (1989): "Nothing is gained by omitting the final comma in a list, while clarity can be lost in some cases through misreading."

---

* *The Associated Press Stylebook and Briefing on Media Law* 329–33 (Norm Goldstein ed. 2002).

- Maxwell Nurnberg, *Questions You Always Wanted to Ask About English* 181 (1972): "[W]hen we say 'The colors of our country are red, white, and blue,' there's a little pause after *white* that seems to ask for a comma to make *blue* just as important as *red* and *white*, and not merely a combination of white and blue."

- Patricia T. O'Conner, *Woe Is I* 137 (1996): "[M]y advice is to stick with using the final comma."

- R. M. Ritter, *The Oxford Guide to Style* 121 (2d ed. 2002): "If the last item in a list has emphasis equal to the previous ones, it needs a comma to create a pause of equal weight to those that came before."

- William A. Sabin, *The Gregg Reference Manual* § 123b, at 15 (9th ed. 1999): "Some writers prefer to omit the comma before *and*, *or*, or *nor* in a series, but the customary practice in business is to retain the comma before the conjunction."

- *Scientific Style and Format* § 4.15.6, at 49 (6th ed. 1994): "Some writers prefer to omit the comma before the closing conjunction, but routine use of this comma saves having to take time to consider possible ambiguities."

- Kate L. Turabian, *A Manual for Writers of Term Papers, Theses, and Dissertations* §§ 3.68, 3.70, at 50–51 (5th ed. 1987): "A series of three or more words, phrases, or clauses (like this) takes a comma between each of the elements and before a conjunction separating the last two."

- *U.S. Government Printing Office Style Manual* § 8.42, at 131 (2000): "The comma is used after each member within a series of three or more words, phrases, letters, or figures used with *and*, *or*, or *nor*."

- *U.S. News & World Report Stylebook* 41 (Robert O. Grover ed., 9th ed., 2001): "Items in a series are divided by commas: *On his farm he grew soybeans, peanuts, and corn.*"

Part G

Becoming Proficient in Designing Text

63

In the argument section,
use argumentative headings.

Quotable Quotes

"Remember that the court usually gets its basic impression of the nature of your legal argument from these headings, because the usual practice is to turn to the index, where such headings should be inserted verbatim, and read it before reading the brief."

—Raymond E. Peters, *The Preparation and Filing of Briefs on Appeal*, 22 Cal. St. B.J. 175, 179–80 (1947).

"Headings should always be argumentative rather than topical or even assertive. For instance, write 'This suit is barred by laches because brought twenty-five years after the issuance of the original certificate' rather than 'This suit is barred by laches.' The first gives the argument in a nutshell, the second does not—though certainly the second assertive heading is infinitely more effective than the merely topical 'The question of laches.' Similarly, say 'Appellant had notice of the defect and therefore is not a holder in due course' in preference to 'Appellant is not a holder in due course' or to 'Appellant's contention.' Otherwise stated, employ the technique of the American newspaper headline rather than that of the English: our journalists say 'Bums Down Braves, 9–2,' whereas theirs write 'Test Match at Lords.' "

—Frederick B. Wiener, *Briefing and Arguing Federal Appeals* 67 (rev. ed. 1967).

"When headings are interspersed within the argument itself they should be phrased in argumentative form, and not as mere topical references. If they are so worded, the judges will see immediately not only what the section concerns, but what the advocate argues."

—Girvan Peck, *Writing Persuasive Briefs* 149 (1984).

"The point heading should be a clear and complete statement, forcefully written. It should not be a statement of an abstract principle of law, but should contain the conclusion that must follow the application of a principle of law to the facts of the case."

—Edward D. Re, *Brief Writing and Oral Argument* 147 (6th ed. 1987).

"Appropriate headings and subheadings increase clarity. They explain where the brief is going and provide signposts along the way. The captions should be as brief as possible, but sufficiently explicit to describe the point. Numbering the subpoints may also be helpful. That tells the reader that the brief is turning to a different but related aspect of the same subject."

—Daniel M. Friedman, "Winning on Appeal," in *Appellate Practice Manual* 129, 133 (Priscilla A. Schwab ed., 1992).

Explanation

Although it's fine to use topical headings in a statement of facts (e.g., "The May 2003 Meeting"), you should punctuate the body of your brief with headings that capsulize an argument. Each heading should be a complete sentence ending with a period, set in boldface type, and preferably no more than two lines long (single-spaced). A good argumentative heading is essentially a "super topic sentence." The paragraphs that follow it should elaborate the point in the heading—without merely repeating it.

As the Wiener quotation above suggests, a good heading will often contain a logical connective such as *because* or *therefore*. That way, you're sure to include some reasoning instead of merely stating a conclusion.

If you follow this tip, your table of contents will reveal the full argument, assertion by assertion. Your brief will become more skimmable. And in the weary eyes of a busy judge, that means a lot.

The following tables of contents show how easy it can be to track the argument if well-organized headings contain assertions. Notice that the headings are all set in roman type in the table of contents even though in the text of the brief they should be set according to tip #64.

Example A is drawn from a brief filed by the Solicitor General's Office in July 2001. In a brief with only one main argument, the SG traditionally puts an unnumbered heading followed by argumentative headings preceded by capital letters: A, B, C, etc.

The headings in Example B appeared in a brief to the Supreme Court of Mississippi in a case decided in 2002. Many lawyers were involved in the case: William R. Keffer of Dallas; Reuben V. Anderson, Luther T. Munford, Michael B. Wallace, Amanda K. Jones, and Christopher B. Green of Jackson; Robert Meadows and C. Camille Nurre of Houston; and Robert O. Allen of Brookhaven, Mississippi. LawProse, Inc. acted as editorial consultants. Interestingly, the Supreme Court of Mississippi closely followed the organization and expression of the headings in its opinion.

Example C, from a brief by Harry M. Reasoner of Houston, is to the Texas Supreme Court on the question whether alcohol manufacturers have a duty to warn of the dangers of alcohol.

Example D shows headings in a fuller context, with the surrounding text. It comes from a brief opposing a motion to dismiss. Notice how the headings are short enough to capture the reader's attention, yet complete enough to reveal the gist of the argument.

Some Uncommonly Good Examples

Example A

Table of Contents

Example B

Table of Contents

Example C

Table of Contents

Example D

SouthTel Corporation's Opposition to Alpine Systems' Motion to Dismiss and Request for Postponement

SouthTel Corporation opposes Alpine Systems' motion to dismiss because SouthTel's tariff establishes the jurisdiction of the Arbitrator to decide this claim. SouthTel also opposes Alpine's request for an indefinite postponement because the schedule Alpine requests will unnecessarily delay these proceedings. SouthTel asks the Arbitrator to issue an order denying Alpine's motion to dismiss and requiring Alpine to serve an answer within seven days after service of the Arbitrator's ruling.

1.   The Arbitrator has jurisdiction to rule on SouthTel's claim against Alpine for outstanding Tariff charges.

A.   SouthTel's Tariff defines the terms for service to Alpine including the arbitration of payment disputes.

Alpine ordered telecommunications services, and SouthTel provided them, under the terms of SouthTel Tariff F.C.C. No. 1 ("Tariff"). The law is well settled that the tariff of a telecommunications common carrier controls the rights and liabilities between the carrier and its customer.[1] Unlike mere contracts, federal tariffs are the law.[2] Here then, Tariff § B-7.13 governs the legal rights of Alpine and SouthTel to arbitrate payment disputes.

B. Tariff § B-7.13 permits either the customer or SouthTel to initiate arbitration of a payment dispute. Once begun, both parties are bound to arbitrate the claim.

Section B-7.13 provides a choice of forums for the resolution of payment disputes. "All disputes concerning or affecting payment of invoices . . . may be resolved through binding arbitration." When a customer contests SouthTel invoices totaling over $10,000, the customer may choose to arbitrate the dispute. Likewise, when a customer fails to pay invoices totaling over $10,000, SouthTel may choose arbitration.

But the right to arbitrate would be empty without a corresponding requirement to arbitrate. "Once SouthTel or the customer has commenced arbitration of a dispute, arbitration shall be mandatory." Thus, § B-7.13 ensures the right. Once either a customer or SouthTel has commenced arbitration, the other party must arbitrate the initiating party's claim. Alpine argues that the right and the requirement to arbitrate are inherently contradictory. (Alpine's Motion, p. 2.) To the contrary, the requirement guarantees a right that would otherwise be meaningless. Alpine's argument fails because it rests on a false conflict.

C. Tariff § B-7.13 permits, but does not require, a customer to allege a counterclaim in an arbitration that SouthTel has initiated.

Section B-7.13113 defines a counterclaim as "[a] claim the Responding Party has against the Claiming Party which concerns or affects the payment of invoices that are the subject of the Notice of Claim." This rule limits counterclaims in arbitration to claims that arise out of the same transaction as the Claiming Party's claim. Section B-7.13 provides that such a counterclaim "may be asserted." Thus, a Responding Party (like a Claiming Party) has a choice of forums for the resolution of its claim. The Tariff does not require a Responding Party to assert any counterclaim it may have in arbitration; but the Tariff allows the Responding Party to assert a counterclaim. And if the party chooses to arbitrate a counterclaim, then § B-7.13272 directs the party to file its counterclaim together with its answer.

---

[1] *See MCI Telecomms. Corp. v. Graham*, 7 F.3d 477, 479 (6th Cir. 1993); *American Tel. & Tel. Co. v. Florida-Texas Freight, Inc.*, 357 F. Supp. 977, 979 (S.D. Fla.), *aff'd per curiam*, 485 F.2d 1390 (5th Cir. 1973).

[2] *See Western Union Tel. Co. v. Esteve Bros.*, 256 U.S. 566, 572 (1921); *Western Union Int'l v. Data Dev., Inc.*, 41 F.3d 1494, 1496 (11th Cir. 1995); *MCI Telecomms. Corp. v. Garden State Inv. Corp.*, 981 F.2d 385, 387 (8th Cir. 1992).

So when SouthTel initiates arbitration, a customer has the option of arbitrating its counterclaim. Alpine's assertion that the Tariff requires a customer to arbitrate counterclaims ignores the key language in § B-7.13, "counterclaims may be asserted." (Alpine's Motion, p. 3.) It is only after a customer has opted to arbitrate its counterclaim that arbitration of the counterclaim becomes mandatory upon both parties.

D.   Arbitration of SouthTel's payment dispute does not impair Alpine's right to assert a counterclaim in another forum.

Alpine complains that § B-7.13 deprives a SouthTel customer of the private right of action and the remedies provided by §§ 206 and 207 of the Communications Act, 47 U.S.C. §§ 206, 207 (1995). (Alpine's Motion, pp. 2–4.) This argument rests upon a misreading of the Tariff, as explained in part C above. No Tariff provision requires Alpine to allege a counterclaim in arbitration. Alpine may pursue any claim it has against SouthTel in the forum of Alpine's choice. If Alpine legitimately believes that SouthTel's actions have violated the Communications Act, Alpine may seek relief from the Federal Communications Commission or in federal court. The question presented by SouthTel's Notice of Claim is whether Alpine is liable to SouthTel for the Tariff charges detailed in the Statement Account. The Arbitrator's ruling on this question will perforce decide the validity of Alpine's defenses to SouthTel's claim. But such a ruling will not bar Alpine from asserting an independent claim against SouthTel in the forum of Alpine's choosing. Section B-7.13 expands rather than limits the forums available to Alpine to raise such a claim.

E.   Section 7.13 vests the Arbitrator with jurisdiction to decide SouthTel's claim against Alpine.

The Statement of Account attached to SouthTel's Notice of Claim shows that SouthTel has not received payment from Alpine on invoices issued since April 10, 1994, which total more than $220,000. Under the terms of § B-7.13, this payment dispute may be resolved through binding arbitration. Since SouthTel has served a Notice of Claim, the dispute is subject to arbitration. Accordingly, the Arbitrator has jurisdiction to decide SouthTel's claim. Alpine's motion to dismiss for lack of jurisdiction must therefore be denied.

64

Format headings with an Arabic-numbered outline system in this sequence: boldface large; boldface; boldface italic; italic. Position all headings flush left.

Quotable Quotes

"Subheads and sub-subheads may be differentiated by different sizes or kinds of type."

—*Words into Type* 14 (3d ed. 1974).

"Whatever organization you choose, convey the organization in clear headings that communicate your assertions. This will help the reader understand your logical development and your point. Also consider dividing larger sections with subheadings. Subheadings give the eye a respite and the mind a map, and can encourage your reader through the document. When you subdivide, moderation is the key. Avoid headings that fragment, rather than organize, your text."

—Mary Barnard Ray & Barbara J. Cox, *Beyond the Basics: A Text for Advanced Legal Writing* 229–30 (1991).

"Subheads . . . are each set on a line separate from the following text, the levels differentiated by type style . . . ."

—*The Chicago Manual of Style* § 1.74, at 25 (15th ed. 2003).

"Most readers find subheads useful, especially in longer articles."

—Colin Wheildon, *Type & Layout* 127 (1995).

"State and federal judges routinely emphasize . . . that headings and subheadings help them keep their bearings, let them actually *see* the organization, and afford them mental rest stops. Another advantage they mention is that the headings allow them to focus on the points they're most interested in."

—Bryan A. Garner, *Legal Writing in Plain English* § 4, at 14 (2001).

Explanation

When typewriters were the only means of producing briefs, the conventions for emphasizing text were extremely limited: all capitals, initial capitals, underlining, and indenting. Often lawyers and their secretaries would progressively indent headings to the point where a small heading would appear in the middle of the page. That type of heading is hard to read, and it doesn't display the structure of the argument very well.

Although it's possible to use progressive indents, the better technique is to use a combination of size, character weight, and roman-vs.-italic to signal gradations in headings. The problem with progressive indenting is that it doesn't mix well with double-spacing. It's good for the table of contents—use the progressive indents there—but not in text.

The sequence in text, then, should be as follows:

---

1.   Main heading in large boldface.

A.   Subhead in regular boldface. Notice that in this heading, as in the ones below, the indent is "hanging"—the second line of text doesn't begin at the left margin. This enhances clarity.

(1)   *Second-level subhead in boldface italic. Notice that the italicizing makes the heading a tad smaller even though the typeface specifications are otherwise the same.*

(a)   *Third-level subhead in italic. Rarely will you need this level, but it's good to have it available.*

The tip says how to do it, but the examples demonstrate how it works in practice. First, to see an example that goes all the way down to a third-level subhead, see the ADA brief in tip #5 (pp. 34 through 42). For a before-and-after version through the second-level subhead, see the example below.

One caution: if you were ever to indent headings, you'd need to set your tabs a little differently from the half-inch default settings that come with most software (see #66). The big tabs contribute to the unsightliness of the "Before" example.

A Before-and-After Example

Before   **II.   Being at the apex of their organization, the Burgesses are not subject to deposition.**

          A.   The Burgesses are at the apex of a large conglomerate of related business of which Burgess Gibraltar is only a part.

The court of appeals held that the Burgesses' status as co-chairs of the REIT (Burgess Gibraltar Group, Inc.) is not enough to trigger the apex-deposition doctrine, given that Burgess Gibraltar is not a party. But the court of appeals failed to mention that Burgess Gibraltar is at the core of a huge conglomerate of related entities, and that the Burgesses are officers, directors, or owners of many of those entities, several being named defendants here—the so-called "Burgess Defendants." Categorizing the Burgess Defendants is the best way to understand the Burgesses' relationship to this lawsuit.

> (1)   The Burgesses controlled the mall's prior ownership.

First, there is the prior owner of the mall—Gibraltar Mall Development Co., L.P. The Burgesses were two of the general partners of that limited partnership. The other two general partners were Gibraltar Mall, Inc. and ILG Shopping Malls, Inc. Millard Burgess was the chair of those two corporations, while Jeffers Biltmore was the president of each. The Burgesses also owned all of the stock in ILG Shopping Malls, Inc., while Gibraltar Mall, Inc. was a wholly owned subsidiary of Millard Burgess & Associates, Inc., a corporation whose stock is solely owned (directly or indirectly) by the Burgesses. Since that time, Gibraltar Mall, Inc. has been merged into Millard Burgess & Associates, Inc.

The Burgesses are at the apex of the structure that encompassed the prior ownership of the mall: Gibraltar Mall Development Co., L.P., Gibraltar Mall, Inc., ILG Shopping Malls, Inc., and Millard Burgess & Associates, Inc. And overlaid on that structure were the numerous partnerships and other Burgess affiliates that owned and controlled the Burgesses' portfolio of 97 shopping centers at that time. Thus, the entire structure—with the Burgesses at the top—constituted a huge conglomerate.

> (2)   The Burgesses control the mall's current ownership.

The second category of Burgess Defendants consists of those entities . . . .

After   **2.   Being at the apex of their organization, the Burgesses are not subject to deposition.**

A.   The Burgesses are at the apex of a large conglomerate of related business of which Burgess Gibraltar is only a part.

The court of appeals held that the Burgesses' status as co-chairs of the REIT (Burgess Gibraltar Group, Inc.) is not enough to trigger the apex-deposition doctrine, given that Burgess Gibraltar is not a party. But the court of appeals failed to mention that Burgess Gibraltar is at the core of a huge conglomerate of related entities, and that the Burgesses are officers, directors, or owners of many of those entities, several being named defendants here—the so-called "Burgess Defendants." Categorizing the Burgess Defendants is the best way to understand the Burgesses' relationship to this lawsuit.

(1) *The Burgesses controlled the mall's prior ownership.*

First, there is the prior owner of the mall—Gibraltar Mall Development Co., L.P. The Burgesses were two of the general partners of that limited partnership. The other two general partners were Gibraltar Mall, Inc. and ILG Shopping Malls, Inc. Millard Burgess was the chair of those two corporations, while Jeffers Biltmore was the president of each. The Burgesses also owned all of the stock in ILG Shopping Malls, Inc., while Gibraltar Mall, Inc. was a wholly owned subsidiary of Millard Burgess & Associates, Inc., a corporation whose stock is solely owned (directly or indirectly) by the Burgesses. Since that time, Gibraltar Mall, Inc. has been merged into Millard Burgess & Associates, Inc.

The Burgesses are at the apex of the structure that encompassed the prior ownership of the mall: Gibraltar Mall Development Co., L.P., Gibraltar Mall, Inc., ILG Shopping Malls, Inc., and Millard Burgess & Associates, Inc. And overlaid on that structure were the numerous partnerships and other Burgess affiliates that owned and controlled the Burgesses' portfolio of 97 shopping centers at that time. Thus, the entire structure—with the Burgesses at the top—constituted a huge conglomerate.

(2) *The Burgesses control the mall's current ownership.*

The second category of Burgess Defendants consists of those entities . . . .

65

Put a little more white space above a heading than below.

Quotable Quotes

"A subheading that's correctly spaced has more white space above the heading than below. This signals the reader that the head and the following text function as a unit."
—Philip Brady, *Using Type Right* 34 (1988).

"Use an extra line or half-line of space above headings; the distance helps cue readers to expect a change of subject."
—Bryan A. Garner, *The Redbook: A Manual on Legal Style* § 4.22(b), at 74 (2002).

Explanation

It makes perfect sense to group closely related things together. So why should headings be equidistant between the end of one segment of text and the beginning of the next? Though it's a common practice, it makes no sense at all. And professional typesetters know better. Start looking at books, magazines, even advertisements. There's a lot to be learned from examining how professionals use type.

You can see good examples of properly spaced headings in tips #63 and #64.

66

Use the power of your computer. Set sensible defaults, and use macros to make writing easier.

Quotable Quotes

"[P]eople tend to look at a business document in plain old typewriter-style Courier typeface the way they look at a salesman with a patch on his jacket."
—Grant Buckler, *Color Keeps Moving into the Mainstream*, Computer Dealer News, 27 July 1992, at 14.

"Too many laser printers are trapped in the typewriter's rut. . . . [T]he aesthetics leave much to be desired. At the root of the problem is this: Too many laser printers are cursed by Courier. Relying on that default typeface alone, they never take advantage of today's font technology . . . ."
—Winn L. Rosch, *The Right Type*, PC Sources, Aug. 1992, at 316.

"In the old days, you didn't have to spend much time designing your documents because all you had to work with was the Courier typeface. Paragraph indentations and margin widths were your only formatting concerns. But now that word-processing packages are becoming more like desktop-publishing software, expectations are higher."
—Catherine Kenny, *Ami's Got Plenty of Style*, PC World, Aug. 1993, at L37.

"In our law firm, some of the most hallowed truths of legaldom are falling by the wayside—such as the age-old truth that legal documents must always use a 10-pitch, double-spaced courier typeface. . . . You don't want to be beaten in court or in the marketplace because your opponent presents a more readable, emphatic document."
—Gene Barrett, *The New World Order of Windows and Word Processors*, Mich. Law. Wkly., 21 Mar. 1994, at 5.

"Using your laser printer to print documents in a proportionally spaced typeface instead of the conventional double-spaced Courier gives a clean, elegant and professional appearance that puts your best face to the world."
—Daniel B. Evans, *You Are What You Print*, Law Prac. Mgmt., July–Aug. 1994, at 58.

"For large areas of text, it is usually better to use a serif type (that is, a type with tiny strokes or projections at the end of most of the letters). The serifs guide the eye horizontally and put light and shade on the page because the letters have thick and thin strokes. Serif types tend to look authoritative, classical, and official . . . . The sans-serif types (types without serifs) tend to be more useful as headings and in forms, catalogues, and flyers . . . ."

—Martin Cutts, *The Plain English Guide* 151 (1995).

"Body type must be set in serif type if the designer intends it to be read and understood. More than five times as many readers are likely to show good comprehension when a serif body type is used instead of a sans serif body type."

—Colin Wheildon, *Type & Layout* 60 (1995).

"I have seen firms spend hundreds of thousands of dollars on technology only to make their briefs and other documents look like they were typed on a 1940 Underwood. Never use Courier."

—Mark P. Painter, *The Legal Writer* 40–41 (2d ed. 2003).

Explanation

Your initial settings from the software manufacturer will lead you astray. Your margins will be too small, you won't be able to make effective bullets because your tabs will be much too large, and your typeface will probably be the drabbest of all: Courier.

My recommendations:

Margins	1.2 inches on each side, 1 inch on top and bottom.
Tabs	The equivalent of 5 characters for first tab; after that, evenly spaced tab settings every .15 inch.
Typeface	CG Times, Times Roman, Times New Roman, Palatino, Garamond, or some other serifed typeface.
Typesize	13 points (10–11 in footnotes); in federal court, 14 points.
Right Margin	Ragged, not justified.

Many lawyers seem to puzzle over the recommendation for a ragged right margin. Here is what two experts say on this point:

- "Text with a ragged (uneven) right margin is easier to read. When each line looks different, readers are less likely to stray to another line. This is because they can quickly separate and identify each line without having to adjust to the different spacing between letters and words."*

- "Unjustified type ('ranged left' or 'flush left') tends to produce a more relaxed, informal look."**

---

* Robert D. Eagleson, *Writing in Plain English* 78 (1990).
** Martin Cutts, *The Plain English Guide* 154 (1995).

Once you get in the habit of using a ragged right margin, you'll find it irritating to look at other lawyers' briefs with words spaced out in an unsightly way merely to justify the right margin. Still, book publishers that employ professional typographers will continue to prefer the polished look of a justified right margin—skilled hands can make it work. And there's some empirical evidence that in such hands, it leads to even greater readability. But with most law-office word processing, the ragged right margin is a better bet.

As you experiment with improving the design of your briefs, you ought to bear in mind that court rules are becoming more sophisticated on these matters. In December 1998, Rule 32 of the Federal Rules of Appellate Procedure was amended in two important ways. First, it replaced the age-old 50-page limit with a 14,000-word limit. Second, it mandated 14-point type (although individual circuits may allow a smaller size). In the years to come, more and more state courts are sure to follow this lead. Even if your court's rules aren't as specific as Rule 32, you should consider following that rule because it will make your brief much more readable than most.

One last point. Up to the late 1990s, most word processors made it difficult for you to use special characters like dashes and section symbols. So you'd have to create macros as shortcuts for recurrent keystrokes. Here are the ones I've used:

Alt-B	Bullet-dot + left indent
Alt-M	Em dash + hard space (see #57)
Alt-N	En dash
Alt-P	Close quotation mark (a smart quote: ")
Alt-Q	Open quotation mark (a smart quote: ")
Alt-S	Section symbol + hard space

To be sure, software developers come out with improved programs every six months or so. The point is that you need to know how to produce each of those marks quickly and accurately, regardless of the software you use.

67

Indent your paragraphs only a quarter of an inch or so. Avoid the puzzlingly common double-indent.

Quotable Quotes

"The indention of paragraphs should be in proportion to the width of the page. An em space [the width of a capital M] is enough for a page less than 27 picas—4½ inches—wide. An em and a half looks better for widths from 28 to 35 picas; 2 ems for 36 picas or more."

—*Words into Type* 246 (3d ed. 1974).

"[T]he plainest, most unmistakable yet unobtrusive way of marking paragraphs is the simple indent: a white square. How much indent is enough? The minimum normal indent is one em. . . . Where the line is long and margins are ample, an indent of 1½ or 2 ems may look more luxurious than one em, but paragraph indents larger than three ems are generally counterproductive. Short last lines followed by new lines with large indents produce a tattered page."

—Robert Bringhurst, *The Elements of Typographic Style* 38 (1992).

Explanation

Many lawyers seem to think it's their firm's trademark to double-indent paragraphs. But if so many believe this, how could the practice be truly distinctive? And where do legal secretaries learn this? To anyone who can supply the answer to this riddle, I'll be grateful.

Meanwhile, if your secretary has the habit of hitting the tab key twice at the beginning of a paragraph, issue a cease-and-desist order.

If you want to know how paragraphs should look, examine any book from a reputable publisher.

A Before-and-After Example

Before   Records are subject to public inspection only if they are "public records" under the CPRA. Cal. Gov't Code § 6253. To be public records, they must have been prepared, owned, used, or retained by a state or local agency. *Id.* § 6252(d). Unless BDI or PrimaCare is considered to be a state or local agency, the information they keep from the County cannot be public records. *Id.*

On their face, the statutory definitions of "state agency" and "local agency" do not include PrimaCare. *See id.* § 6252(a), (b). The only argument for calling PrimaCare a state or local agency is that PrimaCare will take over the County's function of providing health care to the inmates and the poor, and thereby obtain government status.

No California court has considered whether a private entity taking on a government function is considered to be a state or local agency under the CPRA.

After   Records are subject to public inspection only if they are "public records" under the CPRA. Cal. Gov't Code § 6253. To be public records, they must have been prepared, owned, used, or retained by a state or local agency. *Id.* § 6252(d). Unless BDI or PrimaCare is considered to be a state or local agency, the information they keep from the County cannot be public records. *Id.*

On their face, the statutory definitions of "state agency" and "local agency" do not include PrimaCare. *See id.* § 6252(a), (b). The only argument for calling PrimaCare a state or local agency is that PrimaCare will take over the County's function of providing health care to the inmates and the poor, and thereby obtain government status.

No California court has considered whether a private entity taking on a government function is considered to be a state or local agency under the CPRA.

68

Avoid all-caps and initial-caps text. But if you do use initial caps, don't capitalize any word shorter than five letters if it's an article, a preposition, or a conjunction.

Quotable Quotes

"Never set headlines using capital initials and lowercase on every word—unless your intention is to create visual hiccups. This is a bad and outmoded convention left over from nineteenth-century newspapering days . . . . [S]uch heads are extremely difficult to read and there is no longer any functional reason . . . to continue using them. . . . Use all-capital setting only when the lines are very short . . . . In bulk, [all caps] are hard to read . . . ."
—Jan V. White, *Editing by Design* 91 (2d ed. 1982).

"Large areas of text set in all capitals take more time to read than text set in lowercase."
—Bill Gray, *Tips on Type* 41 (1983).

"What an odd phenomenon it is that lawyers—whenever they want to draw special attention to passages, such as main issues in a brief or warnings in drafted documents—make them typographically impenetrable. Using all caps is bad enough; underlining them is even worse."
—Bryan A. Garner, *A Dictionary of Modern Legal Usage* 130 (2d ed. 1995).

"Text set in capitals is difficult to read."
—Colin Wheildon, *Type & Layout* 127 (1995).

Explanation

What's the problem with using all capitals? Because all the characters are uniform in size, it's hard to distinguish one from the next. The text letters don't have what typographers call "ascenders" and "descenders," the parts of letters that go above (*b*) and below (*p*) the line of type. That using all caps causes difficulties in reading is largely a physiological matter, not a question of taste.

In the days of typewriters, we had two options for highlighting text: capitalizing and underlining. But today, of course, we have many other options, chief among them being boldface type, larger typesizes, and italics.

When initial caps are appropriate, as in a boldfaced heading, the prevailing style is to leave articles and short prepositions and conjunctions lowercase. What is "short" is a question of style, but four letters or fewer is the most common answer. Watch out for short words that may be used as prepositions or adverbs, such as *in*, *by*, and *up*. If the word functions as a preposition in the sentence, it's lowercase (Merritt Was Bound by the Contract). But if it functions as an adverb, as in a verb phrase, it is capitalized (Merritt Stood By as Its Agent Breached the Contract). Although it is also part of a verb phrase, the *to* in an infinitive is considered a preposition and is left lowercase.

In the following example, the first version is from a brief actually filed in the Courier typeface. The second version—with initial capitals but still in Courier—is little better. The final version shows how it might have been done.

A Set of Examples

Before (all caps)   TABLE OF CONTENTS

Before (initial caps)   TABLE OF CONTENTS

After

Table of Contents

69

Generally, spell out numbers one to ten, and use numerals for numbers 11 and above.

Quotable Quotes

"In deciding whether to use numerals or spell out numbers, the nature of the writing should be considered and literary style distinguished from technical and scientific style. At one extreme is the formal style of the Bible, proclamations, and similar writings, in which all numbers, even of years, are spelled out; at the other extreme is the statistical style, in which all numbers are expressed in numerals."

—*Words into Type* 125 (3d ed. 1974).

"[M]ost numbers represent significant quantities or measurements that should stand out for emphasis or quick comprehension. . . . Spell out numbers from 1 through 10; use figures for numbers above 10."

—William A. Sabin, *The Gregg Reference Manual* 111 (9th ed. 2001).

"When science and mathematics aren't involved, the best practice is to spell out numbers, cardinal or ordinal, smaller than 11."

—Bryan A. Garner, *The Elements of Legal Style* 79 (2d ed. 2002).

Explanation

Editors used to spell out everything from 1 to 100. That's the hyperformal way—and the slow way. If you want to be solemn and stately, do that. If you want to get your information across quickly, use words only for one to ten.

But this spell-out-ten-and-under rule has several exceptions:

1. If a passage contains some numbers below the cutoff and some above, don't mix words and numerals. If the things being counted all belong to the same category or type, use numerals consistently:

Sirotka requested 20 yellow legal pads but used only 5. (But: *He asked for shipments of 300 cars on six different days in May.*)

2. Spell out approximations: *About a hundred protesters showed up for the rally.*

3. For millions and billions, use a combination of numerals plus words for round numbers (*$4 million*) and numerals for other numbers (*$4,637,888.84*).

4. Use numerals for percentages (and use percent signs): *8%, 50%.*

5. Spell out numbers that begin sentences: *Fifteen people were injured in the blaze.*

Two additional points. First, unless you're working in mathematical columns, avoid putting ".00" after a round number. Second, don't double up words and numerals, the way you do in checks and negotiable instruments. Are you really afraid that the judge or a court staffer will fraudulently alter a number?

Some Before-and-After Examples

Example A

Before   This amendment was enacted in 1975 to eliminate stale malpractice actions. The legislature accomplished this objective by (1) placing limitations on the tolling provision for minors under the age of ten (10) and (2) restricting the maximum possible tolling period for citizens over the age of ten (10) to four (4) years.

After   This amendment was enacted in 1975 to eliminate stale malpractice actions. The legislature accomplished this objective by (1) placing limitations on the tolling provision for minors under the age of ten, and (2) restricting the maximum possible tolling period to four years for citizens over the age of ten.

Example B

Before   Currently there are thirty (30) named members in the plaintiff class, which will likely increase in size to approximately three thousand (3,000) members upon discovering who else has purchased Whizzer Mobiles.

After   Currently there are 30 named members in the plaintiff class, which will likely grow to about 3,000 members upon discovering who else has purchased Whizzer Mobiles.

Example C

Before   As noted above, Gibson falsely advised Jennings that the purchase price was $25,000.00, when the purchase price was actually $20,500.00.

After   As noted above, Gibson falsely advised Jennings that the purchase price was $25,000, when the purchase price was actually $20,500.

70

Use charts, diagrams, and other visual aids when you can.

Quotable Quotes

"The need for graphic presentation of matters difficult to describe otherwise . . . justifies inclusion in the brief of maps, charts, or patent drawings. You must have those visual aids in your brief so that the judges can study them at their leisure when the case is under consideration."
—Frederick B. Wiener, *Briefing and Arguing Federal Appeals* 330 (rev. ed. 1967).

"Use diagrams, photographs, and tables, if they will clarify your argument. If you think you need it in your brief, it is surprising how much ingenuity a printer can exercise to see that it gets there. If a picture was necessary to make the facts clear to the jury, it is going to be equally helpful in making the facts clear to the court, and there is only one copy of the picture or diagram in evidence as an exhibit. If you want to have it in the hands of all members of the court, it has to be in your brief."
—Arno H. Denecke et al., *Notes on Appellate Brief Writing*, 51 Or. L. Rev. 351, 363 (1972).

"Words are not the only way to present information. There are visual devices familiar to readers; [these] will help you to avoid using long, involved description. Use maps, diagrams, formulas, photographs, and drawings if they present the information more clearly and efficiently for readers."
—Robert D. Eagleson, *Writing in Plain English* 66 (1990).

"[C]harts or tables may inform the judge at a glance of what he or she could similarly understand only with minutes of reading and of puzzling out words and figures. Complex machines or locales, such as unusual intersections, may also be quickly demonstrated or understood by a diagram, where it might take hours for counsel to write (and minutes for the court to read with understanding) words purporting to convey the same information."
—Albert Tate Jr., "The Art of Brief Writing: What a Judge Wants to Read," in *Appellate Practice Manual* 197, 206 (Priscilla A. Schwab ed., 1992).

Explanation

Some information is best conveyed not through words, but through graphics. In every case, you'd be well advised to think about which ideas are best suited to graphic depictions. Then try to make the graphics as simple as possible so that someone looking at them will immediately see the point you're trying to make. Finally, look for ways to make the graphics dovetail into the argument. Refer to them in your text. Explain them.

Some advocates have gone so far as to file videotapes to accompany their briefs. In a notable example, Randall Miller of Tulsa and William Keffer of Dallas produced and then filed a video in support of a summary-judgment motion in an environmental-contamination case. The video showed—as no mere words could—the extent of the environmental damage, as well as its causes.

But you don't always have to go that far. Even in the traditional hard copy of a brief, opportunities arise for the creative use of graphics. For example, George M. Sirilla and David W. Long of Washington, D.C., adopted the unusual strategy of reproducing a 1978 Mad Magazine cover to make a substantive point before the Federal Circuit (see Ex. A). A patentee was claiming that every time a bar code got scanned on any item, he should receive a royalty for the technology. Representing the National Retail Federation on the defense side, Sirilla and Long argued in favor of prosecution laches: the plaintiff had delayed far too long in trying to enforce his patent claim, which dated back to the mid-1950s (with continuation patents issued up to 2000). On pages 2–3 of their brief, they showed a Mad Magazine cover with a caption that read: "Mad Magazine hopes this issue jams every computer in the country . . . [oversized bar-code illustration] for forcing us to deface our covers with this yecchy UPC symbol from now on." The point was that bar codes were very much a part of American culture by the late 1970s—and that no one should be allowed to begin enforcing a patent to collect royalties in the late 1990s. It was an important case in which the Federal Circuit first definitively established that prosecution laches is a good defense.* The court's opinion tracked the Sirilla–Long reasoning.

Graphics don't always have to be creative or ambitious. I once used the diagram in Example B and table in Example C in an appellate brief involving breaches of an ethical wall inside an insurance company. The defense team wasn't supposed to communicate with the coverage team because it would create a conflict of interests. But things went awry with the insurer's employees, and the graphics helped illustrate a complicated set of facts.

When a statement of facts relies heavily on visualizing how events unfolded in a location, nothing helps more than a map and photographs. Kathleen Flynn Peterson, Randall Tietjen, and Anne E. Workman included both in a 1999 brief to the Minnesota Supreme Court (see Ex. D). They were representing the parents of a girl who was assaulted in a locker room at her high school by a stranger who had been seen by three school employees. Circled numbers on the map pinpoint positions where events described in the statement of facts took place. The brief also contains four

* *Symbol Techs., Inc. v. Lemelson Med., Educ. & Research Found. Ltd.*, 277 F.3d 1361 (Fed. Cir. 2002).

police photos that help the reader get a better mental image of what happened and where.

For a brief to the New Jersey Superior Court, John K. Nelson of Toledo, Ohio, created Venn diagrams (see Ex. E) to show why a change in corporate structure did not affect insurance coverage of one facility that was transferred from a division of the parent company to a wholly owned subsidiary. Venn diagrams are handy for showing what characteristics are shared by individuals in a group. Typically the circles (which represent universes of characteristics, such as "all people over 6 feet tall") overlap (e.g., with another circle showing "all people from Phoenix") to show the individuals who fit both descriptions. Here, there is no overlap, but the inclusion of all the elements within the large circle tells the whole story.

A picture can be worth . . . well, it can help win a lawsuit.

Example A

Cover of April 1978 issue of "MAD" magazine,
used to substantiate the defense's claim that the patentee had waited until
UPS codes were widely used in commerce before suing for infringement.

Example B

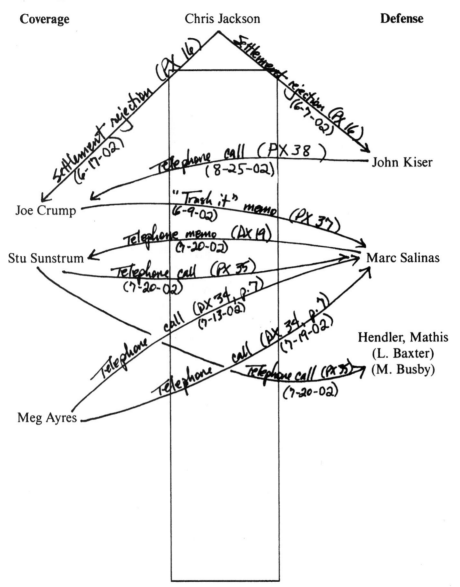

Coverage   Chris Jackson   **Defense**

Settlement rejection (PX 16) (6-17-02)

Settlement rejection (PX 16) (6-7-02)

John Kiser

Telephone call (PX 38) (8-25-02)

Joe Crump

"Trash it" memo (6-9-02) (PX 37)

Telephone memo (DX 19) (7-20-02)

Stu Sunstrum

Marc Salinas

Telephone call (PX 35) (7-20-02)

Telephone call (DX 34, p. 7) (7-13-02)

Telephone call (DX 34, p. 7) (7-19-02)

Hendler, Mathis (L. Baxter) (M. Busby)

Telephone call (PX 35) (7-20-02)

Meg Ayres

Example C

Calendar of Relevant Events: *Airhart v. National Indemnity*

Dec. '01	Jan. '02	Feb.	March	April	May	June	July	Aug.	Sept.
12-18-01: Airhart and Cowser file suit (PX 20)			3-30-02: Airhart and Cowser offer to settle for $600,000 (DX 26)	4-10-02: Kiser directs Hendler, Mathis to withdraw (PX 31)	5-4-02: Hendler, Mathis files cross-claim against Claude's estate (PX 29, ex. 13)	6-3-02: Salinas writes to decline $600,000 settlement offer—no counter (PX 43)	*7-13-02: Meg Ayres, of the coverage team, calls Marc Salinas (DX 34, p. 7)	8-9-02: Judgment became final	9-7-02: National Indemnity sues Airhart and Cowser for declaratory judgment
				4-11-02: Kiser's memo that Hendler, Mathis has observed that Josephine is a defendant, too (PX 31)	5-17-02: Hendler, Mathis replaced by Marc Salinas (PX 29, p. 14)	*6-7-02: Joe Crump writes memo re acquiring Hendler, Mathis memo (PX 37)	*7-19-02: Meg Ayres again calls Marc Salinas (DX 34, p. 7)		9-14-02: Salinas signs covenant not to execute against Josephine's estate (DX 9)
				4-11-02: Hendler, Mathis memo to National Indemnity explaining Josephine's estate's liability (PX 14)	*5-25-02: Kiser telephones Joe Crump (PX 35)	*6-9-02: Salinas sends Crump Hendler, Mathis memos with note to "trash it" (PX 37)	*7-20-02: Salinas calls Sunstrum re $600,000 (DX 19)		9-16-02: Airhart and Cowser send DTPA letter to National Indemnity (PX 64)
				4-13-02: Hendler, Mathis requests authority to settle for $150,000 (DX 15)	[5-25-02]: Undated Kiser memo that Joe Crump may need to write a reservation (PX 34)	6-14-02: Kiser writes Jackson recommending $600,000 agreed judgment (PX 15)	*7-20-02: Sunstrum calls Busby of Hendler, Mathis, as well as Salinas (PX 35)		
					5-26-02: Airhart and Cowser offer again to settle for $600,000 (PX 42)	6-17-02: Jackson rejects Kiser's view as not being in National Indemnity's best interests (PX 16)	7-21-02: Trial court's judgment		
						6-23-02: Kiser writes Kluver that $600,000 is over the limits—will offer "vigorous defense" (PX 18)	7-21-02: Sunstrum calls Salinas		

*Indicates a breach of the Chinese wall.

Example D

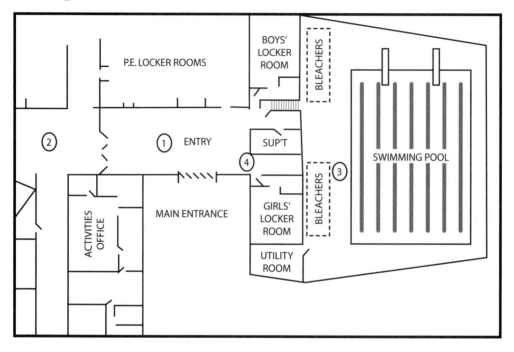

Example E

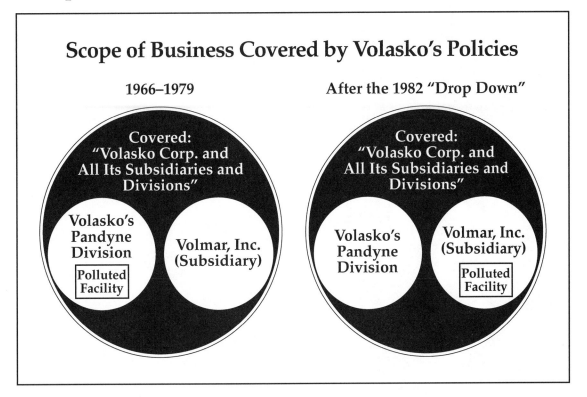

Part H

Sidestepping Some Common Quirks

71

Never distort the facts or the law. Avoid hyperbole and personality attacks.

Quotable Quotes

"Avoid scandal, impertinence, and sarcasm. In pointing out your adversary's misstatements of fact or law, be courteous about it—strive to find a charitable cloak for his improprieties. In other words, it is proper to annihilate your adversary—but do it gracefully."

—Raymond E. Peters, *The Preparation and Filing of Briefs on Appeal*, 22 Cal. St. B.J. 175, 183 (1947).

"[Y]ou must appear to be fair—*absolutely* fair. There must be no misrepresentation of your opponent's case. The method of fairness is the giving of full recognition to the weight of evidence for the contrary proposition."

—Gorham Munson, *The Written Word* 112 (rev. ed. 1949).

"Overstatement of the facts, which is not at all the same as a confident presentation of them, should always be avoided. Few things are so damaging as an exaggeration . . . that can be exposed by the other side, and the worst of all is a quantitative exaggeration that can be exposed without possibility of escape."

—Frederick A. Philbrick, *Language and the Law* 8 (1949).

"[N]ame-calling is a contest no one can win."

—Frederick B. Wiener, *Briefing and Arguing Federal Appeals* 125 (rev. ed. 1967).

"[G]ranted that your opponent's disbarment is long overdue, granted in any event that his conduct in the particular case was shameful and thoroughly unprofessional, take those matters up with the grievance committee, and don't inject them into either the written or the oral argument of an appeal."

—*Id.* at 258.

"When you overstate, the reader will be instantly on guard, and everything that has preceded your overstatement as well as everything that follows it will be suspect in his mind because he has lost confidence in your judgment or your poise."

—William Strunk, Jr. & E.B. White, *The Elements of Style* 72–73 (3d ed. 1979).

"Understatement will serve you far better [than hyperbole]. If you establish a reputation for understatement, judges will consider your contentions carefully even if they appear erroneous on first blush."

—Harold G. Christensen, *How to Write for the Judge*,
Litigation, Spring 1983, at 25, 26.

"The better the writer, the greater the detail and sensitivity of the observation. But distortion of the observation or making up what you haven't observed is a violation of the rules a [writer] must live by."

—George Kennedy et al., *The Writing Book* 13 (1984).

"*Never* misrepresent the opposition. A sure way to lose an argument is to make the opponent more of a 'bad guy' or simpleton than the facts warrant. Be sure your interpretation of opposing viewpoints is in no way distorted."

—John M. Lannon, *The Writing Process* 332 (1989).

"Omit irrelevancies, slang, sarcasm, and personal attacks. These serve only to weaken the brief. Ad hominem attacks are particularly distasteful to appellate judges. Attacks in the brief on brothers and sisters at the bar rarely bring you anything but condemnation by an appellate court. All that scorched-earth, take-no-prisoners, give-no-quarter, hardball stuff is out. And never, *never* attack the trial judge."

—Roger J. Miner, *Twenty-Five "Dos" for Appellate Brief Writers*,
3 Scribes J. Legal Writing 19, 24–25 (1992).

"Overstating the facts or the law damages your credibility as an officer of the court; if you fudge here or there, you are bound to be found out. Conscientiously avoid overstatements of any kind, lest you undermine not only your immediate client's cause, but also your own credibility and therefore the chances for future clients."

—Bryan A. Garner, "The Language of Appellate Advocacy," in *Appellate Practice Manual* 188, 190 (Priscilla A. Schwab ed., 1992).

"I like, to the point of being unduly swayed by, a brief that contains not one pejorative adjective or innuendo concerning one's opponent or the trial judge."

—Frank M. Coffin, *On Appeal: Courts, Lawyering, and Judging* 120 (1994).

"A lawyer shall not knowingly make a false statement of material fact . . . to a tribunal."

—*Model Rules of Professional Conduct* 3.3(a)(1) (2001).

Explanation

If you distort or even fudge, you'll be found out. And if you're found out, you've lost everything there is to lose. You've lost credibility.

And when you focus on personalities—especially, on the opposing counsel's personality—you suggest to the seasoned reader that you're weak on the merits. Besides, judges say they're weary of the endless petty attacks that counsel launch against each other.

Following are two examples. In Example A, hardly a phrase doesn't distort or exaggerate. The underlining, by the way, appeared in the original brief. Example B is the skeleton of an overblown brief: some of the substance has been removed, but you get a good idea of the brief's raucous stridency.

Two Egregious Examples

Example A

There is little apparent reason for why the trial court <u>ignored</u> the facts, <u>ignored</u> the law, <u>ignored</u> the lease, <u>ignored</u> the unit agreement, <u>ignored</u> Henkel's admissions, <u>ignored</u> Henkel's broken promises and misrepresentations, and <u>ignored</u> Henkel's repeated changes of position and fatally inconsistent testimony. Perhaps it was because the trial court had decided, based upon an apparent misunderstanding, that "this was the way the case ought to come out."

Example B

In its third point of error, Appellant showed that the trial court allowed evidence that was clearly incompetent, highly inflammatory, prejudicial, hearsay, and improper character testimony, designed to inflame and improperly influence the jury. In its fourth point of error, Appellant showed that the trial court's refusal to disqualify Appellees' counsel tainted the entire proceeding and made it impossible for Appellant to receive a fair trial.

Appellees' arguments in response to Appellant's first point of error are without merit . . . . Appellees fail to address the trial court's improper denial . . . . Appellees' assertion that Appellant could have called witnesses to testify as to Appellees' conspiratorial scheme is meritless . . . . Appellees' assertion is also disingenuous . . . . Evidence of Appellees' conspiracy was also highly probative in showing that Appellees had individually engaged in acts of wrongdoing.

Appellees' responses are meritless and misleading . . . . In reply, Appellant shows why Appellees' arguments are without merit . . . .

Appellees' points in response are meritless. . . . Appellees are incorrect as a matter of law and fact . . . . Appellees misstate the facts and mischaracterize the relief Appellant is seeking from this Court. . . . Appellees totally fail to address these additional critical categories of documents.

Appellees' argument is both legally and factually untenable . . . . Furthermore, Appellees' assertion is disingenuous factually. Appellees know that Brad Simonson—one of the Appellees and the quarterback of the *Surrey* conspiracy—refused to come to trial, preferring to remain safely ensconced in his Los Angeles office and outside the trial court's subpoena power. This was just one more instance of Appellees' efforts to keep *Surrey* and other critical information away from Appellant and from the jury.

First, Appellees' argument conveniently ignores the facts . . . . Second, Appellees have improperly and artificially attempted to narrow the relevance and significance of the denied requests . . . . Appellees clearly misstate New York law . . . . Moreover, Appellees ignore Appellant's claims that the individual defendants also conspired . . . . Thus, Appellees' contention that Appellant did not move to admit this evidence is, at best, disingenuous.

Appellees utterly fail to address Appellant's argument . . . . Appellees' assertion is clearly contradicted by the record . . . . Appellees hammered away at this theme in their First Amended Counterclaim and continued to deliver it throughout pretrial discovery, the trial, and closing argument. It is completely disingenuous of them . . . .

Appellees' attempts to preserve their improperly granted money judgment also must fail. They simply cannot overcome the unmistakable truth that their proof falls far below the standard needed to support damages.

Appellees conveniently ignore long-standing New York law . . . . Appellees' reliance on various documents suggesting a security interest in "accounts receivable" is entirely misplaced . . . . Appellees' failure in their brief to include the remainder of the language reveals the weakness of their desperate efforts to support the trial court's judgment.

72

Counter the Rambo writer with the deflating opener.

Quotable Quotes

"A successful brief will 90 percent of the time reflect courtesy, respect, dignity and calm—not only as pertains to the court of review, but to the lower court, the parties and the adversary. The inner attitude of the attorney will invariably control the style of the discussion."

—John Alan Appleman, "Tactics in Appellate Briefs," in *Advocacy and the King's English* 440, 457 (George Rossman ed., 1960).

"The seasoned advocate accordingly reins in any emotions, so that he or she can concentrate on the factual, legal, and equitable issues. The advocate knows that an argument in court is not an occasion for anger, like a squabble among bad-tempered relatives."

—Girvan Peck, "Strategy of the Brief," in *Appellate Practice Manual* 214, 220–21 (Priscilla A. Schwab ed., 1992).

Explanation

Assume that your opponent is trying to lay waste to you or your client. You know that you must counter it, but how do you do so without getting down into the muck?

Judge Thomas Gibbs Gee showed the way. After he resigned from the Fifth Circuit in 1991, he wrote some stunningly good briefs.* In one of them, he used what I call the "deflating opener." You simply collect the worst rhetorical outbursts from your opponent, recite them in summary form—not characterizing them too much, but quoting them word for word—and then move above and beyond.

Examples A and B—both drawn from reply briefs—illustrate the deflating opener. Example A is Judge Gee's. Example B (consciously modeled on Example A) is by Lann McIntyre of San Diego. Example C illustrates a credibility-enhancing gesture toward the opponent in the very place in which most advocates would whip out a machete.

---

* Judge Gee died in 1994. *See* Bryan A. Garner, *Remembering Judge Thomas Gibbs Gee*, 15 Rev. Litig. 169 (1996).

Some Unusually Good Examples

Example A

Short on nouns and long on adjectives, Plagiar's brief proceeds on the theory that the gross imbalance between the sanctions imposed by the district court and the well-intentioned procedural irregularity by which Schilling obtained discoverable matter can be equalized—and the scales leveled—by heaping imprecations on Schilling's side. And what a prodigious flow of pejoratives it is!

In what must be some kind of record, the 31 pages of Plagiar's brief contain more than 200 expressions bordering on the hysterical: the leader by all counts is *abusive* and its variations (17 appearances), next followed by permutations of the root word *fraud* (fraudulent, defrauded) (14), then *extort* (extortion, extorted) (13), and close behind it *phony* (12). Other items of invective in hard use are *bad faith* (6), *falsify* (4), *flagrant* (4), and *distort* or *distortion* (3). To round it all off suitably, Plagiar refers to Relators' *seemingly endless stream of perversions*. Such a diatribe would be embarrassing in a barroom, let alone this Court.

We concede defeat in the ranting contest—which we never entered—and turn once more and briefly to the facts, beginning with the uncontested ones: . . . .

Example B

Lacking in authority, Pound resorts to hyperbole to obscure the facts that support the valuation opinions. He denigrates Holden's damage proof with pejoratives such as "inflated," "overreaching," "cavalier," "breathtaking," "speculative," "cosmetic," "tinkering," "*deja vu* all over again," "fantasy," "evasive," "inherently unbelievable," "baseless," "not grounded in fact," "unfounded," "highly prejudicial," "extravagant," "grandiose," and "wildly prejudicial." He belittles the company with still more dismissive adjectives such as "troubled," "moribund," "demoralized," "teetering on the brink of bankruptcy," "toxic milieu," and "awash in a sea of red ink." All the while, though, Pound provides no references to the record to support these fantastical characterizations. While Pound's approach is concededly imaginative, Holden suggests a return to the facts and the law to resolve the issues raised by this appeal.

Example C

The commissioner's reliance on the plain wording of the law as a defense here should not be interpreted to indicate agreement with the factual recitation that forms the foundation of the plaintiff's equitable arguments. The "facts" as recited by the plaintiff are, in several instances, mere speculation as to motive or intent, and are in a few instances simply incorrect. This is not to allege or imply impropriety on the part of plaintiff's counsel—indeed, defense counsel does not believe that to be the case—

but merely to say that the "facts" presented in opposition to this motion were presented by an advocate in as good a light as could possibly be cast for the benefit of his client.

The commissioner will not present evidence here to create a factual dispute. Instead, the commissioner will show that, despite the plaintiff's version of the facts, the commissioner is entitled to judgment dismissing the case as a matter of law.

73

Swear off the hence-the-title principle.

Quotable Quotes

"Every professor who teaches the writing art should devote a couple of weeks each semester to a single topic: the lead sentence. In the writing of prose, a conclusive ending is desirable and a well-developed middle is essential, but it is the lead that can make or break a composition."
　　　　—James J. Kilpatrick, *Fine Print: Reflections on the Writing Art* 79 (1993).

"The selection of the starting words should always make the audience want to hear more."
　　　　—Jeffrey McQuain, *Power Language: Getting the Most Out of Your Words* 109 (1996).

"If, at the very outset, a writer seems bored, unwilling to use his imagination, indifferent to his reader, and unclear in his thinking, he's apt to remain that way. But if his opener reveals passion, a clear, perceptive mind, and a flair for drawing in the reader, the odds are he'll stay true to form."
　　　　—John R. Trimble, *Writing with Style* 26 (2d ed. 2000).

Explanation

Formulaic phrases are easy to adopt, particularly when every beginner wonders just what court papers are "supposed" to look like. Once you find out what they do look like, you start making them all look that way.

Perhaps this is how litigators got into the habit of wasting their openers by repeating—more or less verbatim—the very words of the title. In some states, it's with the "Comes now" phraseology; in other states it's "Now comes." In still other states, no one uses that stale jargon, but even there litigators typically do nothing but repeat the title.

This practice led Kevin McDonald, a splendid lawyer in Washington, D.C., to coin the phrase "hence the title." That's the statement a judge might make after reading the typical opener to a court paper.

Why do lawyers repeat their titles? Well, one justification is to define the parties in that paragraph—so that you can say:

HBL Corporation ("HBL"), Sym Industries, Inc. ("Sym"), and Huron Importers, Inc. ("Huron"), collectively referred to herein as "Defendants," file this their Motion to Dismiss, and respectfully state: . . . .

But do you really suppose that, without the definitions, any reader could be confused by a later reference to HBL, Sym, or Huron? Or that a reference to Defendants would be confusing? That's hardly conceivable.

The no-nonsense approach is to abstain from definitions unless they're necessary. If they are genuinely helpful, define the parties briefly as they come up, but don't waste a paragraph on it.

In other words, don't treat the judge like a dunce—a dunce who's supposed to say, after reading your first paragraph, "Oh, I get it. That's why you used that title up above! Thank you for telling me that this isn't a falsely labeled court paper!"

Some Before-and-After Examples

Example A

Before   **The New York Bureau of Securities' (1) Objection to Ronald A. Needham's Motion to Prevent the Examiner from Barring the Debtor and His Counsel from Attending Depositions, or Alternatively (2) Application in Support of Cross-Motion to Prevent the Examiner from Barring the Bureau of Securities and Its Counsel from Attending Depositions, Including the Deposition of Needham**

THE NEW YORK BUREAU OF SECURITIES ("the Bureau"), by and through its counsel, Neill, Ripoll, Aronson, Seckler & Goldstein, hereby (1) objects to the debtor, Ronald A. Needham's ("Needham" or "the Debtor") motion to prevent the Examiner, Brian F. Bloodworth ("the Examiner") from barring Needham and his counsel from attending the deposition of certain witnesses; or alternatively hereby (2) cross-moves to prevent the Examiner from barring the Bureau from attending these same depositions, including the deposition of the Debtor.

[A lengthy "Background" section follows.]

After   **The Bureau's Objection to Needham's Motion to Prevent the Examiner from Barring Needham's Participation in Depositions; Cross-Motion to Allow the Bureau to Participate in All Depositions**

The Court now faces two straightforward issues:

(1) [Statement–Statement–Question]

(2) [Statement–Statement–Question]

[A brief "Factual Background" should follow.]

Example B

Before   **Memorandum in Support of Plaintiffs' Motion to Compel Discovery**

Plaintiffs MTM Fuel Management Company ("MTM") and Swanson Pipe Line Company ("SPLC") respectfully submit this Memorandum in Support of Plaintiffs' Motion to Compel Discovery.

[The heading "Procedural History" follows, and then two pages of a largely irrelevant recitation of things that have happened in the case.]

After   **Memorandum in Support of Plaintiffs' Motion to Compel Discovery**

MTM and Swanson bring this motion for two reasons. First, Greenbrier Associates has unilaterally declared an exemption from discovery because it believes that discoverable information will eventually be held inadmissible once the court applies the parol-evidence rule. Second, Greenbrier asserts that it can refuse to answer discovery requests because it considers the lawsuit "meritless" and plans to file a motion for judgment on the pleadings.

Because Greenbrier's positions are legally and factually untenable, this Court should compel discovery and consider making any other orders that the Court finds appropriate.

[This new opener was possible only after long, hard study of the original motion to compel.]

Example C

Before   **DEFENDANT'S REPLY TO PLAINTIFF'S RESPONSE TO MOTION TO DISMISS**

Defendant, Lucky Seven Casinos, Inc. (misnomered as Lucky Seven Casino, Inc.) ("Lucky Seven"), files this, its reply to plaintiff's response to its motion to dismiss for lack of personal jurisdiction.

After   **Lucky Seven's Reply to Bohanon's Response to Motion to Dismiss**

The fatal flaw pervading Bohanon's arguments is that she cites and discusses specific-jurisdiction cases when this Court is undeniably presented with a general-jurisdiction issue. But before clarifying that muddlement, Lucky Seven must set the facts right.

Example D

Before   **RECEIVER'S RESPONSE TO SPECIAL EXCEPTIONS OF DEFENDANTS SAFFRAN SILBERT ASSOCIATES, SAFFRAN SILBERT, INC., AND EMILY DEMPSIE**

TO THE HONORABLE JUDGE OF SAID COURT:

Plaintiff Diversified Life Insurance Company, an Arizona corporation in receivership, by and through Jeff K. Harlan, Receiver for Diversified Life Insurance Company (the "Receiver"), files this its Response to the Special Exceptions to Plaintiff's Original Petition ("Original Petition") filed by Defendants Saffran Silbert Associates, Saffran Silbert, Inc., and Emily Dempsie. Defendants Saffran Silbert Associates, Saffran Silbert,

Inc., and Emily Dempsie are hereinafter referred to collectively as "Defendants." In response to those Special Exceptions, the receiver would respectfully show the court the following:

A.   Defendants Are Not Entitled to the Relief of Dismissal on the Pleadings as Sought in Their Special Exceptions

Although Defendants ask this Court to require the Receiver to replead its petition, ...

After   **Receiver's Response to Defendants' Special Exceptions**

A.   Defendants Are Not Entitled to the Relief of Dismissal on the Pleadings as Sought in Their Special Exceptions

Although Defendants ask this Court to require the Receiver to replead its petition, ...

74

Describe actions, not filings, when possible. And refer to filings generically—not with titles of court papers.

Quotable Quotes

"In order to tell a clear and coherent narrative, a writer must keep in mind the importance of selection and proportion. Inclusion of unimportant or irrelevant details clogs the flow of narrative . . . ."
—Kendall B. Taft et al., *The Technique of Composition* 461 (1963).

"The great virtue of narration . . . is its vividness, its dramatic immediacy. We can see what is happening; we can feel as well as conceptualize events."
—John Halverson & Mason Cooley, *Principles of Writing* 259 (1965).

"When telling a story, you maintain an effective narrative pace by focusing on your point and eliminating any details that don't support it. A good narrative depends not only on what is included, but also on what has been left out."
—Judith Nadell et al., *The Macmillan Writer* 188 (2d ed. 1994).

Explanation

To tell a compelling story, you have to focus on the parties' actions—not on their filings. Thus, the presumption ought to be that you avoid using titles of court papers. With the initial capitals, these titles can easily get in the way of what you're trying to convey.

So instead of writing "the plaintiff filed a Motion to Compel Answers to Plaintiff's Interrogatories and Request for Production," simply write "the plaintiff asked the court to order the defendant to answer the interrogatories and produce the requested documents."

Some Before-and-After Examples

Example A (Shinsato's opposition to Gibson's motion to amend a complaint)

Before
Background

Seven years ago, Shinsato *filed a Motion to Dismiss* Gibson's federal and state claims and a *Memorandum in Support* thereof in Pennsylvania federal court. On the first page of Shinsato's *Memorandum*, it states: "This Court lacks subject-matter jurisdiction over this dispute in that . . . (a) the alleged diversity of citizenship is not complete." Gibson agreed that the *Complaint* did not establish diversity in its *Response to Shinsato's Motion to Dismiss*. Gibson admitted that only federal-question jurisdiction was established and that if Gibson's federal claims were dismissed, Gibson would have to replead to establish diversity jurisdiction and dismiss non-diverse parties. Gibson subsequently *filed a First Amended Complaint* that did not alter the jurisdictional allegations.

After
Background

Seven years ago, Shinsato moved in federal court to dismiss Gibson's federal and state claims. On the first page of its memorandum supporting that motion, Shinsato stated: "This Court lacks subject-matter jurisdiction over this dispute in that . . . (a) the alleged diversity of citizenship is not complete." In response, Gibson agreed that the complaint did not establish diversity. Gibson admitted that only federal-question jurisdiction was established and that if the federal claims were dismissed, Gibson would have to replead to establish diversity jurisdiction and dismiss nondiverse parties. Gibson then amended but did not alter the jurisdictional allegations.

Example B

Before
Following a hearing on January 3, 1997, attended by counsel for both parties, Magistrate Judge Eagan granted Stanley's Application for Pre-judgment Remedy. Magistrate Judge Eagan also granted Stanley's Motion for Disclosure of Assets.

After
After a hearing on January 3, 1997, attended by counsel for both parties, Magistrate Judge Eagan granted Stanley's request for prejudgment garnishment. He also ordered Shaw to disclose all his assets.

75

Avoid voluminous quotations.

Quotable Quotes

"Briefs should not be overlarded with long quotations from the reported opinions, no matter how pat they seem; nor over-crowded with citations designed, it would seem, to certify to the industry of the brief-maker rather than to fortify the argument."

—John W. Davis, "The Argument of an Appeal," in *Advocacy and the King's English* 212, 214 (George Rossman ed., 1960).

"It is a good, sound rule of thumb that quotations from opinions should be included only when they add something, and that, whenever possible, they should be short rather than long."

—Frederick B. Wiener, *Briefing and Arguing Federal Appeals* 242 (rev. ed. 1967).

"Avoid quotations from cited material. Quotation is usually the lazy lawyer's outlet, and it interferes with readability and effective argumentation. Develop the art of clear and concise summarization."

—Mario Pittoni, *Brief Writing and Argumentation* 39 (1967).

"[D]on't fill your brief with extensive quotations . . . . [S]ome lawyers [seemingly] write briefs by reading several (hopefully relevant) cases, copying down several paragraphs from each opinion, and then putting all these quotations into the brief. The only thing the lawyer adds is a phrase introducing the quotation: 'As the United States Supreme Court recently said.' Sometimes the lawyer tries for a bit of variety, and the introductory phrase might come out: 'In *Smith v. Jones*, the Supreme Court had occasion to make the following observations.' This is what some briefs come into the world as: a series of quotations linked together with those introductory phrases."

—Harvey C. Couch, *Writing the Appellate Brief*, 17 Prac. Law. 27, 31 (1971).

"Novice writers . . . quote too much [other] writing. They overquote for two reasons. First, they are insecure and crave any support they can get. Rather than stand up, say something, and dare the lightning, they prefer lying low and letting someone else say it, or something like it. . . . The second reason novice writers quote so much is that they have been taught to . . . in English courses . . . ."

—Bill Stott, *Write to the Point* 113 (1991).

Explanation

The writer's job is to write. That means you're doing more than merely stockpiling what others have said—even if those others happen to be judges. You shouldn't see yourself as a mere quotation-assembler.

If you do, your writing won't have a clear analytical line. How could it, if you're just linking (or not even linking) quotation after quotation?

What you quote should be distinctly subordinate. Even if your quotations come from the U.S. Supreme Court, they're supporting matter: they support what you're saying. And that means you must have something to say. So say it, and then support it (if necessary) with a well-chosen, deftly integrated quotation. (For the deft lead-in, see tip #76.)

The common mistake is to pack page after page with long quotations. This won't earn you any points with your reader. Even the friendliest, most patient reader will eventually begin to skip the quoted passages. The busy judicial reader may well toss your brief aside and pick up another—probably your opponent's.

For writers inclined to engage in this literary cannibalism, three cures are at hand. Learn to paraphrase more; learn to summarize more; and learn to quote in smaller chunks.

A Before-and-After Example

Before   The doctrine of primary jurisdiction requires legislative action supplanting and superseding common-law rights and remedies and even then does not always vest exclusive jurisdiction of every question in an administrative agency. According to the Supreme Court of Missouri:

> Where a <u>claim</u> is <u>originally cognizable in the courts</u> and the enforcement of the claim requires the resolution of issues which, under a regulatory scheme, have been <u>placed within the special competence of an administrative agency</u>, the judicial process is suspended pending referral of such issues to the administrative agency for its views. Under the primary jurisdiction doctrine the courts cannot or will not determine a controversy involving a question which is within the jurisdiction of an administrative tribunal prior to the decision of that question by the administrative tribunal (1) where the question demands the exercise of administrative discretion requiring special knowledge, experience, and services of the administrative tribunal; (2) to determine technical and intricate matters of fact; and (3) where a uniformity of ruling is essential to comply with the purposes of the regulatory statute administered.

Lamar v. Ford Motor Co., 409 S.W.2d 100, 106 (Mo. 1966) (emphasis added) (quoting 2 Am. Jur. 2d *Administrative Law* § 788). "The Worker's Compensation Law is wholly substitutional in character and . . . any rights which a plaintiff might have had at common law have been supplanted and superseded by the act, if applicable." *Killian v. J & J Installers, Inc.*, 802 S.W.2d at 160 (quoting *Jones v. Jay Truck Driver Training Ctr., Inc.*, 709 S.W.2d 114, 115 (Mo. Ct. App. 1986)). "The rights and remedies granted under this Act [the WCL] are exclusive of all others at common law." Mo. Rev. Stat. § 287.120.2 (1994).

After   To take effect, the primary-jurisdiction doctrine requires legislative action that replaces common-law rights and remedies. Even then, the doctrine does not always give an administrative agency exclusive jurisdiction over every question.

In *Lamar v. Ford Motor Co.*, the Missouri Supreme Court declared that if a claim can be judicially enforced only by resolving questions that a regulatory statute has placed within an administrative agency's "special competence," then the judicial process will be suspended while those questions are referred to that agency.[1] The Court described three circumstances in which an agency, under the primary-jurisdiction doctrine, must decide a question before a claim can be adjudicated:

- when the question involves the agency's special knowledge, experience, and services;

- when the question involves technical and intricate facts; and

- when uniformity of ruling is necessary to comply with the purposes of the regulatory statute.[2]

The Worker's Compensation Law is the type of regulatory statute contemplated by the primary-jurisdiction doctrine: it is "wholly substitutional in character"; it replaces common-law rights and remedies.[3]

76

When you have a lengthy quotation, supply an informative lead-in. Assert first, and then let the quotation support your assertion.

Quotable Quotes

"Try . . . to make the quotation a part of your own work; introduce it in your own words; substitute your own paraphrase when it becomes prolix; steel yourself to junking the best passage unless it is relevant; chop up the rest and throw away the remains."

—Sherman Kent, *Writing History* 66 (1941).

"The [best] practice is to state the upshot of the quotation in the lead-in. With this method, the lead-in becomes an assertion, and the quotation becomes the support. The reader feels as if the writer has asserted something concrete and often, out of curiosity, wants to verify that assertion."

—Bryan A. Garner, *A Dictionary of Modern Legal Usage* 730 (2d ed. 1995).

Explanation

This tip, more than most others, can help your writing immediately stand out as unusually good.

Brief-writers quote frequently because we work within a system based on precedent. And, seemingly, quite a few brief-writers want first to draw attention to the caselaw and then to discuss it. The result, though, is that you're asking the judge to slog aimlessly through a quotation before you get around to saying why you've quoted it.

If, in your lead-in, you say what the quotation does for you, you'll accomplish four things. First, you'll be more likely to get the quotation actually read, because the judge will know why you've quoted it. Second, once the judge confirms that the quotation does for you what you say it does, you'll have enhanced your credibility. Third, because you'll be forcing yourself to assert just why it is you're quoting something, your quotations will almost certainly become shorter and more pointed. And fourth, even if the reader were to skip your quotation, your train of thought would still be easily discernible.

That second point is the clincher, though: every time you do this, you enhance your credibility.

The following examples illustrate variations on a theme. In Example A, the first sentence has the real meat, and then the second—which begins with a dreadful citation—spoils what is to come because the reader nearly forgets the earlier sentence. In Example B, the same thing happens. But in Example C, it's not till the follow-up that the point of the quotation becomes clear: the sentence after the quotation needs to be tightened and moved up. As these examples show, focusing on the lead-in will inevitably result in other contextual improvements. In Example C, for instance, the "Before" version has 269 words; the "After" is reduced to 216.

Some Before-and-After Examples

Example A

Before   By statute, federal courts have only limited authority to enjoin state-court actions. 28 U.S.C. § 2283, the so-called "Anti-Injunction Act," provides as follows: "A court of the United States may not grant an injunction to stay proceedings in a State court except as expressly authorized by Act of Congress, or where necessary in aid of its jurisdiction, or to protect or effectuate its judgments." The general rule holds that a federal court should enjoin a state-court action only where potential conflict threatens to undermine the authority of the federal court.

After   Under the Anti-Injunction Act, federal courts have only limited authority to enjoin state-court actions: "A court of the United States may not grant an injunction to stay proceedings in a State court except as expressly authorized by Act of Congress, or where necessary in aid of its jurisdiction, or to protect or effectuate its judgments."[47] The general rule holds that a federal court should enjoin a state-court action only if potential conflict threatens to undermine the federal court's authority.

Example B

Before   Indeed, in 1990 the D.C. Circuit held that an SEC rule barring securities exchanges and associations from listing the stock of corporations that nullify, restrict, or disparately reduce shareholders' per-share voting rights was beyond the SEC's authority and impermissibly intruded on legitimate areas of state regulation. *Business Roundtable v. SEC*, 905 F.2d 406 (D.C. Cir. 1990). The Court stated:

> [T]he SEC's assertion of authority directly invades the "firmly established" state jurisdiction over corporate governance and shareholder voting rights [citation omitted]. Upholding the Commission's advance into an area not contemplated by Congress would circumvent the legislative process that is virtually the sole protection for state interests.

Id. at 413.

After   Indeed, in 1990 the D.C. Circuit held that an SEC rule barring securities exchanges and associations from listing the stock of corporations that nullify, restrict, or disparately reduce shareholders' per-share voting rights was beyond the SEC's authority. The court said that the SEC had impermissibly intruded on legitimate areas of state regulation:

> [T]he SEC's assertion of authority directly invades the "firmly established" state jurisdiction over corporate governance and shareholder voting rights [citation omitted]. Upholding the Commission's advance into an area not contemplated by Congress would circumvent the legislative process that is virtually the sole protection for state interests.[17]

Example C

Before   The Third Circuit liberalized the person–enterprise distinctiveness requirement somewhat in *Jaguar Cars, Inc. v. Royal Oaks Motor Car Co.*, 46 F.3d 258, 268–69 (3d Cir. 1995), when it allowed corporate officers and employees to be named as defendants and their corporation as the enterprise. But the rationale of *Jaguar*, recognizing that corporate employees may act as defendant persons to further purposes distinct from those of the corporate enterprise they direct or participate in, does not apply to the instant fact situation. In *Jaguar*, the named defendants were individual officers of a corporation who conducted racketeering activity through that corporation, the RICO enterprise. Thus, it was the individuals who were named as defendants, not the corporation. The court stated:

> In a § 1962(c) action against officers conducting a pattern of racketeering activity through a corporate enterprise . . . the plaintiff can recover against the defendant officers and cannot recover against the corporation simply by pleading the officers as the persons controlling the corporate enterprise, since the corporate enterprise is not liable under § 1962(c) in this context. Instead, a corporation would be liable under § 1962(c) only if it engages in racketeering activity as a "person" in another distinct "enterprise," since only "persons" are liable for violating § 1962(c).

Id. at 268. *Jaguar* recognized that individual employees or officers are legally and factually distinct from the corporation that employs them, and further recognized that individuals may act to further their own interests not shared by the corporation by conducting racketeering activity through the corporation. The corporation, on the other hand, cannot act other than through its officers, agents, and employees.

After   The Third Circuit has somewhat liberalized the person–enterprise distinctiveness requirement. In *Jaguar Cars, Inc. v. Royal Oaks Motor Car Co.*,[63] the court allowed corporate officers and employees to be named as defendants and their corporation as the enterprise. But the rationale of *Jaguar* does not apply here because the named defendants were individual corporate officers who conducted racketeering activity through the corporation, the RICO enterprise. The corporation was not named as a defendant. *Jaguar* recognized that individual employees or officers are legally and factually distinct from the corporation that employs them:

> In a § 1962(c) action against officers conducting a pattern of racketeering activity through a corporate enterprise . . . the plaintiff can recover against the defendant officers and cannot recover against the corporation simply by pleading the officers as the persons controlling the corporate enterprise, since the corporate enterprise is not liable under § 1962(c) in this context. Instead, a corporation would be liable under § 1962(c) only if it engages in racketeering activity as a "person" in another distinct "enterprise," since only "persons" are liable for violating § 1962(c).[64]

The court further recognized that individuals may act to further their own interests by conducting racketeering activity through the corporation.[65] The corporation, on the other hand, cannot act other than through its officers, agents, and employees.[66]

77

If you can improve on the language of a statute, contract, or case, then paraphrase.

Quotable Quotes

"[A] dull or incomprehensible or badly thought-out idea does not gain in credibility or excitement merely through being sandwiched between quotation marks. Improperly used quotations can say as much about your writing as improper table manners can say about your upbringing. They can say, for instance, that you lack confidence to draw conclusions of your own, or that you lack originality to cast your own sentences, paint your own prose pictures, turn your own phrases."
—Judi Kesselman-Turkel & Franklynn Peterson, *Good Writing* 235 (1981).

"Distill your copy. Rid it of impurities. Make every word earn its own way. When you think you are done, try shortening your copy by one-third. Paraphrase to tighten yawning quotations. Sharpen the focus."
—George Kennedy et al., *The Writing Book* 35 (1984).

"If you have not made other people's knowledge your own by mixing it with your thoughts and your labor of recomposition, you are not a writer but a compiler; you have not written a report but done a scissors-and-paste job. And the chief defect of such an evasion of responsibility is that the piece will probably be tedious to read and lacking in strength and light."
—Jacques Barzun & Henry F. Graff, *The Modern Researcher* 236 (6th ed. 2004).

Explanation

How often have you struggled through the labored prose of a statute, contract, or case? Don't make your reader do the same; paraphrase for clarity and brevity.

It's rare that you'll need to excerpt entire sections from source material. Try instead to boil the source down to its essence and put it in your own words. Or else preserve some of the original while paraphrasing to give the context needed to understand the shorter snippets. If necessary, you can include longer extracts verbatim in an appendix.

The example that follows shows the modern use of an early-20th-century quotation that, to a modern reader, sounds a little quirky: *this* appears twice as shorthand for *this case*, and the entire quotation is hard to follow out of context. With some paring down and paraphrasing, the passage becomes much more comprehensible. The case involves the constitutionality of sanctioning a defendant by entering a default judgment.

A Before-and-After Example

Before   The conflict here surrounds the meaning of *Hammond Packing Co. v. Arkansas*, 212 U.S. 322, 29 S.Ct. 370, 53 L.Ed. 530 (1909). In *Hammond*, the defendant declined to comply with a pretrial discovery order. As sanction therefor, the Arkansas court struck the defendant's pleadings and rendered a judgment against it, "as by default." 212 U.S. at 349, 29 S.Ct. at 379. The United States Supreme Court affirmed the state court's decision, thereby distinguishing the earlier case of *Hovey v. Elliott*, 167 U.S. 409, 17 S.Ct. 841, 42 L.Ed. 215 (1897), which held that to punish for contempt by rendering a judgment of default violated due process. The Court in *Hammond* stated in pertinent part:

> The difference between mere punishment, as illustrated in *Hovey v. Elliott*, and the power exerted in this, is as follows: In the former, due process of law was denied by the refusal to hear. In this, the preservation of due process was secured by the presumption that the refusal to produce evidence material to the administration of due process was but an admission of the want of merit in the asserted defense.

Hammond Packing Co., 212 U.S. at 351, 29 S.Ct. at 380. [193 words]

After   The conflict here surrounds the meaning of *Hammond Packing Co. v. Arkansas*,[62] decided by the Supreme Court in 1909. In that case, the court sanctioned a defendant who had violated a pretrial discovery order. The sanction entailed striking the defendant's pleadings and rendering a default judgment. The Supreme Court affirmed despite its earlier holding in *Hovey v. Elliott*,[63] which disallowed a default judgment as punishment for contempt. But in *Hammond*, the Court distinguished between two types of cases: (1) the "mere punishment" in *Hovey*, where due process was denied by a refusal to hear the plaintiff's case at all; and (2) the "preservation of due process" secured by presuming that the defendant's refusal to produce material evidence showed "want of merit in the asserted defense."[64] [124 words]

78

Abbreviate words as appropriate in case names. Know the other elements of correct citation form.

Quotable Quotes

"Neophytes often cite cases found elsewhere in the brief by the use of the words 'Supra' and 'Infra.' They feel it makes them sound lawyerlike. It is not so."

> —Mario Pittoni, *Brief Writing and Argumentation* 42 (1967).

"Nothing exposes the second-rate lawyer more quickly than an obvious error in citation form."

> —Irwin Alterman, *Plain and Accurate Style in Court Papers* § 7.09, at 116 (1987).

"Abbreviate case names in citations by abbreviating any word listed below . . . . It is permissible to abbreviate other words of eight letters or more if *substantial* space is thereby saved and the result is unambiguous. Unless otherwise indicated, plurals are formed by adding the letter 's.'"

> —*The Bluebook: A Uniform System of Citation* § T.6, at 302 (17th ed. 2000).

"[I]ncorrect citations can impair a writer's credibility and call an argument's validity into question."

> —Bryan A. Garner, *The Redbook: A Manual on Legal Style* § 8.1, at 105 (2002).

Explanation

It's hard to find a quotable quote in the *Bluebook*, a work not known for pithy sayings. But the one given above is especially apropos for brief-writers. Perhaps the most widely ignored *Bluebook* rule is the one relating to abbreviated case names. And violations are easy to spot.

So who cares? Don't forget that the initial reader of your brief is often a law clerk, not a judge. And who are law clerks? Usually, former law-review editors—and recent ones, at that. And what do former law-review editors, especially recent ones, have in common? A *Bluebook* fetish.

You get the idea.

But even if that weren't so, it's simply more economical to abbreviate appropriately—particularly if you're citing cases in the text.

By the way, the *Bluebook* isn't the only kid on the citational block. Various jurisdictions have their own style manuals.* Know the standards that govern your briefs. And recognize that the *Bluebook* may not be at the zenith of citational authorities much longer. The *ALWD Citation Manual*, written by Darby Dickerson and sponsored by the Association of Legal Writing Directors, has admirably streamlined the task of citing authorities. And it has made great headway in American law schools (more than half have now adopted it). *ALWD* is well organized and attractively laid out—a real pleasure to use. (When was the last time you heard anyone describe the *Bluebook* in those terms?) It's easy to find citation styles, many on-target examples are given, and the table of contents and the index make the whole system easily accessible. Be aware that there are discrepancies between the styles of *ALWD* and the *Bluebook*. For example, *Department* is abbreviated *Dep't* in the *Bluebook* (as a contracted abbreviation) but *Dept.* in *ALWD*. And *ALWD* abandons the *Bluebook's* penchant for small caps, preferring italics set downstyle. It's a cleaner system. If you're a citation jock, you'll want to check this one out.**

For now, though, the *Bluebook* still reigns among brief-writers. Listed below are the words to be abbreviated in case names appearing in citations. But remember a few nuances. First, don't abbreviate any word (except for *&, Ass'n, Bros., Co., Corp., Inc., Ltd.,* and *No.*) if the case name appears in a textual sentence. Second, plurals are formed by adding an *s* to the abbreviation: hence *Associates* is abbreviated *Assocs.*; *Center* is abbreviated *Ctrs.*; etc. Third, in *Bluebook* style, contracted abbreviations (with letters removed from the middle) don't have periods: *Association* becomes *Ass'n* (no period); *Commissioner* becomes *Comm'r*; etc.

Keep the following list handy when citing cases; using it will help you save space and clean up the appearance of your citations.

Words to Be Abbreviated in Case Name***

Academy	Acad.	Atlantic	Atl.
Administrat[ive, ion]	Admin.	Authority	Auth.
Administrat[or, rix]	Adm'[r, x]	Automo[bile, tive]	Auto.
Advertising	Adver.	Avenue	Ave.
Agricultur[e, al]	Agric.	Bankruptcy	Bankr.
America [n]	Am.	Board	Bd.
and	&	Broadcast [ing]	Broad.
Associate	Assoc.	Brotherhood	Bhd.
Association	Ass'n	Brothers	Bros.

Building	Bldg.	Financ[e, ial, ing]	Fin.
Business	Bus.	Foundation	Found.
Casualty	Cas.	General	Gen.
Cent[er, re]	Ctr.	Government	Gov't
Central	Cent.	Guaranty	Guar.
Chemical	Chem.	Hospital	Hosp.
College	Coll.	Housing	Hous.
Commission	Comm'n	Import [er, ation]	Imp.
Commissioner	Comm'r	Incorporated	Inc.
Committee	Comm.	Indemnity	Indem.
Community	Cmty.	Independent	Indep.
Company	Co.	Industr[y, ies, ial]	Indus.
Compensation	Comp.	Information	Info.
Condominium	Condo.	Institut[e, ion]	Inst.
Congress [ional]	Cong.	Insurance	Ins.
Consolidated	Consol.	International	Int'l
Construction	Constr.	Investment	Inv.
Cooperative	Coop.	Laboratory	Lab.
Continental	Cont'l	Liability	Liab.
Corporation	Corp.	Limited	Ltd.
Correction[s, al]	Corr.	Litigation	Litig.
Defense	Def.	Machine [ry]	Mach.
Department	Dep't	Maintenance	Maint.
Detention	Det.	Management	Mgmt.
Development	Dev.	Manufacturer	Mfr.
Director	Dir.	Manufacturing	Mfg.
Discount	Disc.	Maritime	Mar.
Distribut[or, ing]	Distrib.	Market	Mkt.
District	Dist.	Marketing	Mktg.
Division	Div.	Mechanic [al]	Mech.
East [ern]	E.	Medic[al, ine]	Med.
Econom[ic, ics, ical, y]	Econ.	Memorial	Mem'l
Education [al]	Educ.	Merchan[t, dise, dising]	Merch.
Electric [al, ity]	Elec.	Metropolitan	Metro.
Electronic	Elec.	Municipal	Mun.
Engineer	Eng'r	Mutual	Mut.
Engineering	Eng'g	National	Nat'l
Enterprise	Enter.	North [ern]	N.
Entertainment	Entm't	Organiz[ation, ing]	Org.
Environment	Env't	Pacific	Pac.
Environmental	Envtl.	Partnership	P'ship
Equality	Equal.	Person [al, nel]	Pers.
Equipment	Equip.	Pharmaceutic[s, al]	Pharm.
Examiner	Exam'r	Preserv[e, ation]	Pres.
Exchange	Exch.	Probation	Prob.
Execut[or, rix]	Ex'[r, x]	Product [ion]	Prod.
Export [er, ation]	Exp.	Professional	Prof'l
Federal	Fed.	Public	Pub.
Federation	Fed'n	Publication	Publ'n
Fidelity	Fid.	Publishing	Publ'g

Railroad	R.R.	South [ern]	S.
Railway	Ry.	Steamship [s]	S.S.
Refining	Ref.	Street	St.
Regional	Reg'l	Subcommittee	Subcomm.
Rehabilitation	Rehab.	Surety	Sur.
Reproduct[ion, ive]	Reprod.	System [s]	Sys.
Resource [s]	Res.	Technology	Tech.
Restaurant	Rest.	Telecommunication	Telecomm.
Retirement	Ret.	Tele[phone, graph]	Tel.
Road	Rd.	Temporary	Temp.
Savings	Sav.	Transcontinental	Transcon.
School [s]	Sch.	Transport [ation]	Transp.
Science	Sci.	Trustee	Tr.
Secretary	Sec'y	Turnpike	Tpk.
Securit[y, ies]	Sec.	Uniform	Unif.
Service	Serv.	University	Univ.
Shareholder	S'holder	Utility	Util.
Social	Soc.	Village	Vill.
Society	Soc'y	West [ern]	W.

79

Shun *clearly* and its allies.

Quotable Quotes

"[I]t seems to be a familiar joke among some ironic observers that when a judge (some other judge) begins a sentence with a term of utter conviction (*Clearly, Undeniably, It is plain that . . .*), the sentence that follows is likely to be dubious, unreasonable, and fraught with difficulties."
—Walker Gibson, *Literary Minds and Judicial Style*,
36 N.Y.U. L. Rev. 915, 925 (1961).

"Argument by adverbs, such as 'clearly' and 'obviously,' indicates that the argument is not being fully developed. If it is a legitimate issue on appeal, it may not be clear or obvious to the appellate court. Rather than concluding that the court should rule in your favor, explain why it should reach that conclusion."
—Richardson R. Lynn, *Appellate Litigation* § 9.7, at 186 (1985).

"The claim that a particular statutory provision covers the case does not gain strength by stating that it 'clearly,' 'plainly,' or 'patently' does so. Nor is the phrase 'the purpose of the rule' improved by inserting the word 'plain' or 'clear' before the word 'purpose.' Indeed, words like 'patently' or 'obviously' suggest that what follows is the *ipse dixit* of the writer, rather than a necessary conclusion."
—Daniel M. Friedman, "Winning on Appeal," in *Appellate Practice Manual* 129,
133–34 (Priscilla A. Schwab ed., 1992).

"*Obviously*, like other dogmatic words (*clearly, undoubtedly, undeniably*), is one that 'lawyers tend to use when they are dealing with exceptionally obscure matters.' "
—Bryan A. Garner, *A Dictionary of Modern Legal Usage* 611 (2d ed. 1995)
(quoting Grant Gilmore, *The Death of Contract* 116 n.63 (1974)).

Explanation

The words *clearly* and *obviously* protest too much. They signal weakness. It's paradoxical but true. If you haven't been aware of this, start looking at any sentence in which one of those words appears. Remove the adverb, and the sentence will be stronger.

Let the court decide for itself what is clear or obvious. Your arguments and supporting evidence should be able to stand on their own.

Not persuaded yet? Consider that in a 2001 survey of a California appellate court, 73 of the respondents agreed with this statement: "I notice, and it bothers me, when a brief uses adverbs like 'clearly' and 'obviously' to support arguments."*

Some Before-and-After Examples

Example A

Before   In sum, *it is clear that* the only requirement to qualify as a consumer under the DTPA is that one must acquire goods or services, either directly or indirectly. There *clearly* is no requirement that one acquire goods or services directly from the defendant or have any direct relationship with the defendant.

After   In sum, the only requirement to qualify as a consumer under the DTPA is that one must acquire goods or services, either directly or indirectly. Neither the statute itself nor the courts have ever required that one acquire goods or services directly from the defendant or have any direct relationship with the defendant.

Example B

Before   Schafer's arguments to foreclose the application of an appeal-bond requirement in this case should *clearly* be overruled. *Obviously*, since this is a civil-contempt case, Schafer cannot appeal his jail sentence. No right to a jury trial exists, so *patently* no such right could be burdened by the requirement of an appeal bond. *Clearly*, the appeal bond should be set to equal the arrearages so that Mary Sue Neufeld can get satisfaction of that amount.

After   Schafer's request to avoid an appeal bond should be denied. Because this is a civil-contempt case, he cannot appeal his jail sentence. And because no right to a jury trial exists, no such right could be unconstitutionally "burdened" by the appeal bond. This Court should set the appeal bond at an amount equal to his child-support arrearages. Only then will Mary Sue Neufeld be assured that Schafer can satisfy any judgment rendered against him.

---

* *California Appellate Practice Handbook* 237 (7th ed. 2001).

80

State the facts powerfully— in chronological order. Never give a witness- by-witness account.

Quotable Quotes

"[C]onfine your facts to the absolutely relevant and the absolutely important. To violate this principle in argumentative writing is to court disaster."
—Gorham Munson, *The Written Word* 112 (rev. ed. 1949).

"The court wants above all things to learn what are the facts which give rise to the call upon its energies; for in many, probably in most, cases when the facts are clear there is no great trouble about the law."
—John W. Davis, "The Argument of an Appeal," in *Advocacy and the King's English* 212, 217 (George Rossman ed., 1960).

"[T]he first objective of the advocate must be so to write his Statement of Facts that the court will want to decide the case in his favor after reading just that portion of his brief. . . . [I]t is a mistake to assume, as many lawyers apparently do, that it is necessary to set out the testimony in the same order in which it was presented at trial."
—Frederick B. Wiener, *Briefing and Arguing Federal Appeals* 45–46 (rev. ed. 1967).

"Set forth your statement of facts in logical, coherent order. Evidence necessarily has to come in one witness at a time, but that's not the way you argue a case, either at trial or on appeal. Your statement of facts should group items of evidence relating to a particular subject so that the court will readily grasp the whole picture. A statement of facts consisting of nothing but a rehash of what Jones testified, followed by what Smith testified, followed by what Thompson testified, is next to worthless."
—Arno H. Denecke et al., *Notes on Appellate Brief Writing*, 51 Or. L. Rev. 351, 359 (1972).

"No part of the brief is more important than the statement of the facts, for however much the court may know about the applicable principles of law, it knows nothing of the facts of the case before the lawyers submit their briefs. . . . Briefwriters should avoid giving a mere summary of the various witnesses' testimony in the order in which they appeared at trial. The purpose of the statement of facts is not to rehash indiscriminately the trial testimony, but rather to organize the facts of the case in such a way as to focus on the issues on appeal."

—Myron H. Bright, *Appellate Briefwriting: Some Golden Rules*,
17 Creighton L. Rev. 1069, 1072 (1984).

"Whenever the narrative can be stated in chronological order it should be, for this is the natural way to tell any story, and the easiest to understand."

—Girvan Peck, *Writing Persuasive Briefs* 117 (1984).

"Some lawyers have the bad habit of presenting the facts by summarizing the testimony of each witness. We much prefer a narrative of the facts."

—Roger J. Miner, *Twenty-Five "Dos" for Appellate Brief Writers*,
3 Scribes J. Legal Writing 19, 22 (1992).

"*Tell the story*. Every case, murder or tax, negligence or antitrust, records the unique history of a human transaction. Perhaps it is the sort of transaction that only a student of a particular discipline will appreciate, but it contains drama nonetheless. By plan or accident, the actors did what they did. They responded to their own ideas or the acts of others. Legal rules may have shaped the actors' plans; their actions and reactions will have legal consequences. In urging the application of particular rules, do not forget the story that calls them forth."

—John E. Nelson, "Building a Brief," in *Appellate Practice Manual* 228,
230 (Priscilla A. Schwab ed., 1992).

"While there are lots of ways to write a statement of facts, a good one passes two essential tests: First, it stands alone. Anyone reading your statement of facts should understand what the case is about without having to look at anything else. Second, the statement of facts should make the reader take your side. It should be persuasive without being argumentative."

—James W. McElhaney, *The Art of Persuasive Legal Writing*,
ABA J., Jan. 1996, at 76, 78.

Explanation

In narrating the facts, you have an opportunity to shine as a storyteller. To succeed, you have to be creative in the way you approach chronological events.

Many brief-writers, though, seem least comfortable with the factual statement. These writers don't tell the story at all. In an appellate brief, for instance, they'll tell the story of how the story unfolded at trial. This means a witness-by-witness account of the testimony, usually dictated as the "writer" reads through the record. Rarely will you find this type of account anything other than wretched.

A statement of facts should instead express a so-called clean narrative line. Professor John Trimble, a LawProse faculty member, uses this term to describe a story that progresses naturally—often dramatically—from beginning to end. Such a story is told like a story, not like a series of witness interviews.

What follows are four splendid examples. Examples A and B are by James L. Turner, an assistant U.S. Attorney in Houston, whose knack for orderly exposition is aided by the fascinating subjects he writes about. Example C is by David Crump, a law professor at the University of Houston. It's a good example of drafting in extremely sensitive circumstances: some unpleasant facts must be conceded, but some countervailing facts bear on the legal issues, and these must be developed in a way that isn't heavy-handed toward a sympathetic plaintiff. Example D is the work of Steven A. Hirsch of San Francisco. It lucidly explains an intricate procedural history that would scare off many writers—and does so engagingly. Notice the effective use of present tense in the headings, giving the narrative a feeling of immediacy; notice also that Hirsch, like many other good brief-writers, puts even the record citations in footnotes (see tip #22). (For yet another example of that point, see the statement of facts in Appendix B.)

Recommendation: Each time you must write a statement of facts, pause for 15 minutes to read or reread one of these examples.

Some Unusually Good Examples

Example A

Statement of Facts

1. Preface: Outline of a narcotics-trafficking organization by an expert.

Drug Enforcement Administration (DEA) Special Agent Roy Dunlap was qualified and offered as an expert witness on narcotics trafficking. The district court accepted the government's offer and allowed Special Agent Dunlap to give expert opinions (4 R. 7). In his capacity as an expert, Dunlap related that a narcotics trafficking organization "operated much like any other business" (4 R. 7) and that every participant in a conspiracy had a defined role.

In a trafficking organization, one routinely found transporters or "mules," and one found "brokers" (4 R. 8). According to Dunlap, a broker or "overseer" was the person responsible for the contraband—the person responsible for the transaction. Upon the broker fell the responsibility for securing a "stash location"—the place where the cocaine was held pending delivery—and for orchestrating the delivery of the contraband. The broker orchestrated delivery but did not necessarily have to participate in it (4 R. 8). On many occasions, the broker or overseer would assume a position from which he could observe a transaction: "watching what players [were] involved, looking for surveillance, looking for police in the area" (4 R. 8).

In Special Agent Dunlap's opinion, it was not unusual for an overseer to minimize his contacts with the people under him:

> The overseer—that's the idea of the organization. He has people that work for him. And because it's a criminal activity, he wants to isolate himself from the actual deal itself, the actual crime. The actual hands-on dirt of the transaction.
>
> So he orchestrates it from afar and he insulates himself the best he can from actually being present during the time of the deal (4 R. 9).

In his experience, Dunlap observed that many criminal organizations were made up of family members or lifelong friends (4 R. 12).

2. The arrival of Jose Rodriguez.

In April 1993, a DEA confidential informant advised Special Agent Roy Dunlap that he would be receiving 40 kilograms of cocaine at the Marriott Hotel, Intercontinental Airport Houston (4 R. 10). The contraband was to be delivered by one Jose Rodriguez of Roma, Texas (4 R. 17; 5 R. 30). The DEA agents were led to believe that the cocaine was to be drawn from a 300-kilogram "stash" that was reported to be stored in a house located somewhere between Cleveland and Conroe, Texas (4 R. 13).

On April 1, 1993, the informant called Rodriguez to discuss the delivery. They agreed to meet the next day, April 2, 1993. Rodriguez was to arrive around 3:00 p.m. The informant and he were to meet at the airport. Rodriguez requested a vehicle; the DEA, fully anticipating this request, had a van ready for him. The informant and Rodriguez settled on a price of $16,500 per kilogram—a total price of $660,000 (4 R. 14, 15; 5 R. 33).

At 3:00 p.m. on April 2, 1993, the informant greeted Jose Rodriguez as the latter arrived on a Continental Airlines flight from McAllen, Texas (4 R. 19). Before the informant and Rodriguez left the baggage area, DEA Special Agent David Preston watched Rodriguez make a telephone call from the baggage area (5 R. 60, 61, 63). The informant and Rodriguez then proceeded from the terminal, through the pedestrian tunnel linking the terminal to the Marriott Hotel, to the hotel parking lot (4 R. 19).

In the parking lot, the informant gave the keys to the van to Rodriguez (4 R. 20). Rodriguez then took the van and left the airport. The informant and Special Agent Dunlap remained at the Marriott, where they were to await Rodriguez's return with the cocaine (4 R. 20).

3. The exchange: an orange pickup for a beige van.

From the airport, Jose Rodriguez drove to an Econolodge located at 9535 Katy Freeway (the intersection of Interstate Highway 10 and Bunker Hill) in Houston (4 R. 21; 5 R. 35). Rodriguez was followed to the Econolodge by a DEA surveillance team. Special Agent Preston noted that Rodriguez arrived at the Econolodge around 4:00 p.m. (5 R. 65) and checked into room number 265 (4 R. 22; 5 R. 36). Rodriguez remained in room 265 between 40 and 45 minutes (4 R. 22; 5 R. 65).

Rodriguez related that the delivery had been arranged in Roma, Texas. Rodriguez was given two telephone numbers: one to a pager and one to a residence, either a house or an apartment (5 R. 36). He had been instructed to meet a person driving an orange pickup truck at a specified service station between 5:00 and 6:00 p.m. (5 R. 37). Rodriguez was to signal his readiness to receive the cocaine by calling one of the two telephone numbers. Rodriguez made his first telephone call from the hotel— he futilely tried to place a call to the pager (5 R. 40–41). When it became apparent that he would not be able to make the call to the pager, he called the other number.

The call to the residence was taken by a woman, who told Rodriguez that no one else was there. Rodriguez gave the woman the hotel telephone number and his room number and asked the woman to place a call to the pager (5 R. 42). Rodriguez waited for perhaps 10 to 15 minutes; when no one called him back, he set out for the designated meeting place (4 R. 44).

From the Econolodge, Rodriguez drove to a Chevron station located at the intersection of Little York and T.C. Jester (5 R. 45). While there, Rodriguez again tried to call the pager number but was rebuffed by the fact that the public telephone at the service station did not allow incoming calls (5 R. 45–46, 66). Rodriguez called the residence. The same woman Rodriguez had talked to earlier again received his call. She told him that the orange truck was on the way (5 R. 46–47).

Between 5 and 15 minutes later, a 1981 orange Ford pickup truck pulled into the Chevron station and parked at the pumps (5 R. 48, 67). The truck was being driven by Arthur Marquez, a man Rodriguez had once seen in Roma (4 R. 23; 5 R. 48). Rodriguez walked over to the pumps and asked the driver if that was the truck he was supposed to pick up. Marquez replied that it was and that it needed gas (5 R. 49). Rodriguez finished pumping the gas, went into the station, and paid for it (5 R. 50). Rodriguez told Marquez that he would call him when it was time for him to return the orange pickup for the beige van (5 R. 50). Marquez gave Rodriguez the keys to the truck, Rodriguez gave Marquez the keys to the van, and they parted company (4 R. 23; 5 R. 51–52).

Thus far the entire transaction had proceeded as it had been planned in Roma, Texas (5 R. 53). Rodriguez had been told to meet a young man driving an orange pickup truck—the cocaine would be found in the truck's toolbox. In Marquez, Rodriguez had indeed met a young man driving an orange pickup truck (5 R. 56).

4. Rodriguez returns to the airport . . .

Rodriguez left the Chevron station and returned to the airport (4 R. 23). He drove directly to the parking lot of the airport Marriott and parked the pickup about two places away from the spot where he had picked up the van. He walked into the hotel and met with the informant. Moments later, Rodriguez and the informant walked out to the pickup. Rodriguez reached over and opened the toolbox built into the truck's bed. The informant looked into the toolbox and confirmed that the cocaine was present. Rodriguez closed the toolbox, and they started back to the hotel. Rodriguez never made it back to the hotel. As Rodriguez closed the toolbox, the informant gave the surveillance team the prearranged arrest signal: Rodriguez was arrested (4 R. 24, 29; 5 R. 13, 14, 53, 54, 69–70).

5.   . . . while Marquez goes home to watch television.

Another surveillance team consisting of DEA Special Agents Jennifer Maxey, Frank Stevens, Kevin Pittman, and Tom Anderson followed Marquez and the van about a block and a half from the Chevron station to the Arbor Oaks Apartments (4 R. 31; 5 R. 83). They watched Marquez park the van and go into an apartment located somewhere in the 900s. After Rodriguez was arrested and information of that arrest had been conveyed to the surveillance team, the agents approached the apartments' management personnel to find out where the owner of the orange pickup truck lived. They were advised that he lived in apartment 901 (5 R. 84).

The agents went to apartment 901. It was about 6:45 p.m. The door to apartment 901 was opened to the agents by Anna Santiago and Elena Marquez (5 R. 86). Anderson identified himself and his fellow agents and showed them his credentials (5 R. 86). He told them why they were there and asked if they knew who owned the orange pickup (5 R. 86). The women replied that they owned the truck and granted the agents' request to come in and look around (4 R. 31, 32; 5 R. 88, 110).

Upon entering the apartment, the agents initiated a protective sweep that led them directly to Marquez, who was sitting on a bed in one of the bedrooms watching television (4 R. 33; 5 R. 88, 111). Despite the fact that Marquez had changed his shirt, Special Agent Pittman recognized Marquez as the driver of the orange pickup truck (5 R. 89, 91, 112). Marquez disavowed any knowledge of an orange pickup truck and denied having driven such a vehicle (5 R. 90, 112). But Marquez was betrayed by his surroundings: in the bedroom the agents found the camouflage hat he had been wearing at the Chevron station, as well as his shirt (5 R. 68, 90). In addition, the agents found the keys to the beige van sitting atop Marquez's television (5 R. 92).

With the discovery of the keys, Marquez was escorted to the front porch, where he was interviewed by Special Agents Pittman, Stevens, and Maxey (4 R. 34; 5 R. 90). After this interview, the agents shifted their attention to Marquez's father-in-law, Roberto Santiago (5 R. 105, 114).

6. Friends, family, and cocaine: Santiago and the ties that bind.

The special agents ran a check on the registration of the orange pickup truck driven by Marquez. The registered owner of the pickup proved to be Annabelle Santiago (5 R. 85). Special Agent Anderson also discovered that the address on Anna Santiago's license was not that of the Arbor Oaks Apartments—the address on the license was a post-office box in Cleveland, Texas (5 R. 93). The explanation for this variance between addresses is that Elena Marquez, Marquez's wife, was the registered lessee of the apartment (5 R. 137–38). Elena's father, Santiago, and his wife, Anna, also lived there. So the agents learned that Marquez resided in an apartment with his in-laws—Anna and Roberto Santiago (5 R. 138).

The agents remained at apartment 901 for perhaps 45 minutes (5 R. 93). Since Santiago had become a suspect in the conspiracy and since his return to the apartment was uncertain, several agents were left at the apartment to continue surveillance while the rest took Marquez to the Harris County Jail. The agents had hardly gotten out of the apartment complex when they were advised that Santiago's four-door Geo Prizm had been spotted near apartment 901 (5 R. 94, 115, 119). Santiago was instantly arrested and transported to the Harris County Jail.

At the jail, Special Agent Frank Stevens asked whether Santiago had been subjected to a thorough search; he was told that no, Santiago had not been searched (5 R. 120). Stevens noted that Santiago smelled as if he had been drinking—the odor was especially pungent (5 R. 120). Special Agent Stevens ordered Santiago to take off his boots. Stevens banged on the heel of one of the boots and turned it over. A plastic baggie containing a white powdery substance (GX 18) was field-tested: it proved to be 11.8 grams of cocaine (4 R. 36; 5 R. 121–22).

Special Agent Anderson related that among the personal effects taken from Santiago after his arrest was a pager. While inventorying Santiago's personal property, he noticed that "there [had been] several pages into this beeper" (5 R. 95). Anderson pulled up three numbers on this pager. One of these numbers was 467-4411, the number of the Econolodge motel located on the Katy Freeway. This number was followed by the number 265—Jose Rodriguez's room number (5 R. 96). Of the other two numbers, one matched the number to Jose Rodriguez's pager (5 R. 96).

The cocaine taken from Santiago's boot was later analyzed by DEA forensic chemists. One of those chemists, George Phillips, confirmed that the substance was cocaine and that it was 87 percent pure (5 R. 146). Phillips also had an opportunity to examine a sample drawn from the 40 kilograms of cocaine that had been found in the toolbox of the orange pickup truck. That cocaine proved to be 89.9% pure (5 R. 148).

7. Starr County–crossed friends: past deeds recalled.

Sergeant A.J. Paulsen of the Houston Police Department recalled a 1984 encounter with Santiago (5 R. 151). According to Sergeant Paulsen, Santiago was one of several people he saw going into and coming from room 358 of the Beechnut Motor Inn during a 32-hour surveillance on that room in January 1984 (5 R. 153, 154). At about 2:15 p.m. on January 25, 1984, Sergeant Paulsen secured a search warrant authorizing him to search room 358 (5 R. 154). Santiago and his brother were among the people the searching officers encountered in room 358. When he was arrested, Santiago was carrying cocaine (5 R. 155). In addition to Santiago and his brother, four other people who were arrested in room 358 hailed from Starr County, Texas (5 R. 158).

8. Epilogue: Expert opinions and the jury's verdict.

Special Agent David Preston, without objection, testified that in his opinion and based on his experience, a callow youth like Arthur Marquez would not be left in control of the delivery of 40 kilograms of cocaine. Special Agent Preston was convinced that someone like Santiago would be assigned that responsibility (5 R. 78–79). After due deliberation, the jury agreed with Special Agent Preston's assessment of the transaction and found Santiago guilty of conspiracy to possess cocaine with intent to distribute and with aiding and abetting the possession of cocaine with intent to distribute (6 R. 3). This appeal followed.

Example B

Statement of Facts

1. The advertisement—commercial alchemy.

The advertisement had all the earmarks of alchemy:

> CASHLESS INVESTMENTS
> We pay you a fee for your creditworthiness—assume all liability and keep
> your credit line open for repeat investments. (Government's Exhibits 39, 40.)

In a time of cash deficits and credit crunches, here was a plan to transmute one's creditworthiness into real cash. But just as the efforts of the alchemists proved to be contrary to the laws of nature, this "cashless investment" scheme proved to be contrary to the law of the land.

Roger Daniels and Jim Arnold were the wizards behind this grand scheme to convert an individual's credit into at least $2,000 cash (5 R. 168). Daniels met Arnold sometime in the early 1980s: Daniels was the proprietor of a health-food store—Arnold was one of his regular customers (5 R. 158). Besides health food, Arnold and Daniels discovered other common interests, including a fascination with the real-estate market. Daniels was a licensed real-estate broker and believed that Arnold had an agent's license (5 R. 159). In either 1983 or 1984, they decided to capitalize on this common interest in real estate by forming Homeview Partners.

According to Daniels, Homeview was originally formed to facilitate the purchase of investment homes in Spring, Texas (5 R. 160). Unfortunately, the Bellaire market proved to be prohibitive and Homeview Partners had to seek houses from other builders (5 R. 161). Arnold and Daniels proposed to purchase houses at discounted prices. They would borrow enough money to meet the purchase price and create "additional money," a "surplus," over and above the buyout price (5 R. 62). Many builders were called, but Keystone Homes proved to be the most promising.

Appraisals were critical to the Homeview scheme. Keystone properties were appraised, and the appraisals were readily available (5 R. 163). In addition, the Keystone sales personnel impressed Arnold and Daniels with their potential to effect a "turnaround" sale of the property. The Keystone salespeople maintained a list of "bustouts"—people who had contracted to purchase a house but could not qualify for the financing (5 R. 165). Homeview proposed to purchase discounted houses using financially qualified individuals as "straw buyers" and then "flip" the property to unqualified individuals drawn from the "bustout" list (5 R. 256, 257, 7 R. 606). Eventually Homeview purchased 36 homes (5 R. 166).

The first item on Homeview's agenda was to find creditworthy buyers to make the initial purchase. To this end they placed an advertisement in the Houston Chronicle: "CASHLESS INVESTMENTS" (5 R. 166; Government's Exhibits 39, 40). Arnold and Daniels outlined their scheme to everyone who responded to their advertisement. They explained that the "investor" would use his credit and complete a loan application. After the investor had closed on the house, Arnold and Daniels would buy the house back from them and Homeview would sell the house to people who wanted to live in it. The "investor" could buy up to four houses. The investor would not have to make a down payment and would not be required to make any payments on the house. For their efforts, Homeview promised to pay them $2,000 for every house they "purchased" (5 R. 167, 168).

The down payments and the closing costs were paid by Homeview out of the surplus developed from the initial purchase from Keystone. The payment of the $2,000 was passed through a trust fund that listed an attorney, Michael Lindsay, as trustee (5 R. 169, 173). Daniels illustrated the scheme with this hypothetical: Homeview would purchase a house at 70% of the list price from Keystone. If the house cost $100,000, Homeview would pay $70,000. The investor would apply for a HUD/FHA guaranteed loan, which would cover all but 15% of the original sales price of $100,000, or $85,000. With an "owner/occupant" loan, the amount could go as high as $95,000. So Homeview would realize a profit of $15,000 to $25,000, less the closing costs and the $2,000 investor fee (5 R. 184). Keystone would thus reduce its inventory, the "investor" would realize a profit of $2,000, and Homeview Partners would be recognized as the magicians who had devised a scheme to sell homes in a sagging economy. They would have effected a 20th-century form of alchemy: they would have transmuted credit into cash.

2. The advertisement brings callers.

People responded to the lure of the advertisement. When they did, Daniels and Arnold would prepare them for the loan process (5 R. 184). In addition to a general outline of the scheme, the "investors" were advised to apply for the loan as owner/occupants even if they did not intend to own or occupy the house (5 R. 247; 6 R. 321). They were also advised to indicate that they had enough money to cover the down payment. The loan documentation reflects that the investors complied with these instructions without qualm. The chart below sets forth a list of the investors who testified at Arnold's trial and the location of the supporting documents indicating their involvement in the Homeview scheme:

[Names and addresses of the witnesses listed here.]

All the "investors" indicated that they would be paying the closing costs, even though these costs were being paid by Homeview. Generally, the "investors" represented that they would be owner/occupants even though they had no intention of living in the house they reputedly purchased. The "investors'" sole motivation was to earn the $2,000 without investing anything more than their credit history. As Daniels observed, no one really bought a house; they merely generated a federally insured loan for Homeview (5 R. 188).

3. Cashless investments become criminal indictments.

The Department of Housing and Urban Development initiated an audit of Keystone Homes. The audit was precipitated by a tip that Keystone was engaged in a "strawbuyer scheme," i.e., a scheme whereby people posing as purchasers were allowing their credit to be used to qualify for FHA loans and were buying houses without putting any of their own money down (7 R. 606). Auditor Gordon Taylor noted an unusually high number of "cash sales" on a list provided by Keystone (7 R. 608). This list led Taylor to Southwest Mortgage Company (7 R. 609). Taylor arranged interviews with ten of Southwest's mortgagors (7 R. 610). These interviews ultimately led him to Homeview Partners and Arnold and Daniels.

Arnold and Daniels were fully aware of the audit and Taylor's investigations. One of the first investors called by Taylor was Sam Larsen, who advised Arnold and Daniels of Taylor's impending visit. Arnold and Daniels met with Larsen shortly before Taylor's arrival. Larsen arranged for them to listen in on the meeting from another room (5 R. 182; 6 R. 326). Larsen asked Taylor for a copy of his questions and then passed them to Homeview Partners. Arnold and Daniels then alerted their investors to Taylor's efforts (6 R. 306, 352, 460). Arnold provided Linda Fields with answers to Taylor's inquiries and gave her specific instructions on how to respond to the questions regarding down payment and ownership (7 R. 480).

The magic was gone. The misgivings initially felt by some of the erstwhile "investors" yielded to admissions of guilt on some unspecified charge. They were allowed to plead guilty in exchange for pretrial diversion (Bledsoe, 6 R. 290; Watson, 6 R. 397; Sykes, 7 R. 674; and Clooney, 7 R. 684). None of the investors ever felt that they had violated the law (6 R. 421, 7 R. 460, 7 R. 680).

Daniels conceded that the scheme was too good to be true and was in fact illegal. He entered a plea of guilty and testified on behalf of the government against his former partner, Arnold. Arnold persisted in his plea of not guilty. The jury, however, returned a verdict to the contrary. This appeal followed.

Example C

Factual Statement

The Relationship

Respondent Kay Birling and Petitioner Dan Hull had a casual sexual relationship that began in late May 1985. (SF 852.) They were high-school students: she was then 19 years of age; he was almost 18. (SF 361; 970). Birling first met Hull at a restaurant and then a week or so later saw him at a party where each had different dates. (SF 847.) She began to call him, and Hull eventually agreed to accompany Birling to her senior prom. (SF 848.) According to both Hull and Birling, that was their first and only traditional "date." (SF 368; 951.) In advance of their first date, she arranged for a hotel room for the purpose of spending the night with Hull after the prom. (SF 849.)

Birling testified that before this prom night, she had never had sexual intercourse with anyone. (SF 851; 847–48.) That night, however, Hull and Birling had sexual intercourse in the hotel room arranged for by her. Hull and Birling both testified that, while they were having sexual intercourse, there were three other persons present in the room. (SF 406; 852.) The following summer, Birling and Hull had several sexual encounters. These occurred when they met each other by chance at various places. They would leave to have intercourse at another location and return to the location of the unplanned encounter. (SF 422; 439–41; 784–85; 974–76.) Birling testified that Hull never told her he loved her. (SF 854.) Soon after she went to college at the end of the summer, he ceased to have contact with her. (SF 855.)

On August 10, 1985, Birling asked Hull to accompany her to a wedding she wished to attend. He declined, but did pick her up after the wedding. (SF 855–57.) Before picking her up, Hull went to the home of Defendant Karl Broesche, a friend of his, and arranged to use Broesche's house for sexual intercourse with Birling. Broesche introduced the idea of videotaping the event. (SF 394; 659; 1511.) The record does not reflect what response Hull made, if any. Hull then left to pick up Birling. While Hull was away, Broesche set up a video camera. (SF 1513.)

The resulting videotape (PX 1) consists of three sections. The first section was made by Defendants Broesche, Widner, and Tamborello while Hull was not present. During that period, the three boys predicted in crude language and jokes what would happen when Hull and Birling returned. (PX 1.) The second section of the tape consists of a picture of an empty bedroom, which reflects the fact that the video camera was turned on before the arrival of Birling and Hull. (PX 1.) The third section of the tape records activity between Birling and Hull. All the sexual activity recorded on the tape takes place under a blanket. Hull stated that he used the blanket because he had second thoughts and wanted to shield the sexual activity from being videotaped; the blanket had this effect even in an "enhanced" tape made later. R. 406–07. Hull believes a review of the original tape by the Court will be advantageous to Hull because of the tape's poor quality and nonexplicit nature.

Shortly after the tape was made, Hull took possession of it. He showed it on three occasions, each time in a private residence, to a total of ten persons, each of whom was named by Hull in his testimony. (SF 408–11; 421.)

After she learned of the videotape from a friend, Birling confronted Hull. (SF 873–74; 919.) Birling demanded the tape. After initially resisting, Hull offered to destroy the tape in front of her. She insisted on obtaining it, however, and Hull surrendered it to her. He told Birling that he was sorry and had not meant to hurt her. (SF 875–79.)

The quality of the original videotape was so bad that Birling found it necessary to have an "enhanced" version made. Allegedly, the enhancement was done for the purpose of identifying the boys on the first part of the tape. (SF 1162–63.) Birling's attorney showed only part of the enhanced version to the jury. (SF 401–04.) Even the enhanced version did not show graphic sexual activity, and Birling's attorney showed the jury only the initial and arguably most offensive part, with the boys talking in Hull's absence. The jury never saw the sexual encounter between Birling and Hull on either the enhanced or the original poor-quality videotape.

Birling's Evidence of Damages

Birling's damage evidence, in addition to her own testimony, included testimony of relatives and friends who stated that she had a happy childhood, had adjusted quickly to her parents' divorce, and had suffered emotional distress from the events involved in the present suit. (SF 449–50; 452; 819–20; 1435; 1447.) She and friends described incidents of embarrassment when she heard of other persons' knowledge of the videotape. (SF 896–97; 919–23; 901–02; 961.) Birling also testified that she had experienced nightmares, shaking, dizziness, and stomach upsets (SF 901–02; 904), although a causal link between these symptoms and the videotape could only be inferred. Birling's school records showed frequent absences even before these incidents. She testified to difficulty working and taking finals. (SF 879–82; 904.) The evidence, however, showed that not long after learning about the tape, she changed universities. (SF 925; 932; 984–85.) After that change, she made better grades than she ever had before. (SF 963; 994–95.) She testified to difficulty relating to men, although she had several sustained relationships during college. (SF 925–26; 933; 961; 963; 996–99.)

Birling offered the testimony of George Dempsey, a psychologist to whom her attorney referred her. (SF 929.) Dr. Dempsey's diagnosis was that Birling suffered from "posttraumatic stress disorder," the same disease from which combat soldiers sometimes suffer. Dr. Dempsey opined that the suit had "therapeutic value" for her. (SF 502; 509; 511.)

In response, Hull presented two specialists in posttraumatic stress disorder, Dr. Chester B. Scrignar and Dr. Marco Mariotto. Dr. Scrignar has published many articles and two books dealing with anxiety disorders, including posttraumatic stress disorder, and coauthored an article with Dr. Charles Figley, the preeminent authority on posttraumatic stress disorder as it affects Vietnam veterans. (SF 1051–52; 1054–55.) Dr. Mariotto, who worked with Dr. Figley while at Purdue University, is also a preeminent authority on posttraumatic stress disorder. (SF 1387.) Both experts stated that Birling did not suffer from posttraumatic stress disorder because she had neither the antecedents nor the symptoms of the disease, which cannot be caused by embarrassment but instead arises from personal repeated experience with extreme violence, as in combat. (SF 1397–98; 1056; 1058–59; 1065–66.)

Birling's Abandonment of Intentional Torts

On May 1, 1989, Fort Worth Lloyds, an insurance company, intervened in the case. (2d Supp. Tr. 38.) As shown by the original and amended intervention petitions (2d Supp. Tr. 38; 56), the purpose of that intervention was to obtain jury findings determining whether any wrongful act by Defendants was intentional or negligent. Fort Worth Lloyds made clear that only liability for negligent acts would be covered by the policy; intentional acts would be excluded from coverage.

Just before submission to the jury, Birling abandoned all the intentional torts and all the negligence theories other than negligent infliction of emotional distress and invasion of privacy. (SF 1265; Tr. 40.) Birling's abandonment of these claims was motivated by a desire to reach the proceeds of Defendants' homeowner's-insurance policies. The only jury question requested by Birling was for "negligent infliction of emotional distress." Hull objected, arguing that "negligent" infliction of emotional distress did not authorize recovery. (SF 1268; 1556.) The jury found that Hull had negligently caused Birling mental anguish and apportioned 65% of responsibility to him. The jury awarded $1 million against the Defendants, including punitive damages.

Example D

Statement of Facts

1. Six federal judges agree that the debtors engaged in a fraudulent scheme to deny pension and medical benefits to their employees.

In the late 1980s, the debtors embarked on a fraudulent "double breasted" scheme that converted their union-signatory plumbing contracting business to non-union status. The debtors' purpose in this subterfuge was to avoid their obligations under a collective-bargaining agreement, including making pension, medical, and training contributions to the Trust Funds.

On May 8, 1987, the Trust Funds sued in the Northern District of California to recover those contributions.[1] On preliminary motions, two federal judges ruled that the debtors had fraudulently concealed their scheme to cheat the Trust Funds.[2]

Five years later, in a decision excoriating the debtors' fraudulent conduct, U.S. District Judge Barbara A. Brownfield granted summary judgment for more than $4.5 million in favor of the Trust Funds, including $2 million in punitive damages—apparently the first time that any federal judge had awarded punitive damages on summary judgment.[3] Judge Brownfield then stayed enforcement of the judgment, on condition that defendants post a certified check for $700,000 "as the supersedeas bond" pending appeal.[4] From that moment on, the funds remained under the exclusive control of the district court and beyond the reach of the debtors until the court released them to the plaintiffs. On February 28, 1995, this Court affirmed Judge Brownfield's principal findings but remanded the case for trial on the issue of intent.[5]

---

[1] Request for Judicial Notice ("RJN"), Tab 1 at 8:8.

[2] *See* May 24, 1988 opinion and order of Judge William W. Schwarzer at p. 11 (RJN, Tab 1); Nov. 15, 1990 opinion of Judge Vaughn R. Walker at pp. 4–5 (RJN, Tab 2).

[3] *See U.A. Local No. 343, etc. v. Nor-Wash Plumbing, Inc.*, 797 F. Supp. 767, 772 (N.D.Cal. 1992) (Brownfield, J.); *id.* at 773.

[4] *See* Judge Brownfield's Order Extending Stay of Execution of Judgment Pending Appeal and Setting Conditions of Payment into Court for Supersedeas Bond, dated May 11, 1992 (1 Excerpts of Record ("ER"), 22–23). As used herein, "ER" refers to Appellants' Excerpts of Record originally filed in Ninth Circuit Case No. 99-15413, which has since been consolidated with Case No. 99-15415.

[5] *See U.A. Local 343, etc. v. Nor-Wash Plumbing, Inc.*, 48 F.3d 1465, 1472 (9th Cir. 1995) (Norris, Beezer and Simonfeld, JJ.) (reversing trial court in part but finding that "[t]he appellees presented significant evidence of Martin's anti-union animus and his intent to avoid the collective bargaining agreement with Local 343, including evidence that on numerous occasions he declared 'I'm going to close that frigging Union shop!' "); *id.* at 1474–75 (evidence was undisputed that Martin lied to union representatives and submitted perjured affidavits to NLRB concealing his fraudulent scheme).

2. After this Court's remand, Judge Neufeldt requires the funds to remain in the district court's registry as judgment security pending the jury's verdict.

Shortly after this Court's ruling, the debtors moved the district court for release of the $700,000 security, while the Trust Funds sought a writ of attachment that would have placed "virtually all of defendants' business assets . . . in the possession and control of plaintiffs, pending trial."[6]

Concerned about possible disruption to the defendants' business if she granted the attachment writ, but also convinced that the Trust Funds had established that it would probably win on the merits and therefore deserved some form of judgment security,[7] Judge Neufeldt adopted a compromise suggested by the parties. To avoid attachment,[8] the Martins agreed to (1) withdraw their motion for release of security, (2) leave the funds in the district court's registry, and (3) continue to operate their businesses subject to restrictions that Judge Brownfield had imposed in April 1992 to prevent any attempts to frustrate judgment.[9] The Trust Funds, in turn, consented to the denial of their attachment writ. Judge Neufeldt's order specifically directed that "funds on deposit as security" not be released "pending further order of the court[.]"[10]

So on August 11, 1995—when Judge Neufeldt adopted the parties' compromise proposal—the registry funds ceased to function as security for the then-concluded Ninth Circuit appeal. Instead, the funds remained in the court's registry in lieu of a writ of attachment as security for any future jury verdict, under a court order implementing a compromise suggested by the parties themselves.

3. The jury confirms the debtors' fraudulent intent, entering a $1.8 million verdict that resolves the status of the judgment security.

On the eve of trial, the Trust Funds offered to settle the case for $300,000 and a union contract.[11] Martin rejected the offer and went on to lose at trial, where the jury awarded $1.8 million in damages plus attorney's fees against him, Nor-Wash, and Northern Quay. On April 10, 1996, the jury found for the Trust Funds on their alter-ego claim, and also on a separate claim for fraud under 29 U.S.C. § 185.[12] In addition, Judge Neufeldt has stated that she will determine the Trust Fund's attorney's fees and expenses, estimated at $1.5 million, and award that sum as well,

---

[6] *See* Judge Neufeldt's Order on: Motion to Reconsider Application for Right to Attach Order, Motion to Release Security, and Request for Sanctions, dated Aug. 11, 1995 ("Aug. 11 Order"), at p. 27, lines 1–4 (1ER 24–28) (emphasis added).

[7] Aug. 11 Order at p. 26, lines 15–17; *id.* at p. 27, lines 1–7 (1ER 24–28).

[8] Aug. 11 Order at p. 27, line 12 (1ER 24–28).

[9] Aug. 11 Order at pp. 27–28 (1ER 24–28).

[10] Aug. 11 Order at p. 4 (1ER 27).

[11] *See* Reply of Debtors to Trust Funds' Motion to Amend Findings, etc., dated Jan. 12, 1998, at 3:18–20 (5ER Tab 4) (the debtors—not the Trust Funds—were the first to disclose on the record the information regarding the $300,000 settlement offer).

[12] RJN Exh. 3; judgment was entered on April 18, 1996.

so the ultimate judgment will total more than $3.3 million. That will render the debtors insolvent.

4. Concerned that the Martins will file a bankruptcy petition, Judge Neufeldt orders the remaining judgment security released immediately to the Trust Funds.

After the trial, on May 21, 1996, the debtors asked Judge Neufeldt to stay execution of judgment, without any additional bond, pending the outcome of their appeal or, alternatively, pending a stay application to this Court. Judge Neufeldt refused the request, noting that it would give the debtors time to file for bankruptcy and thus "tie up the funds" held as security in the district court's registry.[13] Judge Neufeldt stated: "[T]he reason I'm concerned is, if there's a bankruptcy filing that intervenes, I think that does make things more complicated than they should be. I don't think that should happen before this court has an opportunity to release the [registry] funds if there is no stay."[14] But Judge Neufeldt offered not to release the security immediately if the debtors would stipulate not to file for bankruptcy until this Court ruled on their stay application.[15] The debtors refused. Judge Neufeldt then said: "Okay. The consequence of that will be I'll sign the order [releasing the judgment security]."[16] Judge Neufeldt immediately signed the following order:

> A judgment having been entered on the jury's verdict herein, the Clerk of the Court is hereby directed to release all funds being held on deposit in this action and to disburse said funds, including accrued interest, to the law firm for the plaintiffs.[17]

Because no one was available in the clerk's office to release the funds after the hearing that evening, the next morning the Trust Funds' counsel, John J. Purvis Jr., accompanied by Judge Neufeldt's courtroom deputy, obtained a check from the court clerk for the remaining balance, $523,117 ($250,000 having been released to the debtors earlier). Counsel deposited the money in a client trust account where it remained until Judge Megarry specifically authorized their distribution to the Trust Funds.

But—just as Judge Neufeldt feared—between the hearing one evening and the release of the funds the next morning, the debtors had filed their bankruptcy petitions.

5. Judge Simon ignores legal arguments disproving the existence of any automatic-stay violation.

Under the Bankruptcy Code's automatic-stay provision in 11 U.S.C. § 362(a), the filing of a bankruptcy petition "operates as a stay, applicable

---

[13] 1ER 64–99 at 91:16–92:15.
[14] *Id.* at 95:2–7.
[15] *Id.* at 95:21–96:3.
[16] *Id.* at 98:19–25.
[17] 1 ER 100.

to all entities," of acts to obtain possession of or control over *"property of the estate*[.]" Postpetition acts that do not affect "property of the estate" cannot violate the automatic stay.[18]

On July 10, 1997—more than a year after filing their petition—the debtors moved the bankruptcy court for an order holding the Trust Funds liable for contempt sanctions and for compensatory and punitive damages under § 362(h) (which penalizes "willful" automatic-stay violations). They also sought an order compelling the Trust Funds to turn over the registry funds to the debtors.[19]

Without citation to any authority, the debtors alleged that the judgment security was their property and therefore became property of the bankruptcy estate when they filed their Chapter 11 petition on May 21, 1996. In the debtors' view, it made no difference that (1) the district court had entered judgment on a jury verdict before the bankruptcy filing, (2) the judgment far exceeded the amount of the security, and (3) the judge ordered the clerk to *immediately* release the money to the Trust Funds, specifically worrying that the debtors might try to evade the order by filing a bankruptcy petition.

The Trust Funds' counsel opposed the debtors' motion on the ground that the judgment security could not have been property of the estate at the time the debtors filed for bankruptcy protection. Counsel cited case-law in support of several theories, including two ultimately accepted by the district court on appeal:

- Judge Neufeldt's prepetition order releasing the judgment security to counsel constituted the "last judicial act" necessary to adjudicate ownership of those funds; the clerk's postpetition drafting of the check was a merely "ministerial" act that involved no discretion and could not have violated the automatic stay.[20]

- Judge Neufeldt's August 11, 1995 order required the disputed funds to remain in court as judgment security for an eventual jury verdict against the debtors. Accordingly, when the court entered judgment on that jury verdict, the debtors lost any remaining interest they could have asserted in the funds.[21]

Judge Simon rejected these arguments without analysis. Instead, he held a hearing on October 29–30, 1997, limited to the issue of sanctions under § 362(h). In violation of basic due process, at no time before or during the § 362(h) hearing did Judge Simon inform counsel that they might be held personally liable for sanctions under § 362(h) or for contempt sanctions.

---

[18] *In re Duplitronics*, 183 B.R. 1010, 1014–15 (Bankr. N.D. Ill. 1995).
[19] Motion for Order Holding Respondents in Contempt, etc., dated July 10, 1997 (5ER Tab 3).
[20] Trust Funds' Opp. at 7 (1ER Tab 2); *see* Jan. 19, 1999 Order at 11–14 (3ER Tab 28).
[21] *See, e.g.,* Opposition to Motion for Order Holding Respondents in Contempt, etc., filed July 31, 1997 ("Trust Funds' Opp."), at 6–7 (1ER Tab 2); *see* Jan. 19, 1999 Order at 9–11 (3ER Tab 28).

6. Judge Simon holds the Trust Funds and their counsel liable for § 362(h) damages based on counsel's receipt of judgment security that Judge Neufeldt ordered released to them *before* the bankruptcy filing occurred.

On December 11, 1997, Judge Simon issued an order holding the Trust Funds *and counsel* liable under § 362(h) ("December 11 Order"). The order apologized to the debtors for having earlier rejected their proposal that the proceedings encompass contempt sanctions as well as § 362(h) damages, noting ruefully that "[n]ow [the debtors] can say 'we told you so.' "[22] Judge Simon added that, based on what he viewed as the unethical conduct of the Trust Funds and Counsel, he was "now persuaded that § 362(h) affords only a partial remedy and that a full-blown contempt proceeding" must be held as well.[23]

That order is notable for two reasons.

First, Judge Simon held that the Trust Funds were bent on "extermination" of the debtors and had committed "stark and seemingly cynical" violations of the automatic stay, but cited no authority to support his pivotal finding that the judgment security had been property of the estate when the debtors filed for bankruptcy protection.[24] In sharp contrast to the words of other judges who have presided over this dispute, Judge Simon had kind words for fraudfeasor Martin, calling him a "rugged individualist" and "able plumbing contractor" who was "not about to be shoved around" by labor-management trust funds trying to enforce collective-bargaining agreements.

Second, Judge Simon did not address any of counsel's arguments that the judgment security never entered the bankruptcy estate.[25] Nor did the judge accord any weight to the fact that the Trust Funds and their counsel had acted under the authority of a district court's order expressly releasing the judgment security to them immediately so that the funds could not be tied up in a bankruptcy proceeding. Instead, the bankruptcy judge implicitly assumed that the district court lacked authority to adjudicate the ownership of the judgment security as long as the debtors' appeal of the jury verdict remained pending in this Court:

> The salient fact about the deposit's status as property of the estate is that if the Martins and Northern Quay were ultimately to prevail [on appeal] . . . , the funds on deposit in the registry of the court would have to be paid to the Martins or Northern Quay. That constitutes an interest in property within the meaning of 11 U.S.C. § 541(a).[26]

Then, Judge Simon imposed personal liability on counsel, despite having failed to provide any notice to them that they might be held personally liable.

On January 28, 1998, the bankruptcy court issued an order to show

---

[22] Dec. 11 Order at 2 (1ER Tab 7).

[23] *Id.* at 3 (1ER Tab 7).

[24] Dec. 11 Order at 2 (1ER Tab 7).

[25] *See id.* at 15 (1ER Tab 7).

[26] *Id.* at 15 (1ER 39).

cause regarding contempt directed to the Trust Funds and their counsel, John J. Purvis Jr., Diane Sidd-Champion, and the law firm of Mac-Cormick, Johnston & Schilling. The bankruptcy court later consolidated the contempt proceeding with the § 362(h) motion.[27]

7. Judge Simon orders the Trust Funds and their individual counsel to give fraudfeasor Martin extensive, highly personal financial information.

On April 6, 1998, the debtors escalated their campaign against the Trust Funds and their counsel by serving on them 18 separate sets of document demands and interrogatories directed to the most minute details of their personal lives. The discovery propounded by the debtors would have required the Trust Funds and counsel to disclose virtually every scrap of property they owned, from their real property, cash, and securities, down to their most personal possessions.

A few examples suffice to demonstrate the invasiveness of the debtors' discovery demands:

- "List all household goods, furnishings, including, audio, video, and computer equipment which YOU owned during the period January 1, 1997, to the date YOU answer these interrogatories, including the date acquired and the purchase price of each item."

- "List all books, pictures, and other art objects, antiques, stamp, coin, record, tape, compact disc, and other collections which YOU owned during the period January 1, 1997, to the date YOU answer these interrogatories, including the date acquired and the purchase price of each item."

- "List all furs and jewelry which YOU owned during the period January 1, 1997, and the date YOU answer these interrogatories, including the date acquired and the purchase price of each item."

- "List any gifts YOU made during the period January 1, 1997, to the date YOU answer these interrogatories, with an aggregate value in excess of $500 to any one person. State the name of the donee, the date of the gift and the value of the gift."[28]

The debtors' counsel later admitted that this discovery mimicked the standard questionnaires that a *debtor* must complete to prove that he is insolvent and therefore entitled to bankruptcy protection from creditors.[29] But in this case, it was the *creditors' lawyers* who had to provide the information—involuntarily, on pain of crippling discovery sanctions.

---

[27] 1ER 148–52.

[28] Movants' First Set of Interrogatories, Propounded to John J. Purvis, Interrogatory Nos. 5, 7, 9, and 32, respectively (5ER Tab 5).

[29] May 26, 1998 Tr. at 4:6–17 (debtor's counsel likens discovery to "a simple bankruptcy schedule" (5ER Tab 7); Opposition of Debtors and Debtors in Possession to Petition for Writ of Mandamus, etc., dated July 24, 1998 (E.D. Cal. Nos. CIV S-98-1175 FCD & CIV S-98-0641 (FCD)) at 12:6–8 (5ER Tab 9).

Counsel moved for a protective order, which Judge Simon entirely denied on May 12, 1998. The May 12 order cited no authority and presented no legal analysis, but intimated that forcing the Trust Funds and counsel to comply with the discovery demands would "facilitate" settlement of the Trust Funds' claims against the debtors:

> [The Trust Funds' counsel assert] that the discovery, which seeks financial information, is not necessary because consideration of the putative contemnors' net worth is neither required nor necessary in assessing punitive damages. The simple answer is that this court believes this information to be appropriate for presentation in this peculiar situation and that *requiring the discovery would facilitate resolution of the matter.*[30]

On June 11, 1998, Judge Simon granted the debtors' motion to compel compliance with *all* of the debtors' discovery on the ground that the Court needed extensive wealth-related evidence to determine the punitive damages it planned to assess.[31] At the hearing on that motion, Judge Simon threatened counsel with issues sanctions[32] and with monetary penalties large enough to trigger the duty to report to the State Bar under Bus. & Prof. Code § 6068(o).[33]

Moreover, the bankruptcy judge rejected counsel's proposal for disclosing the information solely to opposing counsel but not to Martin, on the ground that this restriction would tread on Martin's right to effective representation.[34] The judge also extended the discovery cutoff *for the debtors only*, so they could pursue still more discovery against the Trust Funds and counsel.[35]

8. The district court grants interlocutory review and terminates all bankruptcy proceedings against the Trust Funds and their counsel relating to the putative automatic-stay violation.

Facing the prospect of sullied reputations and imminent contempt and discovery sanctions, and having exhausted every other avenue of relief, the Trust Funds petitioned the district court on June 23, 1998 for a writ of mandamus reversing the bankruptcy court's discovery order. The court responded by granting, *sua sponte*, an interlocutory appeal to determine whether the judgment security ever had been property of the bankruptcy estate for purposes of § 362.[36]

On January 19, 1999, the district court issued an order reversing the

---

[30] Order Denying Motion for a Protective Order, filed May 12, 1998 ("May 12 Order") at 2 (emphasis added) (5ER Tab 6).

[31] Order Granting Motion to Compel Discovery and to Extend Discovery Cut-off for Movants Only, filed June 11, 1998 ("June 11 Order") (5ER Tab 8).

[32] May 26 Tr. at 14–15 (AI could merely determine that for purposes of this litigation each of them has a net worth in excess of some fairly substantial sum . . .") (5ER Tab 7).

[33] May 26 Tr. at 15 (5ER Tab 7).

[34] *Id.* at 14:8–11 (5ER Tab 7).

[35] *Id.* at 16:14–19, 17:20–22, 19:2–19 (5ER Tab 7); June 11 Order at 2 (5ER Tab 8).

[36] Order filed Aug. 5, 1998 (E.D. Cal. Nos. CIV S-98-1175-FCD & CIV S-98-0641-FCD) (5ER Tab 10).

bankruptcy court's liability findings under § 362(h), terminating all adverse proceedings against counsel, and vacating the bankruptcy court's discovery order.[37]

The district court held that no automatic-stay violation had occurred because the judgment security had never become property of the bankruptcy estate. It also rejected the debtors' argument (made again in this Court) that an automatic-stay violation occurred even if the security was *not* property of the estate, so long as the debtors raised a good-faith or bona-fide dispute that it *was*. The Court observed that "there *was not* a good-faith or bona-fide dispute over whether the registry funds were part of the bankruptcy estates at the time bankruptcy commenced."[38] The Court also ruled that the bankruptcy court's failure to afford notice to the Trust Funds' counsel of their potential personal liability "raises serious due-process questions" that are "especially troubling where, as here, the attorneys were acting in accordance with an order from the court and were likely duty-bound to engage in the acts in question."[39]

---

[37] Jan. 19, 1999 Order at 14–15 (3ER Tab 28).

[38] *Id.* at 14 n.7 (emphasis added) (3ER Tab 28).

[39] *Id.* at 14 n.8 (3ER Tab 28).

81

Narrate chronological events using relative times— not a series of dates.

Quotable Quotes

"The indiscriminate use of dates is another Linus blanket for the writer, but cruel and unusual punishment for the reader. I quote from a brief:

> The grand jury returned the indictment March 2, 1974. Defendant was arraigned March 17, 1974. He was tried beginning August 7, 1974. The jurors began deliberating August 9, 1974, in the late afternoon, and returned a verdict at midday August 10, 1974, after deliberating for six hours. The motion for new trial was filed August 18, 1974, argued September 10, 1974, after one continuance and denied by an order entered September 15, 1974. Defendant timely appealed September 20, 1974.

"As I read, I assumed those dates and events were given for some purpose. I attempted to file each in my mind for future recall. Like a person watching a striptease, I assumed that when all the layers had been successively removed I would see something, but there was nothing to see. There was no issue of timeliness or delay in the case. No date—in fact not a word or figure in this entire recital—served any useful function."
—John C. Godbold, "Twenty Pages and Twenty Minutes," in *Appellate Practice Manual* 84, 92 (Priscilla A. Schwab ed., 1992).

"[Advocates seem to operate on the following principles:] [E]very sentence should begin with a date, or at least have a date somewhere in it. No attempt should be made to explain the facts in relative time, such as several months before or several days after. Dates are important, even if they have nothing to do with any issue in the case. A Joycean stream-of-consciousness style is usually very effective, inasmuch as this is ordinarily the way evidence is adduced at trial. Please do not try to limit the factual summary to subjects material to the issues in the case, since the Court's curiosity about irrelevancies is unbounded. Above all, the factual statement should not be at all interesting . . . ."
—Nathan L. Hecht, *Extra-Special Secrets of Appellate Brief Writing,* 3 Scribes J. Legal Writing 27, 29 (1992).

Explanation

The quotations above say it all. The tendency to recite dates ad nauseam is perhaps the commonest—and probably the grossest—type of over-particularization (see #27).

A Before-and-After Example

Before   Plaintiff was injured when she slipped and fell on kiwifruit at the Shop-Rite Supermarket on February 16, 1993. On July 5, 1993, her doctor diagnosed a herniated disk in her lower back. From July 5, 1993 until the present, she has been receiving treatment for this condition. On January 5, 1994, Plaintiff sued Shop-Rite, alleging negligence and gross negligence in maintaining the premises. On September 14, 1994, a jury trial began. On September 15, 1994, the jury returned a verdict in favor of Shop-Rite. On September 16, 1994, the trial court entered a judgment on the verdict. On October 3, 1994, Plaintiff filed a motion for new trial, which was denied on October 5, 1994. On October 26, 1994, Plaintiff timely appealed.

After   On February 16, 1993, Leib allegedly slipped and fell on kiwifruit at the Shop-Rite Supermarket. More than five months later, her doctor diagnosed a herniated disk in her lower back. Leib sued Shop-Rite, alleging negligence and gross negligence in maintaining the premises. A jury returned a verdict in favor of Shop-Rite, and the trial court entered judgment on the verdict. After the court denied Leib's motion for new trial, she timely appealed.

82

Present important ideas in lists.

Quotable Quotes

"Lists are an excellent way to make collections of thoughts or questions more manageable and more visible. They work best if the items are similar in nature and importance and if the items are parallel in structure. Lists are the perfect way to synthesize information into the most usable format. They focus the reader and add some visual interest to the page."
—Veda R. Charrow & Myra K. Erhardt, *Clear and Effective Legal Writing* 190 (1986).

"[O]rganized writers use lists particularly often. A list is all right as part of the text of a paragraph, but it's usually more effective if it's indented."
—Edward P. Bailey Jr., *The Plain English Approach to Business Writing* 43 (1990).

Explanation

You may think I got carried away with lists in this very book. But I've found that when it comes to learning, people crave lists.

Why? Because it's easier to digest information if it can be taken in small bites. Lists are easy to read and remember. And not only do they help the reader; they help you think more clearly as a writer.

With the reward of lists, of course, comes the responsibility of making them parallel (see tip #41). And don't forget that you might use bullets for your lists (see tip #61).

Some Before-and-After Examples

Example A

Before   The writing must be made in the regular course of business, the writing must be made at or near the time of the act, condition or event, a custodian or other qualified witness must testify to the business record's identity and the mode of preparation, and sources of information must indicate its trustworthiness.

After   The writing must be:

(1) made in the regular course of business;

(2) made at or near the time of the act, condition, or event;

(3) authenticated by a custodian or other qualified witness who testifies about its identity and mode of preparation; and

(4) corroborated as trustworthy by other sources of information.

Example B

Before   Plaintiff's Separate Statement of Disputed Facts contains admissions so critical and wide-ranging as to totally eviscerate Plaintiff's case. To illustrate, Plaintiff admits all of the following: that he has no knowledge of the company's bookkeeping practices (Fact No. 17); that he does not know whether the company did or did not improperly fail to pay taxes (Fact No. 17); that Bonderia did not violate state or federal tax law (Fact No. 18); that it is pure speculation on his part that his layoff was related to tax issues (Fact No. 19); that Plaintiff never told Defendant Carbonics that he had a complaint or opposition to defendants' tax practices (Fact No. 21); that his termination was not based upon the receipt or nonreceipt of job evaluations (Fact No. 26); that Plaintiff did not receive arbitrarily unfair or dishonest performance reviews (Fact No. 26); that Plaintiff was not laid off for performance reasons, but for economic reasons (Fact No. 27); that Bonderia discontinued his circuit-board project after Plaintiff was laid off (Fact No. 13); that no one was hired to replace him (Fact No. 13); that Plaintiff's tools were returned to him (Fact No. 38); that Plaintiff has no evidence of lost work opportunities by reason of a lack of tools (Fact No. 33); that retention of Plaintiff's tools cannot constitute a breach of his employment contract (Fact No. 34); and that his alleged emotional distress claims arise out of his termination (Fact No. 50). In addition, Plaintiff failed to respond to Fact No. 5 at all, thereby admitting that he did not possess a written employment contract and was therefore an employee at will.

After   Snyder's statement of disputed facts contains critical admissions that eviscerate his case. For example, the following 14 admissions alone are fatal to his claims:

- He has no knowledge of the company's bookkeeping practices (#17).

- He does not know whether the company did or didn't pay taxes (#17).

- Bonderia did not violate state or federal tax law (#18).

- He is merely speculating that his layoff was related to tax issues (#19).

- He never told Carbonics that he had a complaint or opposition to its tax practices (#21).

- His termination was not based on job evaluations (#26).

- He didn't receive arbitrarily unfair or dishonest performance reviews (#26).

- He wasn't laid off for performance reasons, but for economic reasons (#27).

- Bonderia discontinued his circuit-board project after Snyder was laid off (#13).

- No one was hired to replace him (#13).

- His tools were returned to him (#38).

- He has no evidence of lost work opportunities by reason of a lack of tools (#33).

- Even if Carbonics had retained his tools, it wouldn't have been in breach of his employment contract (#34).

- His alleged emotional-distress claims arise out of his termination (#50).

Additionally, Snyder failed to respond to #5 at all, thereby admitting that he was an employee at will.

83

Rid yourself
of the common superstitions
that will handicap you as a writer.

Quotable Quotes

" 'The man I am talking about' is infinitely better English than 'The man about whom I am talking,' as should be apparent to all familiar with good speech, listening to the two forms. Yet legions of our young folk will leave school having firmly implanted in their heads, and alas their use, that for reasons beyond their ken, the more elegant, dressy, scholar-like way of saying it is, 'The man of whom I am talking'—no matter how strongly their instincts, bless them, tell them it is unnatural and forced."

—Richard Burton, *Why Do You Talk Like That?* 186–87 (1929).

"Next to the groundless notion that it is incorrect to end an English sentence with a preposition, perhaps the most wide-spread of the many false beliefs about the use of our language is the equally groundless notion that it is incorrect to begin one with 'but' or 'and.' As in the case of the superstition about the prepositional ending, no textbook supports it, but apparently about half of our teachers of English go out of their way to handicap their pupils by inculcating it. One cannot help wondering whether those who teach such a monstrous doctrine ever read any English themselves."

—Charles Allen Lloyd, *We Who Speak English:
And Our Ignorance of Our Mother Tongue* 19 (1938).

"Unfortunately many of us have to unlearn our school training, which has made us shun split infinitives as an invention of Satan and taught us never to end a sentence with a preposition—rules that good writers constantly break."

—Gorham Munson, *The Written Word* 198 (rev. ed. 1949).

"It is no wonder that so many capable business and professional people have complexes about written communications. They have been brainwashed into thinking that writing competence is a function mostly of grammar, punctuation, syntax, and the like. Four points off for every split infinitive! Two demerits for a misplaced adverb! What a tragedy. Many first-class writers and potential writers in companies, agencies, and firms across this country do not know a participle from a partitive, an ellipsis from an elision, or the preferred meaning of *presently* from the meaning of *at present*. But they know how to make thoughts flow and ideas fly. They can make a difficult argument persuasive; they can fine-tune the wording of an idea so it sounds just right to an audience. These are the qualities and abilities that make the world go around."

—David W. Ewing, *Writing for Results in Business, Government, and the Professions* 16 (1974).

Explanation

It's surprising, really, just how many false beliefs there are about writing, and how common they are. From the Fowler brothers' *The King's English* (1906) to Trimble's *Writing with Style* (1975; 2d ed. 2000), even to my *Dictionary of Modern Legal Usage* (2d ed. 1995), writing books frequently warn against stylistic superstitions.

You see, when an authority says that it's okay to begin a sentence with "And" or "But," and the like, you shouldn't conclude that the rules have changed. Experts know that the so-called rule was never a rule at all. It's a rank superstition that never should have gotten into circulation.

What are these superstitions? There are many:

- Never end a sentence with a preposition.

- Never split an infinitive.

- Never split a verb phrase.

- Never begin a sentence with *And* or *But*.

- Never write a one-sentence paragraph.

- Never begin a sentence with *Because*.

- Never use *since* to mean *because*.

- Never use *between* with more than two objects.

- Never use the first-person pronouns *I* and *me*.

- Never use *you* in referring to your reader.

- Never use contractions.

For a discussion of these points, see virtually any good book on grammar or usage.

But let me go even further: you should own at least two solid dictionaries of usage by different authors. Essentially, they're grammar books with an alphabetical arrangement. You'll find informative mini-essays on all the important (and many fascinating but less important) issues that confront writers and editors. You can turn to a good usage dictionary if you want to know whether *criteria* and *data* and *none* should be treated as singular or plural; whether *hopefully* has lost the bad odor it acquired in the 1970s; whether *impact* is in good use as a verb; whether *incentivize* passes editorial muster; whether *reason why* is good phrasing;

whether you should say *couldn't care less* or *could care less*, and *between you and me* or *between you and I*. On and on the list goes. With an up-to-date dictionary of usage, you should have reliable guidance on these points within 45 seconds of having the question occur to you.

So which two should you acquire? You might be well advised to get one classic guide and one modern one. Among the classics, Theodore Bernstein's *The Careful Writer* (1965) stands high among the American guides; H.W. Fowler's *A Dictionary of Modern English Usage* (Ernest Gowers ed., 2d ed. 1965) is at the pinnacle of British guides. (The year 1965 was a good one in usage circles.) Among the more up-to-date guides, try either Wilson Follett's *Modern American Usage: A Guide* (Erik Wensberg ed., 2d ed. 1998) or my own *Garner's Modern American Usage* (2d ed. 2003).

Browsing in these books now and then is a great way to sharpen your knowledge of words and language. You'll gradually come to feel more confident in that knowledge. Meanwhile, you'll shed the superstitions that plague so many mediocre writers.

Part I

Capitalizing on Little-Used Persuasive Strategies

84

Show, don't tell.

Quotable Quotes

"Comment is superfluous. If the author makes the scene appear terrible to the reader, he need not say in himself or in the mouth of some protagonist, 'It is terrible!' If the picture is pathetic so that he who reads must weep, how superfluous, how intrusive should the author exclaim, 'It was pitiful to the point of tears.'"

—Frank Norris, "Simplicity in Art," in *Foundations of English Style* 112, 117 (Paul M. Fulcher ed., 1927).

"Don't tell readers what to feel. Show them the situation, and that feeling will awaken in them."

—Natalie Goldberg, *Writing Down the Bones* 68 (1986).

"Don't tell your readers—show them. Many beginning writers make this cardinal error. They describe their thoughts, feelings, and attitudes about a subject rather than allowing the facts, action, and evidence to speak for themselves."

—David L. Carroll, *A Manual of Writer's Tricks* 20 (2d ed. 1995).

"Facts, not opinions, are what convince the reader. When you start interpreting the facts—characterizing what people said and did—you have stopped guiding your reader through the thicket of the lawsuit. Instead, you have popped out the legs on your traveling sales case, hung up the sign on the front of the case and wound up a dozen or so of your little walking dolls, hoping sales will be brisk.

"But you don't want to be the street corner huckster, you want to be the guide your reader can trust. So be careful about every sentence you write. Understate rather than overstate. Better yet, don't evaluate at all. Let your reader do it for you."

—James W. McElhaney, *The Art of Persuasive Legal Writing*, ABA J., Jan. 1996, at 76, 78.

Explanation

Be careful about drawing conclusions. You have to earn your conclusions by showing the reader first.

Don't say that something is unfair; show why it is, and let the reader conclude that it is.

Don't say that somebody acted unprofessionally; explain what the person did, and let the reader decide.

Don't call an argument absurd; show why it is.

If you follow this advice, you'll find yourself being more concrete, more careful in marshaling facts, more adept at arousing the very emotions you feel. You'll find yourself being more persuasive.

Think of your job as this: you're trying to induce the judge to seethe in indignation while never revealing your own indignation. That's a tremendous challenge.

Some Before-and-After Examples

Example A

Before   Upon the resumption of Ms. Koshinsky's examination, Mr. Plaut *engaged in highly unprofessional conduct*, including characterizing the witness's testimony as canned, bullying the witness with threats of monetary sanctions, and falsely stating that counsel for Northern California Hispanic Association was coaching the witness, screaming during the deposition, and slamming the deposition room door. (Irby Decl. ¶ 6; Horton Decl. ¶ 7.) Indeed, Mr. Plaut even *saw fit* to refer to Ms. Irby as that "screaming lady lawyer" for Northern California Hispanic.

After   When Ms. Koshinsky's examination resumed, Mr. Plaut did the following:

- told the witness that her testimony was "utterly canned . . . easy to see through" (Horton dep. at 321);

- bullied the witness with threats of monetary sanctions, saying, "We'll get to the bottom of you, my friend" (Horton dep. at 323);

- claimed falsely that counsel for the Northern California Hispanic Association was coaching the witness (Horton dep. at 325); and

- left hurriedly, slamming the deposition-room door in a way that was audible at least 15 offices down the hall (Symington Decl. ¶ 2).

Just before slamming the door, Mr. Plaut shouted, "I can't take any more of that screaming lady lawyer." (Irby Decl. ¶ 6; Horton Decl. ¶ 7.) This despite Ms. Irby's never having raised her voice. (*Id.*)

Example B

Before   **Introduction**

Survcon's opposition brief confirms that the Hartley and Higson Defendants are entitled to a determination that they are the prevailing parties and that they are entitled to an award of attorneys' fees and costs under Section 15.13 of the Purchase Agreement, applicable statutes, and controlling caselaw. *Survcon's arguments regarding the plain language of Sec-*

tion 15.13 *evince utter desperation; they are incredibly convoluted and entirely dependent upon a hypertechnical reading of that language, which is supported by neither logic nor caselaw.* Indeed, in its own brief, Survcon effectively admits that the operative attorneys' fees clause in Section 15.13 of the Purchase Agreement applies both to contract claims and non-contract claims. *Survcon's analysis of the controlling caselaw fares no better.* For the most part, Survcon attempts to distinguish the language of the attorneys' fees provisions at issue in the cases cited by the Hartley and Higson Defendants in *much the same manner as it parses the language* of 15.13. In other instances, *Survcon ignores critical portions* of the courts' opinions pertinent here. In short, *Survcon's arguments do nothing to refute the Hartley and Higson Defendants' entitlement to attorneys' fees and costs* in this case. Indeed, Survcon even concedes that the Hartley and Higson Defendants are the prevailing parties in this action. At last, the Hartley and Higson Defendants are entitled to recover the substantial attorneys' fees and costs that Survcon forced them to incur over nearly a decade in connection with this meritless action.

After   [I can't write a good "After" version. Even after reading the full brief, I can't tell what the issues are. But I do know this: the author of this "Introduction" hasn't earned the airy conclusions stated there. And they're not convincing. Quite the opposite.—BAG.]

Example C

Before   In the present case, Supreme Systems and PowerGas fail to present any substantive evidence in opposition to EXEP's motion for partial summary judgment. Instead, Supreme Systems and PowerGas *feign ignorance* regarding the meaning of the relevant portions of the PBUOA and request additional discovery under Rule 56(f). The Court should deny their Rule 56(f) motions because neither Supreme Systems nor PowerGas makes the showing—required by Rule 56(f)—that knowledge of the relevant facts is outside its control.

Supreme Systems' and PowerGas's *feigned ignorance is absurd* given their participation in the drafting and negotiation of the PBUOA and their involvement in years of related litigation with EXEP and other working-interest owners. By failing to provide a single affidavit opposing the summary-judgment motion from any of their employees involved in the drafting and negotiation of the PBUOA and by demanding additional discovery from EXEP, Supreme Systems and PowerGas effectively argue that none of their employees has knowledge relating to the meaning of the PBUOA and that such knowledge is within the exclusive control of EXEP. In fact, Supreme Systems and PowerGas have access to numerous current and former employees involved in the drafting and negotiation of the PBUOA. In addition, they have access to their own voluminous files concerning the PBUOA and to innumerable documents produced to Supreme Systems and PowerGas in prior litigation involving the parties.

Despite the availability of all these sources of evidence, Supreme Systems and PowerGas *purport* to say that, without additional discovery, they are wholly unable to adduce any affidavits opposing EXEP's motion for partial summary judgment. *Their argument is entirely without merit.* Neither Supreme Systems nor PowerGas can show that knowledge of the relevant facts is outside their control and that either party attempted to obtain such facts from its own employees or documents. Accordingly, the Court must deny their motions for additional discovery.

After   Here, Supreme Systems and PowerGas have marshaled no evidence to oppose EXEP's motion for partial summary judgment. Instead, *claiming ignorance* about the meaning of the relevant portions of the PBUOA, they request additional discovery under Rule 56(f). The Court should deny their Rule 56(f) motions because neither Supreme Systems nor PowerGas has shown—as required by Rule 56(f)—that knowledge of the relevant facts is outside its control.

This *claim of ignorance* about the PBUOA is belied in two ways. First, both Supreme Systems and PowerGas participated fully—for more than 18 months (see Ex. A)—in drafting and negotiating the legislation. Second, since passage of the Act, they have been continually involved in years of related litigation with EXEP and other working-interest owners.

By failing to come forward with even a single affidavit opposing the summary-judgment motion and by demanding additional discovery from EXEP, Supreme Systems and PowerGas argue, in effect, that (1) none of their employees knows about the meaning of the PBUOA, and (2) this knowledge is within the exclusive control of EXEP. In fact, though, Supreme Systems and PowerGas have access to many current and former employees who helped draft and negotiate the PBUOA. And they both have access to their own voluminous files on the Act and to countless documents produced to Supreme Systems and PowerGas in earlier litigation involving the same parties.

Still, Supreme Systems and PowerGas *are telling this Court* that, without additional discovery, they cannot oppose EXEP's motion for partial summary judgment.

Because they have not shown—and cannot show—that knowledge of the relevant facts is outside their control, this Court must deny their motions for additional discovery.

85

If you're the appellant or petitioner, choose your grounds of complaint carefully. If you're the appellee or respondent opposing a party who hasn't chosen carefully, rephrase and consolidate the issues.

Quotable Quotes

"Avoid a tedious multiplication of points. Study to see what ones may be spared with good effect. This matter of co-ordination and subordination requires the nicest discrimination."
—Brainerd Kellogg, *A Text-Book on Rhetoric* 75 (1881).

"Such interminable assignments [of error], instead of impressing the court with the thought of an imperfect trial, rather cast discredit upon the worth of any of them."
—*Chicago Great Western Ry. v. McDonough*, 161 F. 657, 659 (8th Cir. 1908).

"Strike for the jugular, and let the rest go."
—Oliver Wendell Holmes, *Speeches* 77 (1934).

"When a judge finds a brief [that] sets up from twelve to twenty or thirty issues or 'points' or 'assignments of error,' he begins to look for the two or three, perhaps the one, of controlling force. Somebody has got lost in the underbrush and the judge has to get him—or the other fellow—out. That kind of brief may be labeled the 'obfuscating' type. It is distinctly not the kind to use if the attorney wishes calm, temperate, dispassionate reason to emanate from the cloister. I strongly advise against use of this type of brief, consciously or unconsciously. Though this fault has been called overanalysis, it is really a type of underanalysis."
—Wiley B. Rutledge, "The Appellate Brief" (1942), in *Advocacy and the King's English* 429, 434 (George Rossman ed., 1960).

"Legal contentions, like the currency, depreciate through overissue. The mind of an appellate judge is habitually receptive to the suggestion that a lower court committed an error. But receptiveness declines as the number of assigned errors increases. Multiplicity hints at a lack of confidence in any one. Of course, I have not forgotten the reluctance with which a lawyer abandons even the weakest point lest it prove alluring to the same kind of judge. But experience on the bench convinces me that multiplying assignments of error will dilute and weaken a good case and will not save a bad one."

—Robert H. Jackson, *Advocacy Before the United States Supreme Court*,
37 Cornell L.Q. 1, 5 (1951).

"[B]affled and worried or lightheartedly gambling counsel pile the points high, wide, and hit-or-miss because they have lost understanding of the process and so lack confidence in the simple, the clear, the focused."

—Karl Llewellyn, *The Common Law Tradition: Deciding Appeals* 196 (1960).

"Not every appeal should be reduced to one issue, although probably seventy-five percent could and would, by this means, receive a more favorable reaction from the court. It is much better to weed out trivial assignments of error than to leave that gardening for the court."

—Jean Appleman, *The Written Argument on Appeal*, 41 Notre Dame Law. 40, 41
(1965).

"Insofar as counsel in a criminal appeal has a choice between weak points and strong ones, he owes it to his client to abandon those that are weak lest he dilute those that are strong."

—Frederick B. Wiener, *Briefing and Arguing Federal Appeals*
102–03 (rev. ed. 1967).

"Appellate advocacy on civil appeals calls for courage in the lawyer: the courage to forgo, the willingness to pass, alluring grounds that may exist in the record. The lawyer must make difficult choices. He must make calculated judgments in abandoning points for appeal. The compendious effort that throws everything erroneous or even everything reversible at the court runs the risk of pegging the strength of the appeal on the weakest link. Selectivity then is the key."

—Milton Pollack, "The Civil Appeal," in *Counsel on Appeal*
29, 39 (Arthur A. Charpentier ed., 1968).

" '[A] brief which treats more than three or four matters runs serious risks of becoming too diffuse and giving the overall impression that no one claimed error can be serious.' "

—*Jones v. Barnes*, 463 U.S. 745, 752 n.5 (1983) (quoting Committee on Federal
Courts of the Ass'n of the Bar of New York, *Appeals to the Second Circuit* 38 (1980)).

"Use only your best material. Remember that not all your material is likely to be of equal strength or of equal significance to your audience. Decide carefully which material—from your *audience's* view—best supports your case."

—John M. Lannon, *The Writing Process* 332 (1989).

"When faced with a brief that raises no more than three points, I breathe a sigh of satisfaction and conclude that the brief writer really may have something to say. I probably react in the same manner, or perhaps to a slightly lesser degree, when four or five points are presented. Beyond this point, I must confess, a small beast bearing the name of intolerance begins to nibble at my habitually disinterested judgment. Even when we reverse a trial court, rarely does a brief establish more than one or two reversible errors. When I read an appellant's brief containing more than six points, a presumption arises that there is no merit to *any* of them. I do not say that this is an irrebuttable presumption, but it is a presumption nevertheless that reduces the effectiveness of the writer's brief."

—Ruggero J. Aldisert, *Winning on Appeal: Better Briefs and Oral Argument* 121 (1992).

"Once you identify issues, limit them. Present no more than three or four of your strongest claims that the trial court erred. State them in order of their importance, unless the organization of the brief dictates otherwise."

—Jordan B. Cherrick, "Issues, Facts, and Appellate Strategy," in *Appellate Practice Manual* 73, 75 (Priscilla A. Schwab ed., 1992).

Explanation

Although criminal cases have come to be thought of as an exception, the quotations above might lead to a different conclusion. That is, perhaps it amounts to ineffective assistance of counsel to raise more than a few issues.

Clearly, though, in civil cases . . . . No, let's try that again (see tip #79) . . . . But especially in civil cases, an appellate brief reeks of diffidence—of weakness—if it raises a welter of issues.

Consider the fine example of Charles Neave, the great patent lawyer. In a tribute to Neave, Judge Learned Hand extolled Neave's confidence in choosing arguments: "With the courage which only comes of justified self-confidence, he dared to rest his case upon its strongest point, and so avoided that appearance of weakness and uncertainty which comes of a clutter of argument. Few lawyers are willing to do this; it is the mark of the most distinguished talent."*

If it's hard for the responding brief-writer to answer a scattershot brief, it's equally hard for the judge to write a good opinion. Here are two possible ways of responding in a way that will be helpful to the court. First, you can consolidate and regroup the issues. *Someone* has to think clearly about the case, and it might as well be the appellee if the appellant has failed. Second, if a full reconsolidation is hopeless because the opponent's arguments are thoroughly confused and scattered, you can focus on refuting the most salient ones. This is an old technique that Alexander Bain wrote about in the 19th century: "Many doctrines brought forward in argument are not so much false as confused, being made up of ill-

---

* Learned Hand, "In Memory of Charles Neave," in *The Spirit of Liberty* 127–28 (2d ed. 1951).

defined, incoherent notions. . . . Probably the best way of dealing with a mystifying and confused opponent is to select a *specimen* of his arguments for a full and minute exposure."**

In the following example, Charles Dewey Cole Jr. of New York used the first approach. Even in something as mundane as a statement regarding oral argument, he found it possible to persuade. He convincingly told a federal appellate court that this unremarkable case could be decided (his way, of course) on the briefs alone. Here, the issues were sensibly stated as surface issues, given that it's only a statement regarding oral argument. Elsewhere in the brief, they'd need to be deep issues (see #8).

An Unusually Good Example (for the Appellee)

Statement Regarding Oral Argument

Oral argument is not requested.

The seven issues raised by the defendants can, broadly speaking, be grouped into three larger ones: whether the evidence is sufficient to support the verdict (I, III, IV, VI), whether the district court abused its discretion in asking the jury to resolve what the defendants called a "conflict verdict" (II) and in denying the defendants' new-trial motion (V), and whether the district court properly added prejudgment interest to the damages awarded by the jury (VII).

In each instance (with the possible exception of the last issue, which is controlled by Michigan law), the standard of review and the applicable law are well established. The record is complete and shows that the district court properly denied the defendants' motion for judgment as a matter of law and submitted the case to the jury, that the district court did not abuse its discretion when it denied the defendants' new-trial motion on the ground that the damage awards were excessive, and that the district court correctly added prejudgment interest to the damage awards.

The sole issue raised in the cross-appeal—whether the district court correctly granted summary judgment and dismissed the attorney-malpractice and other claims as barred by limitations—is based on a complete summary-judgment record and, in any event, would not be reached unless this court disturbs the district court's judgment. Thus, oral argument will not aid significantly in the decisional process.

** Alexander Bain, *English Composition and Rhetoric* 196 (4th ed. 1877).

86

If you're the appellee or respondent, draft your brief before seeing your opponent's effort.

Quotable Quotes

"The designated brief-writer should do all he can to prepare as early as he can, and before the briefing schedule itself begins. . . . Tentative arguments or position papers can be prepared, even by the lawyers for responding parties, for they can usually anticipate the opening brief well enough to justify the preparation. To delay is to squeeze the time available for writing and to do that is to jeopardize the effectiveness of the brief."

—Girvan Peck, *Writing Persuasive Briefs* 175 (1984).

"Remember the story . . . about Justice Jackson when he served as Solicitor General of the United States. Jackson asked an Assistant SG how work on the government's brief was coming in an important Supreme Court case. The assistant replied that he was waiting for the opponent's brief, because the government was the Respondent. 'What's the matter?' asked Jackson. 'Don't we have a case?' "

—David L. Lee, *Responding to Arguments*, CBA Rec., June/July 1995, at 58, 58.

Explanation

This tip will help you develop your case as well as you can. You won't find yourself in the defensive posture of merely responding to what your opponent says. Too many responsive briefs are entirely reactive.

If you prepare a draft explaining why the court's decision was correct, you'll be in an enviable position when your opponent's brief arrives. You'll be able to massage the draft to account for your opponent's points. You'll doubtless refine your issues and work in some dialectical argument (see tip #88).

Most important, though, you won't feel defensive when you first start writing.

If you think you can't follow this tip, don't just forget it. Take an hour to go through the madman–architect stages (see tips #2–3). At the very least, devise a short linear outline (see tip #5). And work out your deep issues (see tip #8). Then you'll be able to consolidate the appellant's points under those issues (see tip #85).

87

Say it well and say it emphatically. But reject the idea that you should first tell the reader what you're going to say, then say it, then remind the reader of what you just said.

Quotable Quotes

"There is a corollary to the principle of 'tell it short and plain.' It is 'tell it once—or twice at most.' Erosion by repetition is a poor way to convince. Most judges will catch the point the first time it is developed."
—John C. Godbold, "Twenty Pages and Twenty Minutes—Effective Advocacy on Appeal," 30 Sw. L.J. 801, 816 (1976).

"Be blissfully brief. State your point concisely and once. Nothing is more irritating than to have the same question stated again and again in varying ways for forty-five sleep-inducing pages of redundancy."
—Arthur L. Alarcon, "Points on Appeal," in *Appellate Practice Manual* 95, 97 (Priscilla A. Schwab ed., 1992).

"To be persuasive, a brief must be read. Its chances of being read and assimilated are in inverse proportion to its length. Briefs should be edited and 'boiled down' to eliminate repetition and surplusage."
—Jim R. Carrigan, "Some Nuts and Bolts of Appellate Advocacy," in *Appellate Practice Manual* 102, 104 (Priscilla A. Schwab ed., 1992).

Explanation

Some writers have distorted the advice commonly given to public speakers: "Tell them what you're going to tell them. Then tell them. And then tell them what you just told them." That advice may work for speakers, whose audience relies almost exclusively on what it *hears*—without the reinforcement of print.

But it's an extremely simplistic paradigm for writers. And those who say they follow it are among the most verbose members of the bar. In fact, many times I've seen briefs that have virtually the same paragraph on page 3 as on page 10. (This isn't the same thing, of course, as purposely repeating an issue statement or a point of error.) When the language tracks nearly word for word—it's the same idea being presented seven pages later—the alert reader wonders why the writer hasn't made any progress over the span of seven pages.

This is a difficult subject to discuss in the abstract, because there's certainly something to the idea that you frame the issue at the outset, then elaborate the premises, and then conclude with the reasons why the court should hold as you urge. That's fine—even desirable.

Rather, this tip is designed to counteract the artless tendency to repeat conclusions ad nauseam, the idea being that it will sink in by the fifth or sixth time. Every time I've sat down with a writer who does this, I hear: "Well, I rely on the old rule, 'Tell 'em what you're going to tell 'em . . . . ' "

88

Organize the argument section as a dialectic, so that you deal effectively with counterarguments.

Quotable Quotes

"As a rule, the refutation of objections should be near the middle of the discourse, so that the arguments refuted may not make either the first or the last impression. The beginning and end of an argument, as of a play, are the most important parts."

—Adams Sherman Hill, *The Principles of Rhetoric* 385 (rev. ed. 1896).

"It is best to assume a hearer or reader who holds views opposed to those we advocate, as, if we work with the possibility of hostile criticism in mind, we shall be more careful to build up an irrefragable argument than if we work believing that whatever we say will find easy acceptance."

—Frances M. Perry, *An Introductory Course in Argumentation* 57 (1906).

"Do not avoid important facts in the record because they are against you. State them before your opponent does. This demonstrates your honesty, and the facts will hurt you less."

—Mario Pittoni, *Brief Writing and Argumentation* 31 (1967).

"If your audience disagrees with your ideas or is uncertain about them, present both sides of the argument. Behavioral scientists generally find that if an audience is friendly to a persuader, or has no contrary views on the topic and will get none in the near future, a one-sided presentation of a controversial question is most effective.

. . .

"But suppose your audience has not made up its mind, so far as you know? In this case you would do well to deal with *both* sides of the argument (or all sides, if there are more than two). Follow the same approach if the reader disagrees with you at the outset. For one thing, a two-sided presentation suggests to an uncertain or hostile audience that you possess objectivity. For another, it helps the reader remember your view by putting the pros and cons in relationship to one another. Also, it meets the reader's need to be treated as a mature, informed individual."

—David W. Ewing, *Writing for Results in Business, Government, the Sciences and the Professions* 73 (2d ed. 1979).

"Often, it is wise to deal with opposing arguments obliquely, raising them in dependent clauses, while the main clauses carry the argument . . . . This device raises the issues that the opposition would raise, but keeps clear direction."

—Donald Hall, *Writing Well* 258 (4th ed. 1982).

"Try to anticipate the reader's biggest opposition to your position, and address it in detail."

—John M. Lannon, *The Writing Process* 332 (1989).

"[A] serious controversial argument demands one organizational consideration beyond the simple structure of ascending interest. Although you have taken your stand firmly as a *pro*, you will have to allow scope to the *cons*, or you will seem not to have thought much about your subject. The more opposition you can manage as you carry your point, the more triumphant you will seem . . . . The basic organizing principle here is to get rid of the opposition first, and to end on your own side."

—Sheridan Baker, *The Practical Stylist* 29–30 (8th ed. 1998).

"Successful written argument . . . does not take the most extreme possible position by grossly overstating the merits of one side and ignoring the merits of the other."

—Bryan A. Garner, *The Elements of Legal Style* 197 (2d ed. 2002).

Explanation

The first part of any argument should marshal support for your premises (see tip #4). That is, after you've stated the deep issues at the outset (see tips #8–15), begin the argument under each issue by supporting the legal and factual premises woven into the issue.

Then it's time to rebut. You need to demolish all serious counterarguments. Employing the dialectical method is the best way to do this. A dialectic is something like a pendulum through time. At its simplest, it's in the form thesis–antithesis–conclusion; or, you might say, position–counterposition–resolution.

Brief-writers can use the dialectic in shaping an argument. Of course, the conclusion or resolution always ends up on the advocate's side. Let's assume that, in a given section of the brief, you've made your main point. Then, you'll probably want to end the section with a discussion structured in this way:

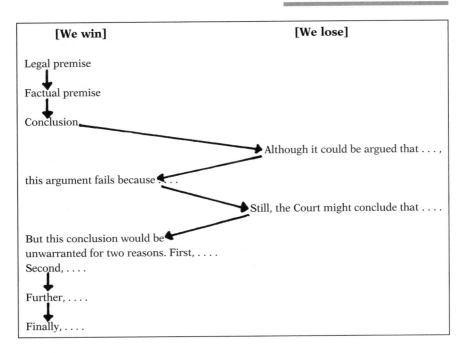

This structure shows that you've considered why the conclusion might be otherwise. You've deflected the counterpunches. The importance of this persuasive strategy can hardly be overstated.

As the first quotable quote explains, you should address the counterarguments in the middle of your argument—not at the beginning and not at the end. Then, knock each one down quickly.

In using a dialectical argument, be sure that you don't start either of two unhealthy syndromes. First, avoid setting out the opponent's points at great length before supplying an answer. Your undercut needs to be swift and immediate. You'll see the poor strategy—highlighting the opponent's argument—in the example below. Second, ensure that you're answering only the most obvious points against you—avoid tipping off the other side to an argument it hasn't yet understood.

A Before-and-After Example of Dialectical Structure

Before   **II. Plaintiff entered into a valid and enforceable arbitration agreement.**

Armando's first substantive argument is that he is entitled to a jury trial on whether he agreed to arbitrate employment disputes with Hamilton Park because (a) he allegedly did not realize that his Form U-4 contained the arbitration clause appearing immediately above his final signature, and (b) Hamilton Park defrauded him by not directing his attention to the U-4's arbitration clause. (Pb18–45.) That argument ignores basic principles of arbitration and contract law and it has been overwhelmingly rejected by courts that have considered these arguments in nearly identical circumstances. In fact, Judge Fisher in the District of New Jersey rejected Armando's exact arguments earlier this month:

> The record is void of any evidence indicating that [Hamilton Park] attempted to procure [Armando's] signature on the application to fraudulently deprive [Armando] of his right to litigate in federal court. In the absence of such a showing, the court will not abandon fundamental principles of contract law and render the contract void. Plaintiff simply failed to read the application carefully. [*Armando v. Hamilton Park Ins. Co.*, Civ. No. 95-5232 (CSF), slip op. at 3 (D.N.J. Apr. 28, 1996) (Exh. E).]

After   ## 2. Armando entered into a valid and enforceable arbitration agreement.

The arbitration agreement for employment disputes is fully enforceable. Although Armando argues that he is entitled to a jury trial on whether he agreed to arbitrate employment disputes with Hamilton Park, he ignores basic principles of arbitration and contract law. His twofold contentions are (1) that he did not realize that his Form U-4 contained the arbitration clause appearing immediately above his final signature, and (2) that Hamilton Park defrauded him by not directing his attention to the U-4's arbitration clause. (Pb18–45.) These contentions have never succeeded in other cases. And in the federal companion case to this one, Judge Fisher in the District of New Jersey rejected Armando's exact arguments earlier this month:

> The record is void of any evidence indicating that [Hamilton Park] attempted to procure [Armando's] signature on the application to fraudulently deprive [Armando] of his right to litigate in federal court. In the absence of such a showing, the court will not abandon fundamental principles of contract law and render the contract void. [Armando] simply failed to read the application carefully.
>
> [*Armando v. Hamilton Park Ins. Co.*, Civ. No. 95-5232 (CSF), slip op. at 3 (D.N.J. May 28, 1996) (Ex. E).]

This Court should not accept Armando's invitation to disturb the settled law.

The following chart compares the structures of the preceding arguments. Notice that the "After" argument puts the advocate's point in the topic sentence of the paragraph. In the "Before" version, the topic sentence favors Armando.

Structure of the "Before" Argument	Structure of the "After" Argument
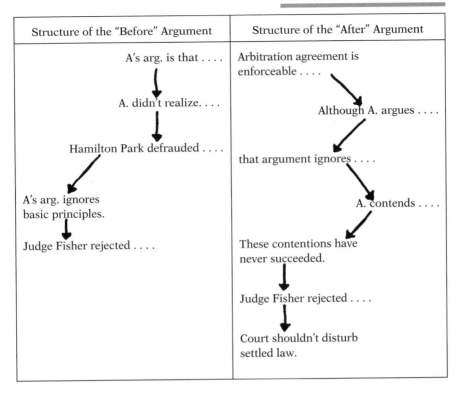	

89

Conclude powerfully. Avoid weak phrases such as "Wherefore, premises considered," "For the foregoing reasons," and "For the reasons stated."

Quotable Quotes

"In running the hundred-yard dash, you start quickly, settle into an even, steady pace, and just before you reach the tape put on your highest speed. Adopt the same system in your writing. But to do so, you must know from the start where you intend to finish."

> —James Weber Linn, *The Essentials of English Composition* § 13, at 19 (1916).

"The ending of an essay should be brief, and it should draw attention to the central part of your thesis. It should never be glued to the body of your paper with a deadly, mechanical phrase such as *in conclusion, thus we have seen,* or *thus it is clear.* For a long essay (but almost never for a short one) a straightforward summary of major points is often effective."

> —Steward La Casce & Terry Belanger, *The Art of Persuasion: How to Write Effectively About Almost Anything* 30 (1972).

"Most readers (including you) know when your concluding paragraph is merely a pro forma bundle of words; use the conclusion to show the reader there is a thinking mind behind those words."

> —Jeanne F. Campanelli & Jonathan L. Price, *Write in Time* 113 (1991).

"The conclusion in a brief is not just the major thing; it's the only thing. It's the only game in town. The purpose of a brief is to convince the court to accept your conclusion—to reverse, vacate, or affirm the lower court's judgment. The only purpose of the brief's contents that precede the conclusion—statements of jurisdiction, standards of review, issues, facts and the discussion of legal precepts—is to set the stage for logical premises to justify the suggested conclusion."

> —Ruggero J. Aldisert, *Winning on Appeal: Better Briefs and Oral Argument* 19 (1992).

Explanation

Like your opening words, your closing words are critical. They're your leave-taking. And you should no more use a formulaic closer than you should send off a trusted ally on an important mission with a perfunctory "See ya."

Yet the classic "Wherefore, premises considered, . . ."—a form with regional variations throughout the country—is just that type of closer.

One way to conclude strongly is to capsulize the two or three or however many reasons why the court should do what you urge. And leave it at that. But put it in a nutshell, without any reference to "foregoing reasons" (which few ever bother to name). Count the reasons and list them, as in Example A (see #82). Your argument will look substantial. Or summarize a little more freely, as in Example B, by Neil Fried of Washington, D.C.

Another way to conclude is to find a different slant or angle on the dispositive arguments. With this approach, you don't merely sum up what has preceded—you discuss it from a different point of view. This approach is nicely illustrated both in Example C, by Elizabeth S. Kerr of Fort Worth, who consistently writes strong briefs with powerful conclusions, and in Example D by Gideon Kanner, a professor emeritus at Loyola Law School in Los Angeles. Kanner reports that he can't recall ever sweating over a passage in any brief more than this one. Read it and you'll see why.

Some brief-writers frame their work with an explicit tie-in between the introduction and the conclusion. This technique works especially well when you've begun with the issues. At the end, you're able to wrap them up, as Dennis J.C. Owens of Kansas City does in Example E, from a brief to a Bankruptcy Appellate Panel. Notice how well he frames the deep issues (see tip #8) and then uses them again at the end.

Example F was the closer in a successful motion for rehearing that I wrote a few years ago. The quotation from Justice Robert H. Jackson is effective because it appeals to the best judicial instincts: it good-humoredly points out that there's no shame in recanting.

Some Good Examples

Example A

Conclusion

Brewer provides no evidence on any of the critical allegations about his SPR credit report:

- that it was inaccurate;

- that it contained obsolete information;

- that any inaccuracies caused him any harm; and

- that SPR failed to maintain reasonable procedures.

In the absence of any evidence, SPR is entitled to summary judgment on all of Brewer's claims.

Example B

Conclusion

ConTel never chose to get into the telephone-leasing business. Instead, the FCC directed ConTel to lease CPE [customer-premises equipment] as part of the Commission's initiative to open up competition in the phone-equipment market. ConTel fully complied with the FCC's directive, doing business subject to its authority and reporting requirements. Under that regime, the issues involved in this case were resolved between ConTel and the FCC from 1990 to 1996. It would be grossly unfair now to subject ConTel to another review of those issues—this time before a state court with the risk of monetary liability—just for complying with the FCC's own mandates. States are preempted from imposing utility-type regulation of this market, but that is just what this suit would amount to if the FCC lets it go forward.

Yet apart from the unjust harm this suit would do to ConTel, allowing claims in an Illinois court would bring chaos to the CPE market. Issues long resolved by the FCC would be reopened in state courts across the country—at a time when the marketplace desperately needs certainty. The dangerous precedent of allowing 50 sets of de facto state regulations would shatter the FCC's unified jurisdiction. And it would impede the FCC's deregulatory goals, regarding not just CPE but a whole range of fields, such as broadband deployment. It doesn't matter whether the state courts end up ratifying the FCC's decisions: the harm comes from allowing state courts to review decisions that the FCC has chosen to preempt.

The FCC must intercede now and reaffirm in a declaratory ruling its previous decisions on the issues raised by the Plaintiffs. Otherwise, the FCC will face more of a drain on its resources and more challenges to its decisions on issues far harder to resolve. This class action is just one of 16 pending in state courts across the country. If the FCC does not act now to protect its preemptive authority and primary jurisdiction, it may later find itself forced to intervene in 16 appeals spinning out of control. And the lawsuits won't stop there, either: other plaintiffs will be encouraged to sue, both in the CPE market and elsewhere.

ConTel asks the FCC to grant declaratory relief and stop this attack on its jurisdiction.

Example C

Conclusion

Divorces are never pleasant. They are less so when a third party is involved, and even less so when one spouse has transferred money to that other person. But there is a reason that the law imposes a burden on the complaining spouse to prove actual knowledge on the third person's part of a spouse's intent to defraud, and that reason is that any punitive or equitable measures should be taken first against the spouse who has purportedly done something wrong.

Here, the Glassmans' community estate was more than sufficient to have allowed the trial court simply to make a disproportionate award to Ms. Glassman, or to have ordered Mr. Glassman to pay her the $61,753.

Here, the evidence showed that Mr. Glassman was transferring money to Ms. Oliver to cover his living expenses, and during the period in question there were indeed withdrawals from the account totaling well over $61,753—none of which went to Mr. Glassman.

And here, the record is devoid of any evidence showing that Patti Oliver was a schemer, with Mr. Glassman, in a plot to cheat Ms. Glassman out of anything.

In short, there is no evidence to support the court's fact findings that were used to divest Ms. Oliver of almost as much money as she herself had when Mr. Glassman began making deposits in her account; accordingly, the trial court's adverse judgment should be reversed and rendered.

In the alternative, the evidence was factually insufficient to support those findings, and Ms. Glassman's claims against Ms. Oliver should be remanded for a new trial.

Example D

Conclusion

Midwestern's Submission Is No More than a Sought-After Result in Search of a Rationale

If legal arguments were olives, Midwestern's doctrinal overreach would have to be labeled "super colossal." After all, Article I, § 19 and a century of settled caselaw construing it could not be more clear, and Midwestern's counsel could not be more experienced or more skilled. How then can Midwestern, with a straight face, successively assert and shed legal theories like soiled socks? What in the world is *really* going on here?

The plain though unhappy answer is that Midwestern's real challenge is not so much to the Dariens' legal position as it is to legal doctrine. Midwestern cares only about the result, law or no law. The result Midwestern seeks—explicitly revealed to the Court of Appeal—is to coerce the Dariens to settle by blocking the compensation that was to be "first" paid to them on the taking of their land.

In recent books, two distinguished commentators, Harvard law professor Mary Ann Glendon and former presidential adviser Sol M. Linowitz, observe that the difference between the best lawyering of bygone days and that of today is that then good lawyers saw themselves as professionals ready to tell an overreaching client—in the words of Elihu Root—that he was a damn fool and to cut it out while in today's legal climate, lawyers too often view their work as a lucrative trade and expertly do whatever they can in pursuit of whatever result the client desires, whether or not doctrinally or morally sound. (Glendon, *A Nation Under Lawyers* 37, 75 [1994]; Linowitz, *The Betrayed Profession* 109 [1994].)

At first blush, these assessments may seem unduly harsh. But on reflection, how else can one explain the spectacle of distinguished lawyers presenting a "brief" to the Court of Appeal on a constitutional issue of eminent-domain law that fails to discuss the constitution or to cite a single eminent-domain case? How else can one explain the present *ad hoc* concoction of a "constitutional right to appeal" that Midwestern's own lead counsel exposes as baseless in his widely distributed treatise, citing *Powers* for that proposition there while ignoring *Powers* here?

What is before the Court is not really a *legal* submission by Midwestern, but a crudely posited result in search of a rationale. It is, in the final analysis, an *ad hoc* assault on an important constitutional guarantee, on the integrity of settled caselaw, and in the end on the judicial process itself.

None of these considerations lose their force just because large sums are at stake here. As this Court aptly put it, the need to compensate is greatest where the loss is greatest. (*Klopping*, 8 Cal.3d at 43.) And so it is. The Dariens are entitled to a large sum as their just compensation because Midwestern took hundreds of acres of their valuable land and has left the residue of their family ranch under the menacing shadow of a huge earthen dam holding back a billion tons of water. But the Dariens, the same as the owners of humble family homes bulldozed for a freeway, are entitled to have their constitutional rights observed. *All* Americans are.

Midwestern has now had three opportunities to come up with a semblance of legal theory capable of abrogating the Dariens' entitlement to invoke the explicit guarantee of Article I, § 19—which is as crystal clear as is its consistent judicial application.

The Dariens are sorry that they must impose on this Court for an expeditious determination. But Midwestern's intransigence has made that necessary. The Dariens pray that the petition for review be denied so they may get on with their lives and Midwestern's substantive appeal may be properly processed below.

Example E

Introduction

Appellants Earl and Carolyn Robb urge the Panel to deny the motion to dismiss and to allow this appeal to be decided on the merits. It is not moot. The motion to dismiss presents the Court with three straightforward issues:

- **Bona Fide Purchaser.** Under § 363(m), if an authorization for the sale of property in a bankrupt estate is modified on appeal, the validity of a sale to a bona fide purchaser is not affected. USLIFE purchased the property knowing of the Robbs' leases; if USLIFE had instead foreclosed, its interest would have been subordinated to the leases. Given USLIFE's knowledge, can it meet the standard of a bona fide purchaser who wipes out the Robbs' leases?

- **Modification of Sale.** Even assuming the sale had been valid, § 363(m)—the "mootness rule"—states only that if an authorization for the sale of property in a bankrupt estate is reversed or *modified* on appeal, then the validity of a sale to a bona fide purchaser is not affected. Given that the Robbs seek merely to modify a sale to account for their leases, not to invalidate a sale, can § 363(m) render their appeal moot?

- **Opportunity to Object.** The mootness rule presumes that interested parties have had the opportunity to seek a stay. Here, the Robbs had no knowledge of the authorization for sale until three days after the sale took place, and they then acted promptly to seek a stay. Given that they had no opportunity to object—beyond that which they are now exercising—does the mootness rule apply to their appeal?

Section 363(m) of the Bankruptcy Code provides that the reversal or modification on appeal of an authorization of sale . . . .

Conclusion

The three questions presented by the motion to dismiss should be answered in a straightforward fashion:

- No, USLIFE is not a bona fide purchaser. Thus, the mootness rule does not apply to this appeal of an order authorizing a sale.

- The mootness rule applies to place only the validity of a sale beyond review. Here, one relief sought is modification. Therefore, no, the rule does not bar this appeal.

- The presumption of the mootness rule that the aggrieved party had a fair opportunity to seek a stay is not valid in this case. The Robbs did not have that chance. As a result, no, the mootness rule cannot fairly apply to their appeal.

The Robbs ask the Panel to deny the motion to dismiss.

Example F

Conclusion and Prayer

We are asking this Court to change its mind. We think this to be not only possible, but necessary. And there is a long tradition of great judges who have thought better on second thought, as Justice Jackson once observed when doing an about-face:

> Precedent . . . is not lacking for ways by which a judge may recede from a prior opinion that has proven untenable and perhaps misled others. See Chief Justice Taney, *License Cases*, 5 How. 504, recanting views he had pressed upon the Court as Attorney General of Maryland in *Brown v. Maryland*, 12 Wheat. 419. Baron Bramwell extricated himself from a somewhat similar embarrassment by saying, 'The matter does not appear to me now as it appears to have appeared to me then.' *Andrews v. Styrap*, 26 L.T.R., N.S. 704, 706. And Mr. Justice Story, accounting for his contradiction of his own former opinion, quite properly put the matter: 'My own error, however, can furnish no ground for its being adopted by this Court . . . ." *United States v. Gooding*, 12 Wheat. 460, 478. Perhaps Dr. Johnson really went to the heart of the matter when he explained a blunder in his dictionary—'Ignorance, sir, ignorance.' But an escape less self-depreciating was taken by Lord Westbury, who, it is said, rebuffed a barrister's reliance upon an earlier opinion of his Lordship: 'I can only say that I am amazed that a man of my intelligence should have been guilty of giving such an opinion.' If there are other ways of gracefully and good-naturedly surrendering former views to a better

considered position, I invoke them all. [Footnoted citation to *McGrath v. Kristensen*, 340 U.S. 162, 177–78 (1950) (Jackson, J., concurring).]

Reynolds prays for even one such invocation.

In particular, Reynolds asks the Court to grant this motion for re-hearing and provide the following relief (in the alternative):

- affirm the trial court's judgment against Fuller Indemnity; or

- reverse the judgment and render judgment for a lesser amount; or

- reverse the judgment and remand the case to the trial court.

Respectfully submitted, [etc.]

90

Make clean, crisp photocopies
of the one or two most important cases,
highlight up to two inches of text,
and bind the cases with your brief.

Quotable Quotes

"[A] good many judges read briefs while sitting in easy chairs, and it is therefore going to advance your case if you . . . satisfy their curiosity without discommoding them and making them get up—particularly if their reading takes place where they do not have ready access to the law library."
—Frederick B. Wiener, *Briefing and Arguing Federal Appeals* 242 (rev. ed. 1967).

"Briefs are sometimes, but not very often, read in a cloistered setting, a quiet library room where the only sound is a softly ticking clock. Briefs usually must compete with a number of other demands on the judge's time and attention. The telephone rings. The daily mail arrives with motions and petitions clamoring for immediate review. The electronic mail spits out an urgent message or another judge's draft opinion, the reviewing of which is given a higher priority than drafting your own opinions. The clerk's office sends a fax with an emergency motion. The air courier arrives with an overnight delivery. The law clerks buzz you on the intercom because they have hit a snag in a case. So the deathless prose that you have been reading in the blue- or red-covered brief must await another moment. Or another hour. Or another day."
—Ruggero J. Aldisert, *Winning on Appeal: Better Briefs and Oral Argument* 25 (1992).

Explanation

Judges read briefs in all sorts of circumstances—sometimes on planes, sometimes at home, and sometimes on the run. If you assume not only that there's a law library nearby, but also that the judge will have time to go find the books, you're almost certainly assuming too much.

If court rules don't prohibit it, bind one or two crucial cases with your brief. (You're almost always allowed to staple them to a motion.)

The decisions you include—whether with a motion to dismiss or an appellate brief—are likely to receive the most judicial attention.

Beware, though. Your reputation is on the line. If you submit largely irrelevant cases, the judge will inevitably draw conclusions about you—and very likely about your case as well.

Part J

Hitting Your Stride as a Brief-Writer

91

Visualize the reader.
Assume an intelligent, impatient reader who knows nothing about your case— assume neither an idiot nor a genius.

Quotable Quotes

"The universally best style is not a thing of form merely, but must regard the expectations of the reader as to the spirit and occasion of what is written. It is not addressed to the learned, but to all minds. Avoiding book-words, it will use only the standard terms and expressions of modern life."
—L.A. Sherman, *Analytics of Literature* 327 (1893).

"Don't 'write down' to the reader. The star newspaper correspondent, Raymond Clapper, used to say: 'Don't overestimate the public's knowledge. Never underestimate the public's intelligence.' The reader's shortcomings are a challenge to write better."
—Gorham Munson, *The Written Word* 48 (rev. ed. 1949).

"[W]hile the judge who writes the opinion may carefully study your brief, the other judges read it rather hurriedly. So your brief must catch their attention and invade their thought processes."
—Harvey C. Couch, *Writing the Appellate Brief*, 17 Prac. Law. 27, 29 (1971).

"[Those] on the other side of the bench are not super-human in . . . their capacity to understand or to accomplish. If you overload them with irrelevant matter, or bore them to tears with tedious and repetitious arguments, you can only reduce their receptivity to your real points. Anything you can do to make your brief shorter, lighter, and more readable, will improve your chances of getting your point across."
—Arno H. Denecke et al., *Notes on Appellate Brief Writing*, 51 Or. L. Rev. 351, 359 (1972).

"No one can write decently who is distrustful of the reader's intelligence."
—William Strunk, Jr. & E.B. White, *The Elements of Style* 84 (3d ed. 1979).

"Do not use technical language [or] institutional jargon, or refer to most statutes simply by sections. You may be so familiar with tax law, or some other specialty, that just saying a number means something to you. It does *not* to me. In fact, it is irritating to have counsel refer to a statute just by letters or numbers. I will generally interrupt and ask what you're talking about."

—Joe R. Greenhill, *Advocacy in the Texas Supreme Court*,
Tex. B.J., June 1981, at 624, 628.

"When writing, you should imagine yourself sitting across from your most important reader. Write your paper as if you were talking to that reader. This doesn't mean that your writing should be informal. Rather, it means that you should rid your writing of needless formality. The purpose . . . is to inform, not to impress."

—Michael Alley, *The Craft of Scientific Writing* 40 (1987).

"When I start a writing project, I picture the audience with as much specificity as I can—even if I have to make up some of the details. I sometimes name the people I'm writing to. . . . When I really get stuck on what to say or how to say it, I stop and tell it out loud to this imaginary audience. First I tell it just to get the point straight, then I tell it again to make it a little more interesting. But I rarely write a word that isn't addressed to someone in particular."

—Elizabeth Warren, *How I Write*, 4 Scribes J. Legal Writing 71, 76 (1993).

Explanation

Write for a human being. Imagine the person. Talk with the person.

Don't write for some abstract "court." If you do, you won't be writing for anybody in particular, and your aimlessness will show.

Imagine a judge sitting uneasily in a chair, with a thousand papers scattered nearby, all crying out for the judge's attention. Imagine that the judge is looking for an excuse to put your brief down and do something else. Your job is to get the judge to sit back and read—intently.

There's something enormously appealing about a straight-talking advocate who writes as if speaking to the court. As an advocate, Frank Easterbrook provided a good example. When he was Deputy Solicitor General, his brief to the U.S. Supreme Court in *Broadcast Music, Inc. v. Columbia Broadcasting System, Inc.** read in part:

> At the risk of repeating what is clear, we emphasize that our discussion does not indicate approval of the blanket licensing system as applied to television networks. The blanket licenses must be evaluated under the rule of reason, which the court of appeals did not apply. This Court need not decide, and we therefore have not discussed, that rule-of-reason issue.

It's often useful, in other words, to tell the court what you're doing and why.

---

* 441 U.S. 1 (1979).

92

Watch out for potential miscues.

Quotable Quotes

"Write so that no one can help seeing your exact meaning at first glance."
—Charles Coppens, *A Practical Introduction to English Rhetoric* 122 (1880).

"Nobody tells a young writer that many of those who read him are going to read him wrong."
—Bernard de Voto (as quoted in Rudolf Flesch, *The Art of Readable Writing* 181 (1949; repr. 1967)).

"[A] good edit must involve the kind of skeptical reading in which one imagines how one reader in ten might misread the sentence."
—Bryan A. Garner, *A Dictionary of Modern Legal Usage* 564 (2d ed. 1995).

Explanation

When it comes time for editing, you need to read the way a stranger would—with nothing but the words on the page to convey your inflections and tone. Predict the word-association problems that some of your wordings may cause. For example, I once saw a brief describing a man who had suffered a severe brain injury, one result of which caused him to "utter inappropriate comments that were sexual in orientation." I immediately wondered what homosexuality, bisexuality, or heterosexuality might have to do with his comments because the usual phrase in that context is *sexual orientation*. But in fact the writer had merely meant "comments that were sexual in nature" or (to save some words) "comments about sex."

In the examples that follow, you'll find miscues that attentive self-editors could have prevented.

Some Typically Bad Examples

- Ms. Connally knew Denby before she had her surgical procedure on a casual basis. [Surely the surgery wasn't casual.]

- The wrongful death beneficiary would in reasonable probability have received this sum if the decedent had lived. [This sounds macabre—as if one could be a beneficiary of a wrongful death.]

- The City participates by developing programs with guidelines and requests an allocation from HUD either as rental rehabilitation or as CDBG. [*Requests* might be read at first as a noun that is parallel to *guidelines*, as opposed to a verb parallel to *participates*.]

- All litigators have had the experience of trying to settle cases before trial, starting trial, and then achieving settlement during trial. [The legal reader expects to read about some type of case that litigators *try*.]

- She was hitting him in his most vulnerable area—his chest. [He must have been wearing an iron codpiece.]

- Mr. Hughes initially went to bed around midnight, but was aroused by Ms. Lounsbury at around 1:00 a.m. to catch a rat. [In a sentence that mentions both sexes and has to do with bedtime—but has nothing to do with sex—it's unwise to use *aroused* in the sense "awakened."]

- The Court recognized that the predeprivation notice and hearing were necessary prophylactics against a wrongful discharge. [The miscue speaks for itself.]

93

Never write a sentence that you couldn't easily speak.

Quotable Quotes

"In fact, very few of us these days write as idiomatically and naturally as we speak."

—L.A. Sherman, *Analytics of Literature* 274 (1893).

"[S]tandard doctrine though it be to compare the writer–reader relationship to the speaker–listener relationship, this fundamental conception is too often consigned to things we take for granted and never give a thought to. It should, on the contrary, be brought to the foreground of our consciousness and never forgotten."

—Gorham Munson, *The Written Word* 27 (rev. ed. 1949).

"Generally, style becomes perfect as it becomes natural—that is, colloquial."

—A.R. Orage (as quoted in Rudolf Flesch, *The Art of Readable Writing* 210 (1949; repr. 1967)).

"Try to get your speaking voice in your writing. You would never say, 'This radio needed repair from the date of purchase'; you would say, 'This radio hasn't worked since I bought it.' In talking, you tend to use short sentences, plain words, active voice, and specific details. You don't worry about beginning a sentence with 'and' or 'but.' You don't use words like 'shall' or 'secondly' or 'societal.' You would never say 'My reasons were the following' or 'Quiet was the night.'"

—Daniel McDonald, *The Language of Argument* 238 (5th ed. 1986).

"Lawyers are not listening to themselves. I do mean 'listen.' When one receives language, written or otherwise, it seems to me that what one does is to listen to it, not to see it. It does not enter the perceiver's mind through the eyes; it enters through the ears."

—Robert Sack, *Hearing Myself Think: Some Thoughts on Legal Prose*, 4 Scribes J. Legal Writing 93, 97 (1993).

"If you've written a paragraph that sounds labored, back off and ask yourself, 'How would I *say* this to a friend?' Then go ahead and talk it out loud. Afterward, write down as nearly as you can recall what you said. Chances are, most of your talked-out sentences will shame your earlier, written version of them."

—John R. Trimble, *Writing with Style* 81 (2d ed. 2000).

Explanation

We lawyers could save ourselves from many preposterous sentences if we'd just use the mind's ear a little better. It's not that good writing is the same as speech. Far from it. Rather, good writing is speech "heightened and polished," as Judge Jerome Frank once said. You ought to be able, without embarrassment, to say aloud any sentence you've written. Your writing ought to sound that natural. If it does, it will read well, too.

Some Before-and-After Examples

Example A

Before   Johnson had the perception that there was a lack of diligence on the part of OHA in its selection of candidates.

After   Johnson thought that OHA wasn't diligent in selecting candidates.

Example B

Before   The firm of Bradley, Fitch, Hall & Russkind was retained to represent Portnoy Medical Center, Inc. ("Portnoy"), a property-damage claimant, in the above-captioned case on or about July 2, 1996. Portnoy was selected as a member of the Official Unsecured Creditors' Committee on or about July 28, 1996. Merton Yibber ("Yibber"), a member of the law firm of Bradley, Fitch, Hall & Russkind, has represented Portnoy in the meetings of the Official Unsecured Creditors' Committee and in negotiations with Nimbus Corporation ("the Debtor") and other claimholders regarding the terms of the plan of reorganization and the disclosure statement.

After   The Bradley Fitch firm has represented Portnoy Medical Center since early July 1996; Merton Yibber has handled much of the work. Late in that month, when Portnoy became a member of the unsecured creditors' committee, Yibber began representing Portnoy in committee meetings and in negotiations with the debtor, Nimbus Corporation.

94

Try to come in well under
the relevant page limit.

Quotable Quotes

"Praised be he who can state a cause in a clear, simple and succinct manner, and then stop."
— *Jungwirth v. Jungwirth*, 240 P. 222, 223 (Or. 1925).

"Eye fatigue and irritability set in well before page 50."
— Patricia M. Wald (as quoted in Mark Rusk, *Mistakes to Avoid on Appeal*, ABA J., Sept. 1988, at 78, 78).

"Remember, you are writing a 'brief,' and if you do not need the page limit to set forth your arguments, stop."
— Malcolm M. Lucas (as quoted in Ruggero J. Aldisert, *Winning on Appeal: Better Briefs and Oral Argument* 196 (1992)).

"Let me add an incentive to the production of short and pertinent briefs. The longer you make your brief, the more likely that most of the pre-argument analysis of your case will be turned over to a law clerk who just finished the bar exam."
— Arthur L. Alarcon, "Points on Appeal," in *Appellate Practice Manual* 95, 97 (Priscilla A. Schwab ed., 1992).

"There are complicated and difficult cases that require lengthy exposition, but most briefs could be improved by tightening and sharpening. The shorter the brief, the more effective it will be."
— Daniel M. Friedman, "Winning on Appeal," in *Appellate Practice Manual* 129, 135 (Priscilla A. Schwab ed., 1992).

"Sharing a common failing of young lawyers, I almost surely wrote longer briefs than are necessary. There are several reasons for such a mistake. One of them is the pleasure of displaying the writer's often newly acquired erudition on the legal points covered by the brief. Another is the temptation to discuss supporting authorities tendentiously, as if each issue they considered had never been ruled on before. There is also an urge to treat the court as a blank slate on which the unlikeliest legal arguments may be successfully pressed. I am sure I burdened courts with superfluous issues and argument, even though I tried not to drown out the important points in a sea of useless ones."

> —Edith Hollan Jones, *How I Write*, 4 Scribes J. Legal Writing 25, 26 (1993).

"You want your brief to be as readable as possible . . . . If I pick up a brief of 49 and a half pages, it has a little less credibility than one that succinctly argues its points in 25 pages . . . . There's nothing better to read than a well-written brief from a really good lawyer."

> —Jerry E. Smith (as quoted in Bryan A. Garner, *Judges on Effective Writing: The Importance of Plain Language*, 73 Mich. B.J. 326, 326 (1994)).

"Effective writing is concise writing. Attorneys who cannot discipline themselves to write concisely are not effective advocates, and they do a disservice not only to the courts but also to their clients."

> —*Spaziano v. Singletary*, 36 F.3d 1028, 1031 n.2 (11th Cir. 1994).

Explanation

It's a funny thing how legal writers are socialized. Throughout our undergraduate years, we're told to meet a certain page limit, but it's almost always a *minimum* page limit. And we struggle to write 15-page papers explicating a poem—all the while feeling as if we just don't have 15 pages' worth of things to say.

We don't write much in law school, typically, and if we do there's usually a minimum page requirement for everything except briefs. The idea is to bulk up the text.

Then we start writing briefs, and we're given a 50-page limit. Many seem to think that instead of coming in just over the limit (the undergraduate habit), we should come in just under the limit. And anything short of about 50 pages just isn't a very good job. That's the mind-set.

Well, anybody who believes this should understand that Judge Jerry E. Smith's quotation above expresses the view of many judges. The shorter, the better. Less is more.

Yet brevity doesn't come naturally to lawyers. Before page limits arose in the early 1970s (and then word limits in the late 1990s), judges used to complain about briefs over a thousand pages long. It seems hardly believable that lawyers could produce such volume on typewriters, but they did.

In some quarters this extreme volubility lives on. For example, in 2002, the New York Court of Appeals received the full briefing on the first death-penalty case since New York reinstituted the death penalty in 1995. No page limits apply to this type of case. Here's what the Court received: an appellant's brief of 875 pages (prepared by 4 main authors); a government brief of 1,175 pages (prepared by 25 prosecutors); an appellant's reply brief of 345 pages; and an amicus brief of 300 pages. The briefing raised a total of 28 issues discussed in 2,795 pages. This is a pity: the lawyers certainly decreased the likelihood that any of the judges would plow through the massive verbiage. Anyone who had tried to distill the main points in 50 pages would surely have found an eager readership.

Try this: whenever you have a page limit or word limit, cut it in half. Try to stick to that limit—with 14-point type and 1.2-inch margins (see tip #66). Sometimes you'll think that this self-imposed limit is all but impossible—occasionally it will be—but you'll probably force yourself to write with much greater focus. And you'll probably earn some judicial gratitude. One last thing: vow never (or never again) to request leave to file a brief that exceeds page limits.

What follows is a memorable example of pithiness. In 1992, Charles Alan Wright filed a brief opposing a petition for certiorari in the U.S. Supreme Court. There's a 40-page limit on briefs of that kind, and he came in at 6. It's wonderful reading and will be well worth your time.

An Unusually Good Example

No. 92–75

In the

Supreme Court of the United States

October Term, 1992

THE LUBRIZOL CORPORATION,

Petitioner,

vs.

EXXON CORPORATION, *et al.,*

Respondents.

On Petition for a Writ of Certiorari to the United States Court of Appeals for the Fifth Circuit

BRIEF FOR RESPONDENT EXXON CORPORATION

REASONS FOR DENYING THE WRIT

Despite the attempts of Lubrizol to convince this Court otherwise, there is neither a conflict among the courts of appeals nor any conflict between the decision below and the decision of this Court in *Salve Regina College v. Russell,* 111 S. Ct. 1217 (1991).

2

Lubrizol candidly admits that its complaint is not that the opinion of the Fifth Circuit violated the holding of *Salve Regina,* but is rather that the court below ignored the "spirit" of that decision. (Pet. at 6). As shown below, the Fifth Circuit is well aware of *Salve Regina* and violated neither its holding nor its spirit in this case.

The holding of *Salve Regina* is that "courts of appeals review the state-law determinations of district courts de novo." 111 S. Ct. at 1225. "Although the considered decision of a district judge naturally commands the respect of an appellate court, a party is entitled to meaningful review of that decision just as he is of any other legal question in the case, and just as he would have been if the case had been tried in a state court." *Id.* at n. 5 (quoting 19 C. Wright, A. Miller, and E. Cooper, Federal Practice and Procedure, § 4507, pp. 106–110 (1982)).

The Fifth Circuit has fully accepted the sound teaching of that case. In at least 17 cases in the 16 months since *Salve Regina* was decided, the Fifth Circuit has announced that it is reviewing the district court's determination of state law de novo. As Judge Jones explained in *City Public Service Board v. General Electric Co.,* 935 F.2d 78, 80 (5th Cir. 1991), the Fifth Circuit had "often held that a district court's interpretation of the law of the state in which it sits is entitled to 'special deference' on appeal and will be reversed only if 'obviously wrong.' " Those earlier decisions, she said, are "no longer authoritative. Under *Salve Regina College,* this court will undertake plenary review of the district court's interpretation of Texas law." 935 F.2d at 80. Undoubtedly there are many more cases, including this one, in which the Fifth Circuit has in fact followed *Salve Regina* and reviewed de novo even though it did not mention those magic words.

3

The issue in *Salve Regina* is somewhat different from the issue Lubrizol claims to discern here and about which it asserts that there is a conflict among the circuits. It is true that in the notorious case of *Factors Etc., Inc. v. Pro Arts, Inc.,* 652 F.2d 278 (2d Cir. 1981), the Second Circuit held that it was bound by a decision of the Sixth Circuit concerning Tennessee law, except in "the rare instance when it can be said with conviction that the pertinent court of appeals has disregarded clear signals emanating from the state's highest court pointing toward a different result." That decision has been criticized: "It is hard to see why the decision of one court of appeals should have more than persuasive effect on a coordinate court on an issue as to which neither of them can speak with authority." C. Wright, Federal Courts 376 (4th ed. 1983).

But in this case there is not the slightest indication that the Fifth Circuit reviewed the decision of the district court in any fashion other than the de novo method required by *Salve Regina.* Nor is there any indication that either the district court or the court of appeals felt bound in any way by the decision of the Second Circuit in *Artvale, Inc. v. Rugby Fabrics Corp.,* 363 F.2d 1002 (2d Cir. 1966).

It is common ground that in New York, as generally, attorney's fees are not recoverable for breach of contract. The issue in *Artvale,* as here, is whether this general rule applies in the special case of a suit for breach of a covenant not to sue. After a careful examination of the law, the Second Circuit concluded that the recoverability of attorney's fees in a covenant-not-to-sue case should turn on what the parties fairly contemplated, or would have had they addressed their minds to the problem. The court held that, by this standard, liability for fees can be imposed only where the covenant is expressly drafted to allow for fees or "for suits brought in obvious breach or otherwise in bad faith." 363 F.2d at 1008.

4

The district court correctly understood this. It described the holding of *Artvale,* and of a later Second Circuit opinion that restated the *Artvale* principles, *Bellefonte Re Ins. Co. v. Argonaut Ins. Co.,* 757 F.2d 523, 529 (2d Cir. 1985), and said:

> The New York state courts, however, have continued to hold that attorney's fees are not recoverable for breach of contract . . . [citing cases]. The New York state courts have not, though, specifically addressed the recoverability of attorney's fees for breach of covenant not to sue, nor have they disapproved of *Artvale* or *Bellefonte.*

(App. 45a–46a). The Fifth Circuit, in turn, recognized that the district court had relied on *Artvale,* which, the Fifth Circuit said, is "a case that both frames the issue before us and sets a standard for resolving it." (App 9a). In a footnote the Fifth Circuit added that the *Artvale* rule "has been applied by courts deciding cases under New York law." For this proposition it cited three cases, only one of which had been cited by the district court (App. 10a at n. 5).

It is of the essence of the common-law method that courts consider and often rely on decisions from other courts, even when those decisions are not binding on them. The district court and the Fifth Circuit were in no way bound by the Second Circuit's decision in *Artvale.* But in the absence of other cases casting doubt on whether *Artvale* correctly stated New York law, they were entitled to give that decision persuasive effect, as they did. Indeed in the common-law tradition, decisions of other courts vary in the respect they are given. They "should be accorded such a measure of weight and influence as they may be intrinsically entitled to receive." H.C. Black, The Law of Judicial Precedents 11 (1928) (quoted in R. Aldisert, The Judicial Process 778–779

5

(1976)). The power of the court's reasoning and the reputation of the court and of the judge who wrote the opinion are factors taken into account.[1] The *Artvale* decision was by Judge Henry J. Friendly, a distinguished New York practitioner before he went to the bench and "universally recognized . . . as one of our wisest judges." *Finley v. United States,* 490 U.S. 545, 565 (1989) (Stevens, J., dissenting).

Of course even an opinion by Judge Friendly would have had to yield if there were evidence that he was wrong in his assessment of New York law or if more recent decisions had shown that New York law is not as he then thought it was. All of this was argued below. Lubrizol devoted eight pages of its opening brief in the Fifth Circuit and four pages in its reply brief to its argument that *Artvale* is inconsistent with New York law. It cited the same New York cases that it now relies on (Pet. at 8–9) in support of that position. Exxon in its brief below showed why those cases were inapposite and its analysis was accepted by the Fifth Circuit.

What Lubrizol cannot avoid is this simple fact, quickly and easily verifiable by computer-assisted research: despite the fact that *Artvale* is now 26 years old, no New York decision has ever

---

1. Lubrizol claims that what it thinks the proper approach to appellate review "is most starkly demonstrated by *Gruver v. Midas Int'l Corp.,* 925 F.2d 280 (9th Cir. 1991)." (Pet. at 10). Yet in *Gruver* the Ninth Circuit did just what Lubrizol criticizes the courts below for doing in this case. Oregon law was controlling in that case. Oregon strictly adheres to the American rule barring recovery of attorney's fees in breach-of-contract actions except where the contract provides for them. The Oregon decisions do not speak to the special case of breach of a covenant not to sue, but the Ninth Circuit found in a 1990 Colorado decision what it called "[t]he most recent and comprehensive review of the cases in this area" and concluded that Oregon would reach the same result as Colorado. 925 F.2d at 284.

6

criticized it or disapproved of it. In fact, the only New York case that ever cited it did so as the controlling rule of law and followed it to award attorney's fees under an indemnity agreement that made no express reference to attorney's fees, legal expenses, or the like. *Breed, Abbott & Morgan v. Hulko,* 139 A.D. 2d 21, 531 N.Y.S. 2d 240 (A.D. 1988), *aff'd,* 74 N.Y. 2d 686, 543 N.Y.S. 2d 373, 541 N.E. 2d 402 (1989). The *Breed* decision was fully discussed by both sides in their briefs below. Had the Fifth Circuit added a citation to that case in footnote 5 of its opinion, where it cited three federal cases applying *Artvale* under New York law (App. 10a), Lubrizol would have had no possible basis for complaint. Surely this Court has more pressing business than to take a court of appeals to task for the lack of a citation.

CONCLUSION

The petition for a writ of certiorari should be denied.

Respectfully submitted,

CHARLES ALAN WRIGHT
State Bar No. 22023000
727 East 26th Street
Austin, Texas 78705
(512) 471-7188

RICHARD B. MILLER
MILLER & FRANKEL
S.D. of Tex. ID 3080
State Bar No. 14107000
3862 First City Tower
1001 Fannin Street
Houston, Texas 77002
(713) 759-1234

7

W. ROBERT BROWN
Counsel of Record
S.D. of Tex. ID 5238
State Bar No. 03178000
THOMAS C. WRIGHT
BROWN, CAMPBELL,
HARRISON & WRIGHT
4000 Two Houston Center
909 Fannin Street
Houston, Texas 77010
(713) 752-2332

Counsel for Respondent
Exxon Corporation

Of Counsel:

EXXON CORPORATION
K.C. JOHNSON
S.D. of Tex. ID 2347
State Bar No. 10760500
800 Bell, Room 1839
Houston, Texas 77002
(713) 656-1719

95

In an appellate brief, always state the standard of review.

Quotable Quotes

"An appellate court will apply specific standards of review based on the nature of the question or questions presented.* It is absolutely essential that the attorney demonstrate how these standards apply to the case . . . and why they require that the case be reversed or affirmed."

> —Edward D. Re, *Brief Writing and Oral Argument* xxii (6th ed. 1987).

"[I]t is important that counsel help us in their briefs by identifying the standard of review. Sometimes there will be issues requiring different standards, as when a judge's conclusion presents a mixed question of fact and law. A clear, succinct, and authority-supported statement of standard of review gets me off to a good start."

> —Frank M. Coffin, *On Appeal: Courts, Lawyering, and Judging* 114 (1994).

Explanation

Under federal appellate rules, of course, the standard of review is required for each issue presented. But even if you're not required to state the standard, you're wise to do so. If the standard happens to be a tough one, you'll enhance your credibility by your unflinching approach.

In stating the standard, avoid using the boilerplate that clutters the first few pages of so many briefs. Notice how Example A—taken from an appellee's brief—presents the standard simply and directly, yet in a fresh way. After reading this, you get the feeling that the appellant's case is already sunk.

Examples B and C come from the same criminal case, in which the trial court entered a judgment of guilty after a seven-week jury trial. The statements are unimaginative but straightforward. Example B makes the judge work harder than necessary by referring to a case rather than explaining the standard for reviewing the trial court's refusal to give a defendant's proposed instruction. But otherwise B is probably superior

---

* Fed R. App. P. 28(a)(6).

441

to C in not requiring the judge to flip back to the statement of the issues to see which standard relates to which issue. Both could be improved.

Example D is by Raymond P. Ward of New Orleans. The standard-of-review section was the first subsection in the argument. Notice how the lead candidly acknowledges the appellants' weakest point—the deference owed to the trial court's factual findings. Then Ward boldly predicts that the appellants will carry their burden on appeal. He then discusses the manifest-error standard of review in an appellant-friendly way.

Example A

Standards of Review

In this appeal, Chronon will attempt to run five hurdles set at high-jump levels.

The first is the great deference that a reviewing court accords to issues determined by a jury, indulging every legitimate conclusion in favor of the judgment. As the Court well knows, it may not "substitute its own judgment for that of the finder of fact." *Lofton v. Texas Brine Corp.*, 777 S.W.2d 384, 387 (Tex. 1989).

The second and third hurdles stand in the way of Chronon's primary points, based on insufficient evidence and no evidence. In reviewing an insufficient-evidence point, this Court must weigh the evidence and uphold the judgment unless it is "so contrary to the overwhelming weight of the evidence as to be clearly wrong and unjust." *Cain v. Bain*, 709 S.W.2d 175, 176 (Tex. 1986). Before setting aside a jury's factual determination, the reviewing court must "articulate why the original finding is manifestly unjust, shocks the conscience, or clearly demonstrates bias." *Sosa v. City of Balch Springs*, 772 S.W.2d 71, 72 (Tex. 1989). And in reviewing a no-evidence point, this Court may consider only the evidence and inferences favorable to the judgment and must disregard all contrary evidence and inferences. *State v. $110,114.00*, 820 S.W.2d 783, 785 (Tex. 1991).

The fourth hurdle is the rule that any element omitted from the jury charge but supported by the evidence must be deemed to have been found by the trial court. Tex. R. Civ. P. 279. Even assuming that Chronon had properly preserved error on its complaints about the jury submissions, the standard of review would be abuse of discretion. *Texas Dep't of Human Servs. v. E.B.*, 802 S.W.2d 647, 649 (Tex. 1990).

The fifth and final hurdle involves the trial court's broad discretion in admitting expert testimony. In complaining of the court's decision to allow Lewis and O'Brien's expert witness to testify, Chronon once again confronts the abuse-of-discretion standard. *See First Coppell Bank v. Smith*, 742 S.W.2d 454, 458 (Tex. App.—Dallas 1987, no writ).

Example B

Statement of Standards of Review

This Court's review of constitutional, statutory, and regulatory questions (issues 1–6) is de novo. *United States v. Presley*, 52 F.3d 64, 67 (4th Cir. 1995). The standard governing a trial court's failure to give a defendant's proposed instruction (issues 2A and 5C) is set out in *United States v. Lewis*, 53 F.3d 29, 32 (4th Cir. 1995). A trial court's ruling regarding expert testimony (issues 5A and 5B) is reviewed for abuse of discretion. *United States v. Myers*, 66 F.3d 1364, 1373 (4th Cir. 1995).

Example C

Statement of Standards of Review

Issues 1 and 2 are questions of law, which are reviewed de novo. *United States v. Fiel*, 35 F.3d 997, 1005 (4th Cir. 1994). Issue 3 is a question of the sufficiency of the evidence, the standard being whether the evidence, when viewed in the light most favorable to the government, could support the finding of the essential elements of the crime beyond a reasonable doubt by any rational trier of fact. *Jackson v. Virginia*, 443 U.S. 307, 319 (1970). Issues 4 and 6 are reviewed for clear error, while the legal findings relating to those issues are reviewed de novo. *United States v. Jones*, 31 F.3d 1304, 1315 (4th Cir. 1994). Issue 5 is reviewed for clear abuse of discretion. *United States v. Dornhofer*, 859 F.2d 1195, 1199 (4th Cir. 1988).

Example D

Standard of Review

Appellants have the difficult burden of proving that the trial court's factual findings were clearly wrong. They can carry this burden. The manifest-error standard of appellate review does not require the court of appeal to rubber-stamp the trial court's factual findings and credibility determinations. Rather, the court of appeal has a constitutional duty to review facts despite the deference accorded to the factfinder. *Ambrose v. New Orleans Police Dep't Ambulance Serv.*, 639 So. 2d 216, 221 (La. 1994). The appellate review of facts is not completed by reading so much of the record as will reveal a reasonable factual basis for the finding in the trial court. The court must go further by determining that the record shows the finding to be neither clearly wrong nor manifestly erroneous. *Id.* at 220. A trial court's factual findings are not immune from appellate review simply because they appear to be based on the relative credibility of witnesses. Where documents or objective evidence so contradicts the witness's story—or the story itself is so internally inconsistent or implausible on its face—that a reasonable factfinder would not credit the witness's story, the court of appeal may well find manifest error or clear wrongness even in a finding purportedly based upon a credibility determination. *Rosell v. ESCO*, 549 So. 2d 840, 844–45 (La. 1989).

96

State squarely what you want the court to do.

Quotable Quotes

"Tell the court what to do with the case. The conclusion should tell the court exactly what the litigant wants done . . . . Ordinarily, the appellee simply wants the court to affirm the result below. But the appellant may request any number of different results—reversal, remand, vacation, modification, a new trial, dismissal. It often takes the mystery out of a case if the appellant will only tell the court just what relief he wants."

—Myron H. Bright, *Appellate Briefwriting: Some Golden Rules*,
17 Creighton L. Rev. 1069, 1073 (1984).

"Tell us exactly what relief you think we should order. It is helpful if, in your summary, you frame the court's mandate as you would like to have it."

—*Preparing Your Appeal to the Fifth Circuit*, 2 Fifth Cir. Rep. 431, 433 (1985).

"I like to read, at the end of the brief, precisely what counsel wants us to do, giving us a menu of possible dispositions."

—Frank M. Coffin, *On Appeal: Courts, Lawyering, and Judging* 120 (1994).

Explanation

New lawyers in particular seem to worry about telling courts what to do. You see this especially when the prayer for relief reads in passive voice: "For these reasons, a summary judgment *should be granted* in favor of Jackson." The better strategy is to be confident and forthright: "Because . . . , Jackson merits a summary judgment, and this Court should grant it."

Seasoned lawyers routinely use this type of directness. They're not bossy, but they're certainly bold. And as shown by the Fifth Circuit guidelines quoted above, judges are eager to know precisely what the advocate thinks the court should do.

Some Before-and-After Examples

Example A

Before   In addition, a ruling on qualified immunity should be made before discovery commences because the doctrine of qualified immunity provides
that government officials are fully entitled to avoid the expense of discovery . . . . Therefore, a ruling as to the qualified immunity of Defendant
Hutchinson should be made before discovery commences.

After   In addition, a ruling on qualified immunity would afford these government officials their entitlement to avoid the expense of discovery. . . . This
Court therefore needs to rule on Defendant Hutchinson's qualified immunity before discovery can begin.

Example B

Before   The Circuit Court's dismissal of plaintiff's petition for failure to state a
claim upon which relief can be granted should be affirmed because defendant Northeastern Mental Health Center is protected by the doctrine
of sovereign immunity, and the individual defendants are protected by
the doctrine of official immunity, as codified in § 632.440.

After   The Circuit Court properly dismissed plaintiff's petition because the Center is protected by the doctrine of sovereign immunity, and the individual
defendants are protected by the doctrine of official immunity. This Court
should therefore affirm.

97

If you've shown that the caselaw is on your side, don't stop there: show that the ruling you seek is fair and right under the circumstances.

Quotable Quotes

"[T]he real and vital central job is to satisfy the court that sense and decency and justice require (a) the rule [that] you contend for in this *type* of situation; and (b) the result that you contend for, as between these parties. Your whole case, on law and facts, must make *sense*, must appeal as being *obvious* sense, inescapable sense, sense in simple terms of life and justice."

—Karl Llewellyn, *The Modern Approach to Counselling and Advocacy— Especially in Commercial Transactions*, 46 Colum. L. Rev. 167, 183 (1946).

"Any law library furnishes precedents which can support a fairly plausible argument for either side of almost any legal proposition likely to be involved in an appellate case. Premising an argument on rules of law does not require the ingenuity nor the independent research that is needed to make a persuasive showing that fundamental tenets of justice and fairness support your contention."

—Frank E. Cooper, *Writing in Law Practice* 243 (2d ed. 1963).

"If there is any legitimate way to argue the equities it should be done, though not in the style of a jury summation."

—Murray I. Gurfein, *Appellate Advocacy, Modern Style*, 4 Litig. 8, 9 (Winter 1978).

"The goal of a judge is not merely to reach a decision supported by a rule of law, but to dispense justice to the parties. Accordingly he will be uncomfortable with an argument based on precedent alone, unless it is clear to him where the equities lie."

—Girvan Peck, *Writing Persuasive Briefs* 78 (1984).

Explanation

Increasingly, courts don't want to know simply that there are cases on your side. They want to know that the legal rules announced in those cases make good sense—that the rules you're asking them to apply are sound public policy.

Some writers believe—I think rightly—that our sense of *stare decisis* has loosened quite a bit over the past several years. As much as courts may stick to the language of constraint ("We are constrained to hold . . ."), they in fact behave as if they have very few constraints. Because of that, it only makes sense, in your arguments, to show not only what the law is but also why it should be so. That way, you don't seem to be relying on mere technicalities to win the day.

One of the advocate's most important jobs is to make the court feel either satisfied or dissatisfied with the status quo. Plaintiffs and appellants want judges to feel dissatisfied so that they'll change the status quo. Defendants and appellees want judges to feel satisfied—to preserve the status quo.

Making the Court Feel Dissatisfied with the Status Quo

Example A

> *The following excerpt, by Harry M. Reasoner of Houston, is the final paragraph of a reply brief in support of an appeal to the Texas Supreme Court. Reasoner seeks reversal of an intermediate court's imposition of a duty to warn of the dangers of alcohol.*

While plaintiffs implore the court to impose a new duty to warn, the real remedy sought here is the creation of a new, retroactive cause of action for damages in Texas for every consumer anywhere who claims injury from prolonged or excessive consumption of alcohol. The gravity of the radical expansion of tort liability sought here, in its damage to the fabric of Texas law, in the flood of litigation it is bound to inspire, and in its isolation of Texas law from that of the rest of the nation, urges review and reversal by this Court.

Example B

> *Here's another closer by Harry M. Reasoner—the final paragraph of a cert petition. It sums up the argument while making review seem urgent.*

The decision of the court below injects an unacceptable degree of uncertainty into a wide array of pricing decisions. It effectively licenses courts and juries to deem price increases unlawful on the basis of unspecified and indefinite subjective factors, without any measurable effect on competition, merely because they decrease the potential profits of individual competitors. This Court should reaffirm the requirement that even a monopolist's pricing must prevent purchaser-competitors from competing profitably before it can be deemed a violation of Section 2 of the Sherman Act.

Example C

> *In this excerpt, Nancy Bellhouse May of Little Rock, in a cert petition, deftly handles a sensitive issue: intemperate behavior by a trial judge in imposing sanctions. She does this not only by marshaling the relevant caselaw, but also by discussing the issue in the larger context of due process.*

[The following is from the statement of the case:]

The Eighth Circuit's interpretation of district courts' inherent power to sanction in this and subsequent cases places its construction of the bad-faith standard in direct conflict with that of the Second, Sixth, and Ninth Circuits; this case therefore presents this Court with the occasion to resolve a conflict between the circuits. In addition, since the Eighth Circuit affirmed the district court's summary imposition of sanctions, it apparently approved the district court's failure to accord Petitioner the notice and hearing to which he was entitled under the Due Process Clause of the Fifth Amendment. Granting the writ will consequently provide this Court with the opportunity to emphasize the importance of this constitutional right.

[The petition concludes as follows:]

The grant of certiorari is therefore warranted so this Court can further define the boundaries of due process. If fair procedures are required no matter who is being punished or what power is invoked, the Eighth Circuit wrongly endorsed the trial court's semantic dodge in this case; absent guidance, other courts may conclude that they too can escape the reach of due process simply by invoking something other than the contempt power when they sanction.

Making the Court Feel Satisfied with the Status Quo

Example A

> *The following excerpt, by Scott P. Stolley of Dallas, is the conclusion of an introductory part of a brief opposing defendants' special appearances. The preceding portion of the introduction establishes fraud and breach of fiduciary duties, as well as violations of the Texas Securities Act.*

Despite having breached their fiduciary duties, and despite having committed several fraudulent acts directed toward Texas—not to mention having violated the Texas Securities Act—the Defendants resist being haled into a Texas court to answer for their conduct. Instead, they contend that the State of Texas has no power to enforce the Texas Securities Act or to protect an injured Texan who was the target of numerous overt acts that were purposefully directed at, and calculated to cause injury in,

Texas. Contrary to this contention, the Defendants could reasonably foresee that their conduct would subject them to jurisdiction in Texas. Therefore, this Court should deny the Defendants' special appearances.

Example B

The following conclusion, by Jim Harris of Dallas, urges the appellate court to deny what would be a third remand to the trial court. Notice how the passage smartly suggests that enough is enough.

The EPA's apparent view of this litigation is to have it continue until it gets a result that it likes. But of course that standard does not guide this Court in deciding if almost ten years of litigation should come to an end. If Judge Baxter, who has remained in charge of this matter since its inception, does not believe that additional evidence would help him reach a better result, then should he be second-guessed? Sequa submits the answer is no, because his decision not to reopen the case on remand was reasonable. Nor does it serve any legitimate purpose to remand for the empty exercise of having Judge Baxter formalize, under his signature, the analysis that he has already adopted and that is clear in the record.

The Court should therefore affirm.

A Pro-and-Con Example on Motion for Rehearing

Movant's Side

In the following excerpt, Eric Eissenstat of Oklahoma City argues for a rehearing after a Tenth Circuit panel has reduced his client's punitive damages from $30 million to $6 million.

Statement of the Case

This case is on remand from the United States Supreme Court for reconsideration in light of *BMW of North America, Inc. v. Gore*, 116 S. Ct. 1589 (1996). In the panel's first opinion—*Continental Trend Resources, Inc. v. OXY USA Inc.*, 44 F.3d 1465 (10th Cir. 1995)—the Court unanimously held: "our review of the voluminous record reveals several factors that support the amount of punitive damages awarded against OXY." 44 F.3d at 1479–80. The Court observed that the relevant ratio of punitive damages to actual and potential harm was 6 to 1. *Id.* at 1476 n.15. OXY's petition for rehearing and suggestion for rehearing en banc was denied.

On remand, the entire panel agreed that *BMW* was factually distinguishable from this case and that all the indicia identified in *BMW* as being associated with reprehensible conduct and a substantial punitive-damage award were present. (Slip op. at 9–11; dissent at 1.) Nevertheless, the majority ordered a remittitur of $24 million because "the harm in this case, though egregious, was entirely economic" and "the ratio between the award and the harm to these plaintiffs—both actual and potential— is too large." (Slip op. at 18.)

For the reasons set forth below, the majority opinion was erroneous, relied on evidence not introduced at trial, is contrary to decisions of the Supreme Court and this Circuit, and raises issues of exceptional importance. Rehearing—or, if necessary, rehearing en banc—should be granted.

Arguments and Authorities

1. The majority relied on evidence not introduced at trial.

Both the first opinion and the majority opinion approved a ratio of punitive damages to harm of 6 to 1. Faced with the identical record, however, the majority determined on remand that its "best estimate" amount of potential harm to CTR was $1 million, not the $5 million it unanimously found to be the potential harm in the first opinion—and, thus, that $6 million, not $30 million, was the maximum constitutionally permissible punitive-damage award.

The majority erred because the $1 million potential-harm figure was based on evidence never introduced at trial. The majority cited the affidavit of John Brickhill, which addressed only 79 of the 140 producing wells at issue as support for its "best estimate." (Slip op. at 13.) The subject affidavits were submitted in connection with CTR's appeal of the antitrust summary-judgment order and focused on the issue whether the Rodman Gathering System was an "essential facility" for antitrust purposes. The affidavits were not in evidence at trial and were not properly considered by this Court in reviewing the verdict.

Compounding this error, the majority ignored the evidence that the jury did hear on actual and potential harm. . . .

Nonmovant's Side

In the following excerpt, Theodore B. Olson and Mark E. Greenwold, both of Washington, D.C., seek to reassure the Tenth Circuit that its reduction in damages—complained of in the excerpt above—was entirely proper.

Introduction

The Panel issued its decision after the Supreme Court of the United States examined the previous decision affirming a $30,000,000 punitive-damage award in this case, granted certiorari, vacated the original judgment, and remanded the case to this Court with instructions to reconsider the award in light of *BMW of North America, Inc. v. Gore*, 116 S. Ct. 1589 (1996). The Supreme Court remanded and ordered reconsideration of only six of twenty punitive-damage cases pending before it at the time of its *BMW* decision.

The Panel followed the Supreme Court's instructions, first "review[ing] the Supreme Court's [*BMW*] opinion" and then "reanalyz[ing] the award in the instant case under these standards." Slip op. at 4–5. (*Continental Trend Resources, Inc. v. OXY USA Inc.*, Nos. 92-6350, 92-6384, 1996 WL 680337 (10th Cir. Nov. 26, 1996).) The Panel noted that *BMW* established three guideposts for reviewing courts in determining whether punitive-damage awards were excessive (slip op. at 8). It recognized that "[t]he *BMW* Court also places in the constitutional calculus the question of the minimum level of penalty necessary to achieve the state's goal of deterrence" (*id.* at 16). Further, the Panel referred to the admonition in *BMW* that a punitive-damage award "cannot be justified on the ground that it was necessary to deter future misconduct without considering whether less drastic remedies could be expected to achieve that goal" (*id.*).

After taking post-remand briefs from both OXY and CTR, reexamining the massive record in this case, and carefully applying *BMW*'s three guideposts, the Panel found that the $30,000,000 punitive-damage award to CTR was excessive and violated the Due Process Clause of the Fourteenth Amendment:

> With the guidance of the *BMW* opinion, . . . we conclude that $30,000,000 exceeds the constitutional limit. The harm in this case, though egregious, was entirely economic, and thus less worthy of punishment than harm to health or safety. Further, the ratio between the award and the harm to these plaintiffs—both actual and potential—is too large. OXY's wealth is not irrelevant, but $30,000,000 is far more than is necessary to secure its attention and modify its behavior in Oklahoma. [Slip op. at 18.]

The Panel then exercised its "best judgment" and found that "$6,000,000 is the maximum constitutionally permissible punitive-damage award justified by the facts of this case." *Id.* at 20. Even after remittitur, the resulting $6,000,000 award is the largest punitive-damage award ever affirmed by any state or federal court under Oklahoma law, is larger than all but three punitive-damage awards ever upheld by this Court (all of which involved conduct causing death or widespread environmental harm), and is 23 times larger than the compensatory-damage award of $269,000. The Panel also found that the $6,000,000 award was sufficient to punish and deter OXY from future misconduct, holding that this amount was "sufficient to obtain OXY's attention" and "to change its behavior in Oklahoma oil and gas fields." *Id.*

98

Show concern for the court's valuable time— but with more than just lip service.

Quotable Quotes

"Courtesy to the court demands that . . . information should be conveyed in the clearest, most concise manner possible. Self-interest, or the interest of the client, emphasizes and reinforces this demand."
—William M. Lile et al., *Brief-Making and the Use of Law Books* 366 (3d ed. 1914).

"The secret ambition of every brief should be to spare the judge the necessity of engaging in any work, mental or physical."
—Mortimer Levitan, *Confidential Chat on the Craft of Briefing*, 1957 Wis. L. Rev. 59, 63.

Explanation

Courts are busier than ever these days—certainly more than when William Lile was writing in 1914. Coming in under the page limit is one way of showing courtesy (see tip #94). So is framing legal issues well (see tip #8).

But there are other ways. For example, if you're seeking discretionary review, explain why your particular case is worth the court's valuable time. And if you're opposing review, say why it isn't—why it won't further the caselaw in the area, or the like. Often, you can build this into your statement regarding oral argument. The concern for the court and the law, as well as with your client's case, will reflect well on you.

In the following example, Charles Alan Wright addresses this very concern in a petition for writ of certiorari filed in the United States Supreme Court. After reading these excerpts, you'll probably be interested to know that the Court granted cert* and ultimately reversed the Fifth Circuit's decision.**

---

* *See Mississippi v. Louisiana*, 503 U.S. 935 (1992).
** *See Mississippi v. Louisiana*, 506 U.S. 73 (1992).

An Uncommonly Good Example

[The substantive portion of the petition begins as follows:]

Reasons for Granting the Writ

The Fifth Circuit erred as a matter of law in looking only to evidence from 1881 forward, rather than from 1812 when Louisiana became a state, in determining the location of the thalweg of the Mississippi River and the first known existence of Stack Island. It substituted its own evaluation of the evidence for that of the Mississippi District Court, contrary to this Court's pronouncement about the proper scope of review in a case tried without a jury. If this were only a dispute between private claimants to land, these errors might not merit review here, but when they resulted in an erroneous determination of the boundary between the States of Louisiana and Mississippi, they require the attention of this Court. This is underlined by the uncertainty about the binding effect of the judgment below, uncertainty that only this Court can resolve.

[The petition concludes as follows:]

It is not necessary now to say which of these views is correct. Suffice it to say that there is support in reason and precedent for all three of them. Unless this Court settles the matter, the certain consequence will be, as Louisiana predicted in its brief quoted above, that both States will continue to assert jurisdiction over the land in question and that further litigation will take place. To leave this in limbo after many years of litigation is no way to treat even the private parties, much less the sovereign States.

This Court should grant certiorari not only to resolve the important substantive issues the case presents but to settle, as only the Court can, the effect of the judgment on all the states and private interests involved.

99

Use focus groups to evaluate draft briefs, with mock judicial readings. Do it professionally and objectively.

Quotable Quotes

"[Y]ou can't argue with a group-reaction; it's an objective fact hard to explain away."
—Gorham Munson, *The Written Word* 194 (rev. ed. 1949).

"[I]mpose what you write . . . upon friends or selected acquaintances for assessment or criticism before it is delivered. Choose those who have no vested interest in your success, who suffer no ague of insecurity which they must cover by excessive comment. If they be reasonably normal and detached, they can help you beyond reckoning. Some searching question or sage suggestion can send you back to your labors with renewed vigor and discernment."
—Charles W. Ferguson, *Say It with Words* 152 (1959).

"[I]t is no sign of weakness or defeat that your manuscript ends up in need of major surgery. This is a common occurrence in all writing, and among the best writers."
—William Strunk Jr. & E.B. White, *The Elements of Style* 72 (3d ed. 1979).

"Ask other attorneys to review the brief for both form and substance. Especially at the later stages of brief drafting, ask them to comment on the clarity of the writing and to make other suggestions to improve the brief. Seek input from other lawyers about the substance or strategy in the brief. In seeking this help, do not ask only those in your firm. In some ways, they may be less helpful than outsiders, and be unwilling to risk offending you. A friend in another firm or in a different kind of practice will have a fresh perspective."
—Richardson R. Lynn, *Appellate Litigation* § 9.13, at 195 (1985).

"It is not an admission of weakness to ask for help in planning and preparing the presentation of material to other people. And it is not an affront to your professional integrity to have someone say that he or she cannot grasp what you mean by . . . a trial page of text. As we write, our minds get set on particular lines of thought, and we unconsciously ignore side-issues or mentally supply steps in an argument. To someone else, the gaps in our thought are obvious at once. Someone else sees implications other than those that stuck in our minds. Points that seemed implicit from our standpoint are often not at all obvious when viewed from someone else's frame of reference."

—Christopher Turk & John Kirkman, *Effective Writing: Improving Scientific, Technical, and Business Communication* 38 (2d ed. 1989).

"Receiving criticism may not be a natural act, but it is a valuable skill, very much worth developing. A crucial introduction to this development can be the standard workshop practice of requiring an author to be silent during the discussion of his or her work. A workshop where an author can't keep quiet but feels compelled to defend and explain the work under discussion is a counterproductive experience for both the author and the people who are trying to offer helpful criticism. I remind authors that they are not required to accept any of the criticism they are offered, and I suggest that they not be hasty in deciding whether or not to use a piece of criticism or a suggestion. A suggestion that seems insulting during and immediately after workshop discussion may next week be the key to a brilliant revision."

—David Huddle, "Taking What You Need, Giving What You Can: The Writer as Student and Teacher," in *Writers on Writing* 74, 78 (Robert Pack & Jay Parini eds., 1991).

Explanation

Most appellate advocates believe that mock oral arguments can be quite useful. Although a few great advocates dispute this—Charles Alan Wright is a notable example—most seem to become more comfortable with their positions, and their ease in explaining them, when they get a little practice. That much is old hat. Yet it's dubious old hat, especially when you consider that oral arguments sway the decisions in only a small percentage of cases.

Given that a supermajority of cases are decided on the briefs, why not focus your energies on testing your written arguments instead of your oral arguments? This means something more formal than merely walking down the hall to ask a colleague, "Could you read this over?" It means seeking a truly objective view from readers who can't possibly be predisposed.

I've done this over the past few years by conducting focus groups to engage in what I call "mock judicial readings." It's an eight-step process.

1. Hire five or six of the smartest lawyers you know—some women and some men, with various levels of experience and various political philosophies—to participate in the mock judicial reading. If you have a plaintiff's case, hire defense lawyers. Offer to pay a generous hourly rate for two hours of their time. Have them run a conflicts check, but don't disclose what side of the case you're on.

2. On the day of the focus group—say, from 7 to 9 a.m. (when everyone is fresh), about a week before your brief is due—have two sets of briefs ready: your opponent's and your own. If you represent the appellee, your task is easy: just be sure that your brief looks like a

finished, filed product. If you represent the appellant, you'll need to prepare a mock appellee's brief based on your opponent's filings in the lower court. Again, it should look like a final product.

3. Have someone neutral run the focus group. Don't introduce the lawyers involved until after you're finished. Ensure that the brief-writers are there to watch.

4. Explain to the participants that they are playing the role of appellate judges. They should read as if they were judges, and they should try to understand the case that's being presented to them in the briefs. The moderator and others in the room are not there to answer questions but simply to observe. Any questions that participants have should be referred to the briefs.

5. Give the participants the appellant's brief (regardless of which side you're on). Ask them to read in silence for 15 minutes. Then stop the reading and ask them questions such as these: "What's your first impression of the case?" "What are the issues you're concerned about?" "Is the brief giving you what you need to decide this case?" You'll be surprised at how quickly, through discussing the case, the participants will move toward a command of the critical issues. Keep the discussion time to 15 minutes.

6. Ask them to continue for another ten minutes with the appellant's brief. Discuss for ten more minutes.

7. Next, give them the appellee's brief. Repeat steps 5 and 6.

8. By now, you'll be in a position to ask which brief is more persuasive and why. Ask each participant to say how he or she would vote in the case and to explain why. Assume that the case has to be decided right then, and caution that you're asking only for an honest reaction given the limited time frame. Disallow abstentions.

This procedure is always an eye-opener for everyone involved. The "judges" find it intellectually stimulating; the lawyers involved in the case are often shocked at how rapidly the readers dissect even a complex case; and the principal brief-writer typically finds it a nerve-racking and humbling experience.

But in major cases it's well worth the time and the investment. For a relatively modest expenditure, you can simulate a conference in which judges decide your case. And you'll see why it's important to have five or six participants—as opposed to just one colleague—because the participants invariably react to one another and help one another understand the dispositive points.

I first used this technique to preserve a sizable plaintiffs' judgment back in 1993, and I've done it many times since then. In fact, I now have a regular list of mock judicial readers.

When I publicized the use of focus groups on CounselConnect (an online forum for lawyers) in 1994, lawyers throughout the country responded that they had never thought of anything like it. Presumably, these are many of the same lawyers who use jury consultants and who assemble panels of retired judges for mock oral arguments.

Sometimes when I hold focus groups, I'm not a lawyer in the case. For example, a law firm once came to me after its client had received a multimillion-dollar judgment against it. The firm was planning its appeal, and the client had approved the use of a focus group. Because the client was the appellant, the firm had to prepare a mock appellee's brief based on the filings.

As it happened, I didn't have a chance to edit the appellant's brief before the mock judicial reading. Not that a simple edit would have mattered. The appellant lost in the focus group by a 4-to-1 vote.

The client and the lawyers—having lost—were ecstatic. They had discovered how to rewrite the brief in a way that would allay the judges' concerns.

That's precisely what they did. They won their appeal in a unanimous decision. They had erased a huge judgment. And they had learned the value of mock judicial readings.

100

Remember the importance of ethos.

Quotable Quotes

"The success or failure of an advocate comes down at last to this: What manner of man is it who is speaking? This is what Emerson meant when he wrote: 'What you are speaks so loudly I cannot hear what you say.' An advocate might obey every rule that Aristotle and Cicero have laid down, but if he is not sincere in what he says, he will not achieve persuasion."
—Lloyd Paul Stryker, The Art of Advocacy 147 (1954).

"The fundamental thing . . . is not technique, useful though that may be; if a writer's personality repels, it will not avail him to eschew split infinitives, to master the difference between 'that' and 'which,' to have Fowler's Modern English Usage by heart. Soul is more than syntax. If your readers dislike you, they will dislike what you say. Indeed, such is human nature [that], unless they like you, they will mostly deny you even justice."
—F.L. Lucas, Style 49 (1955).

"Almost everybody develops a habit of sizing-up each person he has occasion to deal with: Is he honest? Is he intelligent? Has he been willing to do the necessary work on the matter in hand? Judges, consciously or unconsciously, form similar conclusions as they read each brief."
—Robert N. Miller, "Judges and Briefs," in Advocacy and the King's English 413, 419 (George Rossman ed., 1960).

"Every writer, by the way he uses language, reveals something of his spirit, his habits, his capacities, his bias. . . . No writer long remains incognito."
—William Strunk Jr. & E.B. White, The Elements of Style 66–67 (3d ed. 1979).

"As Aristotle pointed out long ago, most people do not have the patience or intelligence to follow a logical argument very closely. Most people will be persuaded neither by reason nor by emotion, but by the ethos—the character—of the author."
—James C. Raymond, Writing (Is an Unnatural Act) 60 (1980).

"Nothing comes from nothing. Quality writing is done by people of quality. Robert Pirsig, in Zen and the Art of Motorcycle Maintenance, says quality depends on three things: self-reliance, integrity, and gumption. If you are self-reliant, you will not blame your boss, or your mother, or your journalism teacher for the kind of writing you do. Second, you have to like who you are and what you do. If you feel good about what you write, it will show. Third, no matter how many prizes you have won or how much criticism you have received, you have to have the gumption to give it your best, one more time. When Frank Lloyd Wright was 76, someone asked him what his best-designed building was. Without hesitation he replied, 'My next one.' "

> —George Kennedy et al., *The Writing Book* 133 (1984).

"If you work for an institution, whatever your job, whatever your level, be yourself when you write. You will stand out as a real person among the robots . . . ."

> —William Zinsser, *On Writing Well* 186 (5th ed. 1994).

"You want your reader to buy two things: your ideas and you, their source. That is, you want them to view your ideas as sound and interesting, and to view you as smart, informed, direct, and companionable. . . . If you don't persuade them to accept you, it's doubtful that you'll persuade them to buy the ideas you're proffering. We buy from people we like and trust—it's human nature."

> —John R. Trimble, *Writing with Style* 6 (2d ed. 2000).

Explanation

The point of the second-to-last quotation—Zinsser's—holds true unless you're a flake, a rotter, an inflater, a self-indulgent wit, or an otherwise unsavory character. In other words, it is well to think twice these days before advising someone, "Just be yourself!"

The lesson is this: whatever you write reflects who you are and how your mind operates. If you're an unsympathetic bully, that will show in your writing. If you're a hothead, that too will show. If you're a wimp, you won't be able to hide it.

The good news, though, is . . . well, we'll leave that for the self-improvement seminars.

APPENDIX A

What follows at page 463 is a motion to dismiss written in what might be called the "orthodox" style. It's slow and verbose. It doesn't contain any type of summary. In fact, the salient points don't emerge until the fourth page, and one of these (*Younger* abstention) isn't explained until the twelfth page. The motion labors two flimsy arguments, which threaten to spoil the good ones. In short, it's fairly typical.

At page 477 you'll find a complete rewrite of the motion in the high-impact style. It takes 5 pages instead of 14. The deep issues are on the first page, the citations appear as subordinate matter, and the only arguments are the strong ones. As rewritten, the motion shows how the principles in this book translate into practice.

No. 03–462

Michapo Sessatonkin Community, a federally recognized Indian Tribe,	§ § §	
	§	United States District Court
Plaintiff,	§ §	
	§	
v.	§ §	District of Michigan
	§	
State of Michigan; Governor Bill Wilson; and Commissioner of Revenue of the State of Michigan, James N. Nelson,	§ § § §	First Division
	§ §	
Defendants.	§	

DEFENDANTS' MOTION TO DISMISS AND MEMORANDUM IN SUPPORT

Introduction and Background

This Memorandum in Support of Defendants' Motion to Dismiss is submitted by defendants State of Michigan ("State"), Governor Bill Wilson, and James N. Nelson, the State's Commissioner of the Department of Revenue ("Department"). Plaintiff ("Tribe") challenges the validity under federal law of two state fees imposed on petroleum distributors insofar as the fees are levied on distributors who make deliveries to the Tribe on its reservation. Complaint, paras. 6 and 7. A description of the challenged fees and pending actions concerning them appears below.

A.   The challenged fees.

One challenged fee imposes "[a] petroleum tank release cleanup fee . . . on the use of tanks that contain [defined] petroleum products . . . ." Mich. Stat. § 115C.08, subd. 3 (1996). This two-cent per gallon cleanup fee is imposed periodically on fuel distributors to finance a state petroleum tank release cleanup fund ("Petrofund"). *Id.,* subds. 2, 3 and 4.[1] Tank owners or operators who engage in cleanups and other "corrective actions" to remedy petroleum spills, leaks, and other releases are eligible for cost reimbursement from the Petrofund. Mich. Stat. §§ 115C.021, subd. 1 (tank owner or operator within definition of "responsible person") and 115C.09, subd. 2 (1996) (responsible person eligible for Petrofund reimbursement). The Tribe, as a tank owner, is eligible for Petrofund reimbursement. *See* Mich. Stat. § 115C.02, subd. 9 (1996) ("person" includes any legal entity).[2]

The second challenged State fee is "petroleum inspection fee" of less than one-tenth of one cent per gallon, which is imposed on persons who own petroleum products held in storage at a pipeline or river terminal or refinery. *See* Mich. Stat. § 239.101, subd. 3 (1996). This fee finances petroleum, inspection, testing, and monitoring expenses by the Weights and Measures Division of the Michigan Department of Public Service. *Id.*

B.   The pending actions.

1.   The state court action.

Before commencing this action,[3] the Tribe asserted a claim in state court challenging the State's authority to levy the challenged fees on petroleum distributors

---

[1] At one reservation delivery site—a retail gasoline filling station operated by the Tribe—there are four underground storage tanks (*"USTs"*) with a combined capacity of 40,000 gallons. Affidavit of Roger Fisher, para. 4. Four additional USTs with a combined capacity of 21,500 gallons are at three other reservation delivery sites. *Id.*

[2] The State has reimbursed cleanup efforts on Indian reservations at a cost of $476,630.06 since 1990 under the Petrofund program. Affidavit of John R. Houck, para. 4d.

[3] The state court action was commenced on May 29, 1997. *See* Certificate of Service attached to last page of state court complaint; Affidavit of Peter M. Ackerberg ("Ack. Aff."), Exh. A.

who deliver fuel to the reservation. In the pending state court action, the Tribe alleges that B & F Distributing Co. ("B & F"), a Michigan corporation, delivered fuel to the reservation during 1993–95, paid the challenged fees, administratively sought a refund from the Department, and was denied a refund. *Michapo Sessatonkin Community v. Commissioner of Revenue,* No. 97-09022, Complaint, paras. 3–4 (Scott Co. Dist. Ct.); Affidavit of Peter M. Ackerberg ("Ack. Aff."), Exh, A. In Count I, the Tribe alleges that the State lacks authority under federal law to administer cleanup and inspection programs financed by the challenged fees on reservation land. *Id.,* paras. 15–19. In Counts II–IV, the Tribe alleges that the challenged fees violate federal law. *Id.,* paras. 20–29. The Tribe, as B & F's assignee, seeks a refund of fees paid by B & F and a declaration that the State lacks authority to impose the challenged fees on fuel delivered to the Tribe on its reservation. *Id.,* prayer for relief at p. 7.[4]

2. The federal court action.

The Tribe alleges in this action that the challenged state fees impermissibly infringe on tribal sovereignty and are preempted by federal law. Complaint, paras. 26–39. It seeks a Court order declaring that the State lacks authority to enter reservation land to administer petroleum cleanups and inspections financed by the challenged fees. *Id.,* prayer for relief, para. 1(a) at p. 11. In addition, the Tribe seeks declaratory and injunctive relief to prevent imposition of the challenged fees on distributors who deliver fuel to the reservation. *Id.,* paras. 1(b) and 2 at pp. 11–12.

---

[4] The state court action was ordered to be "held in abeyance to allow for settlement negotiations to proceed until further notice by counsel." Order (July 29, 1997); Ack. Aff., Exh. E. The state court has been notified by defendants that settlement negotiations were unsuccessfully completed. Ackerberg-Ess Letter (Feb. 12, 1998); Ack. Aff., Exh. F.

Argument

This action is barred by the Eleventh Amendment and, therefore, should be dismissed. Furthermore, even if the action is not barred by the Eleventh Amendment, it should be dismissed on comity grounds or under the *Younger* abstention doctrine. Finally, if the entire action is not dismissed, Count I of the complaint should be dismissed for lack of a case or controversy.

I.   The action is barred by the Eleventh Amendment.

The Eleventh Amendment bars a tribal action against the State as a named party. In addition, the action against the named individual defendants is effectively an action against the State barred by the Eleventh Amendment.

A.   The action against the State is barred by the Eleventh Amendment.

The Eleventh Amendment provides:

> The Judicial Power of the United States shall not be construed to extend to any suit in law or equity, commenced or prosecuted against one of the United States by Citizens of another State, or by Citizens or Subjects of any Foreign State.

U.S. Const. amend. XI. Although not expressly provided, this provision prohibits any suit against a state in federal court unless the state has unequivocally consented to suit or Congress has unequivocally abrogated the state's immunity from suit. *See Pennhurst State School & Hospital v. Halderman,* 465 U.S. 89, 99, 104 S. Ct. 900, 907 (1984). The state's Eleventh Amendment immunity bars suits against it by Indian tribes. *See Blatchford v. Native Village of Noatak,* 501 U.S. 775, 782, 111 S. Ct. 2578, 2583 (1991).

Congress can abrogate a state's Eleventh Amendment immunity, but it must be "unequivocally expresse[d]." *Seminole Tribe v. Florida,* 517 U.S. 44, 55, 116 S. Ct.

-4-

1114, 1123 (1996) (citation omitted). Thus, the provisions of 28 U.S.C. § 1362, granting federal district courts original jurisdiction in tribal civil actions, do not waive states' Eleventh Amendment immunity. *See Blatchford,* 501 U.S. at 788, 111 S. Ct. at 2586. It cannot be said that Michigan's immunity has been abrogated in the absence of a statute unequivocally expressing Congress' intent to abrogate states' immunity from suit in federal court in cases like this one.

A state may waive its Eleventh Amendment immunity, but immunity will be deemed waived "only where stated 'by the most express language or by such overwhelming implications from the text as [will] leave no room for any other reasonable construction.' " *Edelman v. Jordan,* 415 U.S. 651, 673, 94 S. Ct. 1347, 1361 (1974) (citation omitted). Thus, "a state's waiver of sovereign immunity in its own courts is not a waiver of Eleventh Amendment immunity in the federal courts." *Pennhurst,* 465 U.S. at 99 n.9, 104 S. Ct. at 907 n.9. The courts have repeatedly rejected the argument that the State of Michigan has waived its immunity from suit under the Eleventh Amendment. *See Manypenny v. United States,* 948 F.2d 1057, 1066 (8th Cir. 1991); *Hoeffner v. University of Michigan,* 948 F. Supp. 1380, 1392 (D. Mich. 1996) and *DeGidio v. Perpich,* 612 F. Supp. 1383, 1389 (D. Mich. 1985). It cannot be said that Michigan has waived its Eleventh Amendment immunity in the absence of express waiver language or overwhelming implications of waiver from some text. Therefore, the State should be dismissed from the action.

B.   The action against the individual state officers is barred by the Eleventh Amendment.

The action against Governor Wilson and Commissioner Nelson is also barred by the Eleventh Amendment. Generally, the Eleventh Amendment does not bar an action for prospective relief against state officers. *See Ex Parte Young,* 209 U.S. 123, 28 S. Ct. 441 (1908). *Young* held that a federal court has jurisdiction over a suit against a state officer for prospective relief even if the State itself is immune from suit under the Eleventh Amendment. *Id.* However, *Young* does not apply when the relief sought is indistinguishable from a quiet title action. *See Idaho v. Coeur d'Alene Tribe of Idaho,* 117 S. Ct. 2028 (1997). Here, the Tribe in effect seeks to quiet title in Petrofund and inspection fees payable by petroleum distributors who make deliveries to the Tribe on its reservation. Therefore, the *Young* exception to Eleventh Amendment immunity is inapplicable.

In *Idaho,* an Indian tribe sued state officers, alleged tribal ownership of submerged lands and lake beds, and sought declaratory and injunctive relief. However, the Court held that the suit was barred by the Eleventh Amendment. The Court did not agree on a single rationale for its decision. In an opinion announcing the Court's judgment, Justice Kennedy and Chief Justice Rehnquist called for "a careful balancing and accommodation of state interests when determining whether the *Young* exception applies in a given case." *Id.* at 1038 (Kennedy, J.). They noted that:

> The suit seeks, in effect, a determination that the lands in question are not even within the regulatory jurisdiction of the State. The requested injunctive relief would bar the State's principal officers from exercising their governmental powers and authority over the disputed lands and waters. The suit would diminish, even extinguish, the State's control over a vast reach of lands and waters long deemed by the State to be an integral part of its territory. To pass this off as a judgment causing little or no offense to Idaho's sovereign authority and its standing in the Union would be to ignore the relief of the Tribe demands. . . . It is apparent, then, that if the Tribe were to prevail, Idaho's sovereign interest in its land and waters would be affected in a degree fully as intrusive as almost any conceivable retroactive levy upon funds in its Treasury.

Id. at 2040.

In a concurring opinion joined by Justices O'Connor, Scalia, and Thomas, those justices rejected the principal opinion's "case-by-case balancing approach . . . where a plaintiff invokes the *Young* exception to the Eleventh Amendment's jurisdictional bar, even when a complaint clearly alleges a violation of federal law and clearly seeks injunctive relief." *Id.* at 2046 (O'Connor, J., concurring in part). Nonetheless, the concurring justices stated:

> The *Young* doctrine rests on the premise that a suit against a state official to enjoin an ongoing violation of federal law is not a suit against the State. Where a plaintiff seeks to divest the State of all regulatory power over submerged lands—in effect, to invoke a federal court's jurisdiction to quiet title to sovereign lands—it simply cannot be said that the suit is not a suit against the State.

Id. at 2047.

Thus, a majority of the Court agreed that an action against state officials seeking a decree quieting title is beyond the jurisdiction of a federal court. An action challenging the validity of a state statute requiring contributions to a dedicated state unemployment insurance fund has been deemed analogous to a quiet title action. *See Great Lakes Dredge & Dock Co. v. Huffman,* 319 U.S. 293, 300, 63 S. Ct. 1070, 1074 (1943). There is no basis for concluding that this action, which challenges the validity of required fees for environmental cleanup and other designated state purposes, should not also be deemed analogous to a quiet title action. In *Idaho* and here, a tribe seeks a judicial declaration that certain property claimed by the State—land or potential Petrofund revenue—does not belong to the State. In addition, similar to the divestment of state regulatory authority posed by the tribal suit in *Idaho,* the relief requested here would divest the State of its asserted authority to impose fees on its citizens for conduct widely recognized as potentially hazardous to the State's environment. Thus, here, as in *Idaho,* "it simply cannot be said that the suit is not a suit against the State." 117 S. Ct. at 2047 (Kennedy, J.). Naming individual state officials as separate defendants, in addition to the State itself, does not pierce the State's Eleventh Amendment immunity shield in this case.

This conclusion is especially warranted in light of the principle that the "nature of a suit as one against the state is to be determined by the essential nature and effect of the proceeding." *Ford Motor Co. v. Department of Treasury,* 323 U.S. 459, 464, 65 S. Ct. 347, 350 (1945). In *Idaho,* the state's ability to regulate its claimed submerged lands and lake bed was at stake. Here, the state's regulatory scheme to protect the purity of groundwater within its own territory—a resource that implicates special sovereign interests no less than the land above it—is at stake. The state is the trustee of waters of the state, including groundwater. Mich. Stat. §§ 116.16, subd. I (trustee) and 103G.005, subd. 17 (groundwater) (1996). For more than a century, Michigan has considered "[p]ollution of the groundwater [to be] damage to public property." *Michigan Millery Co. v. Travelers Indemnity Co.,* 457 N.W.2d 175, 182–83 (Mich. 1990). Cf. 42 U.S.C. § 9607(f)(1) (state representatives may act on behalf of public as trustee of natural resources to recover damages under federal Comprehensive Environmental Response, Compensation, and Liability Act).[5]

USTs pose the "most common source of groundwater contamination and . . .

---

[5] The Tribe, no less than the State, recognizes the danger of groundwater pollution to its well-being. A recent "Action Plan" adopted jointly by the Tribe and the United States Environmental Protection Agency ("EPA") identifies "[l]ack of information about groundwater quality and quantity, and lack of planning for water quality protection and water resource development" as a high priority issue. Michapo/EPA Region 5 Action Plan: 1998–2000 at p. 11; Ack. Aff, Exh. D.

petroleum is the most common contaminant." U.S. Environmental Protection Agency ("EPA") Administrator Browner's Letter to Regional EPA Administrators (May 14, 1997); Ack. Aff., Exh. B. Because groundwater is a common source of drinking water,[6] "[i]n many cases, UST releases have resulted in contamination of public or private drinking water supplies." *Id.* As a consequence, Michigan is vitally interested in protecting its groundwater from contamination. *See* Mich. Stat. §§ 103A.204 (1996) (allocating responsibility for groundwater protection among several State agencies), 103H.001 (State goal to maintain groundwater in natural condition whenever practicable), 103F.461 (requiring Board of Water and Soil Resources to develop recommendations for improvement of groundwater education activities), and ch. 115C (1996) (Petroleum Tank Release Cleanup Act).

A leaking petroleum tank on the reservation can contaminate groundwater flowing across its boundaries. Thus, environmental cleanup actions beyond the boundaries of a polluting facility may be necessary because "most forms of pollution, particularly groundwater contamination, do not observe territorial or property boundaries . . . ." H.R. Rep. No. 1133, 98th Cong., 2d Sess. 79 (1984), *reprinted* in 1984 U.S.C.C.A.N. 5649, 5663 (explaining reason for new provision [codified at 42 U.S.C. § 6924(v)] expanding geographical scope of cleanup actions under Resource Conservation and Recovery Act). *See also* 40 C.F.R. § 280.65(a) (1997) (EPA may require owners and operators of leaking USTs to investigate "surrounding area possibly affected by the release . . ." in order to determine groundwater contamination). In

---

[6] Groundwater is a water supply source for nearly 70 percent of Michigan residents. Michigan Pollution Control Agency, Groundwater Monitoring And Assessment Program: Annual Report (1995) at p. 2; Ack. Aff., Exh. C.

this case, the State's interest in the off-reservation effects of leaking reservation USTs is heightened by the fact that reservation groundwater generally flows toward the Muskegon River, an important state resource. *See* Affidavit of Andrew Lutz ("Lutz Aff."), para. 3 (flow direction) and Mich. Stat. § 103F.378, subd. 1 (1996) (State goal to make Muskegon River suitable for fishing and swimming by year 2005). Thus, the possibility of Muskegon River contamination from polluted groundwater within the Tribe's reservation cannot be excluded. Lutz Aff., para. 4.

The State's regulatory scheme to clean up UST petroleum spills—within the reservations of consenting tribes or within State boundaries—is jeopardized if distributors who deliver petroleum to tribes are exempt from the Petrofund fee. The State's sovereign interest in cleaning up groundwater contamination is as weighty a sovereign interest as Idaho's sovereign interest in regulating its submerged lands and lake beds. Therefore, just as the action against state officers in *Idaho* was dismissed on Eleventh Amendment grounds, the action here against Governor Wilson and Commissioner Nelson should be dismissed on Eleventh Amendment grounds.

II. The action should be dismissed pursuant to comity principles and the *Younger* abstention doctrine.

Even if the Court does not dismiss the action on Eleventh Amendment grounds, it should dismiss it under comity principles and the abstention doctrine of *Younger v. Harris*, 401 U.S. 37, 91 S. Ct. 746 (1971).

A. The action is barred by comity principles.

The United States Supreme Court has consistently invoked principles of comity to "bar federal courts from granting injunctive and declaratory relief in state tax cases." *Fair Assessment In Real Estate Association v. McNary*, 454 U.S. 100, 107, 102 S. Ct. 177, 181 (1981). As the Court explained in another case:

> The reason for this guiding principle [of equitable restraint] is of peculiar force in cases where the suit, like the present one, is brought to enjoin the collection of a state tax in courts of a different though paramount sovereignty. The scrupulous regard for the rightful independence of state governments which should at all times actuate the federal courts, and a proper reluctance to interfere by injunction with their fiscal operations, require that such relief should be denied in every case where the asserted federal right may be preserved without it.

Matthews v. Rogers, 284 U.S. 521, 525, 52 S. Ct. 217, 219 (1932). *Cf. Arkansas v. Farm Credit Serv. of Cent. Arkansas*, 117 S. Ct. 1776, 1780 (1997) ("The States' interest in the integrity of their own processes is of particular moment respecting questions of state taxation.").

This principle of equitable restraint regarding state laws is no less applicable to state levies other than taxes.[7] Thus, in *Boise Artesian Hot & Cold Water Co., Ltd. v. Boise City*, 213 U.S. 276, 29 S. Ct. 426 (1909), the Court affirmed the dismissal of a case challenging the constitutionality of a license fee on comity grounds. *Id.* at 287, 29 S. Ct. at 430. It stated: "Here is a case where every possible defense to the collection of the license fee which has been suggested by the company is available to it in the action at law pending in the courts of the state of Idaho, and there is no reason whatever shown why the law should not take its course." *Id.* Similarly, in *Great Lakes Dredge & Dock Co. v. Huffman*, 319 U.S. 293, 63 S. Ct. 1070 (1943), the Court affirmed the dismissal of an action challenging the constitutionality of required contributions to a state unemployment insurance fund. *Id.* at 302, 63 S. Ct. at 1074.

---

[7] The levy challenged in *Matthews* was characterized by the Court as "an annual license or 'privilege' tax." *Matthews*, 284 U.S. at 523, 52 S. Ct. at 218.

It concluded that declaratory relief "should have been denied without consideration of the merits" because

> it is the court's duty to withhold such relief when, as in the present case, it appears that the state legislature has provided that on payment of any challenged tax to the appropriate state officer, the taxpayer may maintain a suit to recover it back. In such a suit he may assert his federal rights and secure review of them by this Court. This affords an adequate opportunity to the taxpayer, and at the same time leaves undisturbed the state's administration of its taxes.

Id. at 300–01, 63 S. Ct. at 1074.

Here, as in *Boise City and Huffman,* there is a pending state case in which the complaining party can obtain all the relief it may be entitled to receive. The Michigan district courts "have original jurisdiction in all civil actions within their respective districts . . . ." Mich. Stat. § 484.01, subd. 1 (1996). There is no reason to assume that Michigan courts cannot properly adjudicate the Tribe's federal claims. *See Idaho*, 117 S. Ct. at 2037 (Kennedy, J.) (noting Court's prior "expression of confidence" in ability of state courts to uphold federal law). Thus, this case should be dismissed on comity grounds.

B.   The action is barred by the *Younger* abstention doctrine.

Even if the action is not dismissed on the ground of comity, it should be dismissed under the *Younger* abstention doctrine, which incorporates comity notions. In *Younger*, the Supreme Court held that the doctrine of abstention precludes enforcement of a state criminal statute by a federal court when state court proceedings related to the enforcement are pending in state court. 401 U.S. at 54, 91 S. Ct. at 755. The doctrine also applies to a state civil proceeding where the proceeding is (1) ongoing, (2) implicates important state interests, and (3) affords an adequate opportunity to raise federal claims. *See Middlesex Ethics Committee v. Garden State Bar Association*, 457 U.S. 423, 432, 102 S. Ct. 2515, 2521 (1982).

All three requirements for *Younger* abstention are satisfied here. There is an ongoing state court proceeding based on federal law in which the Tribe seeks a declaratory judgment and refund of cleanup and inspection fees paid by one of its fuel suppliers. *See* State Court Complaint, paras. 18, 23, 24, 27, and 29 (alleging federal law violations) and prayer for relief at p. 7. In addition, the state court action implicates the State's indisputably important interest in raising revenue for cleaning up petroleum quality. Finally, there is no reason to presume that the state district court does not offer the Tribe an effective forum for adjudicating its federal claims. Each requirement for *Younger* abstention exists here and, therefore, the Court should dismiss the action. *See Quackenbush v. Allstate Insurance Co.*, 116 S. Ct. 1712, 1723 (1996) (noting court's authority to dismiss equitable suit when declining to exercise jurisdiction).

III. Count I of the complaint should be dismissed for lack of a case or controversy.

If the Court does not dismiss the action on Eleventh Amendment, comity, or *Younger* abstention grounds, Count I of the complaint should be dismissed for lack of a case or controversy. Count I alleges that the State lacks authority to enter the Tribe's reservation to administer the petroleum tank release cleanup and inspection programs. Complaint, para. 27. The Tribe seeks a judgment declaring that the State lacks jurisdiction to administer these programs on reservation land. *Id.* prayer for relief at para. I(a) at p. 11. However, the State has no plans to administer such programs and, therefore, Count I should be dismissed because there is no case or controversy.

Article III of the United States Constitution requires a federal court plaintiff to allege an "actual case or controversy." *City of Los Angeles v. Lyons*, 461 U.S. 95, 101, 103 S. Ct. 1660, 1665 (1983). This requirement compels a federal court plaintiff to allege "that he 'has sustained or is immediately in danger of sustaining some direct injury' as the result of the challenged official conduct and the injury or threat of injury must be both 'real and immediate,' not 'conjectural' or 'hypothetical.' " *Id.* at 102, 103 S. Ct. at 1665 (citations omitted). The case or controversy requirement applies to a declaratory judgment action. *See Marine Equipment Management Co. v. United States*, 4 F.3d 643, 646 (8th Cir. 1993). However, the Tribe does not and could not allege that the State has conducted nonconsensual petroleum cleanups or inspections on the reservation. The State simply does not have any such plans. Affidavit of Michael Gideon, para. 4; Affidavit of Peter Ryburn, para. 3. Thus, "the fear of future regulation is not of sufficient immediacy and reality to warrant the issuance of a declaratory judgment." *Marine Equipment Management*, 4 F.3d at 647. Therefore, Count I should be dismissed for lack of a case or controversy.

Conclusion

For all the foregoing reasons, the defendants' motion to dismiss the action on Eleventh Amendment, comity, or abstention grounds should be granted. Alternatively, Count I of the complaint should be dismissed for lack of a case or controversy.

Dated: _____   Respectfully submitted,

                                Attorneys for Defendants

No. 03–462

Michapo Sessatonkin Community, a federally recognized Indian Tribe,	§ § §	United States District Court
Plaintiff,	§ §	
v.	§ §	District of Michigan
State of Michigan; Governor Bill Wilson; and Commissioner of Revenue of the State of Michigan, James N. Nelson,	§ § § § §	First Division
Defendants.	§ § § §	

**Defendants' Motion to Dismiss
and Memorandum in Support**

Introduction

In deciding the Defendants' motion to dismiss, the Court is presented with two straightforward issues:

- **Eleventh Amendment Immunity.** The Eleventh Amendment bars all suits against a state in federal court unless the state consents to be sued or Congress abrogates the immunity from suit. Here, despite the lack of consent and no congressional abrogation, the Michapo tribe has sued the State of Michigan in federal court. Should the court dismiss the State from this suit on Eleventh Amendment grounds?

- *Younger* **Abstention.** Under the *Younger* abstention doctrine, federal courts routinely refrain from hearing cases when a related state case (1) is ongoing, (2) implicates important state interests, and (3) affords an adequate opportunity to raise federal claims. Here, the Tribe has filed parallel state-court proceedings, those proceedings relate to the state's ability to assess taxes, and the Tribe's federal claims have already been raised. Should this Court abstain from proceeding?

Because the Tribe seeks to invalidate state fees—and the Tribe has sued the same parties for the same purpose in state court—the case also raises questions of comity.

Essentially, the Tribe wants a court to declare that petroleum distributors who deliver to the Tribe's reservation cannot be assessed two state fees. The first is a cleanup fee for petroleum-tank leaks—a two-cent-per-gallon fee imposed periodically to fund environmental "corrective actions" intended to remedy petroleum spills. The second is a petroleum-inspection fee of less than one-tenth of a cent per gallon. This fee, imposed on those who own petroleum products held in storage at a pipeline or river terminal or refinery, finances inspection and monitoring services by the Michigan Department of Public Service.

The State imposes these two fees to benefit Michigan residents. The Tribe is one of many potential—and intended—beneficiaries.

Argument

1.   Because neither condition essential to a federal suit has been met here—the State has not consented to be sued, and Congress has not abrogated the State's sovereign immunity—the Eleventh Amendment bars the Tribe from suing the State.

The Eleventh Amendment bars this type of action against the State as a named party:

> The Judicial Power of the United States shall not be construed to extend to any suit in law or equity, commenced or prosecuted against one of the United States by Citizens of another State, or by Citizens or Subjects of any Foreign State.[1]

The Supreme Court has interpreted this provision as prohibiting any suit against a state in federal court "unless the State has unequivocally consented to suit or Congress has unequivocally abrogated the State's immunity from suit."[2] Even more specifically,

---

[1] U.S. Const. amend. XI.

[2] *Pennhurst State Sch. & Hosp. v. Halderman*, 465 U.S. 89, 99, 104 S. Ct. 900, 907 (1984).

the Supreme Court has held that the Eleventh Amendment immunity bars suits against states by Indian tribes.[3]

Although Congress can abrogate a state's Eleventh Amendment immunity, that abrogation must be "unequivocally expresse[d]."[4] Even a state's waiver of sovereign immunity in its own courts does not waive Eleventh Amendment immunity in the federal courts.[5] The courts have repeatedly rejected the argument that the State of Michigan has waived its immunity from suit under the Eleventh Amendment.[6]

The Tribe cannot point to a waiver. There hasn't been one. This Court should therefore dismiss the State from the case.

2. This Court should rely on the *Younger* abstention doctrine—as well as comity—to dismiss the case in its entirety.

In *Younger v. Harris*,[7] the Supreme Court held that the abstention doctrine precludes enforcement of a state criminal statute by a federal court when state-court enforcement proceedings are pending in state court.[8] The Court has extended this doctrine to state civil proceedings that (1) are ongoing, (2) implicate important state interests, and (3) afford an adequate opportunity to raise federal claims.[9]

All three of those requirements are satisfied here. First, the Tribe has filed a

---

[3] *See Blatchford v. Native Village of Noatak*, 501 U.S. 775, 782, 111 S. Ct. 2578, 2583 (1991).

[4] *Seminole Tribe v. Florida*, 517 U.S. 44, 55, 116 S. Ct. 1114, 1123 (1996).

[5] *See Pennhurst*, 465 U.S. at 99 n.9, 104 S. Ct. at 907 n.9.

[6] *See Manypenny v. United States*, 948 F.2d 1057, 1066 (6th Cir. 1991); *Hoeffner v. University of Mich.*, 948 F. Supp. 1380, 1392 (D. Mich. 1996); *DeGidio v. Perpich*, 612 F. Supp. 1383, 1389 (D. Mich. 1985).

[7] 401 U.S. 37, 91 S. Ct. 746 (1971).

[8] *See Younger*, 401 U.S. at 54, 91 S. Ct. at 755.

[9] *See Middlesex Ethics Comm. v. Garden State Bar Ass'n*, 457 U.S. 423, 432, 102 S. Ct. 2515, 2521 (1982).

state-court suit that is now pending; in that case, the Tribe is asking for a declaratory judgment and a refund of cleanup and inspection fees paid by one of its fuel suppliers.[10] Second, the state-court action implicates the State's indisputably important interest in raising revenue for cleaning up petroleum spills. Third, the state district court offers an effective forum for adjudicating federal as well as state claims—something that Michigan courts routinely do. Because each requirement for *Younger* abstention exists here, the Court should promptly dismiss this action.

If there were any doubt about the proper ruling here, the Supreme Court's pronouncements on comity should eliminate it. The Supreme Court has consistently invoked principles of comity to bar federal courts from granting injunctive and declaratory relief in state-tax cases.[11] In approaching questions of comity with "equitable restraint," the Court has respected the powers and the capabilities of state courts:

> The reason for this guiding principle is of peculiar force in cases where the suit, like the present one, is brought to enjoin the collection of a state tax in courts of a different though paramount sovereignty. The scrupulous regard for the rightful independence of state governments which should at all times actuate the federal courts, and a proper reluctance to interfere by injunction with their fiscal operations, require that such relief should be denied in every case where the asserted federal right may be preserved without it.[12]

---

[10] *See* State Court Complaint ¶¶ 18, 23, 24, 27, 29 (alleging federal-law violations); Prayer at 7.

[11] *See, e.g., Fair Assessment in Real Estate Ass'n v. McNary*, 454 U.S. 100, 107, 102 S. Ct. 177, 181 (1981).

[12] *Matthews v. Rogers*, 284 U.S. 521, 525, 52 S. Ct. 217, 219 (1932); *cf. Arkansas v. Farm Credit Servs.*, 520 U.S. 821, 826, 117 S. Ct. 1776, 1780 (1997) ("The States' interest in the integrity of their own processes is of particular moment respecting questions of state taxation.").

This principle of equitable restraint applies not just to taxes but to other state levies. So in *Boise Artesian Hot & Cold Water Co. v. Boise City*,[13] the Court relied on comity to affirm the dismissal of a case challenging the constitutionality of a license fee.[14] This Court should do the same.

Conclusion

The outcome of this motion rests on three legal doctrines:

- Eleventh Amendment immunity;
- *Younger* abstention; and
- federal–state comity.

Supreme Court caselaw on each of these doctrines applies squarely to this case—and in the Defendants' favor. The Court should therefore dismiss the lawsuit in its entirety.

Dated: _____   Respectfully submitted,

                                             Attorneys for Defendants

---

[13] 213 U.S. 276, 29 S. Ct. 426 (1909).

[14] 213 U.S. at 287, 29 S. Ct. at 430; *cf. Great Lakes Dredge & Dock Co. v. Huffman*, 319 U.S. 293, 302, 63 S. Ct. 1070, 1074 (1943) (affirming the dismissal of an action challenging the constitutionality of required contributions to a state unemployment-insurance fund).

APPENDIX B

What follows is an appellate brief written in the high-impact style. Notice how the very first words—in the Statement of the Case—emphasize the case's importance. (That's critical since it's directed to a court with discretionary review.) Notice also how the conclusion sums up the points with a series of questions.

True, the deep issue doesn't come until page vi. But that's only because the applicable court rules specify where the issue must appear. That's fine if the rules are explicit on the point. After all, the judges who wrote the rules know where to look. And in any event, the first paragraph of the Statement of the Case sums up the main issue and theme (see tip #13).

No. _____

In the Supreme Court of Texas

Allied Mutual Lloyds, Inc., Allied Mutual Lloyds,
and Allied Mutual Fire & Casualty Co.,

Defendants,

v.

Beth Thompson and William Stevens,

Plaintiffs.

Beth Thompson's Petition for Review

Joe Hill Jones
State Bar No. 10915000
John E. Agnew
State Bar No. 00933000
Carter, Jones, Agnew & Kruka
2400 One Main Place
1201 Main St.
Dallas, Texas 75202-3973
(214) 742-6261
Fax: (214) 748-9225

Bryan A. Garner
State Bar No. 07672000
5949 Sherry Lane
Suite 1280
Dallas, Texas 75225-8008
(214) 691-8588
Fax: (214) 691-9294

COUNSEL FOR PETITIONER
BETH THOMPSON

List of Parties

Petitioner/Plaintiff

Beth Thompson

Petitioner/Plaintiff

William Stevens

Respondents

Allied Mutual Lloyds, Inc.
Allied Mutual Lloyds
Allied Mutual Fire & Casualty Co.

Counsel

Joe Hill Jones
John E. Agnew
Carter, Jones, Agnew & Kruka
2400 One Main Place
1201 Main St.
Dallas, Texas 75202-3973

Bryan A. Garner
5949 Sherry Lane
Suite 1280
Dallas, Texas 75225-8008

Counsel

_____

Counsel

_____

Table of Contents

Index of Authorities

Statement of the Case

This case presents an important, specific question about the measure of damages in a *Stowers*[1] case when an insurer assumes the defense of an insured without reserving coverage defenses, never offers to settle, allows an excess judgment to be taken, and then allows the deadline for appeal to pass before informing its insured that it wants to contest coverage.

The suit was brought by Beth Thompson, who was shot in the 1987 incident that gave rise to the liability, and by William Stevens, the husband of Thompson's daughter, Brenda Stevens, who was killed in the shootings. The gunman was Richard Bauer, one of Allied Mutual's insureds; the other insured was Richard's wife, Eloise. Thompson and Stevens sued the insureds' estates. After a contested bench trial, Thompson was awarded a judgment of $2.5 million; Stevens was awarded $1.75 million.

After that judgment became final, Thompson and Stevens took an assignment of both estates' claims against the estates' insurer, Allied Mutual. In exchange, they signed postjudgment covenants not to execute.

Thompson and Stevens then sued Allied Mutual for breach of contract, DTPA violations, Insurance Code violations, and other extracontractual torts. They won summary judgment on the issue of coverage for Eloise Bauer's estate, and that part of the case was severed. An appeal followed.[2] On remand, the case was reconsolidated and tried to a jury, which found for Thompson and Stevens on the claims against Eloise Bauer's estate but for Allied Mutual on the claims against Richard Bauer's estate.

---

[1] *G.A. Stowers Furniture Co. v. American Indem. Co.*, 15 S.W.2d 544 (Tex. Comm'n App. 1929, holdings approved).

[2] *See Allied Mutual Lloyds, Inc. v. Thompson*, 791 S.W.2d 542 (Tex. App.—Dallas 1990, writ denied) (per Enoch, J.).

Judge Richard Bosworth of the 354th District Court of Rockwall County held that the amount of the underlying judgment established damages as a matter of law and entered judgment on that basis. The court of appeals, in a published opinion, reversed and remanded, holding that damages were not established as a matter of law and suggesting that the value of the insured's estate is relevant to the measure of damages. Justice Brian Shannon, who wrote the opinion, was joined by Justice Philip Garwood; Justice Edith Benchley, who heard oral argument, left the court before the court of appeals issued its decision.

Statement of Jurisdiction

This court has jurisdiction under Texas Government Code § 22.001(a)(6) because the court of appeals committed a substantive legal error that is of such importance to Texas jurisprudence that it requires correction. The court also has jurisdiction under § 22.001(a)(2) because the court of appeals' decision conflicts with this Court's opinion in *Gandy*[3] and with the important precedent established in *Allstate Insurance Co. v. Kelly*.[4]

Issue Presented

In *Gandy*, this Court said that after an adversarial trial, the amount of the judgment sets the value of the plaintiff's claim in a later *Stowers* action. In this case, there was an adversarial trial in which the defendant was represented by counsel provided by Allied Mutual. The trial resulted in an excess judgment against the defendant. Does that underlying judgment establish the value of the plaintiff's claim?

---

[3] *Allied Mutual Fire & Casualty Co. v. Gandy*, 925 S.W.2d 696 (Tex. 1996).

[4] *Allstate Ins. Co. v. Kelly*, 680 S.W.2d 595 (Tex. App.—Tyler 1984, writ ref'd n.r.e).

Statement of Facts

On a weekend in late June 1987, Richard and Eloise Bauer of Rockwall had family at their home.[5] Eloise was dying of cancer. Her daughter Beth and granddaughter Brenda had come to Rockwall to care for her over the weekend.[6] On Saturday, June 20, Richard became distraught at his wife's predicament, at one point kneeling beside her and sobbing.[7]

Richard spent much of that day drinking.[8] By nighttime, his blood-alcohol level had risen to twice the legal limit.[9] Just after 11 o'clock, Beth was lying in bed with her mother, and Brenda was sleeping out on the porch.[10] Suddenly Richard walked into the room and pulled a handgun from a bedside table.[11] As Beth and Eloise begged him to put it down, 24-year-old Brenda, a newlywed, came in to her grandmother's side.[12] Brenda picked up the phone to dial for help, and just as she reached an operator, Richard shot her in the head, killing her.[13] Then he shot Beth in the head—through the back of one jaw and out the other—and she ran from the house, surviving the grisly event.[14] He shot his wife, Eloise, three times, wounding

---

[5] R 280–81.

[6] R 277–81.

[7] R 286–87.

[8] R 288.

[9] R 2346.

[10] R 285, 289; DX 1.

[11] R 290.

[12] *Id.*

[13] R 291, 292; DX 1, at 3.

[14] R 291, 292–93; DX 1.

Beth Thompson's Petition for Review
Page 1

her nonfatally. Then he killed himself.[15] Eloise died at home three weeks later—of cancer.[16]

In December 1987, Beth Thompson and William Stevens (Brenda's husband) sued the estates of Richard and Eloise Bauer.[17] They sued Eloise's estate on the theory that she was liable for Richard's tort.[18] Allied Mutual, which had issued a homeowner's policy to Richard and Eloise Bauer as separate and severable insureds, initially undertook to defend Richard under a nonwaiver agreement, but later reserved its coverage rights as to Richard because of the intentional-act exclusion.[19] When Richard's estate demanded an unqualified defense, Allied Mutual refused, so Richard's estate retained independent counsel.[20] But Allied Mutual unqualifiedly defended Eloise's estate, never asserting any coverage defense by a reservation-of-rights letter or nonwaiver agreement.[21] Allied Mutual mistakenly claimed that Eloise could have no liability because she did nothing wrong.[22]

Over the eight months between the filing of suit and trial, the plaintiffs in that lawsuit repeatedly offered to settle for $600,000 (for two occurrences).[23] Allied Mutual

---

[15] R 296; DX 1.

[16] R 296.

[17] PX 20.

[18] *Id.*

[19] PX 29; PX 27.

[20] PX 70, 71; R 679, 681.

[21] R 463–64.

[22] PX 32, 70; R 463, 554.

[23] R 359, 1045.

Beth Thompson's Petition for Review
Page 2

repeatedly refused without telling Eloise Bauer's executor why.[24] Allied Mutual's lawyers at Stutz & Leeds asked for authority to settle for $150,000, but Allied Mutual refused their request, insisting that Eloise could have no liability.[25] But on April 11, 1988, Stutz & Leeds alerted Allied Mutual that Eloise's estate did indeed have liability.[26] Allied Mutual never offered any sum to settle the case[27] or initiated any negotiations, though Eloise's estate demanded a settlement within policy limits.[28]

Nor did Allied Mutual ever reserve its rights against Eloise's estate,[29] though a reservation would have put the estate on notice that it might need independent counsel. Despite working vigorously to defeat coverage throughout the spring and summer of 1988, Allied Mutual never informed Eloise Bauer's estate that it was framing a coverage defense.[30]

Even though Allied Mutual had purported to erect a "Chinese wall" between the defense team and the coverage team, it began breaching that wall on May 25, 1988.[31] In all, at least seven breaches occurred before the time of trial in July.[32] Perhaps the most egregious of these breaches occurred when Marcus Brantley, defending Eloise's estate, sent Allied Mutual's coverage lawyer, Joe Stewart, the April 11 Stutz

---

[24] PX 43, 46, 47, 51; R 423, 429, 584.

[25] R 443–45.

[26] PX 14.

[27] R 448–49.

[28] R 359, 1045; DX 15; PX 19; PX 51.

[29] R 463, 554.

[30] PX 34; R 496–98, 701, 703, 934, 1690–91.

[31] *See* Tab G; *see esp.* PX 37.

[32] *See id.*

Beth Thompson's Petition for Review
Page 3

& Leeds memo that provided the basis for a coverage defense.[33] Brantley urged Stewart to "trash it" once he had the "info" he needed.[34]

Prompted by Marcus Brantley's handwritten note—and with the Stutz & Leeds memo in hand—Steven Boyd, another Allied Mutual coverage lawyer, started looking into the coverage question on Eloise's estate, just two days before the trial in July 1988.[35] In a matter of eight hours, he concluded that only the community assets were liable and that therefore, in his opinion, there was no coverage for the estate.[36] He then drafted a letter, for Joe Stewart's signature, opining that Eloise's estate had no coverage.[37]

But even at this eleventh hour, Allied Mutual neither reserved its rights against the estate nor informed the estate of its plans to contest coverage.[38] Instead, it proceeded to trial without informing the estate that it would contest coverage, and the estate suffered a $4.25-million judgment.[39] Liability was clear, and the potential for damages far exceeded the policy limits.[40] Allied Mutual did not appeal, allowed the judgment to become final on August 20, 1988, and then declined to pay the judgment.[41]

---

[33] PX 37.

[34] *Id.*

[35] R 976–77, 993.

[36] R 981–82.

[37] DX 12; R 977.

[38] R 496–98.

[39] DX 17; R 458.

[40] R 458.

[41] R 459.

Beth Thompson's Petition for Review
Page 4

Nearly a month *after* that judgment became final, Eloise's estate, in exchange for a nonexecution covenant, assigned its rights against Allied Mutual to Beth Thompson and William Stevens, who brought this suit to enforce those rights.[42] As judgment creditors and assignees of Eloise's estate's rights, Thompson and Stevens wrote the 30-day demand letter then required by the DTPA and Insurance Code.[43]

As its first notice to Eloise's estate that Allied Mutual sought a coverage defense—in September 1988, nearly two months after trial—Allied Mutual filed a declaratory-judgment action in district court in Dallas.[44] Upon its dismissal, Thompson and Stevens filed this lawsuit and prevailed on summary judgment. The court of appeals (per Enoch, C.J.) reversed and remanded on narrow grounds, holding that if Thompson and Stevens could show at trial that they or Eloise's estate had been harmed by Allied Mutual's conduct—and that Allied Mutual had "knowledge of facts indicating noncoverage"—they would meet the standard of proving estoppel (or "waiver," as some courts have termed it).[45]

On remand, the trial court reconsolidated the previously severed tort claims so that waiver and estoppel, *Stowers* negligence, DTPA, and Insurance Code claims would once again be considered together. The trial court held a two-and-a-half-week trial in August 1992. The jury found that Allied Mutual (1) had engaged in deceptive trade practices, (2) had acted negligently in handling the insurance claim, (3) had waived its coverage defenses, and (4) was estopped to deny insurance

---

[42] DX 9; R 1097.

[43] PX 35.

[44] R 495–99.

[45] 791 S.W.2d at 553.

Beth Thompson's Petition for Review
Page 5

coverage.[46] The trial record contains ample evidence of harm and of Allied Mutual's knowledge of facts indicating noncoverage.[47]

In rough figures, the judgment of $4.25 million,[48] with interest, equaled more than $6 million in 1992. Proper *Stowers* findings having been made, and with proper DTPA findings and Insurance Code findings under art. 21.21, § 16, the trial court trebled the damages to bring the recovery to over $18 million (excluding attorney's fees).

The court of appeals (per Shannon, J.), after finding sufficient evidence to support *Stowers* liability as well as Insurance Code and DTPA violations, nonetheless reversed and remanded, holding that the amount of the underlying judgment did not establish damages.[49] The court directed the trial court to find the value of Eloise Bauer's estate in order to determine the damages that Allied Mutual must pay—despite the insolvency clause in Eloise Bauer's insurance policy, which provided full coverage even if her estate had been valueless.

The court of appeals correctly stated the nature of the case.

Summary of Argument

Under established Texas law, an insurer that (1) undertakes the defense of an insured without reserving its rights to contest coverage, and (2) neither initiates settlement talks nor agrees to settle within policy limits, is liable to the full extent of

---

[46] R 107–10, 115, 116, 118.

[47] *See Allied Mutual Lloyd's, Inc. v. Thompson*, 1997 WL 531027 headnotes 6 & 8 (Tex. App.—1997) (at Tab C).

[48] DX 17.

[49] 1997 WL 531027, at headnotes 8 & 9.

any judgment in excess of policy limits. Here Allied Mutual controlled the defense of the Eloise Bauer estate, never initiated settlement talks even though liability was clear, refused settlement offers within policy limits, and then allowed an excess judgment of $4.25 million to be taken against the insured. Allied Mutual knew of Eloise Bauer's liability on April 11, 1988, but it continued to control the defense (without contesting coverage) through the July 1988 trial date. The judgment became final in August 1988, and a month later Allied Mutual belatedly asserted a coverage defense. The facts here are extremely unusual, but the principle is not: under *Gandy* and *Kelly*, the amount of the judgment establishes damages as a matter of law.

Argument

A.   An insurer that unreservedly controls the defense of an insured and fails to settle within policy limits, despite clear liability in excess of those limits, is liable to the full extent of any judgment that follows.

In *Allied Mutual Fire & Casualty Co. v. Gandy,*[50] decided last year, this Court explained an insurer's range of choices when an insured requests both a defense and coverage by the insurer:

> *I* [the insurer] ordinarily has three options: to accept coverage of *P*'s claim and provide *D* a defense, to provide a defense but reserve the right to contest coverage, or to deny coverage and refuse a defense.[51]

In this case, Allied Mutual accepted coverage—that is, until the judgment became final. And then it tried to choose a "fourth" option that courts have never sanctioned: "Notice that this list does not include the option, 'Pay for the defense of the insured

---

[50] 925 S.W.2d 696 (Tex. 1996).

[51] *Id.* at 713.

Beth Thompson's Petition for Review
Page 7

with an apology and then contest coverage later'. . . ."[52] This particular point—an un-complicated one—has been reinforced by *Gandy*.

In exchange for an assignment of claims against Allied Mutual, Thompson and Stevens gave a postjudgment covenant not to execute. That presents no difficulty un-der *Gandy*.

The relevant question is the measure of damages, and on that point *Gandy* pro-vides guidance in three separate passages:

- "In a subsequent action by *P* against *I*, *P*'s damages are measured by the value of his claim against *D*."[53]

- "If *P* and *D* settle after an adversarial trial, the value of *P*'s claim can be taken to be the amount of the judgment obtained."[54]

- "For example, as we have said, if the settlement follows an adversarial trial, the difficulties in evaluating *P*'s claim are no longer present. That value has been fairly determined."[55]

B.   The court of appeals' attempt to distinguish this case from controlling caselaw is erroneous; more important, it is harmful to the rights of married insureds in Texas.

Despite this Court's clear guidance, the court of appeals decided not to apply *Gandy* or *Kelly*. The court noted that in this case, the judgment specified that it was enforceable against the community estate, whereas in *Gandy* and *Kelly* the judgments didn't appear to contain that specification.[56] In the critical passage containing the

---

[52] *Insurance Corp. of Ireland v. Board of Trustees of S. Ill. Univ.*, 937 F.2d 331, 337 (7th Cir. 1991).

[53] 925 S.W.2d at 713.

[54] *Id.*

[55] *Id.* at 714.

[56] 1997 WL 531027, at *9.

Beth Thompson's Petition for Review
Page 8

error, the word *amount* appears three times, but it changes its meaning in its third appearance:

> In *Kelly*, a simple mathematical calculation provided the difference between the policy limits and the amount of the underlying judgment and, thus, the amount of the "underlying judgment" to be assessed "as a matter of law" in a later suit against the insurer. By contrast, the face of the judgment in this case does not allow a trial court to determine the "amount" of the underlying judgment against the insured. Instead, it requires a determination of the existence and value of certain assets.[57]

Why the quotation marks around the third *amount*? Because, although that word means just what it always means in the first two occurrences, it shifts its meaning to "collectibility" in the third instance. There is nothing else it could mean.

The intermediate court's distinction is fallacious for five reasons.

First, a judgment's collectibility often differs drastically from its amount. When trial judges enter judgments, of whatever amount, they might wonder how collectible the judgment is. But that has nothing to do with the amount they enter.

Second, the underlying judgment merely reflected Texas law: since Eloise Bauer's estate was liable only because she was married to a tortfeasor, her estate is liable only to the extent of community property.[58] Indeed, the same was true in *Kelly*, where the excess judgment against the nontortfeasor spouse would have been enforceable only against his community estate.[59]

Third, statutory exemptions limit the enforceability of almost every judgment, and yet that has never given courts any difficulty in assessing damages and entering

---

[57] *Id.*

[58] Tex. Fam. Code Ann. §§ 4.031, 5.61 (Vernon Supp. 1993).

[59] *Kelly*, 680 S.W.2d at 601.

Beth Thompson's Petition for Review
Page 9

judgments based on those amounts. That is, there are exemptions relating to home-
steads, current wages, agricultural tools, vehicles, retirement plans, and the like.[60] The
fact that such exemptions exist isn't generally recited in the judgment itself, but such
a recital would merely reflect what the law is. And in this type of case, Texas caselaw suggests that such a recital in the judgment should be included.[61]

Fourth, the claim against Allied Mutual—the only thing at issue in this lawsuit—
was (until assigned to Thompson and Stevens) a part of Eloise Bauer's estate.[62] The
Bauers' community estate benefited from the coverage provided by that insurance. To
hold that it is impossible to assess *Stowers* damages against the insurer without first
assessing the value of the community estate—when the full extent of the *Stowers* liability is part of the community estate's value—is a circular argument. And enshrining
that holding in a precedent will create much confusion in Texas insurance law, de-
stroying *Stowers* rights in cases where either insured spouse has died.

Finally, the court of appeals has nullified the insurance policy's insolvency
clause. By delving into issues regarding the value of the community estate, the court
has voided one of the most important promises that the insurer makes in its contract
of insurance. That promise to the insured is stated in the policy issued to the
Bauers:

---

[60] Tex. Prop. Code Ann. §§ 42.001 et seq. (Vernon 1984).

[61] *See First Nat'l Bank v. Finn*, 132 S.W.2d 151, 155 (Tex. Civ. App.—Galveston 1939, writ
dism'd) (noting that, because a spouse's separate property is not subject to liability for a tort
committed by the other spouse, "upon appropriate pleadings or request, seasonably filed, the
judgment *should exempt* [the spouse's] separate property") (emphasis added); *Seinsheimer v.
Burkhart*, 122 S.W.2d 1063, 1067 (Tex. 1939) (deciding—on the court's own motion—that a
similar judgment should be reformed so that the husband's separate property is relieved from
the judgment's operation).

[62] *See In re Edgeworth*, 993 F.2d 51, 55 & n.15 (5th Cir. 1993).

Beth Thompson's Petition for Review
Page 10

[B]ankruptcy or insolvency of the insured or of the insured's estate shall not relieve the company of any of its obligations hereunder.[63]

By remanding for a finding on the estate's value, the court of appeals has resurrected the prepayment rule, which this court flatly rejected in 1971.[64] In light of the insolvency clause, the nature and extent of Eloise Bauer's community estate—or, for that matter, her separate estate—is irrelevant.

Under the court of appeals' decision, the insurance contract and the amount of coverage are no longer what the parties bargained for. If the insured's estate has to be examined to determine whether any damages exist from *Stowers* liability, then Allied Mutual's duties to settle and defend are limited to the amount of the estate's value, and the insurer's analysis becomes purely one of economic expedience. Assume, for example, that an insured wants liability coverage for $500,000. The insured has exempt assets (a homestead, separate property as a nontortfeasor spouse) and nonexempt assets (community property). The nonexempt assets are worth $50,000. The spouse commits a tort that gives rise to a $1-million liability. Under the court of appeals' holding, the insurer would never be liable on a claim against the nontortfeasor spouse for more than the community assets' value—or $50,000—even though it had agreed to indemnify both insureds up to the policy limits.

Under the radically new doctrine announced by the court of appeals, the amount of coverage available to an insured will often be far from what is written in the policy and far from what the insured has paid premiums for: the amount of the insured's nonexempt community assets.

---

[63]   PX 24, at 3 (under "Endorsements").

[64]   *Hernandez v. Great Am. Ins. Co.*, 464 S.W.2d 91 (Tex. 1971) (per Reavley, J.).

Beth Thompson's Petition for Review
Page 11

The Court must reject this new holding. It could harm every married person in Texas who has liability insurance.

Conclusion

The issue in this case might have been stated in various ways. Did the court mean what it said in *Gandy* about damages—not once but three times? Is *Kelly* still good law? Does *Stowers* remain the law of the state? Has the law of Texas reverted to the prepayment rule for nontortfeasor spouses whose community property is not exempt from execution? Does the insolvency clause in insurance contracts protect only certain classes of named insureds, but not all?

For Texans, this case has a tremendous impact on every insurance contract on which an innocent insured spouse is sued. With this precedent, neither the policy limits nor the amount of the excess judgment is significant. Instead, the only significant factor is the value of the innocent spouse's community estate. In short, by not following *Gandy* and *Kelly*, the court of appeals has effectively (1) rendered the face amount of coverage meaningless, (2) voided the policy's bankruptcy and insolvency clauses, and (3) destroyed the *Stowers* rights of innocent insured spouses.

Thompson asks the Court to grant this petition for review, reverse the court of appeals' judgment, and reinstate the trial court's judgment.

Respectfully submitted,

_____

Joe Hill Jones   Bryan A. Garner
State Bar No. 10915000   State Bar No. 07672000
John E. Agnew   5949 Sherry Lane, Suite 1280
State Bar No. 00933000   Dallas, Texas 75225-8008
Carter, Jones, Magee, Rudberg & Mayes
2400 One Main Place
1201 Main St.
Dallas, Texas 75202-3973

Certificate of Service

A copy of this document was hand-delivered on December __, 1997, to the following counsel for other parties:

_____

_____

_____

Bryan A. Garner

Beth Thompson's Petition for Review
Page 13

Index of Works Cited

---

* Recommended for your library.

Subject Index

515

The Winning Brief: Tips 51–100

51 Fix every remote relative pronoun—that is, ensure that *that* or *which* immediately follows the noun it refers to.

52 Resist rabid deletions of *that*. Even so, prefer [verb +-*ing*] over *that* [+ verb].

53 Don't use *such* as a pronoun <rejected such> or demonstrative adjective <such property>.

54 Use well-recognized symbols and abbreviations, but avoid uncommon ones.

55 Generally, dispense with *Mr., Mrs.,* and *Ms.*; use last names alone after the first mention of a party's or witness's name.

56 Shun sexist language, but do it invisibly.

F. PUNCTUATING FOR CLARITY AND IMPACT

57 Use dashes—not parentheses—to highlight interruptive phrases.

58 Hyphenate your phrasal adjectives.

59 Otherwise, be stingy with hyphens—especially after prefixes.

60 Avoid gratuitous quotation marks and other typographic oddities.

61 Use bullets for lists.

62 Use the serial comma.

G. BECOMING PROFICIENT IN DESIGNING TEXT

63 In the argument section, use argumentative headings.

64 Format headings with an Arabic-numbered outline system in this sequence: boldface large; boldface; boldface italic; italic. Position all headings flush left.

65 Put a little more white space above a heading than below.

66 Use the power of your computer. Set sensible defaults, and use macros to make writing easier.

67 Indent your paragraphs only a quarter of an inch or so. Avoid the puzzlingly common double-indent.

68 Avoid all-caps and initial-caps text. But if you do use initial caps, don't capitalize any word shorter than five letters if it's an article, a preposition, or a conjunction.

69 Generally, spell out numbers one to ten, and use numerals for numbers 11 and above.

70 Use charts, diagrams, and other visual aids when you can.

H. SIDESTEPPING SOME COMMON QUIRKS

71 Never distort the facts or the law. Avoid hyperbole and personality attacks.

72 Counter the Rambo writer with the deflating opener.

73 Swear off the hence-the-title principle.

74 Describe actions, not filings, when possible. And refer to filings generically—not with titles of court papers.

75 Avoid voluminous quotations.